D0328754

JACQUES MARQUETTE

Books by Joseph P. Donnelly, S.J.

The American Colonial Policy of James II
The French in the Mississippi Valley (with others)
The Liquor Traffic among the Indians of the New Northwest
Old Cahokia (with others)
The Parish of the Holy Family at Cahokia, Illinois
Thwaites' Jesuit Relations: Errata and Addenda
Wilderness Kingdom: The Journals & Paintings of Father Nicolas Point, S.J.

JACQUES MARQUETTE, S.J.

1637-1675

JOSEPH P. DONNELLY, S.J.

Professor of History, Marquette University

LOYOLA UNIVERSITY PRESS

Chicago, Illinois 1968

Printed in the United States of America
Library of Congress Catalog Card Number: 68-9498

To “. . . *the Blessed Virgin Immaculate,*

for so he always called Her.”

Relations LIX, 207

CONTENTS

FOREWORD

A few searching minds add significantly to the sum of human knowledge. The millions who follow simply learn that which is already known. A brave band of rugged souls carve out a nation. The millions who follow merely live in it.

Try as we will we can never repay the debt which we owe to those few who led the way in the exploration of our great country. Only three hundred years ago it was a wilderness and, except for men like Father Marquette, it might still be a wilderness today. In the great drama of humanity, which we call history, the life of Father Marquette is a part of the saga of discovery. He, and a very few others, plunged from a tiny "known" world to a vast "unknown" world.

Like so many men who have made important contributions to humanity, his deeds were accomplished when he was very young.

When he was thirty he was an undistinguished schoolmaster in France. At thirty-one he arrived at what is now Sault Saint Marie, Michigan. Five years later, when he was only thirty-six, he entered the Mississippi River. Father Marquette was only thirty-eight when he died on the shores of Lake Michigan.

In his brief life he was unhonored and unapplauded. No civic dinners at plush hotels found him at the speaker's table. There were no parades with ticker tape, no plaques, no medals, no eulogies, and no garlands. It is certain that he himself did not realize the importance of what he had accomplished. And yet this young Jesuit priest explored for the many millions who followed him the great upper valley of the Mississippi and determined its flow into the Gulf of Mexico.

The very least that we can do today for a man who endured and achieved so much, is to research, record, and preserve the record of his accomplishments and to revere his memory.

The history of his life also heightens the realization of the need to preserve the land which he turned over to our ancestors and to us. The lakes, streams, forests, and the wildlife of the land which he discovered have been plundered and polluted. Recounting the record of Father Marquette helps to bring attention once more to the need to preserve our heritage and to use our resources wisely and well.

This is why on September 15, 1965, the President and the Congress of the United States created by law a commission for the purpose of commemorating and memorializing the life and deeds of Father Marquette.

The period selected by the commission is 1968 to 1973. In 1668 he arrived at what is now the United States. In 1673 he entered the Mississippi River. The publication of this book which coincides in time with the activities of the Father Marquette Tercentenary Commission provides the scholarly background against which the drama of the Tercentenary celebration is played.

J. C. Windham, *Chairman*
Father Marquette Tercentenary Commission

May 16, 1968

JACQUES MARQUETTE

1

THE MARQUETTES OF LAON

Laon, the native place of the Marquettes since at least the third decade of the twelfth century, is a formidable stronghold perched on the brow of a limestone escarpment rising some three hundred feet above the surrounding plain. From a distance the great triangular hill, its summit crowned with medieval walls and the massive towers of the ancient cathedral, strikingly resembles a gigantic man-of-war doggedly plowing a vast green sea, intent on attacking a powerful armada laying wait just over the horizon. A natural fortress, the place was already a stronghold when Roman legions established a permanent military camp there and named it Laudunum. Throughout the ensuing centuries the people of Laon, perennially jealous of their liberties, grimly defended their village against the assaults of the Franks, the Vandals, and the Huns. In A.D. 497 Saint

Remi, archbishop of Reims and probably a native of Laon, who made a Christian of Clovis, king of the Franks, established an episcopal see at Laon, with papal permission, and appointed his nephew, Gunband, as its first bishop.[1] Charlemagne's grandson, Charles the Bald, king of Neustria (843-877) and emperor of the Roman Empire of the West (875-877), who resided at Laon, enriched the diocese with extensive grants of land. A century later, during the conflict between Hugh Capet and Louis V, the last Carolingian king of France, Laon supported Louis, but Hugh Capet won the town through the connivance of Bishop Ascelin. As a reward Ascelin was made duke of Laon, count of Anizy, and second ecclesiastical peer of the realm with the right of anointing the king, if the see of Reims was vacant when the occasion arose. The territory granted Ascelin and his successors included seventeen villages over which the episcopal lord exercised both civil and ecclesiastical jurisdiction. Relations between the people of Laon and their episcopal seigneur were anything but cordial. In A.D. 1112 the burghers of Laon purchased a communal charter from Louis VI (1108-1137) authorizing them to establish a civil government independent of episcopal jurisdiction. When Bishop Gaudry, an Englishman whom the Laonnais cordially hated, bribed the king to revoke the charter, the townspeople, angered beyond endurance, murdered the bishop, slaughtered his supporters, destroyed the episcopal palace, and burned Laon's ancient cathedral to the ground.[2] A little over sixty years later, in 1175, the episcopal serfs revolted, protesting the injustices visited on them by Bishop Roger de Rozoy. That belligerent ecclesiastic hired professional soldiers who slaughtered the serfs by the hundreds.[3] Vermand Marquette, the first recorded member of the family, was in the prime of life when Bishop de Rozoy's trained militia cruelly murdered the nearly defenseless serfs. He is a shadowy figure about

[1] Achille Luchaire, *Social France in the Time of Philip Augustus,* 441.

[2] *Ibid.*

[3] George B. Adams, *The History of England from the Norman Conquest to the Death of John (1066-1216),* 397.

whom we know no more than his name and the year of his birth and death.[4]

A battle, waged on July 24, 1214, near Bouvines, a village laying ten miles southeast of Lille, ushered the Marquette family onto the stage of history. When the scheming, unscrupulous John Lackland of England (1199-1216) unfeelingly dismissed Isabelle of Glouster, his barren wife of ten years' standing, and unchivalrously contracted an alliance with Isabelle of Angoulème, a twelve-year-old child already betrothed to Hugh of Lusignan, one of John's vassals, the disappointed suitor sought justice from Philip II (1180-1223), king of France and feudal lord of the two contestants. When John ignored Philip's summons, issued in 1202, to appear in answer to Hugh's complaints, Philip declared forfeit John's French possessions of Brittany, Maine, and Anjou. The next year John Lackland's young nephew, Arthur, son of Richard the Lionhearted, heir by right of primogeniture to the throne of England, and ward of Philip of France, was murdered with the consent, if not the actual connivance, of John Lackland. In retaliation Philip II seized John's remaining French territories of Normandy and Touraine, possessions vastly more important than the small island of England. To regain his lost provinces, John arranged a military alliance with his nephew, Otto IV, emperor of the Holy Roman Empire, and Ferdinand of Portugal, count of Flanders, husband of a niece of Philip, king of France. The coalition army carried all before it until the opposing forces joined battle on a hot Sunday midday, July 24, 1214, on the banks of the little Marq River where Philip II ignominiously defeated his enemy. John Lackland and Ferdinand of Portugal were both captured while Otto IV fled. Obliged by this defeat to surrender claim to any French territory north of the Loire, John returned to England in 1215 where his barons, led by Archbishop Langton, obliged him to sign the Magna Carta. Ferdinand of Portugal was imprisoned in the Louvre during the following twelve years as a punishment for supporting John Lackland. Jacques Marquette, Ferdinand's loyal steward, shared the incarceration with

[4] Frantz Funck-Brentano, *The National History of France: the Middle Ages*, 281.

his lord.[5] When Ferdinand was set free in 1226 his wife Jeanne, to show her gratitude, built an abbey near Lille and conferred the Marquette name on it. Not without reason, Alfred Hamy, in his *Au Mississippi*, wonders whether that Jacques Marquette might not have received the family name from the small Marq River near which the abbey once stood.[6] Not long after his release from prison, Jacques Marquette left the service of his noble master and settled at Laon.

During the lifetime of Jacques Marquette, former steward of Ferdinand of Portugal, or certainly during that of his children, Laon became a very important center for the study of theology. Jacques Pantaléon, son of a Laon cobbler, who began his ecclesiastical career as a choirboy, became a canon of the cathedral at Laon. Attracting the attention of Innocent IV (1243-1254) at the Council of Lyons, Pantaléon was commissioned by the pope to revitalize the study of theology in France. The cobbler's son, who later ruled the Church as Urban IV (1261-1264), established a theological center at Laon which attracted students from all over Europe in such crowds, in fact, that they sometimes outnumbered the townspeople. A century earlier Abelard and William of Champeau were at Laon consulting with Anselm of Laon whose exegetical works on the Scriptures were widely respected.[7]

The medieval student who toiled up the zigzag road leading to the summit of Laon's great promontory found himself in a crowded city of narrow winding streets which seemed dominated by a forest of church steeples. Laon boasted sixty-three churches, five abbeys, five convents, two hospitals, and a commandery of the Knights Templar whose establishment gloried in an octagonal chapel. The whole city was surrounded by a stout wall pierced by three gates: Ardon, Chenizelles, and Soissons, beside which stood a famous

[5] Alfred Hamy, *Au Mississippi: la première exploration (1673)*, 31.

[6] *Ibid.* Ferdinand was held prisoner so long because his wife refused to pay a ransom of 50,000 francs demanded by the king as a punishment for the rebellion of her husband.

[7] See Jacques P. Migne, editor, *Patrologiae cursus completus, series Latina*, CLXXVIII, in which one may read a dialogue between Anselm of Laon and Abelard.

leaning tower. The most impressive structure in the town, then as now, was the cathedral of Notre-Dame-de-Laon. Begun by Bishop Gauthier Mortagne in 1170 and completed about 1225, the vast edifice is almost 370 feet long and nearly seventy feet from floor to roof. The building is dominated by massive square towers which soar sixty feet above the cathedral's roof. Notre-Dame-de-Laon, thought to have been the prototype of the Reims cathedral, has a great rose window in its front facade which is considered second only to that in the cathedral of Notre-Dame at Paris. Visitors to Laon always remark on the stone oxen peeping out beneath the arcades of the octagonal upper portions of the cathedral's western tower. Tradition has it that these stone beasts were placed there to commemorate the labor of the oxen in dragging the heavy stones for the church's structure up the tortuous path to the summit of the high escarpment on which the cathedral stands.[8] Medieval Laon was busy, wealthy, crowded, thronged with weavers, wine merchants, students, monks from various monasteries, and, undoubtedly, a drifting, restless crowd of roistering idlers who usually congregated at medieval centers of learning. Maintaining order and suppressing lawlessness would have required a firm hand and a respected reputation. For a time, at least, during the middle of the fourteenth century, a Marquette shouldered the responsibility as sheriff of Laon.

A century and a quarter after the first Jacques Marquette took up residence at Laon, a descendant of the same name was elected sheriff of Laon in 1357.[9] This Jacques Marquette won honor and a patent of nobility for his service to France's King John II, the Good (1350-1364). During the second period of the Hundred Years' War, King John, an incurable romantic, often called the last chivalrous king, though a violent-tempered and emotionally unstable ruler, set out to vanquish Edward, the Black Prince, eldest son of England's Edward III (1327-1377), who, after ravishing Languedoc, was marching toward the Loire. Informed that John was moving against him with an army of 20,000 men, the Black Prince entrenched him-

[8] Marc Thibout, *Eglises gothiques en France,* xv and plates 10, 11, 12. The famous oxen are clearly evident in plate 10.

[9] Hamy, *Au Mississippi,* 32.

self just south of Poitiers on a plateau cut up by hedges and vines which gave him excellent protection against a cavalry charge. On September 19, 1356, against the wise advice of his field marshal, Clermont, John the Good attacked the Black Prince's nearly impregnable position. The flower of the chivalry of France died that day along with 2,400 men-at-arms. King John was captured along with his fourteen-year-old son Philip. Treated with the utmost consideration, King John was taken to London and given his freedom on condition that his son, Louis of Anjou, remain in England as a hostage until his father could pay a ransom of 3,000,000 crowns. The French king promised that if he could not raise the ransom he would, of his own accord, return to captivity. To aid their monarch's financial need, the citizens of Laon raised 240,000 francs which the city's *prévôt*, Jean de Lyssac, and the sheriff, Jacques Marquette, were commissioned, in 1357, to deliver to King John who was at Brétigny, a small town not far southeast of Paris. The commission was not only important to the king and the future of France, but it was dangerous as well since the hundred mile journey to Brétigny must of necessity be made through a countryside alive with marauding English soldiers. One can visualize the commissioners and their escort, mounted on their chargers in the square before Laon's great cathedral, being deluged with sage advice and good wishes for a safe journey. As the little cavalcade clattered across the square and began the steep descent to the plain below, many a burgher shook his head at the thought of the dangerous ride facing their two commissioners. Prudent, sensible men undoubtedly declared that if anyone could accomplish the mission successfully certainly Jacques Marquette could for he was a brave, trustworthy man whose integrity and courage had never been questioned.

When the two citizens of Laon delivered the money safely to their king, the monarch demonstrated his gratitude to them and Laon by ennobling his visitors, granting them the privilege of using the arms of Laon as a family crest.[10] Laon's coat of arms is composed of a shield with three fleurs-de-lis on a white background below which, on a field of azure, are three martins with gilded beaks

[10] *Ibid.*

and claws, set in a triangular pattern of two and one. The newly acquired Marquette crest showed the martins with beaks but no claws to distinguish it from the arms of Laon.[11] When John the Good was unable to collect the full ransom, and his son Louis escaped to France, King John, true to his pledged word, voluntarily returned to captivity in London where he died in 1364 and was succeeded by his son Charles V (1364-1380). For the next century and a quarter the records of the town of Laon are silent regarding the Marquettes.

After 1470, Father Jacques Marquette's ancestry can be traced in detail. That year the acts of the city of Laon reveal that Louis-Nicolas Marquette held the office of *receveur des tailles,* or royal tax collector, a position then not held in disrepute as later when the Bourbons introduced their cruel tax farming system. A son of Louis-Nicolas, Gérard Marquette, who married Antoinette de Francquefort, seems to have succeeded his father as *receveur des tailles en l'élection de Laon,* a title which could be translated as tax commissioner for the town of Laon. Nicolas, Gérard's son, who married Marie Goulard, set himself up as a merchant at Crécy-sur-Serre, a small village situated sixteen kilometers from Laon. If the reader wonders what merchandise Nicolas handled, undoubtedly he was a dealer in wine and cloth, the two commodities produced at Laon. On the plains below the town grapes were the chief agricultural product. These were taken to Laon and made into wine which was stored in the innumerable limestone caves found on the flanks of Laon's jutting promontory. Wine was shipped by water to Paris, as it is even today. This Nicolas Marquette, who was Father Jacques Marquette's great-grandfather, must have done well financially for his son, Michel-Charles, was not only *procureur et receveur des consignations,* a very long title meaning treasurer, but he was also Vicomte de Beaurieux and Seigneur de Gruet et de Cornielle. Despite these very exalted titles, Michel-Charles was not a nobleman. The titles really adhered to lands he owned and because of his ownership of the land, to which these ancient titles pertained, he

[11] See *Larousse du XXe siècle,* IV, 338. A picture of the Laon coat of arms is given here.

was known by them. Michel-Charles, who married Claudine Chertemps, was Father Marquette's grandfather, all of which brings us to the Marquette family which is the immediate concern of this study.

Nicolas Marquette, the father of the subject of this biography, was born at Laon on September 15, 1597, just when France was returning to normalcy under Henri IV (1589-1610) after two decades of bitter struggle during the Religious Wars. In 1591, only six years before Nicolas was born, the Marquettes attained citywide notoriety when the family supported Henri IV while the citizenry generally was loyal to the League. For their stand the Marquettes were stripped of their property and exiled from Laon, which, as it turned out, supported the losing side. When Henri IV subdued Laon he not only recalled the Marquettes from exile, but restored all of their sequestered property and exempted them from the indemnity which he imposed on the rest of the citizens of Laon. As a grown man Nicolas Marquette held the office of *conseiller du roi* and, because of land he owned, was known as the Seigneur de la Tombelle. He first married Antoinette Baillieu, daughter of a prominent Laon family. When his childless wife died, he married Rose de la Salle, the daughter of Eustache de la Salle of Reims. The de la Salles were a well-to-do family of merchants whose residence in Reims was but a stone's throw from the cathedral. The family was well-connected at the University of Reims through Rose de la Salle's nephew, Lancelot, whose wife, Nicole Moet Brouillet, was the niece of Martin Dozet, chancellor of the University.[12] Saint John Baptist de la Salle, Lancelot's son, received a canonry at the cathedral of Reims in 1666 through the generosity of his great-uncle Dozet who resigned the position in John Baptist's favor. Business association may well explain how Nicolas Marquette happened to marry a girl residing in a city thirty miles southeast of Laon. It is certain, whatever the explanation, that Eustache de la Salle did not hand over his daughter to a stripling widower of about twenty-three unless he considered the Marquettes a family of means and respectability.[13]

[12] Edward A. Fitzpatrick, *La Salle, Patron of All Teachers,* 66.

[13] "A Genealogy of Father Marquette," *Woodstock Letters,* XXVIII (1899), 204-05.

Nicolas Marquette and Rose de la Salle were the parents of six children. These were, in the order of their births: Marie, Françoise, Jacques, the subject of this study, Louis, Jean-Bertrand, and Michel. Marie, the oldest, who died on September 15, 1693, at the age of seventy-two, was born in 1621. Françoise, aged seventy when she died at Laon on November 25, 1697, was born in 1627. Jacques was born on June 1, 1637. The year of the births of each of the three younger boys is mostly conjecture, based on the known ages of some of their children. Louis is thought to have been born in about 1640, chiefly because his oldest son, Louis-Hyacinthe Marquette, is known to have been born on May 22, 1669, perhaps when Louis was in his twenties. Jean-Bertrand was probably born about 1648, judging from the birth date of his son Charles Marquette, Sieur de Hauteville, who was born on March 18, 1693. There is no documentation surviving to assist historians in determining the age of the youngest, Michel, who, though married, had no children.[14]

Françoise Marquette was a lady of no small historical importance in her own right. In 1679, four years after the death of her famous brother Jacques, Françoise founded a school for the daughters of the poor of Laon. And certainly the town needed a school, for educational opportunities in Laon were sadly lacking. On May 1, 1578, Laon petitioned Henri III (1574-1589) for a grant of 4,000 ecrus to erect a school building and 2,000 to pay salaries of a faculty. With these funds the cathedral chapter opened a school, conducted by two brothers named Carolez, which was soon closed because the teachers were so derelict in their duty. In 1589, the people of Laon sought to open a Jesuit college in their town, but nothing came of the project. In the middle of the seventeenth century Laon had a college of sorts, but the institution was respected by neither parents nor students. Parents complained that the teachers were unduly severe and the cathedral chapter, responsible for the school, had continued difficulties with the teachers because of their evil ways.[15] If this was the limit of educational opportunity

[14] Hamy, *Au Mississippi*, 34.

[15] Pierre Delattre, editor, *Les établissements des Jésuites en France depuis quatre siècles*, II, 967-70.

for boys of good family, the girls could hardly have fared any better. And certainly no one gave thought to training the daughters of the poor. Tradition has it that Françoise Marquette opened her school in a house on the Champ Saint-Martin which her parents gave to her. Gathering a small group of charitable women around her, Françoise taught the girls their letters as well as to cook and sew and practice their religion faithfully. The little institution was never a large school, but neither was Laon a large town. It had its share of paupers, however, some so destitute that they lived in caves dug in the hillsides, as some do even today.[16]

Françoise was encouraged and assisted by her older sister, Marie, who, as a young woman, married Jean Maynon de Lillepré. After her school had been in operation for six years, Françoise obtained civil approval for it by an act notarized on October 9, 1685. In time Françoise and her companions became a diocesan community of nuns who were known as the Soeurs Marquette. When Marie Marquette Maynon de Lillepré died, in 1693, she willed quite a notable amount of property to the little community, some within the city and some on the plains below. As long as pious old *Tante* Françoise lived, the Marquette family said nothing about the will. But four years later, when Françoise died, the old lady was hardly cold in her grave before the children and grandchildren of Louis and Jean-Bertrand Marquette hauled the Soeurs Marquette into court, suing them for the restoration of the property which both Françoise and Marie had willed to the nuns.[17] Not quite two months after Françoise's demise, a court decision was registered by Laon's notary, on January 10, 1698, whereby the Soeurs Marquette were given legal title to Françoise's property within the city of Laon, but were obliged to return any outside the city. Françoise's little school carried on until 1805 when it was brought to an end by Napoleon who should have been too busy fighting Nelson at Trafalgar to bother with a handful of defenseless nuns conducting a free school for the poor of Laon. Somewhat later the work of the Soeurs Marquette was revived by another diocesan congregation called the

[16] Hamy, *Au Mississippi*, 324.
[17] *Ibid.*, 42-45.

Soeurs-de-la-Providence. The original building in which Françoise had her little school is long since gone, replaced by private dwellings, numbers 3 to 8 rue Marcelin Berthelot.

For five hundred years before Jacques Marquette was born and continuing down to our own day, the Marquettes of Laon served Laon, France, and God well and loyally. At Laon and in other cities of France they held office as mayors, magistrates, royal treasurers, notaries, tax collectors, sheriffs, judges, and advocates. A sense of civic responsibility seems to have been highly developed among the members of the Marquette family. As soon as one of them became financially independent he stood for public office from which he could not hope to earn more than a token salary. Though the military service of the Marquettes for France was noteworthy, the United States has particular reason to be grateful to them. Four Marquettes, all descendants of Jacques Marquette's brother Jean-Bertrand, fought for the American cause during our Revolution. All were sons of Jean-Claude Marquette de Marcy, a noted infantry captain who, on his retirement, became mayor of Laon. It is not inappropriate to devote a brief space to his four sons who bore arms in our Revolution.

In the spring of 1778, when France recognized the revolting British colonies in America as an independent nation, Louis XVI authorized his military forces to participate actively in the Revolution. Besides naval aid, the French sent thirteen trained regiments to participate in our land operations against British troops. One of these was the Touraine regiment which was sent to America on board vessels of Count de Grasse's squadron. Among the approximately 1,400 men of the Touraine regiment were Captain Jean-Charles Marquette, Lieutenant Nicolas Marquette, and Norbert Marquette. In the Poitou regiment, which also came to help us, was François-Guillaume Marquette de Marcy. Sailing on April 12, 1780, De Grasse brought his squadron to Havana where he stopped to borrow 1,200,000 livres from the Spanish governor and took on board 3,400 French troops who were there awaiting his arrival. Sailing to Chesapeake Bay, De Grasse landed the French troops who joined forces with General Washington's soldiers. The two armies slowly pushed Cornwallis and his British soldiers into the peninsula at Yorktown. With the aid of the French militia Washington forced Cornwallis to surrender on October 19, 1782. Of the Marquettes involved in that military operation, Jean-Charles, the captain, died aboard the *Phenix* in 1780 without ever seeing the land he had come to help. Nicolas Marquette was killed at Yorktown on October 5, 1782. Norbert Marquette lost his life on June 10, 1782.[18] François-Guillaume Marquette survived unscathed and returned to Laon where he married Adélaide-Cunégonde-Dorothée de Wimpffen on July 30, 1793. That veteran of our Revolution died on January 6, 1814, leaving no male heirs. One cannot help feeling sorry for a much younger brother of the family, François Guillaume Auguste, only twelve when his great tall brothers swaggered off to war while he, poor lad, was forced to stay at home and go to school.

Strangely, there does not seem to have been any tradition among the Marquettes of serving the Church. One searches in vain for a Marquette who was a bishop, but only a few Marquettes seemed to have entered holy orders. In 1620, a Marquette was curé of Saint-Martin-au-Parvis at Laon, the parish church of Jacques Marquette's father, Nicolas. That Marquette may have been our Father Jacques Marquette's uncle Michel who, quite likely, was our subject's first schoolmaster. If that abbé Marquette was an uncle of the future Jesuit, his name had to be Michel for he is the only one of his generation who did not marry. In 1657, a Marquette was dean of the cathedral chapter of Saint-Pierre-au-Marché. In 1664, one of the canons of the cathedral at Laon was a Marquette. Ten years later, in 1674, the prior of the abbey of Saint-Martin at Laon was a Marquette. At approximately this same time a Marquette held a responsible office among the Franciscans or, as the French called them, the *Cordeliers*.[19]

There are no direct descendants of Father Jacques Marquette's father still residing at Laon. But several of the Jesuit's *petits neveus*, as they call themselves, still run about the streets of Laon playing much the same games that Father Marquette played when he was

[18] H. Mérou, et al., editors, *Combattants français de la guerre Amérique, 1778-1783,* 320, 325, 327.

[19] Hamy, *Au Mississippi,* 36.

a small boy. At Laon there are some twenty indirect descendants of Louis Marquette, Jacques Marquette's younger brother. Of these, the Barbier family is the most prominent. The abbé Pierre Barbier was chaplain for French colonial troops during World War II, ministering to Vietnamese, Moroccan, and Sinhalese soldiers. He spent two trying years as a war prisoner. Louis, Pierre's brother, a Laon jeweler, increased the population of Laon with seven very blond children, a characteristic which causes one to wonder about the physical appearance of Father Jacques Marquette.

Innumerable representations of Marquette have been done in oil, bronze, and stone, from full figures to busts and bas-reliefs. Perhaps the best known is Gaetano Trentanove's marble statue which the state of Wisconsin presented to Statuary Hall in the nation's capital at Washington. The artist modeled the statue's face from a portrait of Father Pierre François Xavier de Charlevoix, a French Jesuit and noted historian of New France whose portrait was painted when he was over sixty and quite aged.[20] Father Marquette was within three weeks of his thirty-eighth birthday when he died in 1675. Donald Guthrie McNab, a Canadian artist of some ability, who was commissioned in the late nineteenth century to produce portraits of early Jesuit missionaries for Collège Sainte-Marie, Montreal, accidentally discovered a quite ancient picture of a Jesuit which, for a time, was believed to be a portrait of Marquette made from life. The face in the picture is that of a dark, balding, almost beardless, prematurely aging, kindly young man. Careful research has demonstrated that the picture cannot be an authentic portrait of Marquette.[21] Herman A. McNeil's series of bronze reliefs, executed for the Marquette Building in Chicago, portray a tall, ascetical actor who is obviously playing a part. William Lamprecht's gigantic picture of Father Marquette addressing a group of Indians at Lake Peoria shows us a handsome, attractive young Bavarian with a great mop of black hair, his flowing ecclesiastical cloak draped gracefully over his left arm. The model Lamprecht used for the picture was

[20] A copy of the portrait was used as the frontispiece for Volume LXVII of *The Jesuit Relations and Allied Documents*, edited by Reuben Gold Thwaites. This collection is hereafter cited as *Relations*.

[21] *Ibid.*, LXXI, 400-03.

Father Francis Xavier Weninger, a rather noted nineteenth-century Jesuit missionary who was a Bavarian as was the artist. This picture became widely known because it was once used on a commemorative stamp issued by the United States. None of these portraits approaches a representation of the actual Marquette.

In 1952, Harry Wood, a contemporary artist, was commissioned to paint a portrait of Father Marquette for a banking firm at Peoria, Illinois. When he failed to unearth any authentic likeness of Marquette, Wood determined to construct a composite picture of the missionary from faces of citizens at Laon. On visiting Marquette's birthplace, the artist met Louis Barbier and his seven blond children. From these Wood made a portrait which shows a tall, spare, athletic blond with very blue eyes, sparse hair, a strong chin, and a high forehead. The figure in the picture is holding a very elaborate calumet in his strong, calloused hands. The costume worn by the figure is an exceptionally ill-fitting, travel-worn soutane. Prescinding from the value of the portrait as a work of art, Wood presented a real person. It is not at all unlikely that Marquette actually was quite tall, blond, and physically strong. Until shortly before his premature death, every one of his superiors referred to him as a strong, robust man.

The heritage which Jacques Marquette received from his ancestors was an enviable one. He stemmed from a long line of courageous, dedicated, devout men who served France and God assiduously without counting the cost. His maternal ancestors were equally as loyal and as dedicated. If ever a child was formed for greatness, that child was Jacques Marquette.

JACQUES MARQUETTE

1637-1654

Jacques Marquette was born at Laon on June 1, 1637, which happens to be the day Spanish Catholics celebrate the feast of Saint Iñigo, an eleventh-century abbot of the Benedictine monastery of Saint Salvador at Oña, whose name was given to Saint Ignatius Loyola at his baptism.[1] Even if Nicolas Marquette, Jacques' father, had been aware of the existence of the Spanish Benedictine saint, he would probably not have given the name to his son, for the Marquettes did not follow the widespread European custom of conferring on children the name of the saint on whose feast day they were born. For centuries the Marquette male children were named Nicolas, Gérard, Jean, Antoine, Charles, or Jacques. When he was

[1] James Brodrick, *Saint Ignatius Loyola*, 24.

baptized, perhaps in the parish church of Saint-Pierre-le-Viel or in the cathedral of Notre-Dame-de-Laon, the new infant was named Jacques. Through no fault of the clergy of Laon, Jacques Marquette's baptismal record did not survive the devastation wrought on ecclesiastical records at so many places in France during the French Revolution. We know the date and place of his birth because when Jacques became a Jesuit in 1654 he was required to present documentary evidence that he had been baptized and confirmed.[2] The bare facts are historically accurate, but one would like to know if he was lovingly gowned in an ancient baptismal dress worn by a long line of Marquettes before him, and if his sister Marie, then sixteen, carried him to the font, and who his sponsors were, and if he cried when the officiating priest put a pinch of salt in his mouth or when the cold water touched his warm little head. Probably the joyous occasion was properly celebrated since Nicolas Marquette was a prominent lawyer at Laon and the Marquettes had been signally honored by Henri IV thirty-six years previously. Perhaps because of this Jacques was baptized with great solemnity by the bishop of Laon and at the font in the great cathedral. We can be quite certain that when the infant was brought home to his mother the house overflowed with guests come to congratulate the parents and exclaim over the new baby. And, as everyone does on these occasions, people surmised about the child's future. He would grow up to be a great lawyer like his father, or a bishop, maybe even a

[2] *Societatis Jesu constitutiones et epitome instituti,* 330. The regulation regarding these documents reads: *"In quavis religione omnes aspirantes, antiquam admittantur, exhibere debent testimonium recepti Baptismi et Confirmationis."* The sentence is translated: "Those who wish to enter must present documentary proof that they have been baptized and confirmed." A confirming proof for the accuracy of Marquette's birth date is to be found in the catalog of the Jesuit Province of Champagne for 1654, the year he entered the Jesuit novitiate. There he is reported as being from Laon and having been born on June 1, 1637. See Louis Carrez, editor, *Documenta ad historiam Societatis Jesu in Gallia concinandam: Catologi sociorum et officiorum provinciae Companiae Societatis Jesu ab anno 1616 ad annum 1773,* V, 210. It should be explained that each Jesuit province issued an annual list of all its members, giving each Jesuit's date of birth and entrance, when he was ordained, where he then was, and what work he was doing. Carrez added the place of origin of each Jesuit.

pope. Why not? Didn't Jacques Pantaléon become Urban IV, and he a Laon cobbler's son?

That we know almost nothing about Jacques Marquette until he was nine years old is hardly surprising. This was not an age when parents kept baby books or bronzed baby shoes. Jacques was not a first child whose very existence awed and astonished two callow young parents, as though they were the only people who ever had a child. Certainly his two sisters, Marie and Françoise, watched his every waking hour, as older sisters usually do. They fed him and gave him a finger to hold as he took his first faltering steps; they cuddled him, played with him, and washed his smeared little face when he got into the jam jar. All too soon he was a toddler, wandering into the sacred precincts of his father's office with its shelves of great law books and stacks of parchment documents which he was forbidden to touch. It did not seem long before he was playing with other small boys, all very busy with sticks and pot covers which were, in the magic world of childhood, anything but what the prosaic passerby saw. It seemed to his mother that one day he was a baby asleep on her shoulder and the next he was a sturdy little boy old enough to be given a schoolbag, dressed in skirts, as French boys of five and six still are, and sent off down the street to begin learning his letters from his uncle Michel, M. le curé de Saint-Martin-au-Parvis.[3] Jacques and the sons of other bourgeois parents copied the beautifully executed letters of the alphabet, so easily formed by their teacher, until they were able to reproduce a reasonable facsimile of them on their slates with their blunt pieces of chalk. Slowly the letters formed words and soon the words were Latin. Then one could hear them chanting declensions and painstakingly pronouncing Latin sentences. At the end of each day Jacques ran quickly up the steep lane to his father's house, bursting with news of his great accomplishments.

[3] It is not certain that Nicolas Marquette's brother Michel was the pastor, but tradition holds that Jacques received his first schooling from a sacerdotal uncle, pastor of the parish noted. At least it is true that, of his Marquette uncles, Michel is the only one concerning whom there is no marriage record. It is considered quite unlikely that the teacher would have been a de la Salle uncle for the position of pastor would not normally have been conferred on a priest not a native of Laon.

Not every day was the same for young Jacques. There were great feast days when the whole family went to the cathedral for the solemn Mass sung by the bishop and the choirboys, of whom, in due time, Jacques might have been one. Oral tradition has it that when Jacques was six he went on a pilgrimage to Notre-Dame-de-Liesse. It was early in May 1643 and all France was praying for the recovery of Louis XIII who lay sick to death at Saint-Germain-en-Laye. The bishop of Laon, Benjamin Brichanteau, organized a pilgrimage, urging all who could to walk the eight miles to Liesse where they would kneel before the miraculous statue of our Lady and plead with her to heal their king. Everyone at Laon knew that the statue had been transported by the angels from Jerusalem during the eleventh century and in its company had come three crusaders from Laon as well as the beautiful Egyptian princess, Ismérie, who had become a Catholic and hence must flee from the anger of her father.[4] One need not be surprised at such a small child going on that long a journey afoot. Everybody walked in those days and, besides, this was a pilgrimage on which people moved sedately, singing hymns and reciting the rosary. If the boy tired, his father could carry him a while, or his twenty-two-year-old sister Marie, or even Françoise who was then sixteen. The fervent prayers of the pilgrims did not obtain a return to health for their king, but they might have helped procure for him the grace of dying well. The moody, brooding Louis XIII, who had much on his conscience when he came to face his God, died piously on May 14, 1643, with Saint Vincent de Paul kneeling at his bedside. His successor, Louis XIV, then a child of five, would have important, if indirect, influence on the career of Jacques Marquette.

When he was a grown man Marquette revealed a quite significant fact about his childhood which permits us a glimpse at what

[4] Edouard Lecompte, "Les Jésuites du Canada au XIXe siècle," *Lettres du Bas-Canada*, IV (1950), 73-94. Marquette would be pleased to know that some of the ashes of the ancient statue of Notre-Dame-de-Liesse are now in the Jesuit church of the Gesu at Montreal. During the French Revolution the shrine at Liesse, including the statue, was burned to the ground. The people of Liesse collected the ashes of the statue and put them within a new one. A Canadian Jesuit, Father François Cazeau, was given some of the ashes which he brought to Montreal in 1877.

sort of a boy he really was. At twenty-eight when he volunteered for the missions a second time he recorded, in his letter to Father John Paul Oliva, general of the Jesuits, that he had ambitioned becoming a missionary ". . . from my earliest boyhood and the first light of reason . . ."[5] It would probably have been surprising if the young son of pious Catholic parents in Marquette's day did not nurture that aspiration. For such a child dreaming of a missionary career would be much like a present-day American boy ambitioning a trip to the moon. During the seventeenth century, Catholic France experienced a remarkable revival of solid religious fervor following the Wars of Religion which had rent the country asunder toward the end of the previous century. From the first decade of the seventeenth century forward France was blessed with a host of sincerely holy men and women, many of them later canonized, who zealously preached to the peasantry, reformed ecclesiastical studies, organized works of charity, established new devotions, and founded a number of contemplative and active religious orders. Pierre de Bérulle started the Oratory in 1611. Vincent de Paul established the Congregation of the Missions thirteen years later. Louise de Marillac began the Daughters of Charity in 1633. Jean-Jacques Olier laid the foundation for the Society of Saint-Sulpice at approximately the same time. A little later the Society for the Foreign Missions had its inception at Paris. Henri de Levis, Duc de Ventadour, established the Company of the Blessed Sacrament, a lay organization dedicated to aiding religious reform. Jerome le Royer de la Dauversière, a married layman, was the founder of a congregation of nursing nuns. The religious vitality of France in those days turned many men's minds to fervor and instilled in them a desire to revitalize the Church.

Concurrently mission activities during the second half of the sixteenth and the whole of the seventeenth centuries were, perhaps, the most important movement within the Church. The Faith, until

[5] Gilbert J. Garraghan, "Some Hitherto Unpublished Marquettiana," *Mid-America*, XVIII (1935), 16. Marquette to Oliva, March 19, 1665. Oliva was vicar-general of the Jesuits from July 27, 1661, to July 31, 1664, when he succeeded Goswin Nickel to the office of general. See Louis Schmitt, *Synopsis historiae Societatis Jesu*, 501.

then nearly entirely confined to Europe and the Near East, was carried to almost every corner of the world by courageous missionaries. In 1622, encouragement of the mission movement was climaxed by the creation of the Sacred Congregation for the Propagation of the Faith, a papal bureau which exercised ecclesiastical jurisdiction over all missionary activities. Catholic Europe was bubbling with interest in the heroic deeds and spiritual conquests of missionaries who were enlightening the spiritual darkness of the mysterious lands of the fabled Prester John, China, Japan, India, Ceylon, the Spice Islands, Brazil, Peru, the Caribbean, and Canada. Francis Xavier, the magnetic apostle of the Indies, was canonized only fifteen years before Jacques Marquette was born. Published accounts written by missionaries, describing mysterious lands and strange peoples, circulated widely. Long before he knew where New France really was, Jacques may well have heard his father read Father Paul Le Jeune's gripping account in the Jesuit *Relations* of 1634 describing his harrowing winter spent in the open with the Montagnais, or the details of Father Jean de Brébeuf's journey to the Huron country.[6] It requires little imagination to picture a pensive Jacques, leaning against an ancient parapet, gazing out across the broad plain three hundred feet below, dreaming of sailing off to the Far East, there to conquer vast multitudes for Christ. Of the hundreds of young French boys who whiled away a lazy summer afternoon imagining themselves preaching to assembled thousands on the banks of the Ganges or discoursing learnedly before a gathering of erudite Persian scholars, not many kept their fancies alive. But Jacques did. When there was company in the house and he was asked the inevitable question posed to all small boys: "Well, Jacques, what will you be when you grow up, a lawyer?" one can hear him reply with settled conviction, "I shall be a missionary." And his mother interjected, laughingly, "Jacques has been saying that since he was a toddler."[7] Yet the boy was in earnest and his

[6] See Le Jeune's description of his winter with the Montagnais, *Relations*, VII, 111-13. The account of Brébeuf's voyage to the Huron country may be read in *ibid.*, VIII, 91.

[7] The conversation is, of course, invented.

tenacity manifests a firmness of will, a developing dedication which he was never to lose.

After Jacques had attended his uncle's school for two or three years and had learned reading, writing, and a little Latin, it was time for his parents to give thought to his educational future. Certainly it would not do to enroll him at the very unsatisfactory *collège* at Laon where he would probably learn nothing and, besides, be exposed to the insobriety and slovenliness of incompetent teachers. Nicolas Marquette, a prosperous burgher, could well afford to send his eldest son away to receive a proper education. Bishop Brichanteau encouraged the Laonnais of quality to enroll their sons in the Jesuit college at Reims.[8] Madam Marquette agreed with the choice, for Reims was only a day's stagecoach ride away and if the boy got lonely he could visit relatives. Jacques probably rejoiced at the choice since he may have thought of it as the first step toward his goal.

Because his years at Reims were the most impressionable of Marquette's life, we must know something about the character of the education he received and understand the ideals which the Jesuit system of education sought to inculcate in students. When Saint Ignatius Loyola agreed to conduct schools he soon formulated objectives which his followers were expected to attain through that apostolate. Education was considered by Ignatius to be a means

[8] Delattre, *Etablissements*, II, 968-69. The Jesuit college at Reims was issued *lettres-patents* by Henri IV on March 26, 1606, probably at the request of François Brulart, abbé de Valroy. The school was first housed in the defunct Collège des Ecrevées whose building was owned by the Reims cathedral chapter. In 1608 Brulart and his brother Nicolas bought the Hôtel de Cerny on the rue Neuve and gave it to the Jesuits. The school opened on October 18, 1608, with an enrollment of 500 students. In time more property was purchased and additions made to the original building until the structure measured 160 meters by 80 meters. In 1609 the school was incorporated as a college of the University of Reims. In 1620 a residence hall was opened, housing about a hundred students. During Marquette's years as a student the school's enrollment was approximately 700. The college owned a country place at Cormontreuil to which the students went for relaxation on Tuesdays and Thursdays. Much of the old college building was demolished during the nineteenth century. The portion of the building still standing is now used as a general hospital. See *ibid.*, IV, 278-302.

of promoting the salvation and perfection of students who would, when graduated, vigorously and intelligently permeate their social environment with the doctrines and spirit of the kingdom of Christ.[9] To attain this objective Ignatius and his followers constructed a curriculum incorporating the best elements of the educational systems of their day. They adopted and refined the system in vogue at the University of Paris, an orderly progression from the study of grammar through the humanities to philosophy and the professions. The Jesuit curriculum was calculated to sharpen the intellect, inculcate balanced judgment, instill an appreciation for culture, and return to society a poised, eloquent, fervent Christian. Though Saint Ignatius himself was unable to complete the formulation of his system before his death, his followers elaborated his ideas into the *Ratio atque institutio studiorum Societatis Jesu* which, after several previous revisions, was adopted in 1599.[10] The *Ratio* emphasized classical learning and philosophy, both because the study of languages in depth provides excellent mental discipline and because the most essential tool of any profession in the seventeenth century was a consummate command of the Latin and Greek classics. The beginning student in the Jesuit college was thoroughly grounded in the grammar and syntax of Latin and Greek. After two or three years the boy was expected to be able to read, write, and, in the case of Latin, speak the language fluently. As his ability increased the student was introduced to the classical authors while, at the same time, he learned history, mathematics, geography, and the ability to handle his native language elegantly. Then the adolescent spent two or three years reading widely in the classics while he acquired written and spoken eloquence, public presence, and unaffected poise. At about fifteen the student began the study of the natural sciences, logic, and metaphysics. When these courses were completed the incipient adult, then about seventeen, was eligible for the degree of bachelor of arts and was thoroughly prepared to begin courses in

[9] George E. Ganss, *Saint Ignatius' Idea of a Jesuit University*, 18.

[10] The best study of the *Ratio studiorum* in English is Allen P. Farrell's *The Jesuit Code of Liberal Education: Development and Scope of the Ratio studiorum.* This study is hereafter cited as *Jesuit Code.*

law, medicine, theology, or any other profession.[11] The end product of Jesuit education was the poised, able, fervent Catholic, eminently prepared to influence the social world which he was about to enter. Through the seventeenth century hundreds of French boys graduated from the seventy-seven Jesuit colleges. Of these, Reims was not the largest or the most renowned; neither was it the smallest or the least known.

A few days before October 18, 1646, when the school term officially opened at Reims, Jacques Marquette, accompanied by his mother, took the stage for Reims and a strange new life.[12] Safely locked in the boot of the coach was the boy's box containing "a sufficient supply of personal linen so that [he could] change it frequently," as well as, "a long robe with a red cincture" cut to the pattern dictated by the college.[13] After a few days' rest with relatives Jacques was dressed in long white stockings, stout, low-cut boots, baggy pantaloons, a white shirt with a very broad, flat collar, a short jacket with ample sleeves, and a sailor hat with a very wide brim.[14] Madam Marquette and her son presented themselves at the college for a formal call on Father Jacques de Marnay, the rector, who was certainly aware of the Marquette connection with the

[11] Joseph Jouvency, *De la manière d'apprendre et d'enseigner*, 120-21. A noted classicist and able teacher, Jouvency was directed to write this little book, first published in 1691, to instruct young Jesuits in the manner of teaching according to the principles of the *Ratio studiorum.*

[12] Though the date of Marquette's enrollment at Reims cannot be ascertained from any document, we know that he had finished at least one year of philosophical studies when he entered the Society of Jesus in 1654. Since his mother came from a family well acquainted with educational life, it is unlikely that she would not have enrolled Jacques in the earliest class for which he was eligible so that he would have the benefit of the complete Jesuit system. This grade would have been the *septième*, and Jacques would have been about nine years old. Reims did not normally have this grade, but the year indicated as that in which Jacques is presumed to have been enrolled Jacques Brion was assigned to teach *infim. gr.*, that is the lowest class. See Carrez, *Catologi*, IV, 144. He probably began the *septième* in 1646. He would then have begun the *sixième* in 1647, the *cinquième* in 1648, the *quatrième* in 1649, the *troisième* in 1650, *humanité* in 1651, *rhetorique* in 1652, and *logique* in 1653.

[13] Delattre, *Etablissements*, IV, 304. A lengthy list of rules is quoted here.

[14] The description of Marquette's costume is drawn from Mathieu Le Nain's painting, *Le repas de famille.* Le Nain was a contemporary of Marquette and a native of Laon.

de la Salles, a prominent Reims family.[15] The duty call completed, Jacques was handed over to Etienne Macheret, a twenty-four-year-old Jesuit scholastic who was prefect of the youngest group of students at Reims.[16] Jacques was given a tour of the school, assigned a cubicle in the dormitory of the *pension,* a place in the refectory, his classroom, and a seat in the chapel.[17] There Jacques prayed for aid to do well at school and Macheret prayed for the future of his small charge. From that moment Jacques was never out of the immediate presence of one or other Jesuit from October 18, Saint Luke's Day, when classes began each year, until September 14, the inception of the short three-week summer vacation. On the feast of Saint Luke the whole student body attended the Mass of the Holy Ghost and after it an assembly at which Father Rector, de Marnay, addressed them, urging them to apply themselves diligently to their studies and to live piously. Then the students dispersed to the various classrooms for *lectio brevis,* a short class period during which the boys met their new teachers. Young Gérard Brion, Marquette's teacher, who was that day beginning his teaching career, called the roll, assigned the first lesson of the year, and then dismissed his pupils for the day.[18]

The following day the rather strenuous regular order of the day began in earnest. At 5:30 Jacques was rousted from his bed by a bell summoning him to morning prayers, which he was at liberty

[15] The rector would certainly have known of the de la Salle family since the chancellor of the University of Reims, Martin Dozet, was an uncle by marriage of Rose de la Salle's nephew, Lancelot. Also, there were de la Salles in the Jesuit college. See Carrez, *Catologi,* VII, lxxiii.

[16] *Ibid.,* 144. In Jesuit parlance, scholastics are aspirants to the priesthood undergoing their training.

[17] Camille de Rochemonteix, *Un collège de Jésuites aux XVIIe et XVIIIe siècles: le collège Henri IV de La Flèche,* II, 29. The dormitories in the *pension* were divided into enclosed cubicles, each having a bed, a table, a chair, and a chest. Students did all their studying in these cubicles. Rochemonteix's work is hereafter cited as *La Flèche.*

[18] Gérard Brion was born at Tilly in 1623 and entered the Jesuit novitiate on May 24, 1645. After his ordination, probably in 1658, he went to the Caribbean islands as a missionary and spent his active life there. He died at Avignon on April 12, 1678. See Carrez, *Catologi,* V, 189.

to attend in slippers and a dressing gown.[19] At the end of prayers and a visit to the Blessed Sacrament, Marquette splashed cold water on his face, donned his formal school gown with its red sash, and promptly began studying. When his turn came he reported to the prefect with his books and written exercises for a review of what had been learned the previous day and the work about to be undertaken today. At 7:45 breakfast was served, a tumbler of wine and chunks of crisp French bread which the boys tore from the loaf with their bare hands.[20] Classes began at 8:00 and continued until 10:30 when the whole student body attended Mass. The major meal of the day was served at 11:45. The menu was hot soup, mutton or beef, vegetables, wine, bread, and a dessert, in fact two desserts at least thrice a week. Recreation followed until 2:00. The younger lads ran about in one of the inner courts, but the sedate elder students paced up and down, discoursing learnedly about philosophy or literature.[21] Classes began again at 2:00 and lasted until 4:00. At 4:30 the boarders raced to the refectory for *goûté*, a light repast to hold them until supper. After their snack everyone went to his desk for study until 6:00, the welcome bell for supper, a substantial meal of salad, boiled or roasted meat, vegetables, the inevitable French bread, and a dessert.[22] The boys were again free for recreation until 7:45 at which time they resumed studying. During that period each boy went to his prefect to review the day's work. At 8:45 all assembled for night prayers, visited the Blessed Sacrament, and were ready for bed by 9:00. As the season advanced the great drafty dormitories grew chill and damp from the fog rising off the Marne River on whose banks Reims stands. Then in the dark mornings there was a roaring fire around which shivering boys huddled. In the late afternoon and evening, when a small lamp was needed at every desk

[19] Rochemonteix, *La Flèche*, II, 29. The students wore their gowns to class and when they went into the town.

[20] Delattre, *Etablissements*, IV, 306.

[21] Rochemonteix, *La Flèche*, II, 35-36, gives a description of a recreation period at a Jesuit college in Germany at approximately this period. The younger boys are described as playing tag or handball while the sophisticated rhetoricians and philosophers gathered on a broad porch, disputing with "ardor and much clamoring."

[22] *Ibid.*, 33.

so that the boys could see to study, many a lad warmed his hands over the chimney of his student lamp.

If the reader is already imagining Jacques Marquette fading to a shadow under the strict regime, let him take heart. Every Thursday was a holiday on which Jacques could stay in his warm bed until 6:45 in the morning. After Mass and breakfast he studied from 9:00 until 10:00, but then he was free to play until dinner. At 1:00 he went to Vespers and heard a sermon. After that he could take a walk with the prefect and his fellow students or sometimes go on a picnic to the college villa at Cormontreuil. Before supper there was a study period and again after recreation in the evening before bedtime.[23] And there were always ecclesiastical feasts, the rector's name's day, the king's birthday, and an occasional unexpected free day in honor of a visiting dignitary such as the Jesuit provincial, the bishop, or other person of quality.[24] On the great feasts there were no classes or study periods at all. And, what was best, the meals were elaborate: two meat courses, assorted cheese, fine wine, and two desserts.[25] On these occasions a student mounted the lectern and delivered a carefully prepared address on a point of philosophy or on some literary subject with the whole faculty present. The older students in turn underwent this ordeal in preparation for which each must have labored long and worriedly, for what if the mind went completely blank! Whatever we think of the practice, con-

[23] Delattre, *Etablissements*, IV, 305.

[24] Rochemonteix, *La Flèche*, II, 42, lists the following ecclesiastical feasts which were holidays: Saint Ignatius Loyola, Saint Francis Xavier, Saint Francis Borgia, New Year's Day, Epiphany, Saints Fabian and Sebastian, the Purification, Saint Matthew, the Annunciation, Saint Mark, Saints Philip and James, Saint Barnabas, the Nativity of Saint John the Baptist, Saints Peter and Paul, Saint Mary Magdalene, Saint James the Apostle, Saint Ann, the Nativity of the Blessed Virgin, the Exaltation of the Holy Cross, Saint Michael, Saint Luke, Saints Simon and Jude, All Saints, All Souls, Saint Catherine, Saint Andrew, Saint Nicolas, the Immaculate Conception, Saint Thomas the Apostle, Christmas, Saint Stephen, the Holy Innocents. Besides these, the students had no class during Holy Week, and they were also free on local feasts, for example, Saint Remi, patron of Reims. In all there were about fifty days on which there was no class.

[25] *Ibid.*, 33. A dish often served on feast days was capon.

temporaries speak of it as a "charming custom."[26] It would be incorrect to imagine Jacques relaxing only by pacing along the streets of Reims behind the prefect followed by a long line of scholars properly dressed in their gowns which identified them as students of the Jesuit college. At home, in the college courts, the small fry played blindman's buff, checkers, quoits, backgammon, and spinned tops. They wrestled and held foot races just as one sees small boys do today. There were billiard tables available as well as tennis courts and handball courts. Those who wished could take dancing lessons, fencing, drawing, and instructions in heraldry, provided their parents were willing to pay the sums each of these lay instructors charged per semester. Also, with parental permission, boys could go into the town accompanied by a prefect, but when they did they must avoid "cabarets and dangerous company."[27] Putting the regular schedule together with the order on feast days and allowing for the numerous days on which the boys were free, the whole regime was hardly one which merits pity for the student undergoing it.

Fundamentally, student discipline was rigidly enforced and academic work was pursued with a singleness of purpose. No boy, least of all a boarder, could escape attending class without homework done and well prepared to participate. Teachers, however, employed all sorts of pedagogical devices to stimulate student interest. Classes were frequently divided into teams for competition; prizes were awarded for academic excellence, not only at the end of the academic year, but quarterly. At frequent intervals visitors were invited to be present at class competitions to act as referees. Basically, the Jesuit teachers were firm, if just, taskmasters. Every day they gave a prelection explaining the matter to be dealt with in the current class.[28] Then the class proceeded to their work, prodded by questions from their teacher who called on various students to recite. Those listening were expected to attend and correct the mistakes of the one reciting. Toward the end of the class, work for the

[26] *Ibid.*, 44.

[27] Delattre, *Etablissements*, IV, 305-06.

[28] Jouvency, *De la manière*, 105, gives an example of a prelection of a passage of Virgil.

following day was outlined and written assignments announced. At the beginning of each class a monitor collected the written homework and woe betide the boy whose assignment was not ready. There was no escaping; perforce the boys learned.[29]

Though extracurricular activities in Marquette's day differed somewhat from those of a modern student, they were engaged in with a great deal of enthusiasm. Each level of the college had its own academy in which the participants pushed their knowledge farther than classwork demanded. There were academies for the philosophers, the rhetoricians, and for the boys studying grammar. But the major activity was the staging of dramatic productions. In his *Die gesellschaft Jesu, ihre statzugen und ihre erfolge,* Moritz Meschler describes the objectives which the Jesuits expected theatricals to attain for their students:

> By means of their theatrical presentations, the young students were intended to become accustomed to a lack of self-conscious constraint in appearing before a large audience, to a nobility of carriage, to an easy grace in the use of gestures, to clarity of diction, to true and just expression of sentiments. Moreover, the memory should be thereby more developed, and their vocabulary enlarged and perfected . . .
>
> The second aim of the Society's dramatic presentations was moral instruction. Its basic principal was the sound one that an extraordinary power for spiritual reform was to be found in a good theatre where by use of various external means it is possible to work upon the will through the senses and the imagination, presenting virtue as attractive and vice as something horrible. The history of the Jesuit theatre gives testimony of a splendid spiritual influence on both actors and audience.[30]

[29] Farrell, *Jesuit Code,* 340, gives a list of the rules pertaining to studies which were for the use of students. We quote a few: "1. Love and obey your professors as you would your parents. 9. Interrupt long and difficult study with some healthy exercise. 15. To sleep in class, to talk, trifle or disturb the professor is wholly unbecoming a scholar. 22. What you cannot retain in your memory, write on paper; and if you are unable to note down in class all the important points of the prelection do it at home. 25. Do not limit your efforts to prescribed study; with the teacher's counsel you can easily undertake further work of reading, writing, and memorizing."

[30] Moritz Meschler, *Die gesellschaft Jesu, ihre statzugen und ihre erfolge,* II, 251.

Eighteen years before Marquette was enrolled, the Jesuit college at Reims had established the tradition of offering dramatic productions for the public as well as for the student body. In 1628 the boarders staged *La conquest du char de la gloire par le grand Theandre*, produced to celebrate the fall of La Rochelle. In 1629 a student cast produced *Recit de l'ombre de Cloridian*, a drama written by Father Pierre le Moyne. In 1631 they staged *Joannes Elumosinarius*, a Latin play honoring the school's founder, François Brulart. *Les feux de joie* was produced in 1631. *Divus Ludovicus*, obviously in honor of Louis XIII, was performed on August 6, 1641. *Demetrius et Antiphilus*, a comedy, was produced on February 19, 1648, while Marquette was a student at Reims. The most ambitious dramatic undertaking was the *Lys sacré, roy des fleurs ou le sacré de Louys XIV* produced in the presence of the sixteen-year-old Louis XIV in June 1654, when the king was at Reims for his royal consecration. Those who saw the color film of the coronation of Elizabeth II of England in Westminster Abbey on June 2, 1953, will have a clear notion of the pomp and splendor surrounding the *sacré* of Louis XIV. Every nobleman of France who could possibly come was at Reims for the great occasion. And each was anxious to be seen at every affair attended by the king and his court. Every student and teacher at the Jesuit college slaved for months in advance preparing the play, the scenery, scrubbing the whole school, including every student and servant. The honor of the whole Jesuit system of education in France was at stake; nothing must go wrong! The actors with speaking parts were drilled until they and the director were ready to drop. The ballet chorus was put through its routines time and again until it was letter perfect. Jacques was not a principal actor, but practically everybody was in the ballet, from the smallest *chou* to the lordly philosophers. At last the royal outriders swept up before the door of the collège followed by the royal coach bearing the young monarch who, for all his small stature, was majesty personified. In his train were the princes of the blood, the constables of France, the cardinal archbishop of Paris, the *noblesse, haute et petite*. Finally, the momentous occasion was over, and without a single misadventure. The actors delivered their lines with verve and effect; the orchestra played beautifully; the ballet routine was done to perfection. Theatricals do, indeed, inculcate poise, grace of manner, control of vocal inflection as they, no doubt, also cause playwrights and directors to have nervous prostration.[31]

Since every student is profoundly influenced by his teachers, it is not amiss to glance at the Jesuits who taught Jacques while he was at Reims. When Marquette completed his year of grammar and started the *sixième,* in the fall of 1647, his teacher was Thierry Beschefer, a native of Châlons-sur-Marne. Born on March 25, 1630, Beschefer entered the Jesuit novitiate at Nancy on May 24, 1646, and was sent, after one year of ascetical training, to teach at Reims. After three years in the classroom Beschefer went to the University of Pont-à-Mousson where he studied philosophy until 1653. Then he taught at Reims, Auxerre, Sens, Reims again, and Bar-le-Duc, after which he went back to Pont-à-Mousson in 1657 for his theology. He was probably ordained in the spring of 1661. He volunteered for the mission of New France in 1663, writing to the Jesuit general that his desire for the missions was ". . . ignited by the flames which crowned Father Brébeuf and Lalemant with a glorious death among the Iroquois."[32] Beschefer reached Quebec on June 19, 1665, and spent twenty-six years as a missionary. He returned to France in 1690 and died at Reims on February 4, 1711. Significantly, Beschefer was inspired to seek the mission of New France at exactly the time he was associating with the young student, Jacques Marquette. Father Paul Ragueneau's *Relations* of 1649 and 1650,

[31] Carlos Sommervogel, *Bibliothèque de la compagnie de Jésus,* X, 1630. He gives complete bibliographical information about these plays. Students at the Jesuit college at Quebec were giving plays soon after the institution opened. See Angus Macdougall, "La réception de M. le vicomte d'Argenson," *Lettres du Bas-Canada,* IV (1950), 95-104. The author presents the complete text of a play given on July 28, 1658, in honor of the arrival of the new governor, d'Argenson. On March 1, 2, 1940, the students of Loyola College, Baltimore, staged an English version of *Cenodoxus Redivivus,* a play written by the Jesuit playwright Jacob Biderman in 1600. See Richard F. Grady, "Cenodoxus redivivus," *Woodstock Letters,* LXIX (1940), 133-39. The principal actors in the *Lys sacré* were Eustache de Conflans, Orgerius Pinterel, Lancelot Thierry, and Nicolas de Lettres. The last entered the Jesuit novitiate with Marquette, but he did not persevere.

[32] Gilbert J. Garraghan, "Some Newly Discovered Marquette and La Salle Letters," *Archivum Historicum Societatis Jesu,* IV (1935), 284.

describing the martyrdom of Brébeuf and his companions, as well as the flight of the Hurons, was certainly known by Beschefer's students who probably heard them read in their refectory or perhaps in class.[33] Knowing from his own statement how profoundly they affected Beschefer, we can be certain that his students were deeply impressed as they listened to their teacher, aglow with missionary zeal, describe the exalted excellence of a missionary vocation which offered the dedicated follower of Christ the opportunity of imitating our Lord even to the shedding of blood. Of all his classmates Jacques was, likely, the most profoundly impressed for he had already chosen this very vocation which might, indeed, lead to so glorious an end in some distant land. Both teacher and student were to realize their goal of becoming missionaries, but neither would be called upon literally to shed his blood.

The other Jesuits who taught Marquette at Reims were equally influential in shaping the future missionary, but their careers were not as colorful as that of Thierry Beschefer's. Adrien Ferlin, who taught the *cinquième* when Marquette was in that class, 1648-1649, was born at Val-Roy in 1623 and entered the Jesuit novitiate at Nancy on August 22, 1642. In the fall of 1651 he began his theological studies at Pont-à-Mousson. On October 20, 1653, he and another theological student, Nicolas Fournier, died on the same day, before either was ordained. Edmond Francelet was Marquette's teacher for the *quatrième*, 1649-1650. Born at Auxerre on June 17, 1623, Francelet became a Jesuit on October 14, 1641. He had completed three years of teaching before Marquette was his student. Francelet began his theological studies in 1652 at Pont-à-Mousson and was ordained at Metz on April 1, 1657. He died at Auxerre, aged seventy-seven, on March 21, 1690.[34] For the *troisième*, 1650-1651, and *humanité*, 1651-1652, the teacher was Pierre Coqueley, a

[33] These accounts may be consulted in *Relations*, XXXIV.

[34] Though there is no positive evidence that Ferlin and Francelet taught Marquette, these two Jesuit scholastics were the only possible teachers of the grade levels assigned to them during the years noted. Carrez, *Catologi*, IV, 150, notes that the annual catalogs of the province for the years 1648 to 1650 are unavailable. He supplies a summary catalog for these missing years. In that, Ferlin and Francelet are both listed as teaching at Reims. Since Ferlin was the younger, he would have been assigned to teach the lower grade.

native of Bar-à-Seine where he was born on October 22, 1625. Since he entered the novitiate on May 5, 1646, he normally would have had but two years of teaching behind him at the beginning of classes in 1650. That he was considered exceptionally capable is indicated by the fact that in 1653 he was sent to Rome for his theology. After his ordination in 1657, and at the completion of his four years of theology in 1658, he returned to his province and spent his life teaching. He died at Metz on May 11, 1704. For *rhetorique,* 1652-1653, Jacques had a priest for a teacher, the first since he started at Reims. Father Louis Marie, a mature man of thirty-seven and a priest since 1645, was not only Marquette's teacher, but he also held the office of prefect of the *Congregation,* a vitally influential factor in every Jesuit college, as will appear later.[35] During his last year at Reims, Marquette's teacher for *logique,* the first year of philosophy, was Father Guillaume Goulet. Aged forty-six when he taught Marquette, Goulet had become a Jesuit at the age of thirty. He was ordained in the spring of 1651 after only one year of theological study which he did at Pont-à-Mousson. Goulet died, aged seventy-two, at Pont-à-Mousson on November 28, 1679.[36]

Some might wish that the Marquettes had saved for posterity the letters which Jacques wrote home while he was away at school. If these had come down to us, they might not have been as revealing as one might suppose. From our point of view, one of the frustrating characteristics Jesuit education inculcated in the student was a reserve and formalism which is nowhere more evident than in correspondence. Of the letters surviving, which Jesuit missionaries in New France wrote home to relatives, only an occasional few are

[35] Louis Marie was born at Auxerre on February 15, 1615. He entered the Jesuit novitiate on September 19, 1630, five months before his sixteenth birthday. Ordained in 1645, he joined the Reims faculty in 1650. He was appointed rector of the Jesuit college of Autun in 1658. He died, aged fifty, at Auxerre on September 11, 1665. *Ibid.,* IV, V, *passim.*

[36] Guillaume Goulet was born at Mézières on July 3, 1607, and entered the novitiate at the unusually advanced age of thirty on October 6, 1637. He had apparently completed some of his theological studies before his entrance since he joined the fourth-year theological class at Pont-à-Mousson when he was sent to study theology. See *ibid.,* IV, 174.

cast in a familiar vein.[37] Apart from the artificial formality considered proper literary style in the seventeenth century, there is another element which must be kept in mind when judging the character of such communications. In all likelihood Jacques Marquette really didn't know his family very intimately. Between 1646 and 1654 he lived at home a little over a month each year, from September 14 when classes ended until October 18 when they took up again. While he certainly dearly loved his parents as well as his brothers and sisters, they could not have been the intimate, pulsing part of his life they would have been had he grown up at home. The year Jacques was enrolled at Reims his sister Marie was twenty-five and Françoise was nineteen. In all probability Marie was a young, married matron before her nine-year-old brother went away to school. It is likely, also, that Françoise had already begun to take an interest in the poor of Laon before Jacques enrolled at Reims. During the brief vacations at home Jacques could hardly have established very close ties with these elder sisters. As for his brothers, we are completely in the dark about what his relationship to them might have been. Certainly the future missionary could not have maintained very close ties with his childhood friends who sat with him long ago learning their letters together. Perhaps we have not suffered any irreparable loss by not having a fat sheaf of letters written home by the young scholar.

While pursuing the rigorous intellectual curriculum of the college, Jacques and his fellows were afforded ample opportunity for spiritual development, insuring that they would acquire ". . . good and Christian morals."[38] If the graduate be expected to exercise a positive Christian influence on society, it is not enough that he be-

[37] A noteworthy exception to this generalization are the touchingly familiar letters which Father Jean Pierre Aulneau (1705-1736) wrote to his mother. These may be consulted in Arthur E. Jones, *Rare and Unpublished Documents Relating to Catholic Canadian History*. Aulneau's letters may be compared with those written by Saint Charles Garnier to his family. For these, see François Roustang, editor, *An Autobiography of Martyrdom*, translated by Sister M. Rennelle.

[38] Ganss, *Idea of a Jesuit University*, 329. He gives a complete translation of the fourth part of the Jesuit constitutions, that pertaining to education, 271-335.

come a negatively good Catholic. He must be inspired to commit himself actively to the cause of Christ. For the commitment to be genuine the student must be drawn to embrace enthusiastically the good, moral, exemplary life, chiefly because he could not be satisfied with a lesser service of a loving God. The means the Jesuits employed to inculcate solid religious fervor were manifold. In the part of his constitutions "pertaining to good morals," Ignatius advised: "It will help much towards this [that is, sincere religious fervor] if all go to confession at least once every month, hear Mass every day, and listen to a sermon every feast day when one is given."[39] The important role of the teacher in drawing students to serving God was set forth by Ignatius thus: "The teachers should make it their express purpose, in their lectures when occasion is offered . . . them . . . to inspire the students to the love and service of God our Lord, and to a love of the virtues by which they please Him. They should urge the students to direct all their studies to this end."[40] The Jesuit faculty at Reims, and at every other college under Jesuit direction, employed a positive approach from the very youngest student to the oldest. Every Saturday afternoon, each class from the *septième*, or grammar, through the *humanité* had a catechism lesson, using Father Jean Chastellier's *Catechismus graeco-latinus.*[41] In those classes students were required to memorize the answers to the questions, just as American Catholic children did the Baltimore Catechism in the early decades of the present century. Beyond the *humanité* the boys were taught catechism but were not required to memorize. The emphasis on catechism would seem quite surprising if it were not that we know how essential it was for Catholic youth of the late sixteenth and seventeenth centuries literally to learn exactly what the Church taught lest the sad failures of previous centuries leading to the Protestant revolt of the early sixteenth cen-

[39] *Ibid.*, 329-30.

[40] *Ibid.*, 330.

[41] The complete title of Chastellier's catechism was: *Petri Canisii, Societatis Jesu theologi, catechismus graeco-latinus, nunc iterum in gratiam studiosae juventutis, opera cujusdam ex eadem Societate editus.* It may be taken for granted that as soon as the boys began studying Greek they were required to recite their catechism in that language. Chastellier was not the author, but the editor. The author was Georg Mayr.

tury be repeated. By the same token, Jesuits laid seemingly undue emphasis on the idea of a general confession of one's whole life, chiefly because it could be reasonably presumed, until long after Marquette was a student, that people were so poorly instructed regarding the practice of confessing their sins that it was necessary, as it were, to begin afresh with a repetition of the sins of their past lives. Hence, students entering a Jesuit college for the first time were urged to begin their new academic life by making a general confession. Parenthetically, it should be noted that Saint Ignatius and his followers who formulated the *Ratio studiorum* warned Jesuits that students should be urged to make a general confession as well as to confess monthly, but if a student refused to do so he was not to be constrained or dismissed from the school for this cause.[42]

An effective means of inculcating a lasting interest in religion may be gathered from the following quotation taken from the Jesuit constitutions: "Also, each week, . . . one of the students will deliver a declamation about a subject that will give edification to those present and lead them to desire to grow in all purity and virtue. The purpose is not only practice in literary style, but also improvement of morals. All those who understand Latin ought to be present."[43] The obligation of giving a pious exhortation to the student body and the faculty was more than enough to try one's soul. How diligently each student must have prepared his talk, polishing the Latinity and practicing gestures in order to do well! The Jesuit in charge of this weekly ordeal must have suffered along with each poor victim, knowing that at community recreation the Jesuits would make each exhortation a major topic of conversation. Since it may be assumed that only the older students were allowed thus to address their fellows, Jacques Marquette's turn must have arrived during his last year at Reims. Did he choose to speak of the missions, expatiating on the heroicity of that vocation and ending with

[42] Ganss, *Idea of a Jesuit University*, 340: "Those who can be easily constrained should be obliged to what has been said about confession, Mass, the sermon, Christian doctrine, and declamation. Gentle persuasion should be used upon the others. They should not be forced, nor expelled from the schools for not complying, provided that immorality or scandal to others is not observed in them."

[43] *Ibid.*

a peroration extolling martyrdom? Perhaps he did; but he may have been so self-contained that he did not choose to reveal his own dream publicly. Or perhaps topics were routinely assigned and he was fortunate enough to give his exhortation during the month of May, on the Immaculate Mother of God. One cannot help wondering what happened to the written copy of the exhortation, neatly penned in Marquette's clear, regular hand. Did he bring it home for his mother to read or did he destroy it when he was packing his books and notes to leave Reims for the summer vacation?

Besides the various means noted above employed to inculcate and solidify staunch religious convictions in the hearts of students, there was in each Jesuit college a unique religious society, the Sodality, or, as the French called it, the *Congrégation Mariale* which exercised a monumental influence upon the religious spirit of the whole student body. The purpose of the organization was to stimulate a desire for a higher level of Christian perfection in the members of the *Congrégation* who, in turn, would by their example induce all students to embrace a more virtuous life. In each college the organization was composed of a moderator, always a priest, elected officers of the *Congrégation*, and the members who were carefully selected. Each candidate was submitted to a period of probation lasting several months, during which he was instructed regarding the purpose of the *Congrégation*, its rules and the particular devotion to the Blessed Virgin Mary which was the central core of inspiration for the members. At the end of his probation the candidate was received into the organization at a solemn religious ceremony which took place during Mass.[44] Customarily the *Con-*

[44] The manual guiding the *Congrégation* was François Vernon's *Manuale sodalitatis Beatae Mariae Virginis, ac juventutis universae selectae gymnasiorum Societatis Jesu, miraculis dictae sodalitatis illustrum* published at La Flèche in 1610. At the reception ceremony each candidate knelt on the steps of the altar, at the Communion of the Mass, and read aloud the following formula: "Most Holy Mary, Virgin Mother of God, I . . . choose you this day to be my Queen, my Advocate and my Mother; and I firmly resolve to serve you evermore myself and to do what I can that all may render faithful service to you. I implore you to number me among your servants forever. Watch over me and desert me not at the hour of death. Amen." Then the candidate received Holy Communion. The formula was not a vow, but a simple promise given on the solemn occasion. Rochemonteix, *La Flèche,* quotes the formula, II, 128.

grégation met in its own private chapel every Sunday and feast day for Mass, the recitation of the Little Office of the Immaculate Conception, and an exhortation by the moderator or one of the members. Each member of the *Congrégation* was encouraged to recite the Little Office daily and to fast each Saturday in honor of the Blessed Virgin. Some of these societies, for example, that at La Flèche and Louis-le-Grand in Paris, engaged in the corporal works of mercy on a rather ambitious scale.[45] It should be noted that membership in the organization was not granted readily, and never for reasons of exalted birth, but only because a prospective candidate had a proven desire to embrace the way of life outlined by the rules of the *Congrégation.*[46] Originally designed for students approaching the age of twenty, the various schools established a *Petite Congrégation* for boys in the lowest grades. By the time Jacques Marquette came to Reims these sodalities for boys aged nine and upward had been in existence since 1610.[47]

Almost certainly Jacques Marquette was received into the *Petite Congrégation* at the age of nine, as soon as he completed his probation after entering the college at Reims. We infer this from a brief biography which Father Claude Dablon wrote of Marquette after his death. Corresponding with Father Etienne de Champs, the current provincial of the Province of France, the Jesuit unit administratively responsible for the mission of New France, Dablon remarked: "All his conversations and letters contained something about the Blessed Virgin Immaculate, for so he always called her. From the age of 9 years, he always fasted every Saturday; and from his tenderest youth began to say the little office of the Conception, inspiring everyone with the same devotion."[48] It may be explained that the Little Office of the Immaculate Conception is composed of short hymns and prayers arranged in nine units or "hours," according to the manner of the Roman breviary. Many a boy, in a spurt

[45] *Ibid.*, 133-37.

[46] Emile Villaret, *Les congrégations mariales*, I, 293. Only about five percent of the students were admitted to the *Congrégation.*

[47] *Ibid.*, 279-87, relates the history of the founding of the *Petite Congrégation.*

[48] *Relations*, LIX, 207.

of religious emotion, has begun this practice, but for one to set aside, regularly, the approximately twenty minutes required to recite the Little Office daily can only be considered a rarity, even among the boarding students at Reims. Fasting every Saturday out of devotion to the mother of God was an heroic sacrifice at boarding school for boys are always hungry, but boys in a boarding school are ravenous. How hard it was for Jacques to decline a proffered piece of homemade cake on a Saturday when one of his companions received a package from home! There was no tomorrow for these gifts; tomorrow the cake would be gone. Jacques Marquette was, therefore, an unostentatiously pious boy, but no drooping, pale shadow of Aloysius Gonzaga. He was a healthy, zestful youth who joyfully loved God and his blessed Mother and intended to devote his life to their cause.

The long years at Reims may have, at times, seemed to Jacques to be plodding by on leaden feet, but all too soon they were at an end. The chubby child of nine stretched out to the lean, sturdy young man with the shadow of a beard on his face. The awkward adolescent became the poised, cultured young adult. Over the years he acquired facility in Latin and Greek, became skilled in mathematics, informed in history, and capable of using the globes. As each Holy Week came, when the students made their annual retreat, Jacques had ample opportunity to reconsider his chosen vocation.[49] Each year found him more firmly convinced that his choice was the will of God. Perhaps during the spring of his last year at Reims he informed the Jesuit authorities of his ambition. He would enter the Society of Jesus and, in good time, volunteer for the missions, probably in the Far East. One day he was summoned to conferences with three of the Jesuit priests in turn. Each asked him a long list of questions, read to him from a printed form, on which each independently recorded Jacques' answers. Each inquirer reported the candidate's date of birth, ancestry of his family, whether he was obligated to support his parents, if he held any ecclesiastical office from which he could not resign, whether he had been engaged to

[49] Rochemonteix, *La Flèche*, II, 141-42, declares that in the Jesuit colleges all of the students made a retreat of eight days during Holy Week each year.

marry, and if so how did that come to pass, if he clearly understood the obligations he would assume as a Jesuit, whether he was willing to accept any work to which he might be assigned, and, above all, was anyone urging him to make this step, especially any Jesuit. If the latter were true, Jacques would have been directed to wait a year or two until he had made up his own mind, independent of anyone's urging. The whole business struck Jacques as very strange. Each of these three priests knew him well and for years. But this was the procedure and no matter how intimately the examiners might know the candidate each question must be asked and answered as though the person seeking admission was a perfect stranger.[50] Each examiner forwarded the results of his inquiry to Father Jean Cordier, the provincial of the Province of Champagne. Then Jacques waited a seemingly interminable time until one day the rector, Pierre Fournier, stopped to tell him that he had been accepted and should report to the Jesuit novitiate at Nancy in the fall. Then came Marquette's last days at Reims. At the final assembly prizes were awarded to the leaders of each class; the graduating group received their degrees of Bachelor of Arts; and the rector gave the students the usual advice to live good lives during the summer vacation and report back on time for the fall semester. Then there was a flurry of packing, arranging transportation, and the final good-byes. The stagecoach rattled out of Reims onto the highway and finally, with the horses panting, it pulled up on the Champ Martin at Laon and Jacques was home. Was it then that he told his parents of his decision to become a Jesuit or had they known all along?

There was not much time before Jacques must leave for Nancy. During those few days Jacques walked the lanes of Laon, stopping now and then to lean against the ancient parapet where as a child he had dreamed of sailing to distant lands as a missionary. Never once had he wavered in that determination. And now the time was at hand for him to take the road which would lead to the realization of that dream. On a crisp autumn morning, with his father's blessing fresh upon him, Jacques Marquette took the stage for Reims on

[50] *Societatis Jesu constitutiones et epitome instituti*, 329-30.

his way to Nancy. With him was Thierry Thuret, also of Laon, who was bound for the same destination. At Reims the two candidates were joined by Nicolas de Lettres who had been one of the principal actors in the play which the Jesuits staged honoring Louis XIV's *sacré,* in June of that year, 1654. The three young candidates together rode the swaying coach through the autumn rain to Châlons-sur-Marne, across the plains to Verdun, then to Metz, and through the grape country along the Mozelle to Nancy.[51]

[51] There is no historical evidence indicating how Marquette got to Nancy. The distance from Laon to Nancy is about 195 miles. Since the three candidates arrived at the novitiate on the same day, it is logical to presume that they traveled together. The route suggested would be the most reasonable one for them to have taken. See M. and S. Chaulanges, *Histoire, 1610 à 1789,* 87, for a picture of a seventeenth-century French stagecoach.

PREPARATION

1654-1666

On October 7, 1654, Jacques Marquette and his companions stepped off the stagecoach at Nancy, made their way to the Jesuit novitiate on the rue Dizier, and timidly rang the bell.[1] Brother Pierre du Pressoir, doorkeeper and infirmarian, welcoming them, helped with their luggage, and brought them to a parlor to wait while he summoned Father Pierre Courcier, the rector and master of novices.[2] An

[1] The novitiate at Nancy was established on April 1, 1602, through the generosity of Antoine de Lenoncourt, a *grand seigneur* of the duchy of Lorrain, who became a priest at the age of thirty-three. He gave the Jesuits his country house on the outskirts of Nancy, including the fifty acres surrounding it. The Jesuits added a wing to the original house and a chapel, Notre-Dame-de-Grace, which was open to the public. See Delattre, *Etablissements*, III, 671-95.

[2] Carrez, *Catologi*, V, 61.

astronomer of note, the fifty-one-year-old Courcier was a deeply spiritual man whose contemporaries reported that " . . . in the various offices . . . which he held . . . he manifested purity of life, piety, regularity and equanimity of soul to an eminent degree. He possessed great constancy of will but a gentleness of spirit which made him completely forgetful of himself. He was so devoted to prayer and study that he continually engaged in one or the other."[3] Greeting the new novices warmly, Father Courcier brought them to visit our Lord in the novitiate chapel, Notre-Dame-de-Grace, and then introduced them to a novice who would act as their host while they underwent the "first probation," ten days devoted to a relaxed form of a spiritual retreat. During those days their host, traditionally known as a "Guardian Angel," was their only contact with the Jesuit community, excepting Father Courcier. He met them several times daily for spiritual conferences and outlined for them the constitutions of the Society of Jesus. Also each of the candidates was obliged to read Pope Julius III's *Exposcit debitum* and Pope Gregory XIII's *Ascendente Domino*, the two fundamental papal decrees which canonically established the Society of Jesus.[4] Probably on October 18, Saint Luke's Day, the new novices received their Jesuit cassocks and, escorted by Father Courcier, met the thirteen other novices

[3] *Ibid.*, VII, v-vi. Pierre Courcier was born at Troyes on September 1, 1603, and entered the Society of Jesus on October 10, 1624. He was rector of the novitiate (1650-1657), rector of the college at Sens (1664-1668), and provincial (1671-1674). He died at Auxerre on January 5, 1692. His published works are: *Astronomia practica* (1653), *Negotium saeculorum* (1662), *Opusculum de sectione superficiei sphaericae* (1663), *Imago B. V. miraculosa* (1672), and *Supplementum sphaerometriae* (1675).

[4] Ecclesiastical approval of the Society of Jesus was first given by Paul III in his *Regimini militantis ecclesiae* of September 27, 1540. Julius III issued the *Exposcit debitum* on July 21, 1550, approving modifications and changes made by Saint Ignatius during the previous ten years. On May 25, 1584, Gregory XIII approved the Society of Jesus in its final form in his *Ascendente Domino.* Candidates are required to read these documents during their first probation to insure that they understand the nature of the Society and the obligations assumed by its members. For the same reason, they are obliged to read the constitutions of Saint Ignatius, at least in summary form.

already in the novitiate.[5] Jacques Marquette, greeted warmly, was welcomed by the older novices to the fellowship peculiar to religious communities. And now began his true novitiate.

Jacques immediately discovered that routine, daily life in a Jesuit novitiate was far more minutely regulated than it was at Reims. Except for the periods of mental prayer, an hour after he rose in the morning and a half hour in the late afternoon, bells were constantly summoning him to fifteen minutes for one task and a half hour for another, with brief periods of free time for private devotions. The seemingly pointless interruptions of his day were designed to develop the spirit of prompt obedience and recollection essential to the religious life. Concurrently Jacques was submitted to a series of what Saint Ignatius called "experiments," which each novice must go through. The first of these, undergone probably during November 1654, was spending a month removed from all companionship making the complete Spiritual Exercises of Saint Ignatius. The Founder himself explained the object of this experiment thus: "The first experiment is to spend a month, more or less, making the Spiritual Exercises, i.e., examining one's conscience and past life, making a general confession, meditating on one's sins, contemplating our Lord Jesus Christ's life, death, resurrection and ascension, and giving themselves to vocal and mental prayer as our Lord draws them to do."[6] In rules pertaining to them, masters of novices were informed that novices did not make the Spiritual Exercises in order to decide whether they should become Jesuits, since that decision had already been made at their entrance to the novi-

[5] Those in the novitiate with Jacques Marquette were: Joseph Amé of Reims, sixteen, who died at Nancy in 1689; Jean-Baptiste d'Ambraine, twenty, of Reims, who left the Society in 1659; Pierre Beguin of Château-Thierry, twenty-one, who died at Ensisheim in 1702; Jean Bordois of Charleville, seventeen, who died at Dijon in 1708; Pierre Chifflet of Bars-Aube, eighteen, who left the Society in 1663; Nicolas de Lettres of Reims who left the Society in 1655 and died shortly thereafter; Claude Nicolas of Nancy, eighteen, who died in 1693; Edmond Poissenot of Chaumont, eighteen, who died at Verdun in 1658; Rodolphe-Alphonse Rigault of Reims, sixteen, who died in 1693; René le Sèvre of Châlons-sur-Marne, seventeen, who died in 1702; Godefroi Thierry of Charleville, seventeen, who left the Society and died in 1675; Thierry Thuret of Laon, nineteen, who left the Society and died in 1675.

[6] Antonius Arregui, *Annotationes ad epitomen instituti Societatis Jesu*, 155.

tiate. Rather, they were to go through the Exercises to purify their souls, meditate deeply on the mysteries of our Lord's life and God's infinite love of men. Giving himself wholeheartedly to the Exercises, Jacques Marquette emerged from this experiment imbued with a lifelong dedication to following Christ's example and laboring incessantly for the triumph of his cause.

The other experiments were undergone by Jacques one by one. He spent a month in a local hospital nursing the sick, "to increase the virtue of humility and reduce one's self-love."[7] Lest the reader imagine Jacques acting the part of a gracious visitor who did not soil his hands while at the hospital, here is a description of the nursing tasks performed by two other Jesuits: "We made the beds, swept the floors, emptied and scoured the utensils, cleaned up the wards generally, carried the bodies of the dead reverently to the graves we had dug for them, and, day and night, attended, hand and foot, on the sick . . ."[8] In those days hospitals were little more than great barns sheltering the incurably destitute and dying. Caring for the intimate needs of those poor unfortunates required courage on the part of tenderly nurtured young men such as Jacques. Even in our day nothing quite so effectively deflates the pride of both patient and attendant as ministering to basic needs of the helpless sick. For Marquette serving the sick was an exercise of the virtue of charity which forcefully taught him that even the most menial task was not beneath him. The object of the hospital experiment comes more sharply into focus if one recalls the overweening pride of ancestry prevalent in the seventeenth century. Practicing the corporal works of mercy obliges one to realize that every man possesses the dignity of a child of God. If this truth was not already deeply rooted in the young novice's soul, his month serving in the hospital firmly planted it there.

If the experiment of tending the sick offered a certain attraction because of its strangeness and the dramatic effect which serious illness and death seem to have for the uninitiated, certainly there was nothing exulting about being bidden to "undertake, with dili-

[7] *Ibid.,* 156.

[8] James Brodrick, *Saint Francis Xavier (1506-1552),* 56.

gence and solicitude, abject and humbling offices and to do this with a good will."[9] Translated into practical terms, this "experiment" really meant scrubbing the floors of the novitiate, washing the pots in the kitchen, helping the cook, cleaning up the refectory after meals, and all the menial chores attached to caring for a rather large community of forty people. Every day Jacques was assigned some janitorial task, sweeping corridors, cleaning the chapel, preparing vegetables for cooking, emptying garbage, helping with the laundry. Perhaps for the first time in his life Jacques stood over a stove with the cook, stirring the soup while perspiration soaked him. Three quarters of a century earlier the English martyr Edmund Campion underwent the same experiment at Prague. Describing the reaction of his fellow novices, he wrote: "Glorious kitchen where the best of friends . . . fight for the pots in holy humility and charity unfeigned! How often do I picture it; one returning with his load from the farm; another from the market; one sweating, sturdy and merry, under a sack of refuse; another toiling along on some other errand! Believe me, my dearest brethren, your dust and brooms, chaff and loads are beheld with joy by the angels . . ."[10] In a caste-conscious age it was no small sacrifice for Campion, an Oxford don, or Marquette, son of an affluent bourgeoise, to replace the scullion, hoe the kitchen garden, or hang out the wet linen which was washed by hand. Jacques was not submitted to these routines in order to break his spirit, but for a far more exalted and reasonable purpose. He who enrolls under the banner of Christ, desiring to join forces with him in the campaign for men's souls, must "put on" the poor, humble, obedient, pure Christ if he hopes to be his ambassador to men.

Of the other "experiments" to be undertaken, teaching catechism to children and making a pilgrimage, Jacques would find the first quite easy since the members of the *Congrégation* at Reims often assisted the clergy in preparing children for their first Holy Communion. The second, however, entailed real sacrifice. Saint Ignatius directed that each novice go "on a pilgrimage for a month without any money; and even to beg, at times, from door to door, so as to

[9] Arregui, *Annotationes*, 157.
[10] Evelyn Waugh, *Edmund Campion*, 78-79.

experience the lack of food and shelter. Thus, deprived of money or any other creature, they may learn to have utter faith in God and love Him with an ardent love."[11] During his second year in the novitiate Father Courcier called Jacques and directed him to make his pilgrimage with a fellow novice. On the face of it, when Europe had not yet completely lost appreciation for palmers wandering the roads, one might consider that two novices on their own would find a month away from the meticulous routine of novitiate life more of a lark than a trial. On the contrary, novices making their pilgrimage from Nancy to Trier and back, a round trip of nearly 200 miles, ". . . traveled on foot, their only resource being public charity, amidst multiple dangers . . ."[12] The physical effort was no burden to the healthy, athletic Marquette, but the dangers arose from the fact that the duchy of Lorraine bristled with hordes of hostile Calvinists who heartily detested the Catholic clergy. And two young novices, dressed in cassocks, ecclesiastical cloaks, and wide-brimmed clerical hats, would be taken for priests, though neither of them might as yet have received the lowest ecclesiastical order. Even excluding possible physical danger from irate "heretics," the month was in no sense a vacation. The wayfarers were expected to conduct themselves modestly and recollectedly, continuing, as far as possible, the pious practices of the novitiate. It was a humiliating experience for Jacques Marquette to beg his bread and a night's lodging from a total stranger. Undoubtedly he was often rebuffed by people who were sick and tired of sheltering lazy priests who acted as though the world owed them a living. At the end of the month a lean, sun-tanned Jacques returned to the novitiate, humbled, indeed, but endowed with an insight into people and conditions which he otherwise would never have had.

During April 1655, seven months after Jacques Marquette entered the novitiate, a triennial report on all the members of the Province of Champagne was submitted to the Jesuit general. The superior of each house filled out a form sheet, listing eight categories, on which he registered his opinion of each member of his community. The cat-

[11] Arregui, *Annotationes*, 156.
[12] Delattre, *Etablissements*, IV, 768.

egories were, and still are: *Ingenium*, or general ability; *Judicium*, or judgment; *Prudentia*, or prudence; *Experientia rerum*, or experience; *Profectus in litteris*, or academic ability such as degrees; *Naturalis complexio*, or temperament; *Vires*, or health; and *Ad quod ministeria Societatis talentum habeat*, or what work does he do best. Father Courcier reported that Jacques Marquette had good general ability, very good judgment, satisfactory prudence, no experience as yet, was a good student, had excellent health; the work he would do best was still undetermined; and temperamentally he would be classified as *melancholica-sanguinea*.[13] When interpreting the meaning of these two Latin words, it is to be remembered that they were used in a spiritual, not a psychological sense. Long before modern psychology attacked a defenseless world, authorities in the science of the spiritual life assigned definite meanings to such terms as sanguine, choloric, melancholic, phlegmatic.[14] This is the sense in which the terms were applied to Jacques Marquette. A melancholic person is defined by spiritual writers as one who is fundamentally serious and given to facing difficulties objectively. If he is excessively melancholic, he tends to exaggerate the difficulties. A sanguine person embraces causes with enthusiasm, but is inclined to pass quickly from enthusiasm to discouragement. Knowing the accepted definitions for the terms normally employed, Father Courcier's problem was choosing the proper combination of these for each subject so that officials at Rome could clearly discern their

[13] The triennial catalogs of the Champagne province have never been published. The original manuscripts are in the general archives of the Society of Jesus at Rome. In that depository the triennial catalog of the Champagne province for 1655 is identified as Camp.11,f.87r. In the document Marquette is characterized thus: "*Ingenium, bonum; judicium, satbonum; prudentium, mediocris; experientia rerum, nulla; profectus in litteris, bonus; naturalis complexio, melancholica-sanguinea.*" All but two of the ten on this page are characterized as having "*judicium-mediocris,*" or satisfactory for their age. All were novices. The archives of the Society of Jesus in Rome are henceforth referred to as ARSJ.

[14] Adolphe Tanquerey, a widely respected authority on the science of the spiritual life, offers a quite complete outline of the terms employed to describe temperaments in his *The Spiritual Life: a Treatise on Ascetical and Mystical Theology*, Appendix II, 11. The interested reader would also find it instructive to examine Conrad Hock's little treatise, *The Four Temperaments.*

characters. Of the ten people listed on the same form sheet with Marquette, three, including Jacques, are characterized as *melancholica-sanguinea.* The term *melancholica* is applied to six of the ten, with varying modifications such as *biliosa, phlegmatica.* Hence, we become aware that in 1655 Jacques Marquette was considered by his superior to be an earnest, pleasant, physically vigorous young man, talented and endowed with the prudence befitting his years. Father Pierre Courcier could in good conscience recommend to the provincial, Nicolas Roger, that Jacques Marquette be allowed to take his vows as a Jesuit when he completed the two required years of novitiate.[15]

There was little time after pronouncing his vows for Marquette to linger at the novitiate for he was assigned to teach the *cinquième* at Auxerre during the academic year 1656-1657.[16] Packing his meager wardrobe and few notes, the young Jesuit took the coach to Epinal, through Langres to Auxerre, a journey of about 150 miles. As the coach drove into Auxerre Marquette's first impression of the town was its antiquity. Auxerre's irregular streets wander up and down a steep hillside on the top of which is the great bulk of the cathedral of Saint Etienne giving the viewer the feeling that it is more a fortress than a church. Auxerre has its foot in the Yonne River, a valuable natural asset, for the Yonne is navigable from here to Paris. Barges loaded with ocher, leather, earthenware, and wine can easily make the ninety-mile trip by water to France's capital. In the ninth century Auxerre was such a noted center of learning that Charles the Bald, king of the West Franks (843-877), sent his son Lothair there for his education. By the late sixteenth century Auxerre had only one school for its youth, and that a poor one. In 1584, Bishop Jacques Amyot opened a new school, Saint-Xiste, and started

[15] Though the date on which Marquette took his first vows is not known, it would have been the first ecclesiastical feast after October 7. He would not have received his vows until he had finished two complete years of novitiate.

[16] It was quite as normal to send young men to teach immediately after finishing the novitiate as it was to assign them to begin their philosophical studies. Of the twelve young men who completed the novitiate with Marquette, five were immediately assigned to teach. These were Le Sèvre, Nicolas, Chifflet, Poissenot, and Marquette. See Carrez, *Catologi*, V, 92, 86, 91, 93, 82. The other seven were sent to Pont-à-Mousson to study philosophy. See *ibid.*, 89.

a quite elaborate building to house it. When the bishop died, on February 6, 1593, his school came into the hands of the citizens of Auxerre. In 1622, at a general assembly of the citizens, the school was confided to the Jesuits, the townspeople agreeing to support them. Four years later the people of Auxerre rioted because of a tax increase which they believed was caused by excessive financial demands made on the town by the Jesuits. On March 29, 1626, a mob pillaged the homes of some of their elected officials and broke into the college, threatening to kill the Jesuits. Thoroughly frightened, the Jesuits fled to the home of a friend at Monéteau, not far from Auxerre. The next day they returned to the college and, on April 3, the people apologized for their disgraceful conduct. When Jacques Marquette came to Auxerre the townsfolk had long since made their peace with the Jesuits who by that time had built a great, large building along the present rue Ferdinand Buisson, including an impressive chapel dominated by four great black marble monoliths sent to Auxerre from Rome by the Jesuit general.[17]

Arrived at Auxerre, Jacques Marquette was welcomed by Father Olivier Bienville, the rector, and Father Etienne le Grand, who had taught at Reims (1651-1653) when Jacques was a student there. The community was composed of eleven priests, five Brothers, and Pierre Modo, the only other teaching scholastic.[18] Hence, the new teacher could look forward to a very busy year for, besides his classwork, most of the extracurricular activities in the school would fall on the shoulders of Marquette and his fellow scholastic. Jacques buckled down to preparing classes for the *cinquième* in which the boys studied the more difficult letters of Cicero, Virgil's *Bucolics*, some choice passages from Ovid, and Phaedrus' Greek *Fabula.* Now Jacques began to put into practice the explicit directives outlined in the Jesuit *Ratio studiorum* regarding the method of teaching the young.

[17] Delattre, *Etablissements*, I, 427-49.

[18] Young Jesuits are known as scholastics, and are called Mister, until they are ordained. The other scholastic with Marquette was Pierre Modo who had entered the Society in 1650 and was, therefore, unknown to Marquette. Auxerre must have had a small enrollment since only seven Jesuits were teaching. See Carrez, *Catologi*, V, 81.

On October 18, 1656, young Master Marquette, accompanied by the *domestique*, met the *cinquième*, the eleven-year-olds who were his charge for the coming year.[19] Within a few days the class was organized, according to the directives of the Jesuit *Ratio studiorum* into *decuriae*, or small groups, each with its leader. Monitors were appointed to collect papers, check absences, tardiness, and to keep a record of those who recited.[20] After prayers at the beginning of the day, the young teacher efficiently proceeded to work. Reading the previously assigned passage from a Latin or Greek author, he explained any obscurities, discussed the meaning of the text, and then quizzed his students, pitting one group against another. Since Auxerre did not have resident boarders, supervising recreation period was also one of the duties of the two scholastics, Marquette and Modo, who must be with the boys. Sometimes contests were held in class, employing the full incentive of emulation.[21] Toward Christmas the young teacher, with justifiable pride, invited the rector, Father Bienville, and Father le Grand, to visit his class while the boys acted out Phaedrus' fable, "The Fox and the Mask." And that was the day chosen by the class problem child to misbehave. For that boy, this was the last straw. His next stop was with the *correcteur* who did not spare the rod.[22] In the early spring, when one of the students was absent for several days, the *domestique* called at the boy's home to discover that he was very seriously ill.[23] Master Marquette urged his students to pray for the boy's recovery

[19] Jouvency, *De la manière*, 117. The *domestique* was a layman hired to perform the secretarial tasks. Usually these people were older students working their way through school.

[20] *Ibid.*

[21] Farrell, *Jesuit Code*, 292-94, gives the rules laid down in the *Ratio studiorum* regarding the employment of emulation.

[22] The *correcteur* was a layman who administered punishment. In his *Good Father in Brittany*, page 58, Martin P. Harney gives an example of a *correcteur* at the Jesuit college in Quimper. This was a young Irishman named O'Callaghan who worked his way through school by filling this office. A rather clever piece of doggerel was composed about him: "Brittany, scene of my labors, I come from a foreigner's strand; King am I (yet without rule); the scepter I swing in my hand."

[23] Jouvency, *De la manière*, 117, indicates that this was one of the duties of the *domestique*.

and added a *Memorare* at the end of the day for that intention. During the lazy summer months of July and August it required every ounce of the teacher's ingenuity to keep the restless boys at their books. Slowly September came with final grades and the awarding of prizes. On the last day the whole *cinquième* gathered around their teacher to bid him good-bye until the end of the short, three-week vacation, assuring him that they would all be back and in the *quatrième*, with him, they hoped, for their teacher. But Jacques Marquette would not be back at Auxerre in October. He had been ordered to report at Pont-à-Mousson to begin his philosophical studies.

The city of Pont-à-Mousson, which straddles the Moselle River, derives its name from the bridge across the Moselle near Mount Mousson which isn't much of a mountain. In 1572, Charles II, duke of Lorraine and Bar, obtained a pontifical charter from Gregory XIII permitting him to establish a full-fledged university at Pont-à-Mousson which the duke considered to be the most effective weapon he could employ against the spread of Calvinism in his duchy. The university had faculties of arts, philosophy, theology, law, and medicine, all under the general direction of the Jesuits, though the schools of medicine and law were administered by laymen.[24] The young Jesuits of the Province of Champagne normally did their philosophical and theological studies at the University of Pont-à-Mousson, with which they were all familiar since it was only seventeen miles northwest of Nancy where they made their novitiate. Of the seventy-eight Jesuits in the community when Marquette arrived in the fall of 1657, thirteen of them were old friends. Father Pierre Courcier, his master of novices, was teaching theology. Father Guillaume Goulet had taught Marquette philosophy at Reims. Jean Husson and François Bourgoin had also been teaching at the college at Reims when Jacques was a student there. They were studying theology now at Pont-à-Mousson. Nine of Marquette's fellow novices were with him in the course of philosophy. The "spiritual father" of the whole community was Father Jacques Pupin, the recipient of the only extant letter written by Marquette from New

[24] Delattre, *Etablissements*, IV, 82-89.

France to a Jesuit back home.[25] With so many friends and acquaintances in the house, Jacques Marquette was immediately at home.[26]

When classes began in October 1657, Father Guillaume Goulet introduced the first-year philosophers to Aristotelian logic and the basic concepts of the exact sciences.[27] During four days of the week Marquette and his companions listened to Father Goulet lecture to them in Latin on the predicamentals, analogy, the divisions of science, abstractions, and diverse methods of proceeding in physics and mathematics. On Saturday the lecturer quizzed his students orally regarding the matter learned during the week. Once a month a delegated member of the class briefly explained a portion of the material already covered and parried objections launched at him by his classmates. The twenty-year-old Jacques had no time to gaze out of the window watching the roiling Moselle flow by. Philosophy is a demanding mistress with her elusive distinctions and enticing traps laid to snare the unwary. Weekly and monthly intellectual jousting culminated with quarterly public disputations at which the faculty and whole theological and philosophical student body were present. He who defended a portion of Aristotle's logic on such an occasion must expect ruthless, if mannerly, attacks by experienced logicians who did not hesitate to try the defendant's metal. At year's end each student submitted to an oral examination of the whole field studied. The examiners were three faculty members, none of whom need be the teacher, Father Goulet. As he stood outside the door of the examining hall, waiting for his half-hour ordeal, no matter how well prepared Jacques might have been, there was always the possibility that under pressure his mind would become

[25] In each Jesuit community of more than six members, one priest is appointed as an official spiritual advisor to assist all in advancing spiritually. All are free to seek spiritual aid from others, but in houses of study each scholastic must visit the spiritual father once a month, even though he does not confide in the spiritual father, but in some other of his own choice. Marquette wrote to Pupin from Cap-de-Madeleine on August 4, 1667. This letter is quoted in full in a later chapter. Pupin was then rector of the Jesuit college at Dijon.

[26] Carrez, *Catologi*, V, 104-06, lists the members of the Jesuit community at Pont-à-Mousson during the academic year 1657-1658.

[27] Farrell, *Jesuit Code*, 343, outlines the content of the curriculum for each of the three years of philosophical studies.

a complete blank, leaving him stammering unintelligible nothings, and in Latin. He need not have been unduly concerned for he did well, passing to the second year of philosophy.[28]

By the spring of 1658 a new triennial report on all of the members of the Province of Champagne was due in Rome. This time the forms for the community at Pont-à-Mousson were completed by Father Philippe Plumeret, the rector. Jacques Marquette was characterized as having satisfactory ability, judgment, and health, no experience to speak of, and no academic degrees, since he was just beginning his higher studies. As to his adaptability for the work of the Society, the rector reported that Jacques was a good teacher and a fine prospect for the missions when the time was ripe.[29] As for his temperament, he was described as "*biliosa melancholica,*" a characterization which, again, requires correct interpretation. The Latin word *biliosa*, far from having anything to do with a queasy stomach, is a synonym for choloric. People with choloric temperaments are described by spiritual writers as enthusiasts who aspire to great and lofty objectives. Such individuals are often endowed with keen intellects and strong wills as well as surging passions.[30] If unbridled, choloric individuals tend to be stubborn, overconfident, and extremely haughty. If a man with choloric tendencies is so fortunate as to also partake in part of a melancholic disposition, he is one whom Johann Kasper Lavater described as: ". . . the choloric who has subdued passion and pride; . . . the melancholy who has dis-

[28] The grade designations were: "*Bene attigit,*" or excellent, "*attigit,*" or good, "*attigit juxta modum,*" or poor, but passing, "*vix attigit,*" or failing. If he had received the last, he would not have been permitted to continue the following academic year to his second year of philosophy.

[29] ARSJ, Camp.11,132v,no.218. The manuscript reads: "*Ingenium, mediocre; judicium, mediocre; prudentia, mediocris; experientia rerum, nulla; profectus in litteris, mediocris; naturalis complexio, biliosa-melancholica; ad qua Societatis ministeria talentum habeat, ad docenum, missionum etc. suo tempore.*" The Latin word *mediocris* cannot be translated as mediocre. The three terms employed are *mediocris, bonus,* and *satbonus*, except when an individual is said to have unsatisfactory talent, and so forth. In this case the term used is *infima*. Hence, *mediocris* must be translated as satisfactory in contradistinction to *bonus* and *satbonus* which should be translated fine, excellent.

[30] Hock, *The Four Temperaments*, 24.

missed avarice and suspicion."[31] In Philippe Plumeret's opinion, then, the young philosopher, Jacques Marquette, was a well-balanced, reasonably talented young man; a competent and successful teacher; one who could, in time, safely and profitably be sent to a foreign mission.

It was during Marquette's second year of philosophical studies that he first formally petitioned the Jesuit general to be allowed to go on the foreign missions. Though the young scholastic's letter did not survive, the response from Father Goswin Nickel, dated February 4, 1659, reads: "I praise indeed the zeal with which, as you say, you are borne towards the foreign missions, especially those of the Indies, where you will devote yourself wholeheartedly to the conversion of the barbarians; but as you have finished only Physics, you shall have to wait until you have completed a course in Theology. Meantime, cherish so ardent and holy a desire and be mindful in your holy prayers of Rome."[32] Though Jacques Marquette's desire to become a missionary reached back to his childhood, requesting permission to be off to the Far East just at this time was certainly in some way linked to the recent presence in Europe of two prominent Jesuit missionaries from China and Vietnam. In 1653 Father Martin Martini, a sinologist and scientist of the first rank, came to Rome from the court at Peking in an effort to clarify to the Vatican the Jesuit position in the growing Chinese Rites controversy. While in Europe, Martini published his *De bello Tartarico historia* and his *Brevis relatio de numero et qualitate Christianorum apud Sinas* which, together, gave Europeans their first extended knowledge of the kingdom of China.[33] Since Martini was in Rome when a General

[31] Johann Kasper Lavater, *Aphorisms on Man,* no. 606. The complete quotation is: "Venerate four characters: the sanguine who has checked volatility and rage for pleasure; the choloric who has subdued passion and pride; the phlegmatic emerged from indolence; and the melancholy who has dismissed avarice and suspicion."

[32] Garraghan, "Unpublished Marquettiana," 15-16.

[33] Martini's two valuable books were published at Rome in 1654 by Ignatius de Lazzeris. They were immediately pirated and published in Antwerp, Cologne, Vienna, and were translated into Dutch and French. See Felix A. Plattner, *Jesuits Go East,* 107. Plattner errs in saying that the books were first published at Antwerp in 1657. Martini's most valuable work was his *Novus Atlas Sinensis* containing seventeen hand-colored maps of China. This appeared in 1655.

Congregation of the Society of Jesus was held in 1653, every returning delegate broadcasted to the houses of his province the news of the great work Jesuits were doing in China and Japan.[34] Successfully completing his mission at Rome, Martini recruited thirty-six young Jesuits to join the Chinese mission and, with them, set out for the Far East only to be captured and plundered by a French corsair in 1656, a fact which made Martini and his mission all the better known in France. While Martini was in Rome, during 1653, Father Alexandre de Rhodes, the Jesuit apostle of Vietnam, arrived for the purpose of inducing the Holy See to establish three episcopal sees in Vietnam as well as to recruit missionaries. He procured the episcopal appointments, but, until he reached France, he was unable to obtain any missionaries. At Paris, de Rhodes was introduced to a group of pious young priests by Father Jean Bagot, their Jesuit spiritual director. Among the members of this group, which later established the congregation known as the *Missions-Etrangères*, de Rhodes found enthusiastic volunteers, not only for the episcopal positions but also many willing to go to Vietnam as simple missionaries. Most of the latter desired to become Jesuits. Twenty volunteers left France for Vietnam in 1655, among whom were several Jesuits, some not yet ordained, and a group of young priests who made part of their Jesuit novitiate during their long sea voyage.[35] All of this exciting news reached Jacques Marquette at

[34] A general congregation of the Society of Jesus is summoned on the death of a general or whenever it seems necessary to discuss the work of the Society. Each province elects two delegates who attend the congregation with their provincial. As soon as the congregation convenes, it has in its hands all governing authority. On their return home the delegates naturally were full of news about Father Martini and Alexandre de Rhodes.

[35] De Rhodes' own account of his work is to be found in *Voyages et missions du P. Alexandre de Rhodes.* Father de Rhodes planned to recruit priests of private financial resources who would become bishops, establish seminaries, and create a native clergy in Vietnam. This episode touched Marquette very closely because one of his former Jesuit teachers, Adrien Ferlin, received permission to go to Vietnam. On October 18, 1653, the day Ferlin was granted leave to go to Vietnam, he died suddenly at Pont-à-Mousson where he was, that very day, beginning his third year of theology. See Carrez, *Catologi*, V, xxx. The circumstances surrounding Ferlin's death would certainly have been announced to the students at Reims where Jacques was then in school.

Pont-à-Mousson and impelled him, as it were, to beg permission to go to the Far East at once, without delaying to finish his studies and receive ordination. If others were doing so, why not he who had so long desired to join the ranks of missionaries in far places? But the Jesuit general had spoken; he must first finish his studies. At the end of his second year of philosophical studies, the young scholastic was sent to Reims for another two years of teaching.

The two years at Reims were pleasant ones for Jacques Marquette. Jean Cordier, the rector, had been provincial when Jacques applied for admission to the Society of Jesus. Father Nicolas Roger was the spiritual father of the community, a coincidence of major importance for it was Father Roger who, seven years later, sent Jacques to New France.[36] As a former student at Reims, Marquette knew the college well, especially all of the secret hiding places and devious routes which all boarding students know about their institution. Jacques was an old and experienced pedagogue when he came before the *quatrième* for its first session. He taught them Cicero's *Letters to Quintus*, the *Dream of Scipio*, Virgil's *Georgics*, Ovid's *Metamorphoses*, Cebes' *Tableau*, and Saint John Chrysostom's *Letters.*[37] Added to his classwork was the office of prefect of all the boarding students, aged about nine to twelve, a task which has tried many a man's soul. In the fall of the year the small boys of nine were homesick and cried for their mothers. After a feast day the child who overate padded to Master Marquette's bed, in the middle of the night, seeking aid for his distressed stomach. During recreation there were always disputes to settle and games to referee. Nightly, each boy came to Marquette to have his lessons heard, as was required by rule. And then there were the inevitable times when the boys were exasperatingly unruly, only because they were restless. But there were consolations too, some of them purely human. Perhaps one of Jacques' aunts called to see how he was or his mother

[36] *Ibid.*, 141-42, gives the list of those in the Reims community during the academic year 1659-1660. Nicolas Roger was born at Fimes, a small town in Switzerland, on December 16, 1602. He entered the Jesuit novitiate on September 11, 1619. He was provincial of the Province of Champagne from 1664 to 1668 and then went to Reims.

[37] Jouvency, *De la manière*, 121.

came with his sister Marie and a gaggle of small, squirming nieces and nephews to visit Uncle Jacques. The school year 1659-1660 soon passed and the next began with Jacques again teaching the *quatrième* to a new group of boys, with the same prefecting responsibilities.[38]

By the spring of 1661 when Marquette, nearing his twenty-fourth birthday, was a grown man with his character solidly formed, it was time for a new triennial report to be forwarded to Rome, compiled on this occasion by the rector of the college at Reims, Father Pierre Beschefer. In his opinion Marquette had satisfactory talent, excellent prudence and judgment, no unusual experience, no higher degrees as yet, and was temperamentally sanguine. The space provided for an expression of opinion as to what work he would do best was left blank.[39] At Rome, the report would be correctly interpreted to mean that Jacques Marquette was an affable, vigorously healthy young man who did his work well and was undoubtedly a very distinct asset to the college. It was probably with no small regret that Father Beschefer learned that in the fall of 1661 Marquette would be transferred to Charleville. This change of assignment was a welcome one since it probably presented young Marquette with an opportunity to visit Laon on his way north to the new post. Charleville is about fifty miles northeast of Laon which, in turn, is approximately thirty miles northwest of Reims. It was good to be home for a few days, though saddening to see that his father, now sixty-four, was beginning to show his age. His sister Marie's children were growing into early adolescence. Françoise had long talks with her Jesuit brother, explaining her dedication to the poor children of Laon and her dream of consolidating her work into some sort of permanent school and, perhaps, even a small religious community. Louis, Jean-Bertrand, and Michel were advancing in the world, ready to marry and establish homes of their own. It was gratifying, but a little saddening, for Jacques was really

[38] Carrez, *Catologi*, V, 161. That year Marquette was prefect of the *quatrième* and the *sixième*.

[39] ARSJ, Camp.11,f.180v,no.321.

a stranger in his own home. He had been away from Laon for seven years and so much had changed.[40]

Charleville on the Meuse, and the Jesuit college in it, were both founded by Charles de Gonzague, governor of Champagne and a collateral descendant of Saint Aloysius Gonzaga of Mantua. The college on the Quai de la Madeleine was really a collection of jerry-built houses constantly in need of repairs. Of the eighteen Jesuits in the community, only eight taught the little more than 180 students, an unruly lot given to engaging in street brawls with gangs from neighboring towns.[41] Marquette taught the *troisième* for two sessions running and then was sent to Langres on the Marne River, well over 200 miles to the southeast of Charleville. The college at Langres, located on the Place Diderot, has, perhaps, only one questionable claim to fame. Denis Diderot (1713-1784), the Encyclopedist, was an alumnus. When Marquette taught there the college, then in its thirty-third year, still did not offer a complete curriculum. Of the thirteen Jesuits in the community, including two Brothers, only seven were teachers.[42] Marquette taught *rhètorique* to students aged about fifteen who were in their last year of classical studies. Since the Jesuits were not particularly well liked by the people of Langres, Jacques may not have been too unhappy to be sent, at the end of the academic year, back to Pont-à-Mousson where he was assigned to teach the *humanité.*[43] When classes opened in the fall of 1664, Jacques was beginning his seventh year of teaching. He could reasonably expect that at the close of that session he would be sent, in the fall of 1665, to finish his last year of philosophical studies and then begin theology.

In the spring of 1665 the fourth triennial report since Jacques Marquette entered the Jesuit novitiate was forwarded to Rome. This

[40] The material presented here is wholly devised. Though no evidence shows that Marquette visited Laon on his way north, it is almost unthinkable that he would not do so.

[41] Delattre, *Etablissements,* I, 1297.

[42] Carrez, *Catologi,* VI, 25-26.

[43] Delattre, *Etablissements,* II, 937-47. Opposition to the Jesuits arose both from the Calvinists at Langres and from a Catholic group which wished the school to be given to the Oratorians. Marquette's assignment to Pont-à-Mousson for 1664-1665 may be verified in Carrez, *Catologi,* VI, 45.

one was vital to the young man's future, though when it was submitted no one was aware of that. Father Charles-François de Haraucourt, the rector of Pont-à-Mousson, who met Marquette for the first time in the fall of 1664, characterized his subject as having satisfactory ability, excellent judgment and prudence, vigorous health, a master's degree, and a sanguine disposition. As to the work he might do best, the rector declared that Marquette was an excellent prospect for the foreign missions.[44] When Father Nicolas Roger, then provincial of the Champagne province, reviewed the report before forwarding it to Rome he must have agreed thoroughly. Marquette was now twenty-seven years old, an experienced professional man, imbued with sufficient initiative to have qualified for a master's degree at Pont-à-Mousson while carrying a full teaching load.[45] Now a well-balanced, mature man, competent to assess the difficulties of missionary life, Jacques Marquette, on March 19, 1665, the feast of Saint Joseph, wrote to the Jesuit general, John Paul Oliva:

> When I have finished my seventh year of teaching at the age of twenty-eight, I shall be facing a further course of studies. I approach his Paternity to ask that which I sought nearly seven years ago from our deceased Reverend Father General, offering myself in every way, with the consent of superiors, that he order me to set out for foreign nations, about which I have been thinking from my earliest years and the first light of reason, so that I wished to go, even earlier than I was aware. I now believe that there is no safer way for me to gain my end [i.e. becoming a saint]. This was the major reason which induced me to enter the Society. I add, furthermore, that I was, once, more inclined to the Indies, but now I am completely ready for absolutely any region, according to his Paternity's intention. I received a reply [seven years ago] that I should complete a course in theology. But, to avoid encouraging hopes whose fulfillment would be unduly prolonged, first because I am certain enough that I am temperamentally too little suited to learning speculative

[44] ARSJ, Camp.11,f.239v,no.200.

[45] Though the college at Pont-à-Mousson was a large establishment with a great deal of prefecting to be done, Marquette had no duties other than teaching during 1664-1665. See Carrez, *Catologi*, VI, 45. Perhaps his lighter duties may be explained by the fact that during this academic year he received his M.A. and probably required the extra freedom to work on the degree.

subjects and [am] clearly lacking in natural endowments; secondly because I have explained this clearly to our Father Provincial; these reasons make it clear that, given my age and strength, I should no longer waste the effort which I can put at the disposal of Christ's cause for so great a return. So this is what I request of his Paternity: that he write to Father Provincial, expressly directing him to handle this matter, so that if the proper occasion arises, and he judge it expedient, without further response from his Paternity, he may, without my finishing theology or, indeed, even beginning it, since I have already dipped into cases of conscience, send me immediately where the first opportunity is presented for seeking out souls. To win souls to Christ, speculative subjects are not particularly necessary. What is profitable is that zeal and fervor so truly worthy of a son of the Society. That, I expect to secure through the prayers of his Paternity.

The humblest servant in Christ and most obedient son,
Jacques Marquette, S.J.[46]

On April 28, 1665, Father John Paul Oliva, the general, replied:

I was delighted with your letter of March 19 from which I learned your ardent desire to go on the foreign missions and especially your praiseworthy spirit, proper to the Society, whereby you indicate that you are no longer inclined to the Orient more than to any other part of the world. As to theological studies, which you wish to omit altogether so as to realize your desire the sooner, in this, as in everything, you should await the wishes of your superiors. I am writing to Father Provincial to learn his opinion and you will hear from him what we judge to be best in the Lord. In the meantime, apply yourself to acquiring those virtues

[46] The original Latin of the letter may be consulted in Garraghan, "Newly Discovered Letters," 284-85. Garraghan printed his translation of the letter in his "Unpublished Marquettiana," 16-17. In his *Marquette Legends*, 6-7, Francis Borgia Steck also has a translation. Neither translation is completely accurate. The translation given here is the work of the present author. Certain passages in the letter require clarification. Marquette's declaration that he had no aptitude for speculative subjects was his personal opinion, not objectively verified by his previous academic record. It is noteworthy that he did not declare that his provincial agreed with the opinion, but only that he had expressed such a judgment about himself to the provincial. Marquette made a point of his assessment of his intellectual ability for a reason internal to the Society of Jesus. If he had completed his third year of philosophy and successfully passed an hour's oral examination on the whole field of philosophy, he would have been directed to complete a four-year course in theology. At the end of that period, Marquette would have undergone a two-hour examination on the whole field of philosophy and theology. Passing that ordeal would have made him eligible, in part, for the profession of four solemn vows.

absolutely necessary to a zealous worker in order to effect those fruits which the Society hopes to produce in the missions.[47]

Jacques Marquette had every reason to rejoice on reading Father Oliva's gracious reply. His petition would receive serious consideration, even the request to be excused from the lengthy course of theological studies. But all in good time. He must possess his soul in peace, carrying on his teaching assignment. When the school year closed, the teaching scholastic was told to change his quarters to that portion of the college set aside for Jesuit students. In the fall of 1665 Marquette was a *repetens* at Pont-à-Mousson, finishing his philosophical studies and preparing for the final examination on the whole field of philosophy in the spring of 1666. Then, providing nothing came of his request to Father Oliva, he would begin the study of theology. But the future would not be so prosaically regular for Marquette; it was really determined at the Jesuit college in Quebec. In 1650, when the Huron mission was abandoned, a considerable number of Jesuits had been sent back to France.[48] Now, fifteen years later when the presence of French regulars in New France warranted hope that the Iroquois would be subdued, the Jesuits bombarded Rome and Paris with pleas for an increase of missionaries so that the Iroquois and the far western tribes might be evangelized. Father Thierry Beschefer, who reached Quebec on June 19, 1665, well knew Jacques Marquette's burning desire to be sent on the foreign missions. If recruits were needed, here was one willing to come and a suggestion to Father François Le Mercier, who became superior of the mission on August 6, 1665, should help matters along. When the fleet sailed back to France that autumn, somewhere aboard one of the ships was a letter suggesting that, in considering new personnel, superiors would do well to give some thought to Jacques Marquette of whom Father Beschefer, his former teacher, spoke highly.

Suddenly Jacques Marquette was caught up in a whirlwind of activity. On December 8, 1665, happily the feast of the Immaculate Conception, the general, Oliva, wrote to Father Roger: "As for Jacques Marquette, Your Reverence will investigate how and when

[47] Garraghan, "Unpublished Marquettiana," 16-17.
[48] *Relations*, XXXVI, 51-53.

he can be dispatched to the Canadian mission, which he wishes and where he is desired as soon as possible."[49] The provincial hardly had time to receive that communication before Father Oliva wrote again, on December 29, 1665, saying: "The Canadian mission is in desperate need of workers. I earnestly call your attention to this, as I do to all of the French provincials, that each may see whom he may have in his province who is fitted to go there. Among others there is Master Marquette who can be sent at the first opportunity, if he is still of the same mind as that which he made abundantly clear to me."[50] Yes indeed! Master Marquette was certainly of the same mind and there was no time to waste if he were to be aboard ship when the fleet sailed for New France in the spring. Certainly no later than the first of February, 1666, the young scholastic knew that his long cherished dream was about to be realized. There would be no examination on the whole of philosophy for him; more pressing matters claimed his attention. First he must receive holy orders. This he did on March 7, 1666, the feast of Saint Thomas Aquinas, in the lovely old thirteenth-century Gothic cathedral at Toul, twenty-five miles southwest of Pont-à-Mousson.[51] It would be gratifying to know that the newly ordained Father Marquette visited Laon before he left France and perhaps he did, since on his journey eastward to the seacoast from Pont-à-Mousson, Laon would not be too far out of the way. So there was a great celebration with a solemn Mass at Notre-Dame-de-Laon. Françoise made her brother a lovely lace alb; young nephews sang in the choir and little nieces were flower girls. The stay was all too short for the young priest must go to Paris and thence to La Rochelle where he must arrive in time to take ship for New France no later than the month of May.

Arrived at Paris, in the company of Jean-François Elie, a young scholastic also assigned to the mission of New France, Father Marquette reported to the provincial of the Province of France, Jacques

[49] Garraghan, "Unpublished Marquettiana," 18.

[50] *Ibid.*

[51] In the recent past a controversy arose among historians regarding the fact of Marquette's ordination. The evidence attesting to his having received holy orders at Toul on March 7, 1666, is so overwhelming that no honest investigator could possibly doubt it. We summarize the evidence in an appendix.

Brodier, who introduced him to the other recruits preparing to sail with him. These were Fathers Jacques Bruyas and Etienne de Carheil.[52] The little contingent spent long hours listening to Father Charles Lalemant, the uncle of Saint Gabriel Lalemant, tell them stories about New France, describing the pioneer days of the mission. There were conferences, too, with Father Paul Ragueneau, home from New France only three years, who had been superior of the mission when the Iroquois had wiped out the Hurons and destroyed that flourishing mission. Now Ragueneau was all business, organizing supplies for New France, packing small parcels for each of the Jesuits in Canada, collecting all the mail forwarded to him from relatives of the missionaries and writing instructions to Father François Le Mercier, the superior in Quebec, informing him of financial arrangements and the like.[53] The Paris which Marquette saw was not the beautiful city of today, but a sprawling, crowded capital dominated by the cathedral of Notre-Dame and the Louvre where Louis XIV lived and reigned while Versailles was abuilding in a swamp. During his brief stay at Paris, Marquette surely had time to make a pilgrimage to the little chapel halfway up the hill of Montmartre where, on August 15, 1534, Saint Ignatius and his companions first vowed to serve God. As he knelt in the chapel, sanctified over a century ago by the presence of Saint Francis Xavier, Marquette prayed earnestly to that great missionary, as well as to Saint Ignatius, his father in God, to grant him the grace of setting New France on fire as Xavier had the Far East.

With the soft breezes of early May caressing them, the four young missionaries sat in the lumbering stagecoach which left Paris

[52] The recruits were Father Jacques Bruyas of the Province of France, two years Marquette's senior; Father Etienne de Carheil, also of the Province of France, four years older than Marquette; and Jean-François Elie, a member of Marquette's own Province of Champagne, aged twenty-five and a Jesuit since 1661.

[53] Ragueneau came back to France in 1662. See *Relations*, LXXI, 142. Paul Ragueneau was born at Paris on March 18, 1608, and entered the Paris novitiate of the Society of Jesus on August 21, 1626. He came to New France on June 28, 1636. He was superior of the Huron mission, 1645-1650, and superior of the whole Jesuit mission of New France, 1650-1653. He went back to France in 1662 to become French agent for the mission of New France. For a brief biography of Ragueneau, see *ibid.*, IX, 312.

and wheeled out onto the plains of France on the way to La Rochelle. At La Flèche they stopped to rest and to confer with aging missionaries now returned from New France to the comfort of the Collège Henri IV where they lived out their declining days. If Marquette had come there in the fall of 1666, he would have met Robert Cavelier de la Salle, then a Jesuit scholastic, who began the study of theology there in October of 1666, but left the Society the following spring. While at La Flèche, a young Jesuit student, Pierre Cholenec, who would write so touchingly of Marquette after his lonely death, brought the missionaries around to see the room which Saint Isaac Jogues had occupied when he was a student and where the grand old patriarch, Ennemond Massé, had held conferences in 1614 with young Jesuits all aglow with eagerness to convert the Indians of New France. La Flèche was a hallowed place in the history of Jesuit activity in New France and Jacques well appreciated the opportunity to visit it. But time was pressing and the little party must hasten on to La Rochelle. Arrived there, Father Jacques Marquette finally found time to write a note of thanks to Father Oliva, the general, on May 31, 1666:

I cannot sufficiently express to your Paternity how much I appreciate the permission you sent to me to go to Canadian territory. Previous to this I was without preference for any particular mission, but now that you have decided, my whole heart is in this one. I am not at all worried over the danger threatening us from the English and the Turks, who according to report are sweeping our seas. Shielded by the divine will as by the firmest of bulwarks, I shall take off shortly from La Rochelle. I follow the voice of God, who will not suffer me to be tempted above my strength especially as I am well enough aware that this whole affair has been taken in hand and negotiated for me by the Most Blessed Virgin. One thing only I now ask of your Paternity and this is that you deign to give me your blessing so that I may show myself in fuller measure a true son of the Society and bring no disgrace on so good a mother whether it be in Africa or England or the most retired wastes of New France.

Very Reverend Father in Christ,
Your most humble servant and most obedient son in Christ,
Jacques Marquette.[54]

[54] Garraghan, "Unpublished Marquettiana," 18-19.

Finally came the day when the four Jesuit missionaries, together with an equal number of Sulpicians bound for Montreal, were rowed out to the ships. Father Bruyas and Jean-François Elie were taken aboard the *Saint-Joseph,* Father de Carheil, the *Sainte-Catherine*, and Jacques Marquette on a craft identified only as the "seventh ship." With much scurrying of deckhands and a volley of shouted orders, sails were bent and the coast of France faded while Jacques Marquette stood looking expectantly across the open water, his heart already in Quebec. Six long, painful weeks of sea travel were ahead of him in an uncomfortable little craft. Jacques shared a crowded cabin with some of the ship's officers which, at that, was far better accommodations than the packed, noisome hold offered the less fortunate passengers. In no time body vermin migrated from the less cleanly to everyone else. Food was barely edible and the weather was dreadful. Scurvy and fever attacked passengers and crew alike until Marquette had his hands full acting as nurse to the sick and pastor to the dying.[55] At long last the chill bulk of Newfoundland loomed out of the haze hanging over the mouth of the Saint Lawrence. The crude chapel high on the cliff at Tadoussac came into view and just below it the mighty Saguenay River tumbling out of its gorge. The Baie-de-Saint-Paul slipped by with snow geese wheeling over it. Soon the sailors were pointing out the tip of Ile d'Orleans and the rough little chapel at Sainte-Anne-de-Beaupré on the north shore of the Saint Lawrence River. Above the already famous shrine the beautiful Falls of Montmorency caught Marquette's eye and, shortly, a tall, massive, brooding granite escarpment, with the little Saint Charles River curling along its base, appeared, as though challenging the approaching ship. There was Quebec, its lower town huddled against the base of the stark cliff with Fort Saint Louis and the steeple of the parish church standing out against the sky. Jacques Marquette was home; this was his "far Cathay." Father François Le Mercier, superior of the Jesuit mission of New France, noted in the *Journal des Jésuites*, under the heading *September*: "The 20th. Father Jacques Marquette arrived, in good health, on the seventh ship."[56]

[55] See *Relations*, LXVIII, 225-35, Father Luc François Nau's description of his Atlantic crossing in 1734.

[56] *Ibid.*, L, 201.

NEW FRANCE

1666

On that crisp autumn day, September 20, 1666, young Father Jacques Marquette paced the deck of the overcrowded ship on which he had spent so many uncomfortable weeks crossing the Atlantic, eagerly awaiting the Jesuits' skiff to bring him ashore. The harbor was crowded with the six ships which had reached Quebec ahead of his that season. Seamen and stevedores strained at the winches, hauling cargo out of the holds while unwieldy bales of odorous furs piled up on the decks, waiting to be stored for shipment to France. Numerous small boats scuttled about bringing officials back and forth from the ships, carrying cord wood, ferrying passengers across the river to Levis or upstream to Cap Rouge. Above the high water mark along the river front was Quebec's lower town, the business center of New France. Fanning out on shore from three rickety docks jutting into the chill waters of the Saint Lawrence was a rabbit warren of jumbled lanes lined with shops and warehouses. Bakeries scented the air with the enticing odor of fresh bread. The sharp, tangy smell of tar and new rope identified ship's chandleries. Sparks flew from the blacksmith's hammer as he shaped glowing iron. Armorers plied their trade, fashioning weapons. In the stonecutter's yards blocks of dark granite were squared into shape for new buildings. Signs hanging outside of shops identified tinsmiths, toolmakers, upholsterers, tailors, coopers, locksmiths, hatters, goldsmiths, notaries, and surgeons.[1] Dominating the whole was the great warehouse of the Company of New France, absentee landlords since 1645, when the Company of Habitants sub-leased its charter.[2] Lounging around the warehouse, the center of Canada's fur trade, was always a collection of *voyageurs*, short, blocky men with massive shoulders and bandy legs, dressed in scuffed leather, their heads covered by long, knitted stockingcaps and short, stubby pipes in their mouths. The narrow lanes could safely be used as foot paths since few horsedrawn vehicles were to be seen. In the whole of New France there were only twelve horses, all sent just a year ago, the first imported since 1647 when one poor lone animal was sent over for Governor Montmagny.[3] Quebec's lower town was drab, a gray huddle, but shops were prosperous and crowded with

[1] The first census of New France was taken in 1666. The trades mentioned here are among fifty listed in the census. See Gustave Lanctôt, *The History of Canada*, II, 239, for a convenient summary of the census. In 1666 Quebec had a population of 547 people.

[2] In 1645 the Company of New France leased its trading rights to the Company of the Habitants, a group of men residing in Canada, but it did not surrender jurisdictional control of the colony. In 1663 Louis XIV dissolved the Company of New France and established Canada as a crown colony. The next year, 1664, the colony was again given to a monopolistic company, the Company of the West Indies. This group refrained from exercising its prerogative of jurisdictional control. In effect, therefore, New France was a crown colony after 1663.

[3] The colonists were not completely lacking in beasts of burden before 1665. That year the census showed that there were 2,000 cows and oxen in the colony. See Lanctôt, *Canada*, II, 240. Eighty stallions and mares were imported between 1665 and 1672. These were distributed to various *habitants* who agreed to pay a foal in return within three years.

soldiers of the Carignan-Salières regiment, arrived the year before with money in their pockets and no place else to spend it.[4]

When the Jesuits' cumbersome rowboat, with two Brothers at the oars, pulled alongside the ship, Marquette, looking down, elatedly recognized his old school prefect, Father Thierry Beschefer, come to meet him.[5] Planting his broad-brimmed ecclesiastical hat firmly on his head and wrapping his heavy cloak tightly about him, against the biting September wind, lithe young Marquette swung over the rail and down the ship's ladder into the arms of his brother Jesuits. His bales and boxes of luggage were handed down and the boat pulled for shore as the two old friends chattered away, exchanging news. On shore the Brothers loaded the baggage on hand carts while the two priests made straight for the rue de la Montagne, that precipitate path, exactly where it is today, which brought them, out of breath and panting, to the plateau before Quebec's parish church.[6] Stopping briefly there to thank our Lord and his Blessed Mother for protecting him from the perils of the sea, Marquette strolled across to the rue des Jardins. Before him was the sturdy, massive structure of the Jesuit college, the architectural wonder of the colony which Brother Jean Liégeois designed and built after a disastrous fire destroyed an earlier wooden building in 1640.[7] Beside it, still abuilding, was a new church whose high

[4] One should not imagine Quebec as swarming with soldiers in colorful uniforms since military uniforms were not introduced until 1670. Previous to that time soldiers dressed in ordinary work clothes. See Robert La Roque de Roquebrune, "Uniforms et drapeau des régiments au Canada sous Louis XIV et Louis XV," *Revue de l'Université de Ottawa*, XX (1950), 327-42.

[5] Since Father Beschefer was at Quebec at that time, he would be the logical one to send. On October 4, 1666, Beschefer wrote home to France: "Father Marquette . . . arrived safely, after a somewhat protracted voyage . . ." *Relations*, L, 173.

[6] This church, originally built by the Jesuits in 1640, was given to Bishop Laval when he reached New France in 1659. The church stood on the site now occupied by Quebec's cathedral.

[7] Narcisse H. E. Faucher de Saint-Maurice gives a description of this building in his pamphlet, *Relation de se qui s'est passé lors des foulles faites par ordre du gouvernement dans une partie des fondations du collège des Jésuites de Québec, précédée de certaines observations.* The building stood on the site now occupied by Quebec's Hôtel-de-Ville. Brother Jean Liégeois, who erected the building, was killed by the Iroquois at Sillery in 1655.

altar would later be graced with four giant pillars of dressed black granite. Waiting to greet Marquette at the door was Father François Le Mercier, superior of all the Jesuits in New France, a grizzled veteran of sixty-four, companion of the martyrs of Huronia, who had been thirty-one years on the mission.[8] Le Mercier had seen New France change from a wild, raw land to a settled colony about which he wrote in the *Relation* of 1666-1667: ". . . we have witnessed a notable change in the appearance of Canada. We can assert that it is no longer that forbidding and frost-bound land which was formerly painted in so unfavorable colors, but a veritable New France—not only in the salubrity of its climate and fertility of its soil, but in the other conveniences of life, which are being revealed more and more every day."[9] For Jacques Marquette the meeting was momentous. Here was the kind, gentle, wise, experienced superior who had asked the Jesuit general to send him this young man. He would decide the mission field in which Jacques Marquette would work.

Once he had been welcomed by the superior and made a visit to the chapel, Marquette was enveloped by the Jesuits of the community, at least by those who were then at home. By all means he must be taken on a tour of the building. First he must see the *grande salle* where all important school functions were held. Had he heard that the first public disputation had been performed there, in June, in the presence of the bishop, the governor, the intendant, and all of Quebec's *haut monde?* The defendant, young Louis Jolliet, a native-born Canadian, had covered himself with glory, even keeping his head when M. l'Intendant objected searchingly in polished Ciceronic Latin![10] Then they showed him the *salle de la Congrégation,* the sacrosanct meeting place of the members of the sodality of the Blessed Virgin, not just the student members only,

[8] François Le Mercier was born at Paris on October 4, 1604, and entered the Jesuit novitiate there on October 19, 1620. He came to New France in 1635. He was superior of the whole Jesuit mission in New France from 1653 to 1656 and again from 1665 to 1671. In 1673 he returned to France whence he was sent to the Jesuit mission on the island of Martinique where he died aged eighty-six, on June 12, 1692.

[9] *Relations*, L, 237.

[10] *Ibid.*, 191.

but the *Congrégation des Messieurs* as well.[11] In the spring of 1660, when an Iroquois threat was at its height, the governor, d'Argenson, ordered the Ursulines to come and sleep at the Jesuit college. They had used the *Congrégation's* quarters as a dormitory for a week, beginning on May 19. The nuns of the Hôtel-Dieu had been made to come too, but the carpenter shop had been cleaned out to provide sleeping quarters for them.[12] They led him along the corridor where the classrooms were so that he could see how exactly they had duplicated the facilities at home. When school opened, of course on Saint Luke's day, there would be some fifty students attending classes, four of them from France. A small handful of the scholars, Louis Jolliet among them, were seminarians destined for the diocesan priesthood. As yet these young aspiring Levites were attending classes with the lay students, but Bishop Laval hoped to be able to open a formal seminary soon. Then there was the spacious garden where, seven years before, the students had staged a drama in honor of the newly arrived Governor d'Argenson. The play was called: "The reception of Monseigneur le vicomte d'Argenson by all the nations of Canada." The boys took the parts of the Huron, the Algonquin, the Stranger from the North, and the Stranger from the South. Each actor spoke in the appropriate native language. The whole colony attended and everyone was immensely impressed.[13] They led him across the plateau of the upper town to the brow of the cliff where they pointed down to the little Saint Charles River, showing him where Notre-Dame-de-Saint-Anges used to be.

[11] The first *Congrégation* in New France was established by Father Chaumonot. See Francis X. Talbot, "Le congrégation huronne de 1653," *Lettres du Bas-Canada,* VII (1953), 159-70. Regarding the *Congrégation de Messieurs,* see Adrien Pouliot, "Troisième centenaire de la congrégation des hommes de Quebec," *Lettres du Bas-Canada,* XI (1957), 28-36. This congregation, which has existed continually since 1657, has its own chapel at Quebec.

[12] See *Les Ursulines de Québec,* I, 256. During that week Mère Marie and three other nuns continued to live at their convent. See also *Histoire de l'Hôtel-Dieu de Québec,* 236, for a contemporary account of the hospital nuns under these conditions.

[13] See Macdougall, "La réception d'Argenson." The article includes the complete text of the play as well as the names of the actors.

That was the place where in the summer of 1625 Charles Lalemant, Jean de Brébeuf, and Ennemond Massé founded the work of the Jesuits in New France after the abortive attempt of Father Pierre Biard and Father Massé at Port-Royal in 1611. The land where Notre-Dame-de-Saint-Anges once stood was now farmed and a herd of cattle grazed over pastures cleared so laboriously back in 1625. Milk and cheese were no longer the rare delicacies they had been forty years ago. Missionary life in the colony was still rugged enough, true, but at Quebec the community no longer lived on *sagamité* plus what wild game one of the Brothers shot. The community was no longer crowded into a hot attic such as Father Paul Le Jeune described in 1632.[14] The college, as Father Marquette could easily see, was an exact duplicate of those in France and the Quebecois students were good Frenchmen, sturdy, a bit inclined to independence and self-reliance, perhaps, but loyal to France and God.

That evening at recreation young Father Marquette was inundated with questions. How was the war with England going? Did his ship encounter any English pirates on the high seas? How was the voyage; very rough? Did he bring many letters from home? Had the mission's agent in France been able to send along the books they had ordered and cloth for cassocks which seemed to wear out so quickly in this new country? Jacques brought out his little presents, sent along for the missionaries from the Jesuits in France. A ream of paper for the superior, some squat fat candles for the altar, a breviary with larger print for older eyes, a warm vest for Brother Bonnemer who was over sixty-five. After eighteen years on the mission he was beginning to feel the cold of the bitter winters. A tiny bottle of wine from the Côte-d'Or was handed to Father Chaumonot. Everybody laughed delightedly at that because they all knew that his people were vintagers just as they knew that he had run away as a lad of thirteen or so, and had wandered through France and Italy until a kind providence landed him at

[14] See Father Paul Le Jeune's description of living conditions at Notre-Dame-des-Anges, *Relations*, VI, 69.

the door of the novitiate in Rome.[15] Finally, when the community night prayers were said, Marquette was free to seek out his simple, sparsely furnished room where he could close the door and kneel at the rough prie-dieu to thank his Mother Immaculate for assisting him to realize, at last, the ambition he had cherished for twenty years. Here he was, a foreign missionary, or at least an apprentice one. And before long he would become one in very fact. But first

[15] These incidents are, of course, supposititious, but the items mentioned appear on lists of requests sent from Quebec to France. The details of Chaumonot's youth are taken from his autobiography, *Un missionnaire des Hurons.* When Marquette reached Quebec, the following Jesuits were in New France:

François Le Mercier, the superior, sixty-six, arrived in 1635.
Charles Albanel, fifty, reached New France in 1649.
Claude Allouez, fifty-three, came to Quebec in 1642.
Claude Bardy, age unknown, arrived in 1665, returned to France in 1667.
Pierre Bailloquet, fifty-four, came to Quebec in 1647.
Thierry Beschefer, thirty-six, reached New France in 1665.
Jacques Bruyas, thirty-one, landed at Quebec on August 3, 1666.
Etienne de Carheil, thirty-three, arrived at Quebec on August 6, 1666.
Pierre Chastelain, sixty-two, reached New France in 1636.
Pierre-Joseph-Marie Chaumonot, fifty-five, came to Canada in 1639.
Claude Dablon, forty-seven, reached New France in 1655.
Gabriel Druillettes, fifty-six, came to Canada in 1643.
Jacques Fremin, thirty-eight, arrived from France in 1655.
Julien Garnier, twenty-three, came to Quebec in 1662 on completing his novitiate in France. He was ordained at Quebec in April 1666.
Jérôme Lallemant, seventy-three, came to New France in 1638.
Simon Le Moyne, sixty-two, reached Quebec in 1638.
Martin Lyonne, fifty-two, came to Quebec in 1643.
Louis Nicolas, thirty-two, reached New France in 1664.
Henri Nouvel, forty-five, arrived in Canada in 1662.
Claude Pijart, sixty-six, came to the mission in 1637.
Pierre Raffeix, thirty-one, landed at Quebec in 1653.
André Richard, sixty-six, came to Canada in 1634.
Brother Florent Bonnemer, sixty-six, came to Canada in 1647.
Brother Ambroise Brouet reached the mission in 1641.
Brother Joseph Boursier *dit* Desforges, forty-one, came to New France in 1654.
Brother Jean Fréville, sixty-six, reached Canada in 1649.
Brother Louis Gaubert, came to the mission in 1636.
Brother Guillaume Lauzier was sent to New France in 1659.
Brother Louis Le Boëme, thirty-four, came to Canada in 1656.
Brother Pierre Masson came to the mission in 1646.
Brother François Malherbe, thirty, reached New France in 1654.

he must become familiar with New France, its government, its institutions, its economic and social life, the various missionary areas in which the Jesuits were working, the character of the Indians, their languages, and their customs.

The experienced and prudent François Le Mercier certainly instructed his new recruit regarding the sensitive situation existing between the colony's royal officials and the ecclesiastics, especially the missionaries. Since 1603 when Henri IV (1589-1610) granted a trade monopoly in America to Pierre du Gast, Sieur de Monts, in consideration for the latter's establishing a permanent French colony, until 1663 when New France became a royal colony, Canada was constantly under the management of one or other monopolistic trading company whose primary interest was financial profit for its stockholders. Each succeeding company was enjoined to "provide for the instruction of the aborigines in the knowledge of God and the Christian religion."[16] In practice, this obligation required company officials to support the clergy requisite to evangelize the Indians and minister to the spiritual welfare of the French who took up residence in Canada. From the very outset, traders and other company officials in New France learned that debauching the Indian was the most effective means of compelling the native to gather a rich fur harvest. Because missionaries could not in conscience tolerate that policy, they were soon at loggerheads with the company's representatives in Canada as well as its officials in France. Before long, company agents in America and those in Paris were writing memorials to the crown complaining that the Jesuits, who for many years were the only ecclesiastics in New France, were pursuing a policy regarding the Indians which was contrary to the interests of the company. Shortly, colonial officials were accusing the missionaries of having designs of assuming civil as well as ecclesiastical control of the colony. Given the Gallican flavor of Bourbon France, the allegation was not entirely discredited at Paris.

[16] The charter of the de Monts company, from which the phrase is quoted, may be consulted in Marc Lescarbot, *The History of New France*, II, 211-12. Lescarbot was at Port-Royal in Acadia from May 1606 to July 1607.

When Jacques Marquette arrived New France was, in effect, a crown colony, though economically it was a monopoly of the Company of the West Indies. Granted a charter in 1664, that company never exercised its prerogative of appointing, with royal approval, the civil officials of the colony. New France's chief executive was the governor-general who was assisted by governors-particular at Three Rivers and Montreal, all of whom held royal commissions.[17] The Sovereign Council, established in 1663 as a counterweight balancing the hitherto unlimited authority of the governor-general, was composed of five councillors, nominated jointly by the governor-general and the bishop; an attorney-general; a secretary; the intendant; plus the bishop and the governor-general who were ex-officio members. This body partook of the mixed character of a high court of justice and a French *parlement,* much like the *parlement* of Paris. It registered royal and other decrees, thus making them official, and approved the disbursement of public funds. In the practical administration of the colony, the governor-general formulated policies regarding external affairs and was commander-in-chief of the armed forces. The intendant was responsible for all internal matters, including justice and the police as well as the actual spending of public funds. The governor-general, the intendant, and many lesser officials were, with few exceptions, Frenchmen, born and bred, who came to New France as mature men, thoroughly in sympathy with the concept of absolutist monarchy existing in France. As the local embodiment of the king, the governor-general tended to arrogate to himself all of the privileges and perquisites pertaining to the royal personage himself. In keeping with the absurd artificiality of French social standards, governors insisted on rank and precedence, not hesitating to involve the whole colony in endless controversies which were carried for solution to the king himself. Aping their betters, lesser officials were equally as sensitive about their supposed social perquisites. Inevitably, ecclesiastics in the colony became enmeshed in these

[17] The Sulpicians, who held the island of Montreal as a seigniory, had the right to nominate the governor of Montreal. Their nominee was issued a royal commission.

altercations since the importance of rank and position did not cease at the church door.

For over three centuries the kings of France had treated the Church as an arm of the state, regulating its life from the appointment of new bishops to assigning benefices and determining parish boundaries. Control of ecclesiastical affairs by the crown was never more effective than it was during the seventeenth century. Louis XIV's mother, Anne of Austria, established a government bureau, the Congregation for Ecclesiastical Affairs, commonly called the Council of Conscience, whose purpose was to deal with all matters concerning religion. No ecclesiastical appointment of any moment was made except through the Council of Conscience unless the crown acted independently of it.[18] Significantly, no churchmen, not even Jesuits, all normally Ultramontanists, found anything objectionable in the royal administration of these details of the Church. Jesuits generally opposed doctrinal Gallicanism, a theory which proposed, in part, that the pope is not free to issue a doctrinal decision without the consent of a general council. But French Jesuits never questioned the royal "right" to appoint bishops or direct the temporalities of the Church. In New France, Jesuits unhesitatingly opened and closed missions at the royal command, never once, apparently, questioning the king's right to order them to do so. Unfortunately, the mind of French officialdom was pre-conditioned to an over-sensitivity towards the possibility of an ecclesiastical invasion of the royal prerogatives pertaining to church matters. In 1662, just four years before Marquette came to New France, the "Affair of the Corsican Guards" in Rome offered the twenty-four-year-old Louis XIV an occasion to clarify his position regarding the Church. He forced the pope, Alexander VII, to apologize for a wholly fictitious insult to the French ambassador arising out of a drunken brawl between the pope's Corsican guards and some mem-

[18] When Saint Vincent de Paul was a member of the Council of Conscience, he opposed the appointment of Beaumanoir de Lavardin to the bishopric of Le Mans because the man was a professed unbeliever. The support of the candidate was so strong at court that he received the appointment despite his irreligiousness. Beaumanoir de Lavardin was a disgraceful bishop. See Jean Calvet, *Saint Vincent de Paul*, 150.

bers of the ambassador's household. By broadcasting the papal apology Louis XIV quite effectively announced that he would continue to rule the Church in France. The fundamental issue of the Gallican Liberties, which constantly disturbed ecclesiastical France throughout the reign of Louis XIV, did not come into the open until 1682, seven years after Marquette had died. But the atmosphere of suspicion towards the clergy on the part of the régime of Louis XIV solidified long before that date. The crown ministers encouraged civil officials to be wary of churchmen lest they insidiously infringe on the royal prerogatives regarding the Church. And, as is always the case, the more removed the official is from the major authority the more the underling tends to exaggerate the policy of the superior. In New France, therefore, Jesuits had long ago learned to step warily in approaching the king's representatives. Father Marquette must understand that governors and other civil officials were very sensitive of their real or imagined rights. Since the conversion of the Indians depended in no small measure on the good will of the colony's officialdom, proper gestures, such as courtesy calls of newly arrived missionaries, as well as consummate prudence in dealing with the king's local officials was a vital quality which every Jesuit must cultivate.

In the absence of the governor-general, Daniel de Remi, Seigneur de Courcelle, and Alexandre de Prouville, Marquis de Tracy, the king's viceroy for North America, who had marched off six days before Marquette's arrival on a campaign against the Iroquois, the new missionary was free to present himself first to François Xavier de Montmorency-Laval, bishop of Petrea, a suppressed diocese in the old Macedonia, and vicar-apostolic of Quebec. Laval was a strikingly impressive prelate of forty-four whose dark, piercing eyes, large forehead, long aquiline face, and tall, slender figure commanded immediate respect. A man of admitted personal sanctity, his life and his fortune were wholeheartedly dedicated to the task of shepherding his people, French and Indian alike, in the paths of righteousness. Laval had received all of his educational training from the Jesuits at La Flèche and Louis-le-Grand in Paris. He was on the best of terms with the Jesuits in New France, especially since they were his most staunch supporters.

Bishop Laval received Marquette at the episcopal residence on the rue de Buade, an unpretentious house in which eight diocesan priests resided with the bishop and formed the nucleus of the seminary which Laval hoped to develop. When Bishop Laval organized his vast diocese, he had confided the Christianizing of the Indians to the Jesuits. Now, before the stately prelate knelt this vigorous young missionary about to begin a difficult and trying career, one which might easily lead to martyrdom or, at very least, to years of gruelling physical hardship and heart-breaking disappointments. What could the bishop say to this missionary Benjamin? Laval must have called to mind his meeting with Father René Ménard in August of 1660. Coming down the river from Montreal, the bishop had encountered a flotilla of Ottawa canoes homeward bound after trading at Three Rivers. Aboard one of the frail crafts was René Ménard bound for the Ottawa country five hundred leagues from Quebec, from which he was never to return. When the bishop expressed concern for the missionary's safety, Ménard asked what he should do. The bishop replied: "Common sense dictates that you should come back with me, but God wishes you to go on."[19] Bishop Laval could do no more than wish Father Marquette well and promise prayers for his physical and spiritual welfare and abundant success in his future work among those hordes of poor, benighted aborigines who were to be his charges.

Though Father Le Mercier could not at the moment formally present his new recruit to the governor-general, Courcelle, and the Marquis de Tracy, lieutenant-general of North America, Marquette could be carefully briefed concerning them. Tracy, a grizzled old campaigner of sixty-four, was a competent strategist, sensitive regarding the homage due his rank, but a solidly religious man. When he stepped ashore at Quebec on June 30, 1665, he was preceded by twenty guards and four pages, all dressed in the royal colors. In solemn state Tracy marched up the rue de la Montagne to the parish church where he was greeted by the bishop and the assembled clergy. When he was ushered to a richly draped prie-dieu to participate in the chanting of the *Te Deum,* declining to use it,

[19] *Relations,* XLVIII, 259.

he knelt on the floor like any simple peasant before his God.[20] Though he was insistant on a proper retinue accompanying him when he left his quarters, Tracy wasted no time in acquainting himself with the military needs of the country. While waiting for the arrival of the full complement of the Carignan-Salières regiment, he hastily built three forts at strategic positions, garrisoned them, and prepared to campaign effectively against the Iroquois. Governor Courcelle, in the meantime, grew restless at being overshadowed by the presence of the royal lieutenant-general. After all, Tracy was but a bird of passage while Courcelle, the governor-general, must remain after Tracy sailed off to France. Chafed and impatient, Courcelle craved an opportunity to demonstrate his ability, gaining thereby, he hoped, the respect of the colonists and the fear of the Iroquois. Bold to the point of brashness, Courcelle insisted on launching a campaign against the Mohawks in the dead of winter with European troops who were completely unprepared to cope with the deep snow and bitter cold. Though the governor was "breathing nothing but war" when he set out on January 9, 1666, before he covered the three hundred leagues to the Mohawk villages he had lost his way and ended near Schenectady, far from his objective.[21] Algonquins, who promised to act as guides, got drunk and did not join him until Courcelle had been obliged to retreat because of lack of food, the cold, and the utter exhaustion of his frostbitten militia.[22] On his way back to Quebec, Courcelle met Father Jacques Fremin at Three Rivers, to whom he said: "My Father, I am the most unfortunate gentleman in the world, and you are the cause of my misfortune."[23] Reaching Quebec on March 17, the governor promptly ". . . had a dispute with Father Albanel, . . ." chaplain at the fort, whom he accused of ". . . having purposely delayed the Algonquins, which was not true."[24] The fiasco

[20] In his *The Old Régime in Canada*, 239, Parkman says that Tracy was tall and portly, " 'one of the largest men I ever saw' writes Mother Mary [of the Incarnation]; but he was sallow with disease . . ."

[21] An account of Courcelle's campaign may be consulted in O'Callaghan, *Documents*, III, 118, and following.

[22] *Relations*, L, 183.

[23] *Ibid.*, 185.

[24] *Ibid.*, 183.

was all the more painful to Courcelle because the Canadians had warned him and predicted failure. Poor Albanel was a handy whipping boy on whom the disconcerted governor inflicted his pique. Thenceforth relations between the governor and the Jesuits were hardly cordial.

But in the fall, under Tracy's leadership, the French struck a crushing blow. At the head of a force of 600 regulars, an equal number of colonials, and a hundred Algonquin and Huron scouts, Tracy invaded the territory of the Mohawks, at the southern end of Lake George. Finding that the enemy had fled, the invading army destroyed all the villages they encountered. Had Tracy been foresighted enough to carry the war to the other cantons of the Five Nations, he might well have ended forever any further trouble from the Iroquois. As it was, the invasion of their country struck such terror into the hearts of the Five Nations that the next summer, on July 10, 1667, they signed a solemn peace with the French and adhered to it for the next eighteen years.

In the absence of the viceroy and the governor-general, the Jesuit superior certainly brought young Father Marquette to pay his respects to Jean Talon, New France's first resident intendant and the most capable man to hold that office in the history of the colony. Born at Châlons-sur-Marne in 1625, Talon, educated by the Jesuits at Louis-le-Grand in Paris, had gained administrative experience as Turenne's military intendant and was intendant of Hainaut when he was commissioned, in 1665, to assume the same office in New France. Despite his years of association with the Jesuits when he was a student, his attitude towards them and ecclesiastics in general was of a piece with that of French officialdom in his day. In the instructions Talon received before he sailed for Quebec, he was advised that the Jesuits ". . . have assumed an authority there that transcends the bounds of their true profession," and that it was the duty of the intendant to ". . . preserve in just equilibrium the temporal authority resident in the king . . . and the spiritual . . . in such manner always as the latter be subordinate to the former . . ."[25] A polished gentleman and no fool, Talon certainly intended

[25] O'Callaghan, *Documents*, IX, 24. He gives an English translation of these instructions.

to comply with his instructions, but he had no intention of accomplishing that objective with a broadsword. A man of remarkable ability, he was perhaps the first French official who grasped the real economic value of New France as a permanent, flourishing colony. Convinced of the soundness of the country's future, he introduced a whole series of profitable new industries such as commercial fishing, lumbering, ship building, sheep raising, textile manufacture, tanning, and even a brewery. Through Talon's efforts, immigration increased Canada's population by nearly a thousand between 1665 and 1668. The vast, unexplored stretches of New France intrigued Talon, impelling him to encourage people to penetrate the unknown. Where did the great rivers end? Was there a navigable water route through the great land mass of North America whereby France could dominate trade with the Orient? Perhaps there was a series of rivers which would make it possible for France to completely encircle the English colonies and confine them to the Atlantic seaboard. Neither the home government nor, certainly, the Company of the West Indies, would subsidize exploration, but missionaries, all well-educated and observant men, would accomplish it at no expense to France. Perhaps this healthy young missionary, paying his polite duty call, might widen geographic horizons, and at no cost to the crown. Jean Talon could well afford to be his most gracious, courtly self in his interview with Father Jacques Marquette.

The first Indian village Marquette encountered lay before him on the plateau of Quebec's upper town. A sad remnant of the Christians from Huronia, scene of the martyrdom of Brébeuf and his companions, had fled from the fury of the Iroquois to Ile d'Orleans in 1651. Father Chaumonot settled them on land owned by the Jesuits and built a new Sainte-Marie to replace the Sainte-Marie in Huronia. In 1656 the Iroquois attacked the poor little palisaded Huron village, massacring some sixty of the refugees. Thoroughly discouraged, the Hurons, accompanied by their pastor, took refuge under the very cannon of Fort Saint Louis, settling on the site where Quebec's *Bureau de Poste* now stands. Defeated, discouraged, dispirited, they huddled together in rude huts reminiscent of their once spacious long houses, existing on a scanty dole which the crown saw fit to grant them.[26] These poor outcasts were hardly an inspiration to a novice missionary with stars in his eyes, dreaming of converting great multitudes of noble, erect, supple savages. Contemplating this hopeless tag-end of human refuse, Marquette could well wonder whether the doctrines of the gentle Christ could ever be so deeply impressed on the minds of the aborigines that they would relinquish their age old practices of cruelty and horrible inter-tribal warfare. Seven years after Marquette saw them, the Hurons were moved to New Lorette, a village located a little more than ten miles north of Quebec. There Father Chaumonot built a replica of the Holy House of Loreto in Italy, dear to the pastor of these Hurons for he felt that it was while visiting the original Loreto that he received the grace to become a missionary. It was not long before Canada's Loreto attracted the French, "coming thither on pilgrimages, for making and fulfilling vows there, and receiving the sacraments . . ."[27] Today the place is Quebec's airport and the town is lined with motels for it is on a major highway from Montreal to Quebec.

Undoubtedly Marquette was brought to visit the Ursulines in their convent on the crest of the hill to the south of the Jesuit college. Every newly arrived ecclesiastic must be introduced to Mère Marie de l'Incarnation, wife, mother, widow, and business woman before she entered the Ursuline convent in her native Tours, leaving her young son to the care of her married sister. She could reminisce interestingly about the Jesuit martyrs, some of whom she had known quite well. When the Huron refugees flocked to Quebec in 1651, they camped around the convent where Mère Marie fed them until her own community nearly starved in the process. When she first reached the colony in 1639, at the age of forty, she tried hard to learn Algonquin from Father Paul Le Jeune and got a severe headache for her pains. Mère Marie and her small community had made a valiant effort at turning Indian girls into sedate French ladies with no success. Just keeping the little savages fairly clean was a full-time chore and one which left the Indian girls

[26] *Relations*, XXXV, 207-09.
[27] *Ibid.*, LX, 75.

completely puzzled. Why should anyone want to wash off good bear grease which protected skin and hair so well? Why did that nice old lady, Madeleine de la Peltrie, lay foundress of the Ursuline convent, want them to learn needlepoint when everyone knew that clothes were only properly decorated by fringes and quills? It was fun to play at attending choir with the nuns or keeping one of them company when she went off to say her rosary alone. These white ladies were very kind, but pathetically helpless. They couldn't make a sturdy dress from a scraped moose hide or fashion a simple moccasin and they were terrible cooks, always fussing with fancy dishes instead of making good, nourishing *sagamité* with a few fish heads thrown into it to give it some flavor. Mère Marie, at least, understood Indians, or at any rate the love-sick ones, as when a great gawk of an Algonquin made a nuisance of himself, "going and coming like an imbecile while the young [Algonquin] lady only laughed at him."[28] With the daughters of the French colonists, who were much easier to manage, the Ursulines exerted themselves to instill into them the refinements of France. That task was not quite as simple for the nuns at Quebec as it was at the Ursuline convent in Tours. Children in New France were robust, hardy, early accustomed to self-reliance and courage in the face of trouble. The influence of the Ursulines went far to smooth the rough edges of their charges, strengthen their religious awareness, and prepare them to mold their future husbands and children into a noble folk. Mère Marie's spiritual daughters still inhabit their ancient location, performing their same gracious duties as they have for three centuries and a quarter.

Northwest of the Jesuit college, towards the edge of Quebec's promontory, was the Hôtel-Dieu where a baker's dozen of the Soeurs Hospitalières from Dieppe nursed the sick. Cardinal

[28] Mother Denis Mahoney, O.S.U., *Marie of the Incarnation, Mystic and Missionary*, 358. This new biography is the most scholarly study of Mère Marie which has appeared in English. See also John J. Sullivan, editor, *The Autobiography of the Venerable Marie of the Incarnation, O.S.U., Mystic and Missionary*.

Richelieu's niece, Marie Vignerot, Duchesse d'Aiguillon, founded the hospital in 1639 and endowed it with an annual income of 3,000 francs. Mère Marie Guenet de Saint Ignace, only twenty-nine at the time, and two companions, Mère Anne de Cointre de Saint Bernard and Mère Marie Forestier de Saint Bonaventure, nursing sisters, came to New France in 1639 on the same ship with Mère Marie and her Ursulines. For a short time after their arrival the Hospitalières lived at Sillery until the workmen sent by the Duchesse d'Aiguillon finished their quarters in Quebec. Having moved to their new building, the nuns nursed French and Indian alike with tenderness and solicitude. The hospital was a useful place for an incohate missionary to visit in order to learn about Indians at first hand. He would find them, stretched on their pallets, recovering from broken bones, fever, or gunshot wounds, stoically indifferent to their suffering, their dark eyes gazing with wonder at the *Mères Blanches* who tenderly washed their bodies, dressed their wounds, and bathed their fevered brows. In the Indians' eyes these good women meant very well, but were abysmally ignorant. They never applied such tried and true remedies as steam baths in an airtight hut or blowing in the ear to drive out the evil spirit causing pain in the belly. Yet they were obviously true believers in their Great Spirit since they asked nothing in return for their ministrations, not even a beaver pelt which all Frenchmen prized. Now and then, but not very frequently, the nuns induced a dying Indian to accept baptism. For those few triumphs, French women of good birth scrubbed floors, made beds, and bandaged infected wounds, while during their community devotions they prayed for the repose of the soul of Armand Jean du Plessis, Cardinal, Duc de Richelieu, who could well use it, and his lovely, generous, pious niece. As dedicated as the Hospitalières were, together with all seventeenth century French of any status, they were sensitive of their perquisites of rank. When the feast of Corpus Christi was celebrated the nuns at the hospital insisted that the solemn procession of the Blessed Sacrament stop first at their convent because the Duchesse d'Aiguillon had ordered the building of their hospital two years before any negotiations had begun for the Ursulines to come to New France. The Jesuits agreed that "this gives the Hospital nuns the privilege of first place."[29] When Marquette saw the hospital the nuns were at their wit's end caring for crowds of sick soldiers. The superior of the hospital wrote home on October 3, 1666: "We have continued the practice of our calling throughout the entire year with scarcely any respite, our halls having been always full of patients – to such an extent that we have more than twelve thousand."[30] Accompanying her letter was a long list of "articles necessary for the relief of the poor patients." Some of the items requested were: fine rhubarb, opium, myrrh, aloes, English alum, sugar, "white and brown as much as possible," wax for ointments, napkins, old linen. "Chilblains, sores, and hemorrhages, the usual ailments of this country, cause us a scarcity of linen . . ."[31] The Hospitalières of the Mercy of Jesus are still nursing the sick at their original location, but in a vastly expanded establishment. The visitor calling at the Hôtel-Dieu is greeted by a notice asking him to pray for the soul of the hospital's generous foundress and her exalted uncle, who might even yet need prayers.

Every newcomer to Quebec was eventually taken to Sillery, four miles up the Saint Lawrence, to visit the model village of sedentary Indians the Jesuits started in 1637 with funds donated by Noel Brulart de Sillery, commander of the Knights of Malta, who sent skilled craftsmen from France to build homes for the Indians as well as a church, a residence for the missionaries, barns, and a small fort. The French laborers also cleared the land and planted crops to give the Indians a start.[32] This "reduction" was begun by Father Paul Le Jeune who firmly believed that Indian nomads could never be converted and civilized until they were gathered together and rendered sedentary. The daily life of the reduction was minutely regulated. Each morning, at an early hour, a bell summoned all to Mass, after which the men went to their work in the fields or

[29] *Relations,* XXVIII, 193.

[30] *Ibid.*, L, 153.

[31] *Ibid.*, 161, 163.

[32] Camille de Rochemonteix, *Les Jésuites et la Nouvelle-France au XVIIe siècle,* I, 466-72. He prints all of the official documents relating to the royal grant of land made to the Jesuits for the site at Sillery. See *ibid.*, 247, for the highly ornate introduction of the document. Rochemonteix's work is hereafter cited as *Jésuites.*

hunting while the women did their housework. The children who were old enough flocked to the pastor's house to be taught their catechism and learn hymns. In the late afternoon the missionaries gathered their flock for instructions, evening prayers, and conferences. On Sundays and feast days the devout manner manifested by the neophytes at their religious duties was so impressive that the French often went there to Mass because they were so edified. The Indians at Sillery were not all members of the same tribe. Some were Algonquin, some Abenaki, with now and then a rare Iroquois or Indian from some other nation. Yet they lived together peacefully and elected officers to manage the village. Sillery was a very useful place at which to learn an Indian language. Once the superior of the mission determined with which nation a newly arrived Jesuit should work, he could go to Sillery and sit at the feet of a member of that tribe, imbibing the language as a child learns it. By the time Marquette reached Canada many of the older missionaries were not only fluent in the native tongues, but they had reduced several of them to writing and formulated the rules which governed speaking them. But at Sillery the beginner could experience his first taste of working with Indians and, from it, begin to understand something about the character of the aborigines with whom he confidently expected to spend the remainder of his life.

During subsequent days Marquette began to sense the pulse of Quebec and the colony of New France whose very life's blood was the fur trade involving the French and the Indians at various centers along the length of the Saint Lawrence. At Tadoussac, perched on a barren eminence between the broadening Saint Lawrence and the Saguenay tumbling out of its forbidding rock gorge, Indians from as far north as Hudson Bay foregathered in the summer to exchange their peltries for warm blankets, lengths of cloth, metal fish hooks, iron cooking pots, a little tobacco, and perhaps a bright ribbon or a small mirror for the women. The nations which frequented Tadoussac were the Montagnais of the North, the Papinachois, the Bersiamites, and the Porcupines. The summer trading fair was the harvest time for the missionary. The few Christians among the visiting Indians received the sacraments and the pagans had the Faith explained to them several times a day. As he sat at the campfire of a visiting tribe, the Jesuit questioned the Indians about still unknown nations and the geography of the country from which the visitors came. When the days grew shorter and the nights more chill, the Indians reluctantly began departing for their homeland. The missionary, too, making up his small pack of supplies, prepared to accompany a group of them, facing another winter of wandering over frozen rivers through the deep snow, living in fetid shelters, stifled with the smoke, always surrounded by screeching children, howling dogs, morally uninhibited adults, always cold, wet, and hungry, hundreds of miles from a fellow Jesuit or even a Frenchman. But, year by weary year, he encountered still another unknown tribe and gleaned one more valuable piece of geographical information. Infrequently a dying child or an ancient Indian was baptized, but there was never the joy of witnessing a whole tribe embrace Christianity. So long as he was with the Indians, the missionary could induce them to adhere to "the prayer," but when he next met them the priest would find his quondam fervent Christians again practicing polygamy and blindly following the lead of their sorcerers. Father François de Crepieul, who spent years on the Tadoussac mission, described that apostolate thus: "The life of a Montagnais missionary is a long and slow martyrdom; is almost a continual practice of patience and mortification; is a truly penitential and humbling life, especially in the cabins and the journeys with the savages . . . Suffering and hardship are the trappings of these holy but arduous missions."[33]

South of the Saint Lawrence, in the present Nova Scotia, New Brunswick, and Maine, were the Micmacs, the Etechemins, and the Abenaki, all of whom traded with and were consistently loyal to the French and bitter enemies of the colonists of New England. The first Jesuit effort to convert the Indians of New France was made by Pierre Biard and Ennemond Massé in 1611 at Port-Royal among the Micmacs. In 1635 Cardinal Richelieu chartered a company, of which he was a stockholder, to colonize Acadia and evangelize the natives through the ministration of the Capuchins. These zealous men established missions at Port-Royal,

[33] *Relations,* LXV, 49.

on the Kennebec River, and on the Penobscot near the present Castine, Maine. In 1640 Richelieu donated his stock to the Capuchins, encouraging them to employ the revenue to establish schools for the Indians in Acadia.[34] In the meantime some Abenaki, in their wanderings, came upon the Indian settlement at Sillery where they embraced Christianity and urged the Jesuits to send them a missionary. In answer to their plea, Father Gabriel Druillettes, then a vigorous young man of thirty-six, was dispatched in August, 1646, to spend the winter with them.[35] The Capuchins treated the visitor with great courtesy, but wrote to Quebec informing the Jesuit superior of their presence and asking that none of his subjects be sent to open missions in that area. However by 1648 the Capuchins of their own accord requested help from the Jesuits. In 1650 Druilletes again visited the Abenaki at Norridgewolk, Maine in the dual capacity of missionary and ambassador to the English at Boston, who had invited the governor-general of New France, d'Ailleboust, to consider arranging a perpetual alliance independent of the attitude of the home governments.[36] Though the diplomatic mission came to nothing, the missionary was greatly consoled by the religious perseverance of the Abenaki with whom he spent the winter. By 1655, when the Capuchins reluctantly abandoned their missions, the Jesuits were unable to supply missionaries to continue them. The Abenaki, however, continued to come to Sillery for trading as well as to receive religious instruction. Christians trained at Sillery became lay apostles to their fellow tribesmen.

Three Rivers, eighty miles up the Saint Lawrence from Quebec, the once crowded trading center attended by the Algonquins of the North, the White Fish, and some of the farther western tribes, was no longer a busy emporium.[37] The Iroquois had ravaged the length of the Saint Maurice River so completely that the Indians, who had hitherto used it as a highway to Three

[34] John Gilmary Shea, *The Catholic Church in Colonial Days*, 236-42.

[35] *Relations*, XXX, 185.

[36] *Ibid.*, XXXVI, 87.

[37] The town of Three Rivers was established in the summer of 1634. Father Paul Le Jeune, then superior of the Jesuit missions in New France, was the first priest to be stationed there.

Rivers, did not venture to risk the journey. But the nearly 500 French residing there bravely held out as did the Indians living a sedentary life near the church of the Immaculate Conception. Ten years after the inception of that reduction, begun by Father Jacques Buteux in 1641, Father Paul Ragueneau wrote home to Paris describing its importance: "Most of the neophytes, of whom there are many, have taken up their residence there through a motive which would not be expected from barbarians but recently converted to the Faith. 'It is,' they say, 'to fight the enemy of the prayer that we willingly expose our lives; if we die fighting, we consider that we die in defense of the Faith.' "[38]

For a brief period, thirteen years before Marquette reached New France, the Iroquois offered to make peace with the French only because they feared an invasion of their country by the powerful Cat nation whom the Iroquois could not defeat if they must also defend themselves against a possible attack by the French. Hoping to impress the French with the sincerity of their deceptively peaceful intentions, the Iroquois invited the governor-general to send them missionaries and a group of colonists to settle among them. In 1654 Father Simon Le Moyne, an accomplished mimic and an expert on the folklore of the Five Nations, went to Onondaga, the Iroquois capital, to ratify the treaty which had been signed at Quebec in 1653. His fluency in the native language and his uncanny ability to imitate to perfection the great chiefs of the Iroquois made his visit a triumph. As he approached the capital the roads were lined with people come out to greet him. "One calls me brother, another an uncle, another a cousin; never have I had so many kinfolk . . . I called by name all the chiefs, families and persons of importance, speaking slowly and in the tone of a chief . . ."[39] Risking the possibility that the Iroquois were deceiving them, a group of colonists with six missionaries, among them Chaumonot, who spoke the language, and Claude Dablon, established a mission near the present Oswego, New York. Before coming out to Quebec, Dab-

[38] *Relations*, XXXVI, 195.
[39] *Ibid.*, XLI, 99.

lon had learned to play several musical instruments, expecting to charm the savages with his music as he had heard the Jesuits in Paraguay were accustomed to do. As to his musical ability, the forthright Father Chaumonot remarked painfully that Dablon enjoyed it himself.[40] Before long the missionaries learned the truth about the Iroquois invitation to dwell among them. When the threatened invasion by the Cat nation evaporated, the Iroquois showed their true colors and plotted to kill the French, laymen and missionaries alike. Since nothing would be gained by martyrdom, the Jesuits and their lay companions escaped by a clever ruse and returned to the colony.[41] Thenceforth, until the Iroquois signed a peace in 1667, the country of the Five Nations was closed to mission activity. Just a little less than two months after Marquette landed, all Quebec flocked to the parish church to sing the *Te Deum* in thanksgiving for Tracy's victory over the Iroquois. The Jesuits quite possibly sang the loudest because the military success almost certainly meant the reopening of the mission effort among the Iroquois.

In 1666 the most westward permanent settlement in New France was the colony of Montreal established in 1642 by the *Société-de-Notre-Dame-de-Montréal.* During the twenty-four years of its existence the colony had grown from an original population of 42 to 625, but its external appearance was still that of the rudest frontier village. The wooden chapel, Notre-Dame-de-Bonsecours, was confided to the care of the Jesuits until 1657 when a contingent of Sulpicians, led by the abbé Gabriel de Queylus, arrived to assume spiritual charge of the island which shortly became their seigniory. Among these new arrivals was the ramrod straight, thirty-

[40] Chaumonot, *Un missionnaire des Hurons*, 52.

[41] *Relations*, XLIV, 179. The French invited the Iroquois chiefs to an "eat-all" feast. Then Father Dablon lulled them to sleep with his music. When the Indians were all sleeping soundly, the French hastily embarked and were far from danger before their guests awoke the following morning. Explaining the reason for their action, Chaumonot, *Un missionnaire des Hurons*, 151, wrote: ". . . seeing, as I say, that their death and captivity would work more harm than profit to the French colony . . . seeing that their death would be of no service to the poor captive church . . . they took flight, hoping to return when times were more tranquil."

year-old former cavalry officer, the abbé François Dollier de Casson, a figure of historically heroic proportions, who labored mightily for the Indians.[42] At the Hôtel-Dieu, Jeanne Mance, then an old lady of sixty, cared for the sick and the wounded, no longer single-handed, as she had for years, but with the aid of the Soeurs Hospitalières de La Flèche, a community of nursing nuns founded by a married man.[43] Marguerite Bourgeoys' little school was housed in quarters more fit for use as a stable.[44] On the Saint Lawrence River side of the island there was a none too formidable fort around which the settlers' houses clustered in a haphazard fashion. Somewhat inland there was a little clutch of homes built around the Godois well. Life at this western bastion of New France was so dangerous that no man dared be more than an arm's length away from his weapons. In every field there was a small redoubt into which workers could take refuge if and when the Iroquois suddenly appeared, as they often did.

West of Montreal the country was still pretty much a *terra incognita.* Since 1642 when Isaac Jogues and Charles Raymbault visited the Saulteurs dwelling near the site of the future mission of Sainte-Marie-du-Sault, the Jesuits had been anxious to evangelize the many nations beyond of whose existence they learned through contacting the Saulteurs. Two efforts, in 1656 and 1660, to open that field ended in disaster.[45] In the summer of 1665, just a year

[42] There is no better account of Montreal's early history than Dollier de Casson's *Histoire de Montréal.* Ralph Flenley has translated and edited the work in English under the title, *The History of Montreal, 1640-1672.*

[43] Jerome le Royer de la Dauversière is a typical example of the vitality of the religious resurgence in seventeenth-century France. In 1631, though married and the father of several children, he took a vow obliging him to establish a community of hospital nuns, begin a colony on the island of Montreal, and transport the nuns there. Though the vow was absurd on the face of it, he literally accomplished his whole commitment to God. The work of his nuns at Montreal may be reviewed in Marie Morin's *Annales de l'Hôtel-Dieu de Montreal.*

[44] Marguerite Bourgeoys was induced to come to Montreal by Paul de Chomedey, Sieur de Maisonneuve, the founder of Montreal and its first governor. In 1659 she founded the Congrégation-de-la-Notre-Dame-de-Montréal which is today the most numerous of the congregations of teaching nuns in Canada.

[45] These two efforts are discussed later.

before Marquette reached Quebec, Father Claude Allouez went west with an Ottawa flotilla.[46] That rugged son of his native Haut Loire was the tailor-made missionary for the West, solid as the mountains of his native land, hardened to heat, cold, and toil, persevering, prudent, judicious, even-tempered, but consumed with zeal. In one of his letters home he delineated the characteristics needed by a missionary in New France and in doing so described himself: "The Jesuits who leave old France for the new should be led to do so by a special and very strong vocation. They must be men who are dead to the world and to themselves, apostolic and saintly men who seek only God and the salvation of souls. They should love crosses and mortification; they should be willing to work on land or sea; they should yearn to convert the savages more than they would desire to gain an empire. They ought to long to come to the forests of Canada as latter-day precursors of Jesus Christ or as a new Saint John, as voices crying in the wilderness, calling the savages to the knowledge of the Saviour. Finally, they must find all their strength, all their satisfaction, all of their treasure in God alone . . ."[47] This was the missionary whom Jacques Marquette would eventually join in that far western land. The new recruit was given but three brief weeks to acquaint himself with all the intricacies of colonial life before he was sent off to begin his apprenticeship for his life's work.

[46] *Relations,* XLIX, 161-63. Claude Allouez was born on June 6, 1622, at Saint-Didier and entered the Jesuit novitiate at Toulouse on September 25, 1639. After his novitiate he studied rhetoric and then philosophy at Billom. He taught there from 1645 to 1651 and then studied theology at Toulouse, 1651-1655. He came to New France in 1658.

[47] Pierre Margry, editor, *Découvertes et établissements des Français dans l'ouest et dans le sud de l'Amérique Septentrionale (1614-1674): mémoires et documents originaux,* I, 59-64. This work is hereafter cited as Margry.

APPRENTICE

1666-1668

On a chilly afternoon, a day or two after reaching Quebec, Jacques Marquette sauntered along the paths in the Jesuits' garden listening intently while Father Thierry Beschefer outlined the glorious apostolic opportunities opening up at that moment. For the past fifteen years, since the Iroquois destroyed the Huron mission, Jesuit missionaries had been "exiled" from the Indian country, constrained to confine their missionary efforts to the settlements of sedentary Indians at Sillery or Three Rivers. But last summer when some Ottawa were trading at Three Rivers, they asked for a Blackrobe to go home with them. Father Claude Allouez departed with the Ottawa on August 8, 1665. Though nothing had been heard from him for over a year, if he succeeded a whole new mission area would soon be available.[1] Perhaps Father Le Mercier

[1] *Relations*, XLIX, 161-63.

might decide to send Marquette to that field, provided the young recruit could learn Algonquin, the root language of all the tribes thus far contacted in the West. Beschefer's countenance lighted up as he explained the distinct possibility that the Iroquois mission might become active again. On June 6, 1666, when a party of Oneida came to Quebec seeking peace, they had been housed at the college.[2] Beschefer had made it a point to become friendly with them, using the occasion to practice his faltering Iroquois so that he might be the better prepared to evangelize that nation. When the Oneida arranged peace terms, Beschefer had been chosen to go to their country to ratify the peace. But, he informed his newly arrived friend, the contingent got no farther than Three Rivers on July 28, 1666, when it was summarily recalled because a Mohawk war party had slaughtered four Frenchmen near the northern end of Lake Champlain. One of the victims was a nephew of the Marquis de Tracy.[3] Even so, it was highly probable that the soldiers, then campaigning against the Five Nations, would crush them, forcing them to sue for peace. If a kind providence gave the French a resounding victory, the Iroquois would certainly ask for missionaries and perhaps Marquette would be sent there as a companion to Father Beschefer. Everything hinged on one's ability to learn the native languages. Some Jesuits simply could not accomplish that feat. Look at Father Noel Chabanel, a man of brilliant intellectual attainments and undoubtedly a martyr. Hard as he tried, he never was able to make himself understood in Huron, even to the day of

[2] *Ibid.*, L, 191, 193. See also Pierre François Xavier de Charlevoix, *The History and General Description of New France*, translated with notes by John Gilmary Shea, III, 87. This study is henceforth cited as Charlevoix.

[3] Charlevoix, III, 87. The murdered nephew's name was de Chasy. On learning the sad news, Tracy dispatched Pierre de Saurel, Sieur de Sorel, captain of the Carignan-Salières regiment to attack the Mohawks. On the way Sorel found the guilty parties who pretended that they were bound for Quebec to make peace. Believing them, Sorel brought them back. At a feast provided for them by Tracy, one of the Mohawks boasted that he had killed de Chasy. Understandably irate, Tracy had the savage hanged on the spot.

his martyrdom.[4] The trick was to become a child again, learning as a child learns, without reasoning one bit about the hows and the whys of the language. Twenty years ago and more, Jean de Brébeuf had advised his brethren who were beginning the study of a native language: "You must be prepared, instead of the great master and theologian you have been in France, to be here a modest pupil – and then – good God! with what teachers! – women, little children and all the savages; and you must be prepared to be exposed to their laughter. The Huron language will be your Saint Thomas and your Aristotle; and, able man that you are and eloquent among learned and clever persons, you must make up your mind to be dumb for a long time among barbarians. It will be a great thing for you if you can begin to stammer at the end of a little time."[5]

Jacques Marquette was not left long in ignorance of Father Le Mercier's plans for him. A few days after he stepped ashore at Quebec, he was on his way to Sillery to learn Montagnais which automatically meant that he was destined for missionary work among the Indians on the lower Saint Lawrence River as far as Tadoussac, a physically difficult and spiritually discouraging mission indeed.[6] The mission of Saint-Joseph-de-Sillery, fitted snugly on a small meadow which sloped gently down to the Saint Lawrence, was a comfortable place for an apprentice missionary to make a beginning. The residence of the missionaries was a two-story, solidly built stone building forty-seven by twenty-six feet in dimensions. A few yards away was the chapel dedicated to Saint-Michel, also a spacious building almost as large as the rectory. A short distance further on was a quite large stone building to which

[4] Rochemonteix, *Jésuites,* II, 103. Many have wondered why some of the Jesuits sent to New France could not learn a native language. Their difficulty, it seems, was more psychological than anything else. The native languages were not orderly tongues. The Jesuit with his intense training in logical thinking found the irregularity of Indian languages a frustrating business.

[5] Jean de Brébeuf, *The Travels and Sufferings of Father Jean de Brébeuf among the Hurons of Canada as Described by Himself,* 84-85.

[6] ARSJ. France 23. Annual catalogs of the Province of France. In the catalog for 1666 Marquette is listed as at Sillery studying Montagnais. He was probably sent there because the superior, André Richard, who had spent years on the Tadoussac mission, was fluent in Montagnais.

were attached stables and a barn. The interior of the buildings were all quite new for only nine years before Marquette arrived they were rebuilt after being gutted by a disastrous fire.[7] Old Father André Richard, approaching seventy with thirty-two years of mission experience behind him, was delighted to be given this new recruit seemingly destined to follow in Richard's own footsteps.[8] Also, there was Father Henri Nouvel, himself almost a neophyte missionary since he had been in New France only since 1662, though he was versed in Montagnais because of some three years spent on the Tadoussac mission.[9] The third member of the community at Sillery was Father Louis Nicolas, a rugged product of the mountain country of southern France, brusque in manner and not afraid of physical hardship.[10] The Indian population of Sillery was not very large for the Algonquins and Montagnais, the original residents, had been slowly decimated by Iroquois attacks, susceptibility to diseases contracted from the Europeans, and the dastardly effects of inebriation. Yet just when Marquette was there the piety of the few residents was most impressive. Noel Tecouerimat, the exemplary Algonquin captain of the village, a convert of forty years' standing and a tower of strength to his tribe, died most

[7] Adrien Pouliot, "La plus vieille maison du Canada," *Lettres du Bas-Canada*, IV (1950), 31. In 1948 the Jesuit rectory at Sillery was restored to its original state and became a museum. The building is considered to be the oldest house in Canada.

[8] André Richard was born in the diocese of Bourges on November 23, 1599 (some say 1600), and entered the Jesuit novitiate at Paris on September 25, 1621. He came to New France on May 17, 1634, and was first stationed at Cape Breton. He was sent to Miscou in 1640 and remained there until 1661, though he went to France in 1658 and 1659. From 1661 to 1662 he was at Chedabouctou. Then he returned to France until 1666. When he returned he was made superior of Sillery. See *Relations*, VIII, 292.

[9] Henri Nouvel was born at Pézenas on March 1, 1624. He entered the Society of Jesus on August 28, 1648, and came to Canada in 1662. He first worked at Tadoussac and then at Sillery. He went to the Ottawa mission in 1671 and remained there until 1695. He was superior of that mission from 1672 to 1680. He returned to France in 1695 and died at Aix-la-Chapelle on January 8, 1696. See *ibid.*, XLVII, 317-18.

[10] Louis Nicolas, born on August 24, 1634, at Aubenas, entered the Jesuit novitiate on September 16, 1654, at Toulouse. He came to New France in 1664. In the summer of 1667 he went to the Ottawa country with Father Allouez. In 1675 he returned to France. Rochemonteix, *Jésuites*, II, 359.

piously on March 19, 1666. Apicanis, a staunch Algonquin Christian, whose life was despaired of, was dramatically cured, as it was piously believed, through the intercession of Father Paul Le Jeune who had died at Paris in the odor of sanctity on August 7, 1664. Charlotte Nestaouip, a very old lady, died after a painful illness extending over seven months during which she exhibited a ". . . state of sanctity and innocence well-nigh unexampled even among civilized communities . . ."[11] Jacques had barely started becoming acquainted with the gutteral native language when he was uprooted and sent to Three Rivers. In the house diary at Quebec, Father Le Mercier noted tersely, on October 10: "Father Jacques Marquette goes up to Three Rivers to be a pupil of Father Druillettes in the Montagnais language."[12]

A raw wind whistled around the little sloop which took Jacques Marquette and a crowd of soldiers eighty miles up the Saint Lawrence, the deck and hold loaded to capacity with supplies for the army campaigning against the Iroquois. Just above Sillery the captain showed the young missionary the mouth of the Chaudière River, the highway to the Abenaki country where Father Gabriel Druillettes had spent the winter twenty years ago. As the sloop mounted against the current, granite walls closed in, crowding the mighty Saint Lawrence into a narrow gorge through which sailing craft passed with difficulty. Above Cap Rouge the river broadened again and the fertile country contained, here and there, the cabin of a *habinant* nestled in a grove of pines along the shore. At the mouth of the little Bastican River a deck hand pointed out a tiny settlement, informing Marquette that some of the best *voyageurs* in the colony might come from Three Rivers, but those from Bastican were respected equally as much. Slowly the high bluff at Cap-de-la-Madeleine appeared and beyond it the mouth of the Saint-Maurice, so cluttered with islands that Champlain and the early French explorers thought that three separate rivers entered the Saint Lawrence here. Above the mouth of the river the ship was warped to a primitive dock at the foot of a path leading to the

[11] *Relations,* L, 119-25.
[12] *Ibid.,* 203.

fort and Father Marquette stepped ashore to begin his life as a missionary in the west.[13]

Three Rivers was a rough and ready river town, a true frontier outpost, constantly threatened by attack from the Five Nations who easily approached the village by way of the Richelieu River which emptied into the Saint Lawrence not thirty miles upstream. The constant presence of danger possibly may explain why the little village gave New France such daring adventurers as Pierre Boucher, Radisson, Grosselliers, Nicolas Perrot, the Papins, the Verendrye family and so many skilled voyageurs.[14] Because it was a handy trading post for all of the Indians of the north and west, Three Rivers partook of a character far different from that of the more orderly, dignified Quebec or the more religiously dedicated Montreal. During the trade fairs Three Rivers boiled with excitement as it was inundated with roistering *voyageurs* squandering their pay and *coureur-de-bois,* those clandestine trouble-makers, come out of the far country to enjoy a wild spree before disappearing again into the endless woods they knew so well.[15] Marquette saw Three Rivers at its boisterous worst for the town was overrun with soldiers of the Carignan regiment left by Tracy to guard his supply lines. Every tavern was crowded and every shop swarmed with Frenchmen buying anything available as a souvenir to take back to France. Crowds of Indian squaws and their children squatted around the fort, waiting patiently for the return of their men who were away aiding the French in the war against the Iroquois. As he walked through all the bustle and confusion with Father Jacques Fremin, Marquette might well wonder if the Jesuit mission at Three Rivers could ever make an impact on this brawling mass of Frenchmen to say nothing of the disheveled, unattractive natives sprawling about in attitudes of evident indifference to their fate.

[13] Grace Lee Nute, *Caesars of the Wilderness*, 14, 19. She gives two maps of Three Rivers showing the village as it was in 1634 and 1650. The Jesuit mission for the Indians adjoined the property of Jean Godefroy.

[14] *Ibid.*, 15.

[15] Thomas B. Costain, *The White and the Gold: the French Regime in Canada*, 196.

French Jesuits had been laboring for the conversion of the Algonquins at Three Rivers since 1634, four years before Marquette was born. Father Paul Le Jeune and his companion, Father Jacques Buteux, went up to Three Rivers in September, 1634, to spend the winter with the Sieur La Violette and some French whom Champlain directed to establish the outpost. Though several of the French died of scurvy that winter, the outpost held on and grew to be extremely important for the defense of Quebec. By 1641 Father Beuteux established his reduction of the Immaculate Conception in imitation of Sillery, striving to induce the Algonquins of the north to settle down there permanently. The little Indian village, begun prosperously with a population of eighty, continued through the next quarter century with indifferent success. The Algonquins were a fickle, inconstant lot, readily influenced by whoever last talked to them. Being worse than indifferent farmers, they were obliged to go off in the spring and fall to continue their age-old practice of hunting, removing themselves from the influence of their missionaries.[16] As Three Rivers grew in French population the Indians at the mission only too readily acquired the vices of their European neighbors, especially addiction to *eau-de-vie* for which they had no tolerance. By 1663 the few Indians at the mission who opposed the use of alcohol shook the dust of Three Rivers from their feet and crossed the Saint-Maurice to Cap-de-la-Madeleine where, on land owned by the Jesuits, they started a new village which was cared for by one of the Jesuits from Three Rivers.[17]

There was little time to give the newly arrived Father Marquette a gentle introduction to the apostolic work. Father Jacques Fremin,[18] the superior, who had been on the Iroquois mission in 1658, momentarily expected orders to return to his former field of labor since all the reports from the army in the field indicated great

[16] Charlevoix, II, 118.

[17] *Relations,* L, 207.

[18] Jacques Fremin was born at Reims on March 12, 1628, and entered the Jesuit novitiate at Paris on November 21, 1646. He came to Canada in 1655. In 1656 he went to Onondaga with an abortive mission which lasted until 1658. From 1658 until 1666 he worked at Miscou and then with the Algonquins at Three Rivers and Cap-de-la-Madeleine.

success. Father Pierre Bailloquet,[19] also stationed at Three Rivers, spent most of his time across the river at Cap-de-la-Madeleine striving valiantly to deepen the faith of those few Algonquins seeking to live a sedentary existence there.[20] Pastoral care of the French inhabitants of Three Rivers, plus the added burden of ministering to the troops of the Carignan regiment, more than occupied most of old Father Gabriel Druillettes' day. Yet somehow he and Marquette must find time for the young man to learn Algonquin. And Marquette could hardly have had a better instructor. Gabriel Druillettes,[21] then fifty-six, had labored twenty-three years among the Indians in New France. Aged before his time, that lean, hardened old warrior had spent many a winter in the open with the Abenaki of Maine, the Indians living north of Tadoussac, and the Algonquins whose homeland was Lake Saint Thomas, a hundred miles up the Saint-Maurice. His calloused hands and bent shoulders were mute witness to the miles he had paddled canoes and the innumerable nights he had crouched in a drafty shelter surrounded by crude natives whose language had become a second mother tongue to him. He could teach young Marquette the lilting multi-inflected language of the Algonquin, but, what was far more difficult to learn, he could instruct the young neophyte in the devious

[19] Pierre Bailloquet was born at Saintes in 1612 and entered the novitiate at Bordeaux on November 20, 1631. He came to New France in 1647.

[20] The property at Cap-de-la-Madeleine was given to the Jesuits in 1646 by Jacques de la Ferté, the abbé de Sainte Madeleine in whose honor the place was named. See *Relations*, XLVIII, 295.

[21] Gabriel Druillettes was born at Gurat on September 29, 1610. He was educated in the Jesuit college at Toulouse and entered the novitiate at the age of nineteen. While teaching at Puy he was profoundly influenced by Saint Francis Regis who wished to go to New France, but was directed by superiors to remain in France and continue his work of giving missions to the rural population of southern France. Druillettes reached Quebec on August 15, 1643. He learned Algonquin at Sillery and spent the winter 1645-1646 with the Algonquins on their winter hunt. In the fall of 1646, at their request he visited the Abenaki. While there, he traveled as far south as the New England settlements. In 1650 and again in 1652 he was sent as an official ambassador of the governor of New France to Boston in an effort to arrange an alliance with the English. He frequently wintered with the Algonquins. See René Barbin, "Le voyageur du Christ (Gabriel Druillettes, 1610-1681)," *Lettres du Bas-Canada*, VI (1952), 41-51, 81-97.

mentality of the aborigines, the do's and the don't's which only long experience with the Indians themselves could inculcate in the European come to live with them and save their souls.

So the daily routine at the mission began. Each morning Father Marquette arose before the dawn to summon the Indians to the chapel where he listened to them recite their morning prayers, attuning his ear to their language. After celebrating Mass, the young missionary gathered the children for their daily catechism lesson and their practicing the hymns and prayers. This was the best time of the day. He and the children together chanted the answers to the catechism questions posed in Algonquin by Father Druillettes. The children were puzzled when Marquette answered with them until they came to understand that they were teaching him to speak their tongue. Soon they were laughing good-naturedly at his mistakes and correcting him with the patience which only children can muster. After the catechism lesson Marquette accompanied Druillettes on his visits to the cabins, listening intently while the old missionary heard out the carping complaints of a shrewish wife or arbitrated a dispute between two old crones, each claiming ownership of a warm blanket. Marquette carefully observed the mannerisms of this experienced older Jesuit, noting that he never showed impatience, never spoke harshly, and always seemed to manifest just the right degree of interest. In the evening when the men came back from the fields or from their hunting, Marquette sat cross-legged at a fire, listening to a dignified old chief discuss the crops, the weather, the possibility of a new Iroquois raid, or narrate ancient tales of the past glory of the Algonquins. Slowly, haltingly, Marquette began to use the native tongue until one day Father Druillettes sent him across the Saint-Maurice, accompanied by just one young Algonquin lad, to anoint an old brave who was dying at Cap-de-la-Madeleine. Then the young missionary was directed to take part in a fishing excursion to Lac-Saint-Pierre, up the river. On these short voyages Marquette learned to paddle a canoe, to sit quietly, to speak only when necessary, and to adapt himself to the Indian mentality. Having a gift for languages, fortunately, it was not long before he was making himself understood by everyone, though, of course, among themselves the Indians laughed at his absurd mistakes. Yet they liked this gentle, cheerful, willing, physically strong, young priest who showed that he respected them and wanted to understand them.

Through the winter and spring of his first season as a missionary, Jacques Marquette witnessed a whole series of stirring events at Three Rivers. Soon after he settled in, the dignified old Marquis de Tracy brought his gloriously victorious army back from its triumph in the Iroquois country.[22] When the thousand men arrived at Three Rivers the jubilant troops erupted like a volcano, intent on celebrating their victory. They brawled in the streets, wrecked the taverns, and scandalized the Indians. Every young girl, Indian or white, had her host of importunate admirers. The weary chaplains of the expedition, Father Charles Albanel and Father Pierre Raffeix, sat up until the wee hours of the morning reporting their experiences to the small Jesuit community at Three Rivers. These two battle-scarred veterans bubbled over with enthusiasm for the Iroquois mission which the coming peace arrangements would certainly make possible.[23] As he watched the superior, Jacques Fremin, beam with delight over the prospect of returning to the Iroquois, young Jacques Marquette pulsed with hope and desire. He had picked up a few Iroquois phrases here and there; perhaps that was enough to qualify him. Just maybe, he too would become a part of that most dangerous of all missions on which Father Isaac Jogues and René Goupil had gained the martyr's crown. When the troops finally left for Quebec and the iron winter settled on the land, the river was closed to traffic until spring. In January, 1667, when the Sovereign Council revived the ordinance forbidding the sale of alcoholic spirits to the Indians, the regulation was so poorly observed at Three Rivers that Father Louis Nicolas took the Indians off to a new location lest the small, faithful remnant of Algonquins not already debauched be lost to the evils of drunkenness.[24]

The spring and summer of 1667 were exciting. Jacques Marquette, tanned and supple from his days of journeying on snowshoes during the hard winter and voyaging by canoe in the spring,

[22] *Relations*, L, 203.
[23] *Ibid.*, 201.
[24] *Ibid.*, 207.

now felt himself to be a vital part of mission life. He spoke Algonquin fairly well, at least enough to teach catechism, preach a simple sermon, and hear confessions, if the Indians spoke slowly enough. Experience taught him that Indian stolidity was merely a pose. When one knew them, the Indians were a simple, credulous folk, inconstant, however, and very vain. The women, who seemed to be little better than beasts of burden, actually wielded a powerful influence. The children, whom their elders never punished, were lovable, affectionate little creatures and quite bright. The more he came to understand the Indian, the more Marquette's sympathy went out to them. The aborigines could be made into excellent Christians and stable citizens if only the French would cease exploiting them. Look at the liquor problem, for instance. Every Frenchman outside of Quebec had, at one time or another, seen the horrors perpetrated by a group of drunken Indians. Yet some of the French, in spite of civil and ecclesiastical prohibitions, would not stop selling *eau-de-vie* to the natives at Three Rivers, even when the governor-general sent the Sieur Goribon up from Quebec in July, 1667, to investigate the flagrant violations of the decrees of the Sovereign Council forbidding the practice.[25]

Perhaps the most noteworthy event to occur at Three Rivers during July 1667 was the arrival of a group of Iroquois envoys on their way to Quebec, accompanied by their wives and children to show Onontio that they came to make peace. Certain that the impending parley would surely include a request by the Iroquois for the return of the Blackrobes to their country, Father Jacques Fremin went down to Quebec so that he would be on hand to return with the Iroquois and reopen the mission. At Quebec the ambassadors "declared among other things, that all their desires were to have . . . our Fathers with them to cement the peace . . ."[26] Granting the request, Father Le Mercier assigned Jacques Fremin and Jean Pierron to work among the Mohawks and Jacques Bruyas for the Oneidas. Leaving Quebec on July 14, the valiant little band of missionaries stopped at Three Rivers where Marquette listened to

[25] *Ibid.*, 211.
[26] *Ibid.*, LI, 81.

them planning their strategy, envying them their lot, wishing that he had been chosen, as he almost was, instead of young Father Jean Pierron, who had been in New France only since June 27, 1667.[27] After a brief delay the missionary contingent was on its way while Jacques Marquette must stay at Three Rivers.

Fremin and his party had hardly left the mission when everyone was elated at the arrival of Father Claude Allouez who had left Quebec for the Ottawa country on May 14, 1665, over two years ago.[28] Warned of the approach of a score of Ottawa canoes, Marquette and Father Charles Albanel, superior at Three Rivers since Fremin's departure for the Iroquois mission, sauntered down to the dock to greet the arriving natives. To their delight, there was Allouez climbing out of a canoe, wading ashore, bronzed from the sun and wind, gaunt from long stretches of near-starvation, his clothing in tatters, but as jaunty and buoyant as a conquering hero. And well he might be for he came back from the ends of the world, a thousand leagues to the west.[29] Marquette and Albanel could hardly contain their curiosity while Allouez thanked the chief in whose canoe he had returned, collected his Mass-kit and was free to go to the mission residence. Finally when the three Jesuits were alone, Marquette laid out clean linen, a less worn cassock, shoes, and stockings for the returned voyager who retired to cleanse himself of the smoke and grime of hundreds of Indian camps. Refreshed and fed, Allouez began recounting his experiences while Marquette and Albanel listened, as to a tale from the Arabian Nights.

The journey westward, begun on August 8, 1665, had started inauspiciously, Father Allouez told his listeners. The Ottawa flotilla, bearing four hundred savages and six Frenchmen besides himself, was barely out of sight of Three Rivers when an Ottawa chief, in

[27] *Ibid.*, L, 213. Jean Pierron was born at Dun-sur-Meuse on September 28, 1631, and entered the Jesuit novitiate at Nancy on November 21, 1650. He arrived at Quebec on June 27, 1667. He returned to France in 1678 and died at Pont-à-Mousson on February 20, 1700.

[28] *Ibid.*, XLIX, 161.

[29] *Ibid.*, L, 249. ARSJ, France 23, 231v, the catalog of the Province of France for 1667 lists Charles Albanel as the superior at Three Rivers.

arrogant and menacing tones, informed the missionary that the Ottawa had no intention of allowing a Blackrobe to enter their country to cast magic spells on their children who, everyone knew, died the moment a missionary uttered his incantations while pouring water on their heads. Rather than allow such a disaster to their children, the Ottawa would abandon Allouez on a desert island.[30] The devil himself seemed to be on the side of these hostile Indians for the canoe bearing all the French became unseaworthy after only two or three days of travel. That evening Allouez persuaded the Indians to divide up the French among the various Ottawa canoes, but the next morning they refused the missionary a place, abandoning him on the shore. Fortunately he was rescued, but no one in the rescuing canoe knew the route west. Finally overtaking some of the Ottawa party, Allouez threatened them "with the displeasure of Monsieur de Tracy, whose spokesman I was."[31] Thenceforth the Indians gave the missionary a place in a canoe but required him to man a paddle and carry his share of the burdens at the portages. After two gruelling weeks the party reached Lake Nipissing, coasted down the French River to Georgian Bay and worked its way to Sault-Sainte-Marie. On September 2 Allouez's canoe emerged onto the broad expanse of Lake Superior, to which he gave the name Tracy "in recognition of the indebtedness to him on the part of the people of these regions."[32]

For the whole month of September, Allouez and his companions followed the southern shore of Lake Superior, passing Sainte Thérèse Bay (Keweenaw Bay) where Father René Ménard spent the winter of 1660-1661. On October 1 Allouez reached Chequamegon Bay, at the foot of which was a great Indian village so populous that it could muster an army of eight hundred warriors. The missionary opened his mission there and called it Saint-Esprit. Luckily the Ottawa, on the point of becoming involved in a war with the Sioux through the imprudence of their young men, had just called a conference of a dozen neighboring nations which Allouez was in-

[30] *Relations*, L, 251.

[31] *Ibid.*, 255. See *ibid.*, XLIX, 249. Allouez bore presents from Tracy to the tribes whom he expected to meet.

[32] *Ibid.*, L, 265.

vited to address. Fluent in Algonquin, the language of the Ottawa, the missionary harangued that exotically apparelled audience, forthrightly asserting the power of the king of France and "spoke to them earnestly concerning the mysteries of our religion."[33] Then began two long, weary years of visiting the Indians who frequented the shores of Lake Superior, "being present everywhere, – in their cabins, at their embarkations, on their journeys . . .,"[34] seeking to enkindle the spark of Faith in their hearts. But the Ottawa were a gross people who adored idols, practiced polygamy, and were given to revoltingly immoral excesses. Their response to Allouez's teaching was to insult him, destroy his little bark chapel, and steal his few possessions. They admitted that what the Blackrobe preached was "very reasonable, but license prevails over reason, and, unless grace is very strong, all our teachings are of slight effect."[35]

Leaving that village of abomination, Allouez took up residence with the Hurons of the Tobacco Nation, living no great distance away, who had been hounded from their homeland in 1649 when the Iroquois invaded Huronia. How engrossing was Allouez's account of that once Christian tribe! He told his listeners of baptizing a very old woman whom the martyred Father Charles Garnier was on the point of baptizing in 1649. Father Allouez restored the Tobacco Nation to its religious duties, sorrowing the while to witness how nearly all knowledge of the Faith had been erased from their minds in the short span of less than twenty years. During the coming year Allouez baptized a hundred children of the tribe and induced their elders to frequent the sacraments and embrace "the pious sentiments they formerly had for the Faith."[36]

In time, Claude Allouez met other nations, hitherto almost entirely unknown to the French. The Potawatomie, whose country lay along the Lake of the Illinois (Lake Michigan), were a populous nation able to field an army of three hundred warriors. On a visit to that country Allouez proclaimed the Faith at a general council

[33] *Ibid.*, 281.
[34] *Ibid.*, 281, 283.
[35] *Ibid.*, 305.
[36] *Ibid.*, 309.

of the whole nation. This was a warlike people, extremely idolatrous and addicted to polygamy, but more docile than other nations and well disposed towards the French.[37] Next to the Potawatomie but south of them, were the nations of the Sac and the Fox who spoke a dialect of the Algonquin tongue. The Fox were "not very far removed from the recognition of the creator of the world; for . . . they . . . related . . . that they acknowledged . . . a great spirit, the maker of heaven and earth . . ."[38] The Sac, however, were a fierce, numerous, nomadic people, given to cruelty and strongly opposed to the French. Hope of converting those two peoples was not so high, but when Allouez spoke of the Illinois his face lighted with excitement. The Illinois dwelt in a country sixty leagues to the south, "beyond a great river which, as well as I can conjecture, empties into the sea somewhere near Virginia."[39] These Indians, whose language was an Algonquin dialect which Allouez barely understood, were once very populous, but continued attacks by the Sioux and the Iroquois had reduced them to only two villages. Of the many spirits to whom they offered sacrifice, one was honored above all others as the maker of all things. Allouez considered that this unique belief of the Illinois would incline them to accept Christianity readily, since it only remained to teach them how they must serve God in order to see him and be blessed. Allouez preached to eighty of the Illinois who carried his word to the whole country of the south.[40] The missionary judged the Illinois to be as affable and humane as their homeland was warm of climate and fertile of soil. His small Jesuit audience of two readily divined that Claude Allouez ached to hasten back to the country of the Illinois.

Almost as an afterthought, Father Allouez mentioned meeting the Sioux and the Cree. The former inhabited a country of prairies on which they cultivated only a little tobacco. But a kind of wild marsh rye grew in sufficient abundance to nourish them. Then, quite casually, Allouez remarked that the Sioux dwelt "to the west

[37] *Ibid.*, LI, 27.
[38] *Ibid.*, 45.
[39] *Ibid.*, 47.
[40] *Ibid.*, 51.

of this place [i.e. Chequamegon Bay], towards the great river named Mesippi."[41] For the first time, a European brought back from the west the name of the mighty river soon to be the object of an intensive search. One cannot help but wonder what Jacques Marquette's reaction was on hearing the word *Mesippi* enunciated by Claude Allouez. Was it merely another of the many Indian words which flowed from the returned missionary whose reminiscences of the past two years poured from him in a flood of eloquence? Or did Marquette roll the word on his tongue, savoring it, wondering where the river was, how large, how long, how many benighted tribes dwelt on its banks awaiting an apostle to draw them to the feet of Christ our Lord?

The rest of Father Allouez's story was quickly told. The Cree, whose usual abode was on the shore of the North Sea, plied their canoes on a river which, Allouez thought must empty into Hudson Bay, since the Cree spoke of seeing there white men living in houses and using books.[42] The docile and kindly Cree asked Allouez to spend the winter among them, but he felt obliged to visit the Nipissings, former neophytes of the Huron mission, who had been without a pastor for nearly twenty years. Setting out from the mission of Saint-Esprit on May 6, 1667, Allouez, with two Indian companions, paddled around the southern end of Lake Superior and followed its shore northward and eastward until he was able to enter Lake Nipigon where he found the Nipissing village on June 3. The difficult and dangerous journey was almost fruitless. The Nipissings had lapsed into idolatry, though twenty of them still adhered to Christianity. Undaunted, Allouez remained with this hardhearted people for two weeks, working as diligently as his health, "broken by the fatigues of his arduous journey, allowed."[43] After accomplishing what he could with the Nipissings, Allouez retraced his route to Saint-Esprit where he joined a flotilla of a score of Ottawa canoes bound for the summer trading at Three Rivers.

[41] *Ibid.*, 53.
[42] *Ibid.*, 57.
[43] *Ibid.*, 69.

The whole of Allouez's saga was long in the telling, but eminently interesting to his listeners, especially to Marquette.[44] But the time came for Allouez to leave. On August 4, 1667, the returned missionary, refreshed in body and spirit, went down to Quebec where he persuaded Father Le Mercier that this new mission field should be expanded at once. Willingly, the superior granted Allouez a fellow missionary, Father Louis Nicolas, as well as "one of our Brothers and four men, to be employed at the scene of action for their maintenance."[45] The basic supplies were quickly assembled and, on the morning of August 6, 1667, Claude Allouez and his small apostolic army was on its way.[46] Louis Nicolas, who was already at Montreal, would join the party there. Allouez stopped briefly at Three Rivers to relay his news and beg the prayers of Marquette and Albanel for the success of the venture. As Jacques Marquette watched Claude Allouez's little flotilla of canoes grow smaller and finally disappear up the Saint Lawrence, he must have longed to have been a member of that party. But departure for the west was not yet for him.

On the evening of August 4, 1667, the day on which Claude Allouez reached Quebec, Marquette wrote his former spiritual director, Father Jacques Pupin, a letter redolent with his enthusiasm for missionary life as it was expressive of his hope to participate in the work progressing in distant areas:

> The missions which are being opened on every side leave me no rest any more than they do Reverend Father Superior, who wishes all the new missionaries to know the principles of all the [Indian] languages or to learn one of them in particular. We have peace at present with the five Iroquois nations and it is confidently believed that it is a firm one, for they never thought that the French would carry the war into their own country. They number over 20,000 souls, according to the report of those who have visited them, and they will be very difficult to convert but

[44] See Marquette's letter to Pupin, quoted below. On August 4, 1667, Marquette wrote that Allouez returned from the Ottawa country "15 days ago." Allouez got to Quebec on August 4 and left there on August 6. It would seem, then, that Allouez spent most of his fifteen days at Three Rivers. See *ibid.*, L, 213.

[45] *Ibid.*, LI, 73.

[46] *Ibid.*, L, 213.

there will be less to suffer, though the only food there is Indian corn and a little fish.

The mission among the Upper Algonquins is a very difficult one. They are 500 leagues from here. There are fifty-six portages to be made before you reach them. During three or four months [of the year] one has nothing to eat except strips of bark. On the shore of a lake over a hundred leagues in length there are twenty or thirty nations. Father Allouez, who returned thence fifteen days ago and who left to go up there again, takes along with him Father Louis Nicolas and one of our Brothers with four men to begin an establishment for the support of the missionaries.

If there had not been need of someone for the Algonquins, I would have gone with Father Fremin to the Mohawks, but Father Pierron took my place three weeks after his arrival. I do not yet despair of going to the Upper Iroquois; at least I shall try to be ready for any sort of mission which they ask for in France.

That Father mentioned above, [i.e. Allouez] has been within eight days of the North Sea [Hudson Bay]. Several Indians assured him that they often saw ships passing there. These could not be taking any other route than the one to Japan or other islands which are not far away.

M. de Tracy is returning with the intention of persuading the King to purchase Manate [Manhattan] from the English and Orange [Albany] from the Dutch. That country is so peopled with savages that, besides their own report [i.e. the Dutch and English], a Frenchman who has seen it says that the route leads you for six days through an almost continual succession of cabins. This being the case, we shall not lack for occupation.

After studying Huron for two months, they were obliged to send me back here for the Algonquin mission. I have counted here thirty-eight canoes a part of which has already left for the hunt and will not return until Saint Luke's Day [October 18]. God has surely had pity on me ever since I have been in this country. I have not felt any dislike for it or had the least desire for France. You know that I had no memory at all when I was over there and yet I find no difficulty whatever with languages which have no relation to ours. Today I began to learn the language of the Manate country and this winter I shall learn Montagnais.[47]

All was well with Jacques Marquette. Everything about New France pleased him. The frontier life, the Indians, the vast stretches

[47] Marquette to Pupin, August 4, 1667, from Cap-de-la-Madeleine. The original of the letter is to be found in the Bibliothèque Nationale, Paris, Collection Moreau, 842, f. 37 v. Garraghan quotes the French in toto in his "Unpublished Marquettiana," 19-20. The translation given here is not that offered in Garraghan's article.

of the rivers, and above all the opportunity to labor for the conversion of the natives satisfied his long-standing desire to be a missionary. And the future held promise of better things to come. Perhaps, even yet, he might be sent to the Five Nations and, if not, then certainly to the Ottawa mission. Meanwhile, he would acquire as many of the Indian languages as opportunity offered in order to be useful in whatever mission his superior chose to send him. Jacques Pupin could rest content about this former spiritual son; he was, indeed, advancing in wisdom and age and grace before God and man.

The autumn and winter of 1667 were busy months for the missionaries at Three Rivers. Once the scanty crops were harvested, the Indians went off hunting to stock the larder for winter. And the youngest missionary, Marquette, went with them, striding along the faint trails, scrambling over rocks and through chill streams, stalking the game. At night, when the late autumn wind nipped at the hunters, Marquette squatted beside the campfire exchanging experiences of the day and leading the Indians in their night prayers. When snow covered the land the hunting was better, but long days on snowshoes toiling over rugged country took their toll. At night Marquette was glad enough to be freed of those torturing racquets which forced the wearer to walk awkwardly, swinging each leg in a sideward arc until the muscles cramped painfully. By late November, when the hunters had bagged enough game, the party came back to the mission of the Immaculate Conception at Three Rivers, picking up the caches of meat they had made as they went along. In mid-December, Andatiakonhons, a Huron who had accompanied Father Fremin and his Jesuit companions to the Iroquois country, stopped on his way to Quebec with letters for the superior, Father Le Mercier. Father Albanel and his small community questioned the Huron eagerly. He told them that the Jesuits were well and had been received hospitably, though there was some grumbling by the young Iroquois braves.[48] In January, Father Bruyas wrote from the chief village of the Oneida that these Indians were "cruel,

[48] *Relations,* L, 219.

secret, cunning and inclined to blood and carnage."[49] A month later, in mid-February, young Father Jean Pierron passed through on his way to report conditions among the Iroquois to Father Le Mercier. He informed his fellow Jesuits at Three Rivers that all the missionaries among the Iroquois were well and living peacefully, but were not making many converts as yet.[50] Among the Mohawks, the missionaries were chiefly engaged in inducing the Huron Christians, long ago adopted by their conquerors, to return to their religious duties. So few of the Jesuits spoke Iroquois well and there was so much missionary work to be done that the mission desperately needed an increase of personnel. Almost certainly, Jacques Marquette must have had a quiet word with Jean Pierron before the latter left for Quebec, begging him to remind the superior of Marquette's willingness to embrace any mission to which it seemed good to send him.

Perhaps unknown to him as yet, Jacques Marquette's future mission was decided in the spring of 1668. On April 21 of that year, Le Mercier noted in the house diary at Quebec: "We are going to embark to go up the river, namely: Father Dablon, Caron, Charles Panie and myself, to la Prairie-de-la-Madeleine, there to conclude all affairs, and to decide as to the manner of granting the concessions; Father Marquette, two men, and a young lad to await an opportunity of going to the Ottawa country; Father Julien Garnier and Charles Bouquet, to go and assist Father Bruyas at Onneiout."[51] Thus it was that a day or so after April 21, while Father Le Mercier was at the mission of the Immaculate Conception at Three Rivers, he called Jacques Marquette to him and told the ardent young missionary that his future lay in the West among the distant nations contacted by Father Allouez.

Much as Marquette wished to rush off at once, he was obliged to wait patiently at Three Rivers until an Ottawa flotilla drifted in, finished its leisurely trading, and could be persuaded to take him back. In the meantime he continued his apostolic work, traveling

[49] *Ibid.*, LI, 123.
[50] *Ibid.*, 145.
[51] *Ibid.*, 149.

about with the Indians. On May 20, eighty miles up river from the mission, Marquette was asked to supply the solemn ceremonies for a child privately baptized previously. The missionary recorded in the register of the parish of the Most Holy Family at Boucherville: "I, Jacques Marquette of the Society of Jesus, have conferred the ceremonies on Marie, daughter of Victor Kiouentaoue and Antoinette de Miskouminich, at the age of two months and baptized privately at Sorel by Monsieur Morel, a priest, the godfather being Ignace Boucher and the godmother Marie Boucher."[52] So the summer wore on until mid-August when an Ottawa flotilla arrived, bringing Father Louis Nicolas back from the West.[53] Marquette hastily arranging to return with the Ottawa, wrapped his Mass-kit and a few spare clothes into a bundle, and, shoes in hand, gingerly eased himself into the canoe, his chariot to the realization of his dreams. At about the time Marquette picked up his paddle on his way to Sault-Sainte-Marie, François Le Mercier was writing to the Jesuit general, giving details of how the newly opened missions were supplied with missionaries, as the general had requested. In his letter of September 1, 1668, Le Mercier informed Oliva that three priests had gone to the Iroquois mission: Julien Garnier, Etienne de Carheil, and Pierre Milet. Le Mercier continued: "Lastly, to Father Claude Allouez (who is in charge of the Ottawa mission, the most arduous of all because of the unheard-of barbarity of the natives, a mission some five hundred leagues away from here) we have sent Father Jacques Marquette, who has a good knowledge of Algonquin, is of sound health and strong body, of excellent character and tried virtue; and, because of his wonderfully gentle ways, most acceptable to the natives."[54]

[52] Louis Lalande, *Une vielle seigneurie Boucherville*, 115.

[53] Charlevoix, III, 119.

[54] Ernest J. Burrus, "Father Jacques Marquette, S.J.: His Priesthood in the Light of the Jesuit Roman Archives," *Catholic Historical Review*, XLI (1955), 264. The document Burrus quotes is to be found in ARSJ, Gal. 110. I, f.44-47v. The date on which Marquette departed for the West is nowhere recorded. Since the Ottawa came to Three Rivers on other occasions during the middle of August, it appears reasonable to presume that this was approximately the time when Marquette would be able to go back with them.

SAINTE-MARIE-DU-SAULT

1668-1669

The summer of 1668 was as eagerly awaited by the merchants and traders of New France as a miser impatient for an opportunity to gloat over a horde of recently acquired, new-minted louis d'or. For the first time in many years the water routes which the Indians traveled from the north and west were safe for them to bring their furs in to Montreal, Three Rivers, or Quebec to exchange them for goods of European manufacture on which they had long since come to depend. The peace treaty, imposed by the Marquis de Tracy, between the Iroquois and the French, including all of their aboriginal allies, was concluded too late in the summer of 1667 for such distant nations as the Ottawa to come down for their trading. Throughout the winter of 1667-1668, licensed merchants in the French centers stocked their shelves to the ceiling with copper cooking pots, knives, blankets, metal axes, bolts of cloth, bright ribbons, small mirrors, and trinkets galore, anticipating the most profitable trading season experienced for many a summer. Up in the Ottawa country, an important source of tobacco and peltries, the Indians, gathering at the Sault, organized a large flotilla for the hazardous journey to Montreal. Father Claude Allouez came in from his distant mission of Saint-Esprit on Chequamegon Bay to accompany the flotilla for a visit to his superior from whom he ardently hoped to receive new recruits to help him gather the rich spiritual harvest he confidently expected. After seemingly endless days of travel, the six hundred savages from the West, all dressed in their outlandish best, loudly chanting boastful greetings, swept up to the beach below the fort at Montreal.[1] Crowds of Frenchmen streamed down to meet their customers while squat little cannons boomed a welcome. Awaiting Allouez, as he waded ashore, was Father Jacques Marquette who delightedly announced that he and Brother Louis Boëme had been assigned to the Ottawa mission. Elated by such good fortune, Allouez promptly brought the newly appointed assistant to meet his Ottawa friends from the Sault. This was his young Blackrobe brother, he told them, who would return to their country to help them learn the great truths taught by the Christian God. The Indians eyed the young priest, noting his strong young body, his frank friendliness, his facility in speaking Algonquin, and his meticulous observance of their Indian courtesies. Poised and composed, Marquette told these Indians that the sun shone brighter because he now met them. He would come to their country, sharing their cabins and their fires, not to ask anything of them but to help their great father, Allouez, teach them the true road which led to eternal life. In the evening with the noises of roistering heard in the background, Marquette and Allouez conferred, planning the work at the Sault and beyond. Though Allouez was obliged to go down to Quebec to report to the superior, Father Le Mercier, Marquette and Brother Louis, with the two laymen accompanying them, were to take the first opportunity to go west for there was much to be done. When they reached the Sault, they must begin at once

[1] *Relations,* LI, 263.

building a permanent mission center at the site already chosen by Allouez.[2] Marquette and Brother Louis, however, waited patiently in Montreal until some of the Indians from the West finished their trading and, surfeited with town life, were ready to go home.

On a shining summer day, probably in mid-August, 1668, delighted as a schoolboy released for his summer holidays, Father Jacques Marquette, vicar-general of the bishop of Quebec, set out for his high adventure.[3] Pushing off into the Saint Lawrence, in two canoes laden to the gunnels with supplies needed for the new mission, the four apostolic *voyageurs* bent their backs to the wearying work of paddling some 1,500 miles north and west, much of that distance up rivers noted for their powerfully swift current. Rounding the eastern end of the island of Montreal, the party worked its way up the treacherous little Rivière des Prairies, thereby avoiding a tiresome portage around the Lachine Rapids which only the foolhardy would attempt negotiating by water. The river widened into the twenty-five mile, elbow-shaped stretch of placid Lake of Two Mountains in which the current grows increasingly stronger as it narrows into the recognizable confines of the mighty Ottawa River. From that point forward it behooved the travelers to be on the alert for, despite the peace, one could never tell whether around the next bend there might not lurk a skulking, hostile band of Iroquois. Each evening at dusk the party landed and, tethering the canoes to a handy tree, ate their meagre meal and got what rest they could. After finishing his breviary by the uncertain light of a small camp fire, Marquette sat gazing out across the giant Ottawa, listening to the intense silence of the wilderness about him. What poor aborigines lay hidden behind these thickly forested hills? How

[2] No document declares that Allouez met Marquette at Montreal before the latter went up to Sault-Sainte-Marie. It would, however, seem logical to assume that such a meeting took place. Brother Louis Boëme was born at Saintes on August 25, 1632. He apparently came to New France when he was a child. In 1648 he went to Huronia, quite probably as a *donnée*. See *ibid.*, XXXII, 91, 97, wherein he is referred to as "little Louis." In 1650 he returned to France and entered the Society of Jesus at Toulouse on November 24, 1650. He returned to Canada in 1656 and died in 1709. See *ibid.*, LXXI, 149, 399.

[3] H. Têtu and C. O. Gagnon, editors, *Mandements, lettres pastorales et circulaires des évêques de Quebec*, I, 274.

many generations of missionaries must undergo hardships before the Indians would all be gathered into the Christian sheepfold? When the travelers were well into the Ottawa, they came to the Long Sault, the site of Dollard's heroic defense of New France eight years ago. This was the first of eighteen tortuous portages, some of them six miles in length. At each one every last item of the cargo had to be unloaded while the canoes were laboriously borne through the overgrown trails on the shoulders of the travelers who were then obliged to repeat the trip many times to transport the baggage to the new launching point. Danger lurked in Lac des Chats in which barely submerged, needle-sharp rocks threatened to rip open the paper-thin bottoms of the canoes. Often shallow water required the travelers to splash their way on foot up the river, dragging the heavy canoes behind them. After negotiating the roaring Chaudière Falls and the treacherous Rapids des Joachims, they toiled on to the picturesque mouth of the Mattawa River, issuing majestically into the Ottawa from between the high walls of impressive mountains. That evening, resting around their small fire, warming themselves, the travelers knew that they were at the halfway mark. In the morning they started up the thirty miles of the Mattawa which brought them, with intervening portages, to the broad, shallow expanse of Lake Nipissing, fifty miles of open water. Not daring to cross in a direct line, the missionary and his companions hugged the southern shore, increasing the distance by twice the length of the lake. Then they entered the black, angry French River which roared westward into Georgian Bay. Paddling past innumerable islands and deeply indented bays, the *voyageurs* were often forced to take refuge on shore to escape lashing autumn storms. On many evenings they huddled together, cold, wet, and weary, after a long, tiring day spent fighting strong winds which contested their advance. At last they swung around Saint Joseph's Island, paddled up Hay Lake, putting ashore just below the roaring rapids of the Saint Mary's River. The right bank of the river was crowded with Indians shouting greetings. Among them were thirty or forty French traders who frequented the Sault to exchange their wares for the peltries gathered by the Indians.[4] Thus, at the age of thirty-one, twenty-four years after he conceived the desire to dedicate himself to evangelizing the peoples beyond the seas, Jacques Marquette was, in very truth, a missionary. The crowd of unprepossessing savages on shore before him and the hardly more attractive Frenchmen were his spiritual charge.

Father Marquette and Brother Louis had made the merest start at becoming acquainted with the people when Father Claude Allouez reached the Sault. Then the three Jesuits spent long evenings in the rude shelter the French erected for them, elaborating plans for the Ottawa mission.[5] Primary consideration was given to the Sault itself and to the vital part the Chippewa band of the Ottawa who lived there could play in effecting the conversion of the nations of the West. Geographically, the location was providentially designed as a herald's platform from which to broadcast the word of God. From early spring until winter, many tribes were attracted to the Sault where they could obtain an ample supply of fish from the Chippewa, who alone had the skill to catch the whitefish streaming through the rapids of the Saint Mary's River. Balancing themselves upright in their frail bark canoes, unconcernedly riding the whirlpools, they "thrust deep into the water a rod, at the end of which is fastened a net made in the form of a pouch, into which the fish are made to enter. This is repeated over and over again, six or seven fish being taken each time, until a load of them is obtained."[6] The almost endless supply of fish brought aboriginal visitors from as far north as the Hudson Bay basin, Sioux and Cree from the west, as well as peoples to the south, Potawatomie, Menominee, Miami, and a few Illinois. Even if only a few visitors from each nation were influenced, a beginning would be made and, perhaps in time, all of those nations would have the Gospel preached to them.

[4] O'Callaghan, *Documents*, IX, 383. In a memoir relative to the limits of New France, Governor Denonville, March 8, 1688, noted that the French had been in the area of Sault-Sainte-Marie for over forty years.

[5] Louise Phelps Kellogg, *The French Régime in Wisconsin and the Northwest*, 157. Though she declares that the French built a house for the Jesuits, she does not document the statement.

[6] *Relations*, LIX, 131.

As for the Chippewa themselves, they were a shrewd, canny lot who understood quite well their economic and geographic importance. Instinctive business men, they were quick to realize that it was good business to maintain friendly relations with the French, who could supply them with European goods which could, in turn, be exchanged at a profit to the nations beyond the Sault. Of Algonquin stock, the Chippewa, who spoke a dialect of Algonquin, which Marquette could understand, were villagers, inhabiting dome-shaped houses constructed of willow poles overlaid with bark. Though their major interest was economic, they were courageous warriors who killed mercilessly, but were not given to torturing their captives. The religious beliefs of the Chippewa were of a piece with those of other aborigines, recognizing a supreme good spirit, who ruled the world through a host of lesser spirits, and an evil spirit whom prudent men also placated with sacrifices.[7] Since the Chippewa considered the good spirit far too awesome to approach, except on special occasions, they peopled their world with lesser preternatural beings, assigning one such to each member of the group. Their somewhat regular contact with French *coureurs de bois,* for better than two score years, probably led them to reject many of their more far-fetched superstitions, but the example set by their European visitors did little to attract the Chippewa to embrace Christianity. Nonetheless, however difficult the task of converting them might prove, Christianizing the Chippewa at the Sault was the first crucial step toward winning the West to the doctrines of Christ. If the Chippewa became staunch Christians all the Indians who visited them would be influenced to do likewise and even the French would be obliged to improve their conduct.[8] Hence, while Brother Louis and his assistants would busy themselves constructing the mission compound, Father Marquette must labor mightily at converting the Chippewa.

When chill mornings and flaming leaves on the hardwoods warned of coming snows, Father Claude Allouez hastened away to

[7] Diamond Jenness, *The Indians of Canada,* 281.

[8] Louise Phelps Kellogg, editor, *Early Narratives of the Northwest, 1634-1699.* When Galinée was at Sault-Sainte-Marie in 1670, there were twenty or twenty-five Frenchmen living there.

his mission at Saint-Esprit, many leagues to the west on Lake Superior, while Brother Louis with his two Frenchmen began felling trees and clearing land for the new mission center. First, they put up a residence for the missionaries, a quite spacious one since it would serve as headquarters, housing, at times, several missionaries, some Brothers, and, perhaps, at times, several *donnés*, those dedicated lay assistants to the missionaries who served them without financial remuneration. Then came the chapel, on which they lavished great care "to adorn it, going farther in this than one would dare promise himself in a country so destitute of all things."[9] Adding barns for storing equipment and supplies, the tireless workers surrounded the whole with a palisade of cedar posts twelve feet high. Possibly in early December, 1668, perhaps on December 8, the feast of the Immaculate Conception, a day particularly treasured by him, Jacques Marquette celebrated Mass for the first time in the new chapel before a small congregation of a few French. Perhaps on that day Father Marquette named the mission Sainte-Marie.[10] Through the remainder of the winter and early spring little Brother Louis, a tireless worker, grubbed away at clearing land outside the palisaded enclosure so that, as soon as possible, he could plant a kitchen garden, for what group of Frenchmen can live happily without herbs and vegetables? In time, enough land was cleared so that grain could be planted, especially wheat. Just two years after the first logs were cut for the new mission compound, the abbé René de Bréhant de Galinée visited Sainte-Marie-du-Sault, on May 25, 1670, and described it thus:

At last we arrived . . . at Sainte-Marie of the Sault, the place where the Reverend Jesuit Fathers have made their principal establishment for the missions of the Ottawas and neighboring tribes. They have had two men in their service since last year, who have built them a pretty fort, that is to say a square of cedar posts twelve feet high, with a chapel and a house inside the fort, so that now they see themselves in the condition of not being dependent in any way on the Indians. They have a large

[9] *Relations*, LIV, 139. This chapel was destroyed by fire in 1671 and replaced by another ". . . yet more beautiful . . ." *Ibid.*, LVIII, 255.

[10] No documentary source proves that Marquette gave the mission its name. This is an assumption.

clearing well planted, from which they ought to gather a good part of their sustenance; they are even hoping to eat bread there within two years from now.[11]

While the mission compound was under construction Father Jacques Marquette enthusiastically launched his crusade for the conversion of the Chippewa, in particular, and those other aborigines who frequented the Sault. This, his first independent apostolic charge, was no cynosure, no pleasant interlude among noble savages similar to the unreal creatures peopling Jean Jacques Rousseau's *Contrat Social.* Just the year Marquette began his apostolate, Father Le Mercier wrote of the Indians at the Sault: "We have to bear everything from their bad humor and their brutality in order to win them by gentleness and affection. One must make himself, in some sort, a savage with these savages and lead a savage's life with them . . ."[12] His eighteen months' apprenticeship at Three Rivers now stood Marquette in good stead. The uncouth habits of the Chippewa, their offensive body odor, their fetid cabins, the constant turmoil of their communal life, even their licentious practices, quite likely affected him hardly at all. When he could gather a group of Indians together, they listened respectfully and they seemed to welcome him each time he visited the sick in the cabins. At night around the fires in the cabins, when the Blackrobe and the whites were absent, the Chippewa, and any chance visitors, held lengthy discussions, analyzing the teachings of the missionary. What he said was good in itself, but very difficult to put into practice. Sobriety, continence, honesty, justice, and living peacefully with neighboring nations were admirable qualities. But the young braves and the sorcerers were quick to point out that the French, who claimed to adore the Blackrobe's God and follow his commandments, were forever casting bold glances at pretty young squaws just as they constantly quarreled among themselves and dealt dishonestly in trading. True enough, the French went to the Blackrobe's chapel, attending the strange rites performed there, but their daily conduct was glaringly at variance with the precepts Father

[11] Kellogg, *Early Narratives,* 205.
[12] *Relations,* LI, 259.

Marquette preached. The elders, however, counselled prudence, diplomacy, and delay. The new Blackrobe was a good young man, kindly, sympathetic, and understanding. It could not be denied that he forthrightly condemned the irregular conduct of his French compatriots. Maintaining friendly relations with the French made good business sense. Listening respectfully to the Blackrobe went far to maintain amicable feelings and it hurt no one; perhaps it might even do some good. The fact was that the Chippewa, as Father Gabriel Marest would declare over four decades later, bore "the impress of the climate in which they live; it is harsh and indocile. Religion does not take so deep root in them as we could wish; and there are only a few souls who, from time to time, give themselves truly to God and console the missionary for his labors."[13]

The Chippewa at the Sault, numbering no more than a hundred and fifty, constituted but a fraction of the aborigines to whom Jacques Marquette's apostolate extended. In his *Relation* of 1667-1668, Le Mercier reported that the place was frequented by "twenty or thirty nations, all different in language, customs and policy."[14] Marquette, himself, estimated that his apostolic effort embraced some two thousand Indians, most of whom were nomads.[15] The greater part of these were Upper Algonquins, a generally docile folk, who had learned something of Christianity over fifteen years ago through their contact with the French and the missionaries at Three Rivers. In 1652 Father Jacques Buteux, whose zeal outstripped the strength of his frail body, lost his life while visiting the Upper Algonquins in their homeland, far up the Saint-Maurice River.[16] Fickle and feckless, these Indians were prone to follow the lead of the last person who harangued them, be he Indian sorcerer or Christian missionary. With most of the other chance aboriginal visitors, the Miami, the Sioux, the Cree, a rare Illinois, and other stray tribesmen, the missionary could only communicate by signs or through an interpreter. If a missionary of less zeal and dedication had submitted a report of Marquette's first year laboring

[13] *Ibid.*, LXVI, 283.
[14] *Ibid.*, LI, 259.
[15] *Ibid.*, LII, 213.
[16] *Ibid.*, XXXVII, 135.

among the Indians at the Sault, he would have been justified in presenting a quite discouraging picture. Not so Marquette, who enthusiastically announced: ". . . the harvest there is very abundant, and . . . it only rests with the missionaries to baptize the entire population to the number of two thousand."[17] Lest it be judged that his opinion was that of a visionary, he immediately added: "Thus far, however, our Fathers have not dared to trust those people, who are too acquiescent, fearing lest they will, after their baptism, cling to their customary superstitions. Especial attention is given to instructing them, and to baptizing the dying, who are a surer harvest."[18] From his report, even including its qualifications, emerges an endearing characteristic of Jacques Marquette. In his eyes the Indian was a naturally good, even noble person, unfortunate and misguided perhaps, but basically well-intentioned. The savages would, unquestionably, embrace Christianity enthusiastically once its profound truths were properly explained to them.

In the spring of 1669 the broad meadow stretching along the right bank of the Saint Mary's River was barely mantled in tender green when Father Claude Allouez returned to Sainte-Marie at the Sault from his distant mission of Saint-Esprit. With justifiable pride Brother Louis showed him the results of the winter's work, the snug residence, the tastefully decorated chapel, the tight storage barns, and the stout palisade beyond which lay the fields already planted and flourishing. Young Father Marquette delightedly reported the spiritual gains of his labors. Many infants had been baptized as well as a number of the dying. Though he had made only a few adult converts, friendly relations had been solidified between the mission and the Chippewa and also with hosts of Indians from other nations who visited the Sault. In turn, Allouez recounted the results of his winter's apostolate. The previous fall he had been so thoroughly discouraged that, in a council of the Kiskakon clan of the Ottawa, he solemnly removed his shoes and, beating the dust from them, declared to his audience that, since only some children and a few women among them were willing to pray

[17] *Ibid.*, LII, 213.
[18] *Ibid.*

to God, he was abandoning them, and so irrevocably, that he would not allow even the dust of their land to stay on his shoes. Fearful of losing the friendship of the French, their only protection against the terrible Iroquois and the equally dangerous Sioux, the Kiskakon, there and then, agreed to abolish polygamy and pagan sacrifices and henceforth to refrain from participating in superstitious and immoral practices if only the Blackrobe would not abandon them. Thereafter, outwardly at least, the Kiskakon manifested an enthusiasm for embracing Christianity, even to the extent of dismantling their cabins and re-erecting them near Allouez's little bark chapel so that during the rigors of winter everyone, including the children, could receive daily instructions. Before he was obliged to leave Saint-Esprit, in the spring of 1669, Allouez was able to baptize a hundred Kiskakon and thirty-nine Hurons living in a neighboring village. The most thrilling news of all was: "In the other nations are counted over a hundred persons more, to whom baptism has been given."[19] Such an outpouring of grace, it seemed to the great apostle of the West, was ample proof that the unnumbered multitudes among the nations southward and westward of Sainte-Marie-du-Sault only awaited laborers to reap the greatest spiritual harvest the Jesuit missionaries ever gathered since they first set foot in New France over a half century ago. Allouez was now on his way to Quebec where, by hook or by crook, he would wangle more missionaries for the Ottawa mission. Before Allouez departed for Quebec he was called upon to exercise all his powers of persuasion with the Ottawa to prevent them from causing a recurrence of hostilities with the Iroquois.

Though the peace arranged between the French and the Five Nations in 1667 included all of the savage allies of New France, among whom were the Ottawa, that irresponsible tribe recently captured a band of forty Iroquois braves discovered passing through the Ottawa country on their way back from attacking the Shawnee whose homeland was far to the south. With the Iroquois was a lone Shawnee whom they had captured and enslaved. Released by the Ottawa, the poor Shawnee gave Father Marquette

[19] *Ibid.*, 207.

"marvelous notions of the South Sea, from which his village was distant only five days—near a great river which, coming from the Illinois, discharged its waters into that sea."[20] The Ottawa loaded the Shawnee with presents, sending him back to his people with a promise that they would come to visit him and his people. As for the forty Iroquois braves, the Ottawa fully intended to kill them. Such a flagrant violation of the peace would undoubtedly reopen hostilities, resulting in untold suffering and loss of life on both sides. The missions among the Iroquois, just barely reopened, would certainly be among the first casualties. And, as for the mission effort in the West, an outbreak of war would immediately close the water route to Sault-Sainte-Marie, for how long no one could possibly surmise. Then all of Claude Allouez's bright hopes for converting the countless thousands of Indians, of whose existence the French had only recently become aware, would be cruelly dashed to the ground. With anxious heart Allouez attended the council meetings held by the Indians to decide whether they would go down to Montreal for the trading that summer. Bravely, he harangued the savages with inspired eloquence, cajoling, threatening, pleading for the lives of the captive Iroquois, graphically describing the unthinkable disasters which would inevitably follow if the Ottawa were so rash as to kill the Iroquois. After hours and days of endless, wearisome meetings, the Ottawa finally agreed to release all of the Iroquois, except three whom they intended to hold as hostages against the possibility that the braves of the Five Nations might attack them for having held their fellows captives. Only after further lengthy conferences and exercise of heroic patience, was Allouez able to persuade the Ottawa to place the hostages under his own protection, promising that he would hand them over to Governor Courcelle who could much more effectively use the three poor wretches as surety against any reprisals by the Iroquois.[21]

Once the catastrophe was averted, Marquette and Allouez were free to consider the implications of the information the Shawnee

[20] Emma H. Blair, editor, *The Indian Tribes of the Upper Mississippi Valley and the Region of the Great Lakes*, I, 336.

[21] *Relations*, LII, 197.

had given them. From the very inception of their apostolate in New France, Jesuit missionaries considered the expansion of geographic knowledge to be an important part of their apostolic effort. During earlier periods in the colony's history, missionaries sought geographical information in order to learn the location of Indian nations hitherto unknown to them so that these could be contacted and, hopefully, Christianized. As the British colonies increased in number and population, a new impetus was added to interest in geographical knowledge. If the English expanded westward they would be the first to open relations with the aborigines still unknown to the Europeans. In that event the poor, unsuspecting savages would be drawn into heresy and perdition. To Marquette and Allouez, therefore, the Shawnee's account of the geography of his country was thrilling news. If there really was a great river flowing through his homeland to the South Sea, its banks were almost certainly peopled by many nations who might easily be converted. Further, the river, if discovered, might well provide an effective barrier preventing the British from expanding their territory, provided the French discovered the river before the English and, thus, legitimately claimed ownership of it as well as of all the territory which it drained. The information so casually passed on to the missionaries by that lone Shawnee was of paramount ecclesiastical importance just as it would be of vital civil value, once the government at Quebec was appraised of it. Surely, when Claude Allouez related this news, together with the glowing report of his own success with the Kiskakon and Marquette's rosy description of the mission at the Sault, superiors, both ecclesiastical and civil, would be only too willing to send help to the mission among the Ottawa. Confident of success, Allouez went off with the flotilla of Indians bound for trading, promising Marquette that he would be back in the late summer, bringing with him a whole contingent of missionaries. In the meantime Father Marquette, exercising patience while waiting out the weeks before Allouez could return, spent the summer catechizing the Chippewa and making friends with the savages of other nations who came to the Sault.

When he had delivered the three Iroquois hostages safely into the hands of Governor Courcelle at Quebec, Father Allouez, submitting the encouraging report of the winter's work, earnestly begged recruits for the Ottawa mission from his superior. Though kindly, generous Father Le Mercier, then beginning his thirty-fifth year as a missionary in New France, was hard pressed for men, due to the recent reopening of missions among the Iroquois, the gracious old patriarch assigned the very apple of his eye, Father Claude Dablon, to work on the Ottawa mission as its new superior. In the *Relation* of 1668-1669, Le Mercier revealed his profound admiration for Dablon in saying: "When Father Aloes [*sic*] went down this year to Quebec, to deliver to Monsieur de Courcelle the Iroquois captives that he had ransomed in his name from the Outaouacs [*sic*], and asked for some aid from our Fathers, the lot happily fell on Father Claude Dablon. He has been sent to be the superior of those upper missions, notwithstanding the abundant fruit he was reaping here, and the pressing necessity felt for his presence here."[22] Among all of the Jesuits in New France at that moment, no better choice could have been made. From the time he was a toddler in Dieppe, where he was born on January 21, 1619, Claude Dablon must have been imbued with the venturesome spirit abroad in the town. A century before Dablon's birth Thomas Aubert sailed the *La Pensée* out of Dieppe to Newfoundland and brought back with him the first Indians ever seen in France.[23] One of France's greatest explorers, Jacques Cartier, sailed from Dieppe on his first voyage westward in 1534. Three quarters of a century before Dablon was born it was a common sight in Dieppe to see in the harbor ships which had plowed the oceans of the world. As a boy, Claude must often have sat, chin in hand, on the high, white cliffs overlooking the Dieppe harbor, watching tall ships beat up the English Channel on their way to the Atlantic, bound for exotic lands. Dablon's father, Nicolas, "*lieutenant-general du bailli de Dieppe,*" might not have been a venturesome character, but one of his uncles was an admiral.[24] Though Dieppe was a Huguenot stronghold, knowledge of the mis-

[22] *Ibid.*, 199.
[23] Lanctôt, *Canada,* I, 46.
[24] Delattre, *Etablissements,* II, 15.

sionary effort in New France was widespread in the town. In 1611 the first Jesuit missionaries sent to New France, Ennemond Massé and Pierre Biard, sailed from Dieppe after circumventing opposition from two Dieppe merchants, a controversy which certainly was well known in the town.[25] By 1627 Dieppe became so regularly the port of departure for Jesuits bound for the missions in Canada that they opened a residence there to house missionaries waiting for passage.[26] When Richelieu's niece, the Duchesse d'Aiguillon, contributed funds for establishing the Hôtel-Dieu at Quebec in 1637, it was nuns from a hospital at Dieppe who went to New France to inaugurate that charitable work. Dablon's family was probably not at all surprised when, as a student, Claude expressed an interest in devoting himself to the conversion of the savages of Canada. They were amused, perhaps, when the stripling began practicing on several musical instruments, expecting to charm his future neophytes with his music as he heard the Jesuits did in Paraguay.[27] At twenty, on September 17, 1639, Dablon entered the Jesuit novitiate at Paris and began his training for a career as a missionary.

The three decades which elapsed between the day Claude Dablon entered the Jesuit novitiate and the summer during which he reached Sainte-Marie-du-Sault prepared him well for his important contribution to the missions of the West. After his novitiate he was sent to the famous Jesuit college of Henri IV at La Flèche where he finished his philosophical studies and taught until 1647. After his theological training, at La Flèche, 1647 to 1651, during which he was ordained, he again taught there until 1653 when he was sent to the Jesuit college at Eu until 1655. That appointment must have pleased him because the house at Eu was often a temporary home for missionaries bound for Canada. Finally, in the summer of 1655, he was permitted to go to New France. He was barely off the boat at Quebec when Dablon was sent with Father Pierre Chaumonot to begin a mission among the Onondaga. Though the young missionary could not speak a word of Iroquois, he enchanted the Indians with his music which attracted everyone in the village

[25] Rochemonteix, *Jésuites*, I, 33.
[26] Delattre, *Etablissements*, II, 15.
[27] Chaumonot, *Un missionnaire des Hurons*, 52.

to gather around the cabin of the missionaries. When Dablon ceased playing Chaumonot preached to the assembled savages. Despite such a propitious beginning within three years the missionaries, and a small colony of French who, at the invitation of the Onondaga, settled around the mission, were obliged to flee by stealth to avoid the fate meted out to Isaac Jogues twelve years before.[28] During the subsequent three years Dablon served his apprenticeship at various sedentary missions in the Saint Lawrence River valley. In the summer of 1661 Claude Dablon and Father Gabriel Druillettes, a man of fifty-one with eighteen years of mission experience, were directed to investigate the possibility of establishing a mission on the headwaters of the Saguenay River and, if possible, to reach Hudson Bay.[29] During that lengthy voyage Druillettes stimulated Dablon's growing interest in exploring the unknown by recounting his own frequent travels down the Saint Lawrence to Tadoussac as well as his trips through the Abenaki country to Boston.[30] After his momentous voyage Dablon devoted himself to routine tasks in the college at Quebec until 1669 when he was appointed superior of the Ottawa mission. That assignment must surely have delighted him since, in effect, it authorized Dablon to formulate plans for expanding activities into a country and among peoples largely unknown. His two subjects, Claude Allouez and Jacques Marquette, were apt companions for a man of vision such as Dablon. Allouez had already spent six years ranging far and wide in the West and the young, vigorous Marquette was willing and able to dare any journey into the unknown for the sake of the souls of the nations still dwelling in spiritual darkness.

Jacques Marquette's weeks of patient waiting to learn the results of Father Allouez's visit to Quebec were finally ended when the Indians rushed to the mission compound, informing the young missionary that the great Allouez was coming up the Saint Mary's

[28] *Relations*, XLIV, 175-81.

[29] *Ibid.*, XLVI, 253-95. Dablon's journal of his voyage up the Saguenay.

[30] *Ibid.*, XXIII, 327. Druillettes went from Quebec to the Abenaki country in Maine where he stayed for a year. During the following three years he wintered with the Montagnais in the vicinity of Tadoussac. In 1651 he went to Boston as an envoy from the Canadian authorities who sought to arrange an alliance with New England.

River and with him was a new Blackrobe whom they had never seen. Hurrying down to the river bank, Marquette hailed the arriving Jesuits, delightedly recognizing Dablon with whom Marquette had spent a few days in the college at Quebec when he first reached New France.[31] He fondly remembered those few evenings during recreation when Dablon had entertained the community with the songs of France and imitated for them the haunting chants of native tribes. When all of the supplies brought from Quebec were safely stored, Marquette and Brother Louis joined Dablon and Allouez to hear all the news. The War of Devolution was finished, successfully concluded by the Treaty of Aix-la-Chapelle last year. The Jesuit Province of France, responsible for staffing the mission of New France, had a new provincial, Father Etienne de Champs. Even if the new provincial should prove less interested in Canada than his predecessor, that old patriarch, Father Paul Ragueneau, who had spent twenty-five years in New France, was still the mission's agent in Paris so all would be well.[32] The newly reopened missions among the Iroquois, begun when the peace was signed with the Five Nations in 1667, were all flourishing and this time there was hope that the work would not be interrupted. Governor Courcelle, while grateful for Allouez's tact in averting that dangerous crisis and rescuing the Iroquois, seemed none too elated when he heard the story of the Shawnee and the great river in his country. However, it was rumored that Jean Talon, that capable intendant, recalled to France in November 1668, was returning to Quebec. He would certainly look into the geographical matter. The best news of all was that Father Le Mercier had approved Allouez's plans for opening some new missions south and west of Sainte-Marie-du-Sault. On their way back from Quebec, as they paddled along day by day, Dablon and Allouez had evolved a plan. As superior, Father Dablon would take up permanent residence at Sainte-Marie, headquarters for the expanding Ottawa mission, where he would minister to the French, the Chippewa, and the members of such savage

[31] ARSJ, France 23, 218-19. When Marquette reached Quebec Dablon was stationed in the college at Quebec where he held the office of treasurer.

[32] Léon Pouliot, "Le Père Paul Ragueneau (1608-1680)," *Lettres du Bas-Canada*, XVII (1963), 143-54.

nations as visited the place. Allouez, after an extended tour south and west, would select locations for new missions, spending the winter working in that country. As for young Father Marquette, having already served an apprenticeship of three years evangelizing the savages, he was certainly well prepared to work alone. He would replace Allouez at Saint-Esprit, a lonely mission many miles from even the crudest European settlement. It was a hazardous appointment, too, because the restless Ottawa were constantly irritating the Sioux, their neighbors, who might well turn on the Ottawa and slaughter them. The Kiskakon Ottawa, recent converts, required someone to strengthen them in their new-found faith. Besides, the poor Christian Hurons at the mission of Saint-Esprit, the tattered remnants of the flock for whom Father Jean de Brébeuf and his fellow martyrs had given their lives, could not be heartlessly abandoned by Brébeuf's successors. Then, too, Saint-Esprit was an excellent place from which to make a beginning among the Sioux and the Cree who, in turn, could inform the missionary about nations west of their own lands.

Since it was well into August 1669 before Father Jacques Marquette was assigned to the mission of Saint-Esprit, it behooved him not to delay his departure for winter, the Indians said, often came early to the shores of Lake Superior, making the long voyage to Chequamegon Bay both difficult and dangerous. With Brother Louis helping, the young missionary prepared his small bundles for the months ahead. The already travel-worn Mass-kit was carefully checked to make sure that there was sufficient sacramental wine and hosts for the celebration of Mass. They patched the young priest's worn cassock, forced on him the warmest cloak, packed their thickest blankets in his packets, and saw to it that the soles of his shoes were sound. Father Allouez spoke seriously to the Kiskakon, who were leaving the Sault with Marquette, impressing on them that they must treat this young Blackrobe with particular care. On his last morning at Sainte-Marie, after saying his Mass and swallowing a hasty breakfast, young Jacques Marquette knelt for his superior's blessing and, rising from his knees, eased himself into a canoe bound for Saint-Esprit to continue Allouez's apostolate, but also to learn what he could of the geography of the land to the south, the land of the Illinois, and the great river rumored to be there.

LA POINTE
DU SAINT-ESPRIT
1669-1671

"One must not hope that he can avoid crosses in any of our missions; and the best means to live there contentedly is not to fear them, and to expect from God's goodness, while enjoying the small ones, to have much heavier ones."[1] Thus Father Jacques Marquette characterized his apostolate at the mission of Saint-Esprit at Chequamegon Bay. Crosses and tribulations were showered on the young Jesuit in abundance from the very outset of his journey to his new post. Departing from Sault-Sainte-Marie in mid-August, 1669, Marquette and his Indian friends faced a canoe voyage of well over five hundred miles. The party had hardly emerged from Whitefish Bay, a twenty-mile wide funnel through which the wa-

[1] *Relations*, LIV, 187.

ters of Lake Superior flow into Saint Mary's River, when bitter winds laden with snow greeted them. Throughout the whole of that seemingly endless voyage, everyone was constantly drenched with icy spume and chilled to the bone by fierce winds against which they barely made headway. It seemed that each day they lost more distance than they gained. At dusk every evening they carefully beached the canoes lest the wind and the waves capture their crafts. Many nights when it was impossible to light a fire the weary, thoroughly drenched travelers curled up on the snow in the lee of a large rock. Sheltered somewhat from the cruel wind, they dozed fitfully until dawn when the weary journey began again. As the days advanced, great chunks of ice began to appear, racing at the paper-thin canoes like so many giant prehistoric monsters bent on devouring them. Day after weary day, the buffeted voyagers toiled along the ruggedly picturesque southern shore of Lake Superior, too absorbed in their battle with the elements to notice the beauty of the scenery. Pictured Rocks at Au Sable Point was only another indistinct pile of snow-plastered stone. Marquette Bay meant little or nothing. Munising Bay was only a stretch of sheltered water, protected by Grand Island. Miles and days went on endlessly before the party reached Keweenaw Bay and the inlet to Portage Lake. Perhaps the exhausted travelers stopped to rest some place along the site of today's Portage Ship Canal, relieved to be protected from the biting wind and off the treacherous, ice-choked lake for a while. Finally, many days and over a hundred miles west of the Keweenaw peninsula, the half-frozen canoeists slipped between Chequamegon Point, a narrow strip of gravel, and Madeleine Island into the welcome shelter of Chequamegon Bay. Following the western shore, they came, at the foot of the bay, to their long journey's end, the mission of Saint-Esprit. Jacques Marquette laconically recounted his gruelling journey thus: ". . . after a voyage of a month amid snow and ice, which blocked our passage, and amid almost constant dangers of death . . . I arrived here on the thirteenth of September . . ."[2]

[2] *Ibid.*, 169. It is well over five hundred miles by water from Sault-Sainte-Marie to Chequamegon Bay. On this journey Marquette averaged no more than fifteen miles a day.

Since the unseasonable winter weather had not touched this far western end of Lake Superior, warm autumn sun caressed his weary shoulders as Father Marquette approached the shore over the placid, shining water to meet the people of his mission. Stalks of ripening corn waved in soft breezes dispersing the smoke rising from the roofs of the cluster of bark cabins resting on a gentle plain sloping down to the attractive bay.[3] As the arriving missionary watched the Indians hurriedly assemble to greet him, he could not help reviewing in his mind everything he had learned about this place and its people. Old Father Gabriel Druillettes had probably related to Marquette the oral traditions of their origins which the Ottawa Algonquin handed down from generation to generation. Hundreds of years ago they had dwelt far to the east on the "great salt water." But the Great Spirit, Ke-Che-mun-a-do, a kindly, benevolent supreme being, caused them to move slowly westward. At the Island of the Great Turtle (Mackinac Island), where the vast waters divide, some of the Ottawa went southward, settling near the "stinking water." These were the Keepers of the Fire (the Potawatomi), the Eastern Earth People (the Delaware), the Wild Rice People (the Menominee), the Southerners (the Shawnee), those at the Bay Entry (the Saulk), the Fox People (the Outagamie) and the People of the Peninsula (the Miami or Maumee).[4] Many of the Trading People (the Chippewa), however, went northward to the place where the waters fall and boil (Sault-Sainte-Marie). There the Chippewa band remained, taking advantage of the abundant supply of fish, nearly always available. The remainder of the Ottawa moved farther westward, disputing possession of the southern shore of Lake Superior with the Sioux, whose homeland that country was. Finally, the Ottawa settled on Madeleine Island, two miles off shore, at the mouth of Chequamegon Bay. On their island home the Ottawa became so prosperous that their village extended two miles in width and three in length. Security and leisure, unfortunately, brought with them vice and corruption until the all-powerful, wanton sorcerers took to practicing human sacrifices and

[3] *Ibid.*, 177.
[4] William W. Warren, *History of the Ojibway Nation*, 31.

cannibalism. At last, after years of groveling fear, the Ottawa revolted against their medicine men and, killing them, fled in horror from that dark and bloody island which, ever after, was held to be cursed. Moving eastward, the Ottawa gradually dispersed. Some settled on Manitoulin Island while others found homes on the upper reaches of the Ottawa River. There Champlain met them and the stripling Etienne Brulé dwelt with them, learning their language and customs. When the route up the Ottawa River to the west became a busy highway over which missionaries went to Huronia and Indians passed back and forth, trading with the French at Montreal, the Ottawa, traders by long tradition, unsuccessfully sought to exact tolls from the travelers. At last the powerful Five Nations, once the undisputed middlemen of the Saint Lawrence River valley, realized that to maintain their economic position they must crush the Ottawa and the Hurons, even to the extent of wiping them out completely. In the early spring of 1649, the Iroquois launched a brilliantly conceived campaign. With war parties totaling little more than a thousand braves, they set out to destroy a population numbering, perhaps, upwards of 30,000. The Hurons and Ottawa, poorly led and completely disunited, were easily defeated. Those who escaped death fled in panic to their ancient refuge on the shores of Chequamegon Bay. Thence, the Petun Hurons wandered aimlessly southward until they finally returned and settled near the Ottawa.

After the Iroquois invasion the French heard nothing from the Ottawa until 1653 when a group of them, plus a few Hurons, risking death at the hands of the Iroquois, came down to Montreal with a supply of rich peltries to purchase desperately needed supplies of European manufacture. Reporting that some 2,000 refugees were gathered at a place 150 leagues west of Huronia, the Indians promised to return the following year with a larger contingent and a much richer cargo.[5] Faithful to their word, six score Indians returned in 1654, bearing news of the existence of a great river which the French conjectured might be a route to the "sea of China."[6]

[5] *Relations*, XL, 213, 215.

[6] Marie (Guyard) de Incarnation, *Lettres de la révérende mère Marie de l'Incarnation*, II, 67.

When those Indians departed for home two Frenchmen accompanied them for the purpose of encouraging continuance of the trade.[7] On the return of the Ottawa to Montreal in 1656, accompanied by the two Frenchmen, thirty French determined to go west with the visitors. The Jesuits appointed Fathers Leonard Garreau and Gabriel Druillettes with Brother Louis Boëme to join the expedition so that the poor, scattered Petun Indians might again have pastors for their souls. The large flotilla was barely out of sight of Montreal before Father Garreau was mortally wounded in an attack which the Iroquois launched against the expedition. This disaster so thoroughly frightened the French that they fled back to Montreal. By then New France was economically prostrate since her one cash crop, the fur trade, had all but disappeared. At that fateful moment two incredibly intrepid Frenchmen, Pierre Esprit Radisson and Médard Chouart, Sieur des Groseilliers, set out clandestinely in August, 1659, to reopen the trade, without which New France would surely die.[8] These two daring, if sometimes nearly traitorous, *voyageurs* penetrated the west, reaching Chequamegon Bay. They built a sketchy fort there, explored quite widely, baptized some dying children, and returned to Montreal on August 20, 1660, with a flotilla of Ottawa whose canoes carried peltries valued at 200,000 livres.[9] The expedition not only saved the colony financially, but it proved that the Far West's rich resources could be reached with safety.

When the Ottawa set out for the west the Jesuits, anxious to rejoin their Huron neophytes, to say nothing of scouting the possibility of Christianizing the many nations of that area, whose names and locations were barely known, sent Father René Ménard, a physically weakened man of fifty-six, to open a mission. The pagan Ottawa treated the holy old man shamefully, abandoning him at Keweenaw Bay where he barely survived the rigors of a terrible winter. In the spring of 1661, when he reached the Ottawa

[7] *Relations*, LII, 219. See also Nute, *Caesars of the Wilderness*, 23, who demonstrates that Pierre Esprit Radisson could not have been Groseilliers' companion on this journey.

[8] Nute, *Caesars of the Wilderness*, 58.

[9] *Relations*, XLV, 161, 163.

villages of Chequamegon Bay, Ménard learned that the Hurons, residing far inland to the south, not only lacked spiritual succor but were starving as well. Charitably setting out with a lay companion, Jean Guerin, Ménard was lost in the woods when carrying the baggage around a rapid while Guerin piloted their canoe through the troublesome white water.[10] Not until 1665 was another attempt made by missionaries to penetrate the west.

During the years elapsing since Ménard visited Chequamegon Bay and Father Claude Allouez's arrival there in the fall of 1665, noticeable changes had occurred regarding the location of tribal groups. The news of the Marquis de Tracy's defeat of the Iroquois had emboldened the Petun Hurons to emerge from their forest fastness on the Black River and join the Ottawa at Chequamegon Bay. The Ottawa themselves, heartened by the Iroquois defeat as well as by the renewal of regular contact with French trading parties, hoped to recapture their once valuable position as middlemen in the economic stream of trade between the French and all of the western tribes. When Allouez spent his first winter at Saint-Esprit two Indian villages were to be found there. One of these was the home of the Ottawa and the other was inhabited by the Petun Hurons, most of whom were Christians, at least in name.[11] These latter were restored to the practice of their religion, but the Ottawa were an entirely different kettle of fish. After spending two trying winters among them Allouez confessed that he found it necessary constantly to entreat God to grant him "patience for the cheerful endurance of contempt, mockery, importunity and insolence from these barbarians."[12] The Ottawa, except for the Kiskakon band, were "so addicted to idolatry, superstition, legends, polygamy, unstable marriages, and every sort of licentiousness, which makes them renounce all natural shame,"[13] that he abandoned his effort to try to convert them. When he returned to Chequamegon Bay, in the fall of 1668, after a flying trip to Quebec, Allouez discovered

[10] A. A. A. Schmirler, "Wisconsin's Lost Missionary: the Mystery of Father René Ménard," *Wisconsin Magazine of History*, XLV (1962-1963), 99-114.

[11] *Relations*, LI, 21.

[12] *Ibid.*, L, 299.

[13] *Ibid.*, LI, 21.

that the Ottawa had, very imprudently, become involved in a quarrel with their hosts, the Sioux, as they had already begun to do when he first encountered them in 1665.[14] Of the three Ottawa bands at Chequamegon Bay, the Sinagaux, the Keinouché and the Kiskakon, the missionary was convinced that only the latter could be readily Christianized. They were "an enemy to warfare, . . . but . . . so addicted to raillery that [they] had, up to that time made child's play of our Faith . . ."[15] During the winter, 1668-1669, Allouez effected a complete change of attitude among the Kiskakon in the dramatic manner previously related. The other two Ottawa bands, however, remained either cooly indifferent or positively hostile to Allouez's advances. The mission of Saint-Esprit was, therefore, no post for a desiccated, timid invalid; it required a missionary with a dynamic personality, one capable of prodding the slothful Hurons, encouraging the barely converted Kiskakon, and boldly challenging the arrogant, licentious Sinagaux, as well as arousing the blandly indifferent Keinouché. The mission equally called for a man of prudence and foresight, one who could accurately estimate the future of the effort. Would the growing hostility between the Sioux and the Ottawa require, in the near future, another migration of the Hurons and Ottawa alike? If so, when was it psychologically and diplomatically propitious to support such a move?

There was a further factor of major import to be kept in mind regarding the mission of Saint-Esprit. The location was a frontier outpost in the civic as well as the religious sense. A missionary of outstanding ability might possibly establish friendly relations with the Sioux as well as their neighbors, the Cree and the Assiniboin. If those tribes embraced Christianity the nations beyond them could be approached with safety, to the incalculable benefit of countless souls as well as to the immeasurable economic profit of New France. Again, no Frenchman, missionary or layman, would fail to be intrigued by the vague but persistent rumors regarding the existence of a mighty river in the country of the Illinois, about

[14] *Ibid.*, L, 279.
[15] *Ibid.*, LII, 205.

whom the French, as yet, knew so little. There must be something geographically solid behind that constantly recurring report. If there really was a great river, and an equally vast drainage system flowing into it, where did all that massive volume of water discharge into an ocean? Was it possibly the long-sought passage to the China sea, piercing the northern hemisphere of the New World? If so, locating and claiming it would, almost inevitably, mean gaining control of the rich trade with the Far East. Tall Spanish galleons and the ships of English and Dutch chartered companies would clamor to pay toll for the use of the passage rather than risk their cargoes sailing around the bottom of South America on their long way home from Cathay. Since decisions of moment locally, and even possibly nationally, might well hang in the balance at Saint-Esprit, none but a solidly balanced, prudent missionary should be assigned to that post. That Jacques Marquette was eminently qualified to be trusted with these responsibilities was attested to not merely by his very appointment to Saint-Esprit, but by important collateral evidence concerning him forwarded to the Jesuit general in 1669. That year Father François Le Mercier was called upon to submit the regular triennial report on each of his subjects. Regarding Marquette, his superior recorded that this man was talented, possessed of noteworthy prudence and judgment, and was now an experienced missionary. Concerning Marquette's intellectual attainments, Le Mercier attested that these were of the highest. By temperament, the young missionary was a stable, balanced individual. As to the apostolic work for which Marquette was fitted, he was unquestionably a born missionary. Father Le Mercier was completely confident that the rigorous and important mission of Saint-Esprit was in capable hands.[16]

As Jacques Marquette waded ashore, at the end of his arduous journey, the first to greet him were the Hurons, proudly usurping that honor by right of spiritual primogeniture. Was it not to the Hurons that the Blackrobes first came, and over forty years ago, in the person of the great Echon, Jean de Brébeuf, in his martyr's grave these twenty years? The Hurons at Saint-Esprit might be

[16] ARSJ, Fr.14f.219r.no.674.

numerically the least of the aboriginal bands at Chequamegon Bay, and, if the truth were admitted, a cringing, cowardly lot, but they were not benighted pagans, sacrificing to false gods and believing in stupid magic. True, Father Allouez often scolded them for participating, shamefacedly, in the licentious practices of their Ottawa neighbors. He did not deny, however, that even if they did so, they knew better. Besides, everyone knew that all Frenchmen spoke the Huron tongue; did anyone ever meet a Frenchman who didn't? Radisson and Groseilliers were not fluent in the jargon which the Ottawa called a language, as those who remembered them must honestly admit. It mattered little, however, because the Hurons interpreted for them and both Frenchmen spoke the Huron tongue.[17] Enjoying their hour of glory to the full, the Hurons escorted the newly arrived young Blackrobe to their village where they assembled the whole band to welcome him, offering a lavish banquet of their poor best. When the feasting slowed its tempo the grave old elders, one by one, rose in impressive solemnity and delivered sonorous speeches of welcome. The sun shone brighter this day because the Blackrobe was again with them to show them the right path. There was only one small cloud in the sky, and that no bigger than a beaver's paw, but there all the same. Their father, Allouez, had not returned to them. But they would heed the word of the new Blackrobe with the strange name as they had that of Allouez. And what was the word of the new Blackrobe to them?

Now that he must reply to the Hurons, Jacques Marquette stood tall among them, reluctant to address them, for his message would disappoint them, causing them to lose face. Speaking slowly, haltingly, for he was not fluent in Huron, the missionary regretfully informed his listeners that their father, Allouez, "who understood them so thoroughly, had been unwilling to return to them for this winter, because they did not take enough interest in the prayer."[18] After four winters among them what Allouez said of the Hurons two years ago was still true. They boasted to the Ottawa that they

[17] Groseilliers probably learned Huron while he was a lay assistant to the Jesuits on the Huron mission. See *Relations*, XXVIII, 229, wherein Groseilliers is reported to have come back from Huronia in 1646.

[18] *Ibid.*, LIV, 171.

alone at Chequamegon were Christians. But, "the intercourse which they have so long had with the infidels has nearly effaced from their minds all vestiges of religion, and has made them resume their former customs."[19] Marquette warned his audience not to expect any other missionary, one who, perhaps, spoke Huron better than he, to come to them. All the Blackrobes who knew their tongue had gone to the newly opened missions among the Iroquois where so many Huron captives now lived. The Petun Hurons at Chequamegon must examine their consciences and desist from boasting to the Ottawa that they were Christians. They could not honestly claim that fair name while their very conduct debased it. For the Hurons this was a hard saying and who could believe it? Yet the young Blackrobe conveyed his disappointing message so diplomatically that he could report: ". . . they acknowledged that they were well deserving of this punishment. Since then they have spoken of the matter during the winter, and resolved to do better, as they have declared to me."[20] Promising to visit the crestfallen Hurons from time to time, Marquette left them to take up his work among the Ottawa.

Of the three Ottawa groups dwelling in the area, the Sinagaux were the least inclined to accept Christianity. Ignorant, arrogant, dominated by their vicious sorcerers, they were inalterably attached to their revolting indecencies and pagan sacrifices. When Marquette sought to instruct them the people ridiculed him and refused to listen. Though he was usually the soul of charity regarding the Indians, the young Blackrobe's judgment of the Sinagaux was: ". . . I think there is so little to be accomplished with this nation that I have not even been willing to baptize the children who were well, or those who seemed able to escape disease, contenting myself with being on the watch for the sick."[21] Despite the opposition of the Sinagaux, Marquette visited their cabins regularly, hoping, at least, to baptize the dying whom these Indians strove to hide from him. But gossip, spreading from one village to another, often revealed what the Sinagaux wished to conceal. On one dramatic

[19] *Ibid.*, L, 307.
[20] *Ibid.*, LIV, 171.
[21] *Ibid.*

occasion, when a dying woman asked for the performance of a singularly indecent dance to effect her cure, Father Marquette boldly entering the cabin where all the elders were assembled, denounced the impiety of the woman and the moral corruption of the sorcerers. One of the more ancient elders spoke out in favor of the missionary, perhaps only for the sake of peace. He declared that the Blackrobe should be given "what he asked, and that it was no matter if that woman did die."[22] On the whole, however, Marquette made no inroads among the flint-hearted Sinagaux.

The Keinouché Ottawa offered a more hopeful field for the young Blackrobe's apostolate. As a group these Indians, rather than rejecting Christianity out of hand, "declared themselves boldly, saying that it was not yet time" for them to accept the missionary's teachings.[23] There was, however, some reason to hope for the eventual conversion of this band for there were among them at least some baptized Christians of exemplary character. One middle-aged man was "looked upon as a wonder among the savages, from his never yet having chosen to marry; and he still persists in his resolution, whatever one can say to him on the subject."[24] This affluent bachelor was continually importuned by his relatives to marry as he must also have been plotted against by every mother with a marriageable daughter. Another outstanding Christian was a newly married young man who had his difficulties avoiding participation in lascivious rites. These degrading practices took place whenever a member of the band dreamed that his manitou required them. No pagan savage would dare disobey a directive thus received since he firmly believed that dreams were inspired by the spirits who would wreck terrible vengeance if the recipient of the dream did not obey literally. Often the young Christian, unaware of the nature of the gathering to which he was invited, escaped morally unscathed only by pretending to be so ill that he was obliged to depart.[25] These two stalwart Christians, together with the young man's mother and some of his sisters, also Christians,

[22] *Ibid.*, 175.
[23] *Ibid.*, 171.
[24] *Ibid.*
[25] *Ibid.*, 173.

consoled Marquette who hoped that their example would eventually change the hearts of the Keinouché.

The Kiskakon, Father Allouez's recent converts, were Jacques Marquette's pride and delight. When he reached Saint-Esprit these new Christians were just beginning to harvest their corn.[26] Immediately they flocked around the new Blackrobe clamoring for news. Where was their father, Allouez, and why had he not returned to them? Were the French abandoning them now that they were nearly all Christians? No, Marquette assured them, they need have no fear of that. The chiefs of another great nation had declared themselves Christians and, in order to instruct them, Father Allouez had gone to that nation. But he had sent a new, younger Blackrobe, who spoke the language of the Kiskakon and already cherished them, to dwell in their cabins and continue to instruct them. Marquette had come "only out of consideration for them and for the Hurons; that they should never be forsaken, but cherished more warmly than all the other nations; and that they had only one common interest with the French."[27] Disappointed at losing their first father in God, the Kiskakon quickly warmed to their gracious, charming young pastor who was obviously already devoted to them.

And so Father Jacques Marquette began his missionary labors among the Kiskakon. After visiting every cabin in the village, to meet each member of the band, the Blackrobe selected one of their poor dwellings where he would live with that family, their dogs, the children, and the swarm of relatives who were constantly in and out, night and day. His first pastoral function, endearing him to all the women, was the joyous ceremony of baptizing all the new babies born since Allouez left the Kiskakon in the early summer of 1669. Each little morsel of humanity must be elaborately admired and an appropriate saint's name chosen for it after a lengthy discussion with proud parents and doting grandmothers.[28] Then the shy, young brides and the great, hulking grooms were assembled to have their marriages blessed, amid much joshing by the assembled witnesses. Each morning Father Marquette visited every

[26] *Ibid.*, 177.
[27] *Ibid.*
[28] *Ibid.*

cabin, inquiring after the ill, doling out simple remedies. And, inevitably, there were the alienated married couples to be reconciled. In a society long accustomed to the easy solubility of marriage, it was irksome for these new Christians to compromise their differences rather than following the easier solution of simply parting. One young Christian matron, abandoned by her husband, was in grave moral danger because her relatives, perhaps irked at the presence of an extra mouth to feed, urged her to find a new husband. Buoyed up by the missionary's assiduous encouragement, the distraught young woman conducted herself as a Christian should, giving no cause for gossip about her. Within a few weeks, exercising his powers of persuasion towards the young husband, Marquette could report that ". . . with the remonstrances I made to her husband, [I] compelled him to take her back towards the end of the winter . . ."[29]

Handling the aboriginal teenagers presented to Marquette much the same problems they offer today. "The elders told me," the missionary related, "that the young people had not yet any sense, and that I must check them in their dissolute conduct."[30] A wise old Christian spoke out at a meeting of all the Ottawa elders, demanding that Christian girls never be permitted to witness the indecent dances performed by the pagans.[31] Winning the support of the mothers, Marquette advised them to prevent the young braves from visiting their daughters at night.[32] Immensely pleased with the cooperation he received from the mothers, the young missionary recorded that, while there was a flood of gossip about the young girls of the other Ottawa bands, he never once heard any unsavory tales concerning the Kiskakon maidens, even though he "knew almost all that was going on among the two nations that were near us . . ."[33] Giving the girls due credit for their virtuous conduct under difficult circumstances, Marquette noted that he knew "well all the importunities they suffered every night, and the courage they must

[29] *Ibid.*, 179.
[30] *Ibid.*, 183.
[31] *Ibid.*, 175.
[32] *Ibid.*, 183.
[33] *Ibid.*

needs have to resist them. They have learned to be modest, and the French, who know them, see plainly that they do not resemble the rest."[34] That triumph in itself went far towards effecting a profound revolution in the moral standards of the Kiskakon.

Having inculcated a proper Christian modesty among the women, Father Marquette tackled the problem of weeding out pagan customs among the Kiskakon. Refraining from acting the imprudent zealot, he understood that while modifying Indian customs he must avoid creating a vacuum. He explained: ". . . in order to effect these changes the more easily, I keep a little of their usage, and take from it all that is bad."[35] A propitious occasion for eliminating certain pagan rites presented itself when the chief of the band permitted a dog to be suspended from a pole near his cabin, "a kind of sacrifice the savages make to the sun . . ."[36] When the Blackrobe informed the chief that this was wrong, "he went himself at once and threw it down."[37] Hitherto none of the Ottawa held a feast without offering some form of sacrifice to their deities and making speeches addressed to them at the beginning of the celebration. Marquette induced his neophytes to dispense with the sacrifices, encouraging them to retain their colorful orations in which they "addressed themselves to God, whom they ask for health and for what they need, saying that it is for this purpose they give the feast."[38] Explaining to the Indians the Christian belief in guardian angels, the young missionary encouraged his people to seek divine aid through the intercession of these angelic spirits rather than appealing to their false manitou, as they had done while pagans. It was not long before "They despised all those little divinities that they had before being baptized; they often make fun of these, and are astonished that they have had so little sense as to offer sacrifices to those false creatures."[39] So, before winter set in Marquette had won the respect and affection of the Kiskakon to

[34] *Ibid.*
[35] *Ibid.*, 181.
[36] *Ibid.*, 177.
[37] *Ibid.*
[38] *Ibid.*, 181.
[39] *Ibid.*, 183, 185.

such a degree that in their councils and in all matters of consequence they consulted him. "It was enough to show them what I wished in order to obtain it when I spoke to them as Christians."[40] As a result of the missionary's influence the Kiskakon "gained the upper hand over the other nations and may be said to govern three others."[41]

With the Kiskakon well in hand Father Marquette looked farther afield, considering how to approach the Sioux, the Cree, and the Assiniboin, all of whom dwelt to the west of Chequamegon Bay. The Sioux, he learned, were a numerous people having many characteristics in common with the Iroquois, except that they never went to war unless they were attacked.[42] Since by custom among them the Sioux received all visitors graciously, though they feared the French, the young Blackrobe sent them a present, by an Ottawa messenger who spoke the Sioux language, informing them that ". . . they must show due recognition to the Frenchman wherever they met him, and must not kill him or the savages accompanying him; that the Blackrobe wished to proceed into the country of the Assiniboin and into that of the Cree; that he was already among the Outagami; and that I should set out this autumn to go to the Illinois, the passage to whom they were to leave free."[43] The Sioux responded cautiously, consenting to the passage of a missionary through their country, but they returned the present, declining to accept it until all of their people assembled at the conclusion of the fall hunt. They promised, however, to come to the mission of Saint-Esprit, in the fall of 1670, "to hold council with the Illinois and talk with me."[44] As for the Assiniboin, Marquette was unable to learn much about them. It was rumored that in their homeland, which was on a lake some fifteen or twenty days journey west of Chequamegon Bay, there was a great river which was thought to

[40] *Ibid.*, 181.

[41] *Ibid.*

[42] *Ibid.*, 191.

[43] *Ibid.*, 193. See Kellogg, *The French Régime*, 158, who says that Marquette sent the Sioux "gospel messages and pictures." Marquette did not say what presents he sent the Sioux. But see *Relations*, LVI, 115, 117, wherein Dablon says the Sioux sent back holy pictures Marquette sent them.

[44] *Ibid.*, LIV, 193.

lead to the Western Sea. One of the Assiniboin told Marquette that once when he was at the mouth of that river, he "had seen Frenchmen and four large canoes with sails."[45] The Cree were nomads, a people of mystery, whose rendezvous was not yet clearly known. They roamed the vast country to the northwest, but came to Chequamegon Bay "to buy merchandise and corn."[46] Concerning the possibility of converting these tribes, Marquette remarked: "I could wish that all of the nations had as much love for God as these people have fear of the French; Christianity would soon be flourishing."[47]

When grim winter closed in on the land Jacques Marquette settled down in his small bark chapel, which also served as his residence, prepared to devote his time to strengthening the religious faith of the Kiskakon and learning what he could about the great nation of the Illinois. At his invitation the Kiskakon moved their cabins close to the chapel "in order that they might pray to God, be instructed and have their children receive baptism."[48] Despite the bitter cold and monotonous diet, the winter was an interesting one for the Blackrobe. Describing these weeks, he wrote: "It is a great consolation to a missionary to see such pliable dispositions in the midst of barbarism, to live in such peace with savages and to pass sometimes whole days in teaching them and making them pray to God."[49] Every day, even in the most severe weather, the neophytes beat a path to the small bark chapel. The unbaptized were prepared to receive that sacrament while the new Christians received further instructions. On cold winter evenings while the Blackrobe sat, cross-legged, before a bright fire, surrounded by the Kiskakon elders, those sage old men listened to their missionary relate bible stories to them and in turn they recounted the history of their people. When they heard, for instance, the story of the tower of Babel, the Indians related that "their old

[45] *Ibid.*
[46] *Ibid.*, 195.
[47] *Ibid.*, 193.
[48] *Ibid.*, 181.
[49] *Ibid.*

men had related to them how formerly a great house had been built, but a strong wind had overthrown it."[50]

During the winter Father Marquette also gathered a noteworthy store of geographical knowledge. By great good fortune he came into the possession of a very precious treasure. In the fall of 1669 a Kiskakon brave fell ill while he was still unbaptized. This sincere soul begged the missionary "to grant him that grace [of baptism], or else to remain near him because he did not wish to employ the jugglers for his cure and he was afraid of hell-fire. I prepared him for baptism, and was often in his cabin, the joy that he felt in consequence partly restoring his health. He thanked me for the care that I had taken of him, and soon after, saying that I had given him his life, he gave me the present of a slave that had been brought to him from the Illinois, two or three months before."[51] Undoubtedly Father Marquette spent many a long winter evening questioning the Illinois youth and slowly, painfully gaining some skill in the boy's native tongue.[52] It was vital to Marquette to learn everything possible about the language and geography of the Illinois country because, even as he was sent to Saint-Esprit in the fall of 1669, his superior informed him that ". . . in the autumn of 1670 I shall go to start the mission among the Illinois in pursuance of Father Superior's orders."[53] From his young Illinois companion Jacques Marquette drew a storehouse of information about the people and the geography of that region. What matter that much of it might prove incorrect; at least what the young missionary heard was something to start with. The Illinois, the boy declared, isolated themselves in a country thirty days journey by land from Saint-Esprit. Enroute there, one encountered the Ketchegamin, a village of twenty cabins, and then the Miami. After that it was necessary to cross a vast prairie, at the end of which the Illinois

[50] *Ibid.*, 183.

[51] *Ibid.*, 177.

[52] *Ibid.*, 187. Marquette says: "With this purpose in view, the Ottawa gave me a young man who had lately come from the Illinois, and he furnished me the rudiments of the language, during the leisure allowed me by the savages of La Pointe in the course of the winter."

[53] *Ibid.*, 185.

would be found inhabiting two great villages containing eight or nine thousand souls. From what his informant attested Marquette believed that the Illinois were a surprisingly moral people, well disposed to accepting Christianity. Fortunately, too, the Illinois lived in a country having a mild climate abounding in game. The people raised corn and vegetables, especially squashes, as large as those of France. Besides there were fruits and berries of various kinds all growing wild. If the missionary went there, the youth declared, the Illinois would believe that his very presence would establish peace everywhere in that great land.[54] How could a zealous young missionary not expand with joy, knowing already that, by his superior's order, he was to be the proto-apostle of the Illinois in the fall of 1670?

The young Jesuit spent long hours closely questioning his Illinois youth about the geography of that country. Marquette learned that when the Illinois came to Chequamegon Bay, as some did to trade, they crossed a great river flowing from north to south. Since the Illinois "did not know what a canoe is," they had not yet heard mention of the river's mouth.[55] "They simply know that there are some very large nations lower down than themselves, some of whom, towards the east-southeast of their country, raise two crops of Indian corn a year."[56] The young Illinois further intrigued the Blackrobe by telling him that during the previous summer (1669), some Shawnee came to the Illinois wearing glass beads. These visiting Indians made an overland journey of nearly thirty days before reaching the Illinois. Reflecting on his newly acquired knowledge, Marquette strove to come to some positive conclusions. "It is hard to believe," he wrote, "that the great river discharges its waters in Virginia, and we think rather that it has its mouth in California."[57] One can sense the suppressed excitement in the young missionary's conclusions: "If the savages who promise to make me a canoe do not break their word to me, we shall explore this river as far as we can, with a Frenchman and this young man who was given me,

[54] *Ibid.*, 187, 189.
[55] *Ibid.*, 189.
[56] *Ibid.*
[57] *Ibid.*

who knows some of those languages and has a facility for learning the others. We shall visit the nations dwelling there, in order to open the passage to such of our Fathers as have been awaiting this good fortune for so long a time. This discovery will give us full knowledge either of the South Sea or of the Western Sea."[58]

Often in the late winter and early spring Jacques Marquette gazed out across the frozen expanse of Chequamegon Bay, willing with all his might that the ice would break up and the snow melt so that he might have the sight of an Illinois contingent trudging into the mission, prepared to take him back with them. But cold held the land in a vice-like grip. Today it was warm and the children ran in and out of his quarters, playing their tantalizing game, "Guess what I am thinking about."[59] If you guessed correctly you had to give the child whatever he asked. The next day wild north wind roared up the bay, so bitterly cold and laden with cutting sleet that everyone stayed close indoors. Finally, the cold relented. The men put the bark canoes back into open water, soaking them after the long winter of drying out, patching seams, and replacing broken struts. Women aired the cabins, prepared the seed corn for planting, and were driven to distraction in their efforts to induce the children to dress warmly in the deceptively bright, but chilly, sunshine. On Easter Sunday, Father Marquette stood before his Kiskakon and preached to them on the joys of heaven, looking fondly at his little flock, his heart rejoicing. The Kiskakon were now nearly all Christians. In the council meetings of the three Ottawa bands, even the most dissolute Sinagaux realized that the Kiskakon were the leaders of the whole Ottawa population at Saint-Esprit. Perhaps the other Ottawa bands did not understand what it was that caused the transformation among the Kiskakon, but it was clear that these faithful followers of the Blackrobe had established a favored relationship with the French. And that, in itself, was extremely useful for the whole Ottawa population, especially lately when imprudent young Ottawa braves, by their feckless raiding, had irritated the Sioux until it was highly possible that

[58] *Ibid.*, 189, 191.
[59] *Ibid.*, 175.

those powerful western tribesmen would rise in their wrath and drive the Ottawa from Chequamegon Bay, slaughtering numbers of the people in the process.

When the Easter celebration, with its attendant lengthy oratory, ended it was time for the Kiskakon, and all the Ottawa and Hurons as well, to leave their villages for the spring hunt. With saddened hearts the Kiskakon gathered to bid farewell to Marquette who had become father, mother, and brother to them. When they returned to harvest their corn and settle down in their village again, their missionary, both he and they fully expected, would be far away in the Illinois country. Solemnly and sonorously, the chief of the Kiskakon promised their Blackrobe that during the hunt and ever afterwards he and his people would remember their prayers and everything that they had been taught so that they would all serve the true Great Spirit faithfully. Since they could not hope to have Marquette with them in the fall, they pleaded, "earnestly begging me to have one of our Fathers go and join them in the autumn, when they should have reassembled. Their request was granted, and if it please God to send some Father to us, he will take my place, while I go to start the mission among the Illinois . . ."[60]

In all of the Indian villages at Chequamegon Bay, the few weeks before Easter had been charged with suppressed anticipation of changes about to occur. In each Ottawa band, and among the Hurons as well, the chiefs and the elders conferred lengthily, deciding which of the braves would accompany the women and children on the summer hunt and which of them would man the canoes carrying the winter's catch of peltries to Sault-Sainte-Marie, or perhaps even to Montreal, to exchange the furs for axes, knives, guns, ammunition, cooking pots, needles, blankets, and simple medicinal remedies, all things the Indians could not, or any longer need not, make themselves. Those going for the trading must not forget a few yards of bright cloth and some ribbons for the women as well as little mirrors, jew's harps, and other small trinkets for the children. And maybe a little *eau-de-vie,* perhaps? Just a jug or

[60] *Ibid.,* 185.

two for medicinal purposes of course! At last, when it was all decided, the women dismantled the cabins, rolling the bark coverings into cumbersome bundles while the braves bound for trading loaded the canoes with the bales of peltries. Then one bright morning after grunted farewells, the chiefs and the braves pushed off on the five hundred mile trip to the Sault. Father Marquette, with his cassock tucked up around his waist and his shoes slung around his neck, waded out to a Kiskakon canoe and, carefully washing the sand from his bare feet, eased his lithe body into the balky little craft, grasped a paddle with practised skill, and set off with the Ottawa-Huron trading flotilla for Sainte-Marie-du-Sault, fully expecting never again to set eyes on Chequamegon Bay and the mission of Saint-Esprit.

During the warm spring weather of April 1670, the voyage back to the Sault took on the aspect of a pleasant vacation. Now Father Marquette, surrounded by friends, had the leisure to enjoy and admire the rugged grandeur of Lake Superior's shore as it unfolded before him day by day. Dark, brooding pine forests, crowding down to the very shoreline, sighed soulfully, hinting at solemn secrets hidden within them. Massive piles of giant rocks gleamed with the colors of the rainbow. Graceful gulls wheeled above gentle waves rolling off the majestic inland sea. At last the party, rounding Whitefish Point, coasted down Whitefish Bay past Naomikong Point and began to feel the increasing strength of the current pulling them into the Saint Mary's River. Every paddler in the flotilla, balancing himself more alertly, struggled to keep the canoes with their valuable cargo of furs upright and dry while they jubilantly rode the racing river to the small mission dock just below the turbulent rapids. Tired, happy, not a little wet from splashing ashore in his bare feet, Jacques Marquette leaped nimbly onto the dock into the delighted amplexus of his superior, Claude Dablon, and his devoted friend, Brother Louis Boëme.[61]

In the days immediately following his return to the Sault, Father Marquette reported orally to Father Dablon and composed,

[61] The probable date of Marquette's arrival at Sault-Sainte-Marie in the spring of 1670 was May 8.

it is supposed, the written account of his winter's activity which was published in the *Relation* of 1669-1670.[62] Yet that account did not give the whole story; a very important phase of it was barely touched upon. With profound concern Marquette informed Father Dablon that there was increasing emnity between the Sioux and their guests, the Ottawa and Huron. Marauding young bucks on both sides were getting out of hand. Despite a peace pact arranged between the Ottawa and the Sioux at a solemn calumet ceremony, a few ambushes had already resulted in bloodshed.[63] It was Marquette's opinion that very likely before long the Christian Hurons and the Ottawa would be expelled by the Sioux. The Sinagaux Ottawa were not naturally belligerent and the Hurons were so few in number that they would probably strive to avoid serious trouble. But braves of the other Ottawa bands were so recklessly imprudent that they could easily precipitate an incident involving a Sioux attack. It seemed prudent to suggest that Father Dablon give some thought to the probability that the mission of Saint-Esprit would not survive. And, if that came to pass, the Christian Hurons and Ottawa would certainly look to the missionaries for help in finding a new location for their villages. Certain that Marquette's assessment of conditions at Saint-Esprit was realistic, Dablon determined to scout the area near the Sault during the coming summer in search of a suitable new home for the Huron and Ottawa neophytes. But throughout the summer Dablon, and everyone else at the mission of Sainte-Marie, was so occupied with other matters that it was well on towards the winter of 1670 before any practical steps were taken in the matter.

During the summer season of 1670 the mission at the Sault was crowded with visitors. On May 25, 1670, Pentecost Sunday, two Sulpician priests, René de Bréhant de Galinée and François Dollier

[62] *Ibid.*, 164-95.

[63] Nicolas Perrot, *Mémoire sur les moeurs, coustumes et religion des sauvages de l'Amérique Septentrionale*, 99.

de Casson, reached Sainte-Marie-du-Sault.[64] They had left Montreal on June 6, 1669, in the company of Robert Cavelier, Sieur de La Salle, who was authorized by Governor Courcelle to search for a great river called the Ohio by the Iroquois which, according to the Indians, emptied into a sea.[65] The Sulpicians hoped to establish a mission somewhere in the southwest, an area about which the abbé Dollier de Casson had learned from an Indian of that land, a slave of a Nipissing chief with whom the Sulpician had spent the winter of 1668-1669.[66] The party moved up the Saint Lawrence into Lake Ontario at whose western end they met Adrien Jolliet.[67] This elder brother of Louis Jolliet had been sent out by the intendant, Jean Talon, in June 1670, to investigate the feasibility of transporting copper from the mine which Father Allouez discovered in 1667.[68] After locating the mine Adrien Jolliet found some Iroquois prisoners among the Ottawa. From one of the Iroquois, whom Jolliet was bringing back to Quebec with him, he learned of the easier water route to the west by way of Lake Erie, the Detroit River, Lake Saint Clair, the Saint Clair River, and Lake Huron.[69] When the Sulpicians determined to follow that route, La Salle abandoned them on September 30, because ". . . he could not make up his mind

[64] René François de Bréhant de Galinée was born in France in about 1645. He entered the Sulpician congregation in 1661 and came to New France in the autumn of 1668 while still a deacon. The year after his journey to Sault-Sainte-Marie, 1671, he returned to France and died in 1678 while on a journey to Rome. It is not known for certain whether he was ever ordained a priest. See Louis Le Jeune, *Dictionnaire général . . . du Canada*, I, 682-84. François Dollier de Casson was born in France in 1636. He became a captain in the cavalry under Turenne, but resigned his commission to study for the priesthood. He joined the Sulpicians and came to Canada in 1666, having already been ordained. After a noteworthy career, he died at Montreal on September 27, 1701. See *ibid.*, 518-20.

[65] René François de Bréhant de Galinée, "Narrative of the Most Noteworthy Incidents in the Journey of Messieurs Dollier and Galinée," in Kellogg, *Early Narratives*, 168.

[66] *Ibid.*, 167.

[67] Jean Delanglez, *Life and Voyages of Louis Jolliet (1645-1700)*, 7-11. Delanglez demonstrates conclusively that the Jolliet whom the two Sulpicians encountered could not have been Louis and must have been Adrien.

[68] *Relations*, L, 265, 267.

[69] Delanglez, *Life of Jolliet*, 8.

to winter in the woods . . ."[70] The Sulpicians spent the winter, fortunately a very mild one, near the present Port Dover, Ontario. On March 23, 1670, Passion Sunday, they resumed their westward journey and reached Sault-Sainte-Marie, on May 25, where they were received by Dablon and Marquette ". . . with all possible charity."[71] Profoundly ignorant of the problems involved in converting an aboriginal people to Christianity, Galinée declared: "I saw no particular sign of Christianity among the Indians of this place, nor in any other country of the Ottawas . . ."[72] This pious cleric's judgment was based on a visit of three days at a mission established not quite two years.[73] After their winter's experience and their brief stay at Sainte-Marie, the Sulpicians gave up their proposal to open a mission and returned to Montreal.

While the Sulpicians were at Sault-Sainte-Marie the place was alive with Indians gathered there to assemble fur flotillas for the trading voyage to Montreal. Nicolas Perrot and a contingent of Frenchmen who had wintered at the new mission of Saint-François-Xavier at Green Bay came in and prepared to go back to Montreal with the Indians, who, all together, numbered nine hundred.[74] Many of these Ottawa and Hurons were so determined to attack the Sioux that at Montreal they traded their whole fur catch for guns and ammunition, vowing that when they reached home they would wipe out their enemy. Nothing which either the missionaries or prudent and experienced traders such as Perrot said could convince these impetuous braves that they could not possibly defeat the Sioux who far outnumbered them.

[70] Galinée, "Narrative," 194.

[71] *Ibid.*, 206.

[72] *Ibid.*, 207.

[73] *Ibid.*, 206. Galinée remarked, at this point in his journal, that Father Marquette never ". . . ventured to say Mass . . ." before the Indians at Chequamegon Bay. The passage, which has frequently been misinterpreted, is probably accurate. It does not mean that Marquette did not say Mass throughout his stay at Chequamegon Bay, but that he did so in private. To the Indians the celebration of Mass would have been a rite which they could not understand. Dollier de Casson acted in like manner. See *ibid.*, 194.

[74] Perrot, *Mémoire*, 119.

The two Sulpicians had only just left Sault-Sainte-Marie when Father Claude Allouez, accompanied by a single Frenchman, reached headquarters after his winter at Green Bay. Allouez left Sainte-Marie on November 3, 1669, with two canoe loads of Potawatomi who came to the mission on the Saint Mary's River begging Allouez to come to their village, ". . . not that they wished to receive instructions there, having no disposition for the Faith, but that I might curb some young Frenchmen, who, being among them for the purpose of trading, were threatening and maltreating them."[75] After a hazardous voyage lasting a month Allouez reached Green Bay on December 2. The next day, the feast of Saint Francis Xavier, the Jesuit said Mass and dedicated the new mission which he began to the great apostle of the Indies.[76] After wintering with the Potawatomi and the Sauks, when spring came Allouez set out to contact the Indians of the interior. On April 20, 1670, a Sunday, the missionary said Mass on the shore of Lake Winnebago.[77] Advancing further, on April 30 Allouez met some Mascouten and Maumee who lived on the upper Fox River. "These people," Allouez wrote, "are settled in a very attractive place where beautiful plains and fields meet the eye as far as one can see. Their river leads by a six days' voyage to a great river named Messi-Sipi, and it is along the former river that the other populous nations are situated. Four leagues from here are the Kickapoo and the Kischigamin, who speak the same language as the Mascouten."[78] After spending nearly two weeks with these friendly aborigines, Allouez returned to Green Bay which he left on May 20 ". . . to go to Sainte-Marie-du-Sault whither obedience called me . . ."[79]

Completing his lengthy account of the winter's work Father Allouez turned to young Marquette, asking for news from Saint-Esprit. Did the Kiskakon live up to his expectations? Had the Hurons seriously returned to the practice of their religion? Did Father Marquette have any success with the other Ottawa bands?

[75] *Relations*, LIV, 197.
[76] *Ibid.*, 205.
[77] *Ibid.*, 217.
[78] *Ibid.*, 231, 233.
[79] *Ibid.*, 241.

Well, no. The Ottawa, except the Kiskakon, were no nearer Christianity than they had been when Father Allouez left them. But the Hurons were coming around and the Kiskakon would delight Allouez's heart. One incident would prove that to him, the fidelity of Marie Movena. "From last spring up to the present she has resisted her relatives: despite all the efforts they have made to compel her to marry her stepbrother, she has never consented to do it. Her brother has often struck her, and her mother has frequently refused her anything to eat, — sometimes reaching such a pitch of anger that she would take a firebrand and burn her daughter's arms with it. This poor girl told me about all this bad treatment; but her courage could never be shaken, and she willingly made an offering of all her sufferings to God."[80]

Listening to Father Allouez's account of his winter's apostolate, Marquette was delighted to learn about the Indians of the interior. It was helpful to know that the Winnebago were in contact with the Illinois, even though the inter-tribal relationship was, at the moment, an unfriendly one.[81] From the geographic information brought back by Allouez it seemed possible that Marquette could reach the Illinois country by water, avoiding long overland journeys which his Illinois friend had described to him during their many conversations at Saint-Esprit. All that he learned from Allouez made the projected Illinois mission seem within Marquette's grasp. But the project depended on many contingencies. If Father Le Mercier at Quebec could send Sainte-Marie more missionaries, perhaps one of those would replace Marquette at Saint-Esprit. If, however, trouble broke out between the Ottawa and the Sioux, an expedition to the Illinois could not safely be dispatched since the party would, quite probably, be turned back by the Sioux. In midsummer one contingency was happily eliminated when a flotilla of Indians, returning from their trading at Montreal, brought with them two missionary recruits, Fathers Gabriel Druillettes and Louis André. Come September 29, Father Druillettes, the grand old elder among the Jesuits in New France, would be an even sixty

[80] *Ibid.,* 239.
[81] *Ibid.,* 237.

years old with twenty-seven years of mission experience to his credit. Louis André, an impetuous little man, was six years older than Jacques Marquette and a Jesuit four years longer. But since André had been in New France only since June 7, 1669, he had much to learn about Indians, though he spoke Algonquin quite well.[82] Father Druillettes could assume responsibility for Sainte-Marie-du-Sault, freeing Father Dablon, the superior, for making a tour of the outlying missions while he searched for a possible site on which to locate the Huron and Ottawa Christians, if that move proved needful. And, Father Marquette could go to the Illinois.

All of these arrangements were hardly thoroughly discussed before the whole plan fell apart. Father Druillettes barely began his apostolate among the Indians at Sault-Sainte-Marie when a grievous disease afflicted the people. Fortunately the disaster ". . . instead of checking the course of the gospel, . . . on the contrary, brought it into greater repute by many wonderful cures."[83] As if that disaster was not enough, suddenly large numbers of Ottawa began streaming into the Sault from Chequamegon Bay, fleeing from the impending wrath of the Sioux whom the Ottawa refugees insisted were about to attack all of the Algonquin tribes south and west of the mission of Sainte-Marie-du-Sault. The Ottawa barely paused in their flight to tell their story to the Jesuits before they hastened onward to their ancient home, Manitoulin Island, east of Sault-Sainte-Marie and off the northern shore of Georgian Bay. Inexperienced though he was, Father André was directed to follow the fugitives and minister to them.[84] Naturally impulsive, André tried to be everywhere at once. He composed Christian hymns in the Ottawa tongue, harried the Indians into building him a chapel, and became somewhat impatient with them when they did not accept Christianity immediately. By the following spring, 1671,

[82] *Ibid.*, 241; LVII, 318. Louis André was born at Saint-Rémy, Bouches-du-Rhône, on May 28, 1631, and entered the Jesuit novitiate at Lyons on September 12, 1650. After his ordination, he came to Canada in June 1669. He labored with the Ottawa until 1684. He died at Quebec on September 19, 1715.

[83] *Ibid.*, LV, 117.

[84] *Ibid.*, 133. André left the Sault on August 28, 1670.

Louis André came back to Sault-Sainte-Marie a much wiser, if far more gaunt, missionary.[85]

If hostilities in the neighborhood of the mission of Saint-Esprit were inevitable, obviously Father Marquette could not be spared to begin the new mission to the Illinois in the fall of 1670. His presence at Saint-Esprit would be essential to the Christians there. None of the Jesuits any longer doubted that the rashness of the Huron and Ottawa braves in their dealings with the Sioux would necessitate transplanting at least the Christians living at Saint-Esprit to some area nearer Sainte-Marie-du-Sault both to save their very lives as well as to prevent them from lapsing into paganism. Because of their confidence in Father Marquette, he was the obvious missionary to return to Saint-Esprit and convince the Christians to migrate. Just as the Jesuits could not abandon the Christians of Huronia after the Iroquois had driven them out of their homeland in 1650, neither could these latterday Christians be left without aid in their distress. The dream of opening the new mission among the Illinois, as well as the search for the location of the great river, simply had to be abandoned at least for the moment. There was nothing for it but to wait until the Huron-Ottawa trading flotilla returned from Montreal. Then Marquette would find a place in one of the canoes going home to Chequamegon Bay for another winter there. This time his major task would be to induce the Christians to abandon their homes in favor of a site near Sault-Sainte-Marie. Father Dablon promised young Father Marquette that as soon as he had visited the new missions opened by Father Allouez, he would seek out a new home for the Christians at Saint-Esprit and prepare it for their coming.

[85] *Ibid.*, 133-55, contain André's account of his work with the Ottawa on Manitoulin Island.

THE MISSION OF SAINT IGNACE

1671-1673

The few weeks of enforced absence from the mission of Saint-Esprit during the summer of 1670 were a great boon to Jacques Marquette. It was comforting to be with his own in a religious community again, even if it was only a small one. During the day the young missionary was busy helping Father Dablon and old Father Druillettes with their pastoral work among the Chippewa, permanent residents at the Sault, and with the crowds of visiting nations who came there to trade. But at night, when the high gate of the palisaded mission compound was closed against the Indians, Marquette could sit quietly with his brethren discussing the problems of his mission with them. Dablon, a prudent superior whom Marquette trusted implicitly, was a good listener and Druillettes, the young priest's first mentor in New France, could draw on his long experience to offer advice. The most precious period of those weeks was the eight days of complete solitude devoted to making his annual retreat.[1] Undisturbed by the constant noise and confusion of an Indian village, Marquette celebrated Mass daily in the peaceful, inspiring chapel at Sainte-Marie. Once again, as he had done annually for the past sixteen years, he meditated prayerfully on the profound truths proposed by Saint Ignatius in his *Spiritual Exercises.* Perhaps Father Marquette made this retreat with a greater fervor than many another, knowing full well that the coming winter would be a most difficult one. If the hot-headed young Huron and Ottawa braves incited the Sioux to attack, it was not at all unlikely that the young missionary, whose overtures the Sioux had already spurned, might fall victim to a hatchet wielded by a Sioux warrior. Was Jacques ready to go back to Chequamegon Bay with that gruesome prospect facing him? If our Lord required the ultimate sacrifice from him was he sincerely willing to follow his Master that far, to the last gasp of love and loyalty? Was it during those days of prayerful solitude that he wrote his little treatise on "the directing care of God over a missionary," a manuscript found among his papers after his death, ". . . in which he shows the excellence of that vocation, the advantages which it affords for self-sanctification, and the care that God takes of the Gospel laborers. One sees in this little abstract the spirit of God which possessed him."[2] Perhaps, also, it was during that retreat that Marquette bound himself by vow ". . . never to leave these arduous but lovable missions except when holy obedience should withdraw him

[1] A spiritual retreat may be described as a period of solitude in which the exercitant devotes himself entirely to prayer and meditation while he is completely free from any other occupation. The obligation for every Jesuit to make an annual retreat of eight or ten days was imposed in 1608, fifty-two years after the death of Saint Ignatius. See Joseph de Guibert, *The Jesuits: Their Spiritual Doctrine and Practice,* 237. The regularity with which the Jesuits in New France fulfilled this obligation, even under very trying circumstances, is evident from the frequency with which it is reported in the *Relations.* Missionaries usually came back from their distant missions to Quebec, or a more stable residence such as Three Rivers or Sainte-Marie-du-Sault to fulfill this obligation, which, obviously, could hardly be performed in an Indian village.

[2] *Relations,* LIX, 211.

from them."[3] Certainly he must have said to our Lord what he wrote a few years later: "I dread nothing – neither the Sioux, nor the reception awaiting me among the nations, dismay me. One of two things will happen: either God will punish me for my crimes and cowardice, or else he will give me a share in his cross which I have not yet carried since my arrival in this country. But this cross has been perhaps obtained for me by the Blessed Virgin Immaculate, or it may be death itself, that I may cease to offend God. It is that for which I try to hold myself in readiness, surrendering myself altogether into his hands."[4]

Towards the middle of August when the trading flotilla returned to the Sault from Montreal, Jacques Marquette was eager to be off, ready to face whatever might happen at Saint-Esprit. On the first evening, with Sainte-Marie-du-Sault a day's paddling behind them, the Hurons and Ottawa gathered around the campfire ready to recount to their Blackrobe what had occurred at Montreal. Nicolas Perrot had proved himself a true friend. At first the trading with the French merchants had gone well. One day, however, a prankish Ottawa had filched some tobacco from a French soldier. That was a foolish thing to do, especially since the Ottawa had ample pelts with which to buy whatever they wanted. But the soldier was a lazy lout and the Ottawa brave thought it would be a good joke to steal from him. But the Frenchman set up a clamor, which brought a swarm of soldiers to his aid. When one of the sentinels, sent to protect the Indians, pointed out the thief, a scuffle ensued which might have led to bloodshed had Nicolas Perrot not rushed up and, with the aid of a few level-headed Ottawa chiefs, put a stop to the fracas. Captain Pierre du Saint Paul, Sieur de la Mothe, commandant at Montreal in the absence of Paul de Chomedey, Sieur de Maisonnevue, called out the troops to quell the riot, but found on arriving at the scene that Perrot and the Ottawa chiefs had already restored order. Nevertheless, the captain arrested the chiefs whom he took to his quarters to examine into the affair.

[3] *Ibid.*, LX, 223. Father Henry Nouvel, Marquette's last superior, reported this after Marquette's death. Marquette revealed the fact to Nouvel in the last letter which he wrote. The vow probably was of long standing.

[4] *Ibid.*, LIX, 211.

There a deceitful Frenchman, who acted as interpreter for the captain, sought to gain the good graces of the Ottawa by falsely accusing the soldier of instigating the trouble, though the Indian chiefs told the simple truth. Abruptly, de la Mothe ordered the soldier punished by placing him on the *chevalet.* Only Perrot's presence of mind and the honesty of the Ottawa chiefs saved the soldier from painful hours of suffering.[5]

The incident badly disillusioned the Hurons and Ottawa who witnessed it. If the great chief of the French at Montreal could be so easily misled by a lying countryman, would he not be as easily deceived by enemies of the Huron and Ottawa? Perhaps it was unwise to maintain an alliance with the French. The one isolated incident at Montreal, in itself, did not mean a great deal if it were not for the conduct of the French who came out to trade at Chequamegon Bay and Green Bay. These men were always deceitful and dishonest. Look how they treated the Potawatomie who induced Father Allouez to come to Green Bay because the French traders there were treating the Indians so abominably. And the Potawatomie were not even Christians![6] What if the French flooded into the whole West? Were they any less a threat to the Hurons and Ottawa than the Sioux? The great friend of the Hurons and Ottawa, Nicolas Perrot, protected them at Montreal, but he could not be everywhere nor would he long be with them for he was mortal, like every other man. Previous to the incident at Montreal some were rather inclined to disparage talk of war with the Sioux. But now many were not so sure that attacking the Sioux might not be the wisest policy, provided the Potawatomie and a few other neighboring Algonquin tribes could be induced to join in the war. This was why, as the Blackrobe perceived, much of the cargo was composed of guns and ammunition rather than of pots and bolts of

[5] Perrot, *Mémoire,* 122-25. Perrot does not say what the Indian took, but it was probably something of no great value such as a twist of tobacco. Punishment by *chevalet* consisted of tying the culprit on a framework like a tall sawhorse. The victim's own weight would cause him to be painfully bruised. Also, the victim was obliged to maintain his balance on his precarious perch.

[6] *Relations,* LIV, 197. Allouez specifically says that the Potawatomie asked him to come to them, ". . . not that they wished to receive instructions there, having no disposition for the Faith . . ."

cloth which the Indians usually brought back with them. And what did the Blackrobe have to say to all of this? Was their logic not reasonable? Was it not better to form an alliance and beat back the Sioux than to be driven away from Chequamegon Bay into the clutches of the scheming French?

Seated cross-legged on the ground among these seriously worried natives, watching the red glow of the fire reflected on their swarthy, earnest faces, Father Marquette well knew that this was, indeed, the moment of truth for him. High-flown eloquence had no place here. The young Blackrobe must reason with these braves, his friends of a year's standing. They were justified, he told them, in disdaining the Frenchman who spoke with a forked tongue, deliberately mistranslating the honest admission of the chiefs. But the Frenchman, who had no understanding of the true character of the Ottawa and the Hurons, was equally disdained by the French, and for the same reason. Look at Nicolas Perrot, who boldly defended them, obliging the great captain of the French to rectify an injustice, even though that official lost face in the process. It was true, unfortunately, that many Frenchmen who came to their villages deceived the Indians and caused trouble by their quarrelsome and vicious habits. But had not their father, Allouez, traveled many days to Green Bay just to force the French there to cease their bad practices? And had he not succeeded? Had they not often seen Marquette himself chide the French at Chequamegon Bay for their deceit in trading and their unchaste glances at the young squaws? Every tribe, everywhere, had among it grown-up children who were not a credit to the group. Marquette could easily name a few such among the Ottawa and Huron themselves, as everyone present knew. The impending trouble with the Sioux was, after all, the result of imprudent activity indulged in by a handful of such persons, foolishly daring young braves whose elders should have controlled them better. Even if the Hurons and Ottawa did succeed in arranging an alliance, would they be able to muster enough braves to invade the vast, often swampy, Sioux country with success? Everyone knew that the Sioux far outnumbered the Hurons and Ottawa. The Sioux, a peaceful people, harbored the Ottawa and Hurons when they had been forced to flee from the fury of the

Iroquois. Did that generosity merit no gratitude? If worst came to worst, however, it was better for the Indians at Chequamegon Bay to migrate eastward rather than precipitate a war which the Hurons and Ottawa could not possibly win. The captain of the Blackrobes, Marquette assured them, was even now searching out a new and prosperous home for them. Father Dablon would have the place ready by spring, if it was needed. As for the French exploiting the Indians if they moved eastward, the Blackrobes would always be present to defend them, even as Allouez had done at Green Bay. Some of those present knew that bands of the Ottawa had already left Chequamegon Bay during the late spring and early summer. They were now settled on their ancient island home of Manitoulin and a Blackrobe, Louis André, was there sharing their hardships, protecting them from exploiting Frenchmen, and helping the migrants to know the way to heaven. If the others at Saint-Esprit moved, Marquette and other Blackrobes would follow them. The Hurons and Ottawa now knew the true Great Spirit and how to serve him. He would be justly angry if they attacked the Sioux. From that evening forward Father Marquette launched a campaign, striving to persuade the Indians to avoid war. With every stroke of the paddle over the long, long miles of water to Chequamegon Bay, the young Blackrobe prayed for the gift of wisdom and the power of persuasion so that he might divert the calamity of bloody conflict and induce the Huron and Ottawa Christians to leave the Sioux country for the physical as well as spiritual safety of a new, attractive home which Father Dablon would surely find for them before the coming spring.[7]

His homecoming to the mission of Saint-Esprit, in the early fall of 1670, was anything but a joyful occasion for Père Jacques. So much had changed since he bade farewell to his neophytes in the spring, only a few months ago. The whole atmosphere of the Indian villages was now shot through with apprehension and unrest. Many Ottawa family groups had already left for Manitoulin Island. The Sinagaux who lingered on constantly encouraged the other Ottawa to discard their Christian teachings and show their loyalty to the

[7] Marquette's action reported here has no documentary basis.

clan by joining in preparations for a war against the Sioux. To Marquette it seemed that the Hurons had taken leave of their senses. This foolish, boastful remnant of the once-proud Huron nation openly bragged that they alone would attack the Sioux if no one else was willing to aid them. Nothing Marquette said to the Hurons seemed to have any effect on them. Feckless young bucks brashly roved in the neighborhood of Sioux villages taunting the inhabitants, daring them to attack. Now and then there was a skirmish in which both Sioux and Huron lost warriors. Finally, in a kind of frenzied madness, the Hurons basely stooped to degrading treachery in order to precipitate the war.

Five years previously, in 1665, a group of Hurons while out hunting captured some Sioux whom they brought triumphantly back to Chequamegon Bay, fully determined to torture them to death. But the Ottawa intervened and Sinagos, an Ottawa chief, accompanied by some of his braves and a few Frenchmen, escorted the Sioux captives safely back to their village. Appreciative of this courtesy, the Sioux "sang the calumet" for Sinagos, thereby making him an honored son of the whole Sioux nation and conferring on him perpetual immunity from harm.[8] At the ceremony all of the Sioux chiefs gave their solemn consent to an inviolable peace between themselves and the Ottawa. Now, in 1670 a group of Hurons, skulking about deep in the Sioux hunting ground, were captured by some young Sioux braves and brought to the village of the chief who had sung the calumet for Sinagos. Presuming the captives to be Ottawa, the chief was incensed at this apparent breach of a sacred pledge. Promptly placing the captives under his personal protection, the Sioux chief sent one of the Hurons home to assure his tribesmen that the captives were safe, treated courteously, and would be returned promptly. The messenger, either of his own accord or at the instigation of others, deceitfully reported that he had barely escaped with his life and did not know whether the Sioux had killed the other captives. The Sioux chief, unaware of the treachery, dutifully escorted the Hurons back to Chequamegon

[8] In her translation of Perrot's *Mémoire*, Emma H. Blair includes the music for the calumet song. See Blair, *Indian Tribes*, I, facing 182.

Bay, taking along a band of his own braves to insure the safety of the Hurons. On his arrival the Hurons bribed the Ottawa, including Sinagos, to kill the Sioux chief and his warriors.[9] The dastardly deed was hardly done when the Hurons were the first to realize its implications. The only hope lay in flight for once the Sioux learned the fate of their chief and his braves, they would certainly wreck a terrible vengeance on both the Hurons and the Ottawa. Now the Indians at Chequamegon Bay were only too willing to listen to their Blackrobe. They begged him to inform Father Dablon that they would migrate eastward the moment they were able to travel in the coming spring.

Father Claude Dablon, faithful to his promise given Jacques Marquette, successfully sought a new, satisfactory home for the beleagured Christians of Chequamegon Bay, after he spent some time visiting Father Claude Allouez's mission territory. Leaving Sainte-Marie-du-Sault on September 6, 1670, Dablon and Allouez went to the mission of Saint-François-Xavier at Green Bay, which they reached ". . . after a voyage of more than a hundred leagues, which we made by canoe without mishap . . ."[10] Arriving at Green Bay, the missionaries found ". . . matters there in a rather bad state, and the savages highly incensed against the French who were trading with them; they were maltreating the latter in deed and word, pillaging and robbing them of their goods, in spite of their resistance, and subjecting them to unbearable insolence and indignity."[11] After restoring order by sharply reprimanding the French, Allouez took his superior on a tour of the interior so that Dablon could meet the various tribes and assess the personnel needs of the mission. The two Jesuits paddled up the Lower Fox River, crossed Lake Winnebago and, entering the upper Fox, ascended it to the village of the "Fire Nation," or the Mascouten, probably near the present Berlin, Wisconsin.[12] Dablon's description of the country through which the upper Fox River flows could be used effectively

[9] Perrot, *Mémoire*, 101-02.

[10] *Relations*, LV, 185.

[11] *Ibid.*, 185-87.

[12] See Arthur E. Jones, "The Site of the Mascoutin," *Proceedings* of the State Historical Society of Wisconsin for 1906, 175-82.

today by the chambers of commerce of Winnebago and Green Lake Counties. The Mascouten showed their visitors every courtesy, treating them as ". . . extraordinary spirits; and so we availed ourselves of this advantage to instruct the people everywhere, and to seek out sick persons in all the cabins."[13] Some Illinois, whom the missionaries encountered at the Mascouten village, gave the visitors a great deal of valuable information about that country. The Illinois, the Blackrobes learned, dwelt in a beautiful region ". . . near the great river named Mississippi . . ." which flows southward ". . . until it empties into the sea – supposed by us to be either the Vermilion or the Florida Sea, as there is no knowledge of any large rivers in that direction except those which empty into these two seas."[14] Much taken with the Illinois, Dablon could not help thinking, perhaps, how delighted Father Marquette would be when he returned in the coming spring, this time, hopefully, really to go to the Illinois. But first Dablon must find a suitable new home for Marquette's frightened flock.

Paddling slowly homeward towards Sainte-Marie-du-Sault along the mainland above the turbulent Straits of Mackinac, Father Dablon noticed a cluster of quite large islands, some five miles off shore, reclining in Lake Huron like mammoth, sleepy sea monsters. Questioning his Indian companions about them, he learned that long ago these islands, and the mainland to the west of them, were the homelands of the Indians whom they had just left at Green Bay. Once, he was told, the great island with the high, rocky ridge dominating it, the one the Indians called Michilimackinac, had thirty villages on it. But the Iroquois came and murdered the people. Once the Ottawa had four villages on the mainland opposite the island. When the Hurons were first expelled from Huronia, many took refuge for a while on Mackinac Island which was an excellent site for an Indian settlement. The soil was supposed to produce good corn and the waters surrounding it were teeming with herring, carp, whitefish, sturgeon, and three or four varieties of trout. The trout were so big and fat that the Indians,

[13] *Relations*, LV, 205.
[14] *Ibid.*, 207.

who loved grease, had difficulty eating them. The fish were so abundant, in fact, that even in winter one man could catch forty or fifty of them with his javelin in no more than three hours' time. After the French forced the Iroquois to cease their raiding a few years ago some few Indian families had drifted back to Mackinac Island, attracted as much by the unending supply of fish as they were by the very island character of the place, a feature which made it easy to defend.[15]

As the Indians finished their tale, they noticed that Father Dablon sat lost in thought, his paddle trailing uselessly while he gazed across the water at Mackinac Island. Why wouldn't the place be a good refuge for Father Marquette's fleeing flock? Mackinac Island, ". . . situated exactly in the straits connecting the Lake of the Hurons and that of the Illinois, . . ." formed ". . . the key and door, so to speak, for all the peoples of the south, as . . . the Sault for those of the north . . ."[16] The island might not only furnish a good home for the Christians from Saint-Esprit, but it could also offer missionaries an opportunity for contacting passing tribesmen from the south. Of course, there were some inconveniences inherent in the fact that the place was an island. Winds booming through the Straits of Mackinac were often very powerful, whipping the waters into waves far too strong for the frail Indian canoes. Yet the island had many advantages well worth considering. The more he reflected on the matter the more Dablon felt that this was the providential place for Marquette's people. The most effective manner of determining whether his judgment be correct was for Dablon to winter on the island with the Indians already dwelling there. In the *Relation* of 1670-1671, Dablon explained: "To promote the execution of the plan announced to us by a number of savages, to settle this country anew, — some of them having already passed the winter here, hunting in the neighborhood, — we have also wintered here in order to form plans for the mission of Saint Ignace, whence it will be very easy to gain access to all the missions of Lake Huron when the nations shall have returned each to

[15] *Ibid.*, 157-61.
[16] *Ibid.*

its own district."[17] By the spring of 1671, before the Indians on the island had planted their corn, Claude Dablon was satisfied that he had found an ideal home for Jacques Marquette's refugees and one, as well, which would enable missionaries to spread the word of God to passing tribesmen.

Marquette's winter at Chequamegon Bay was unbelievably difficult. All of the Indians were restless and unsettled. The young braves and a few less prudent elders among the Hurons and Ottawa boastfully prepared for war, spending long weeks visiting the neighboring tribes whom they hoped to attract into an alliance against the Sioux. Some few argued that even if allies in numbers could be induced to join forces with the Huron and Ottawa braves, the whole area could not muster a force large enough and sufficiently well-armed to defeat the Sioux. In the end, these prophets of doom predicted, the war would be lost and the whole population at Chequamegon Bay would perish in a wholesale slaughter. In that atmosphere of unrest there were constant alarms of imagined surprised attacks, though most of these proved false. Through the whole of the winter and early spring Father Marquette patiently strove to induce everyone to follow him back eastward. And, bit by bit, he began to win grudging support. In the late winter, when rations were short and heavy snow kept most people indoors, a few of the Christian elders began to urge acceptance of Father Marquette's advice. They, in turn, influenced a few more until, when the first puff of spring breathed across the land, it was understood that most of the Christians would migrate eastward with their missionary. A large contingent of pagans, however, forced to make good their boast, determined to prosecute the war with the aid of what braves they could muster from neighboring tribes.

At last, when the ice went out of the Bay and spring flowers dotted the fields, it was time for those following their missionary to make final preparations. The women of the migrating contingent did no planting that spring. Instead, they carefully packed the seed corn in skin bags, wrapping them carefully to keep them dry. Household articles, pots, blankets, and the like, were piled on

[17] *Ibid.*, 161.

shore for stowing in the canoes. There was no point in carrying away the cumbersome rolls of bark coverings for the cabins since more of the same could be found at the new site. In his turn Father Marquette packed his precious Mass-kit, his few books, and his blankets for transfer to the canoe he would share. On their final morning at Saint-Esprit the departing Indians made their farewells, rounded up the straggling children and, in one final gesture of sorrow, set fire to their now abandoned cabins. Many an old Huron and Ottawa squaw, bent with rheumatism, sadly watched the fire consume the cabins. How many times had she watched a similar scene in the past twenty years! Chequamegon Bay had been home for a good ten years and it could continue to be if the foolish braves had any sense. But that was the way of men, always bragging, always restless, and it was ever the women who suffered from their rashness in the end.[18]

[18] Ascertaining the date of Marquette's departure from Chequamegon Bay, and the consequent abandonment of the mission of Saint-Esprit, cannot be determined from available documents. Perrot's *Mémoire* would lead one to believe that the event took place early enough in 1671 for Marquette to have witnessed the *prize possession* which occurred at Sainte-Marie-du-Sault on June 4, 1671. Perrot says that Marquette witnessed the event, but this is a mistake for Dablon does not include Marquette as one of the Jesuits present, as he certainly would have, since he included all the other Jesuits present. See Perrot, *Mémoire*, 128. Perrot also says that the Hurons and Ottawa fleeing from Saint-Esprit did not reach the Sault until after the ceremony. On their arrival, they ". . . consented to all that had been agreed and concluded." See *ibid.* A reading of Perrot's account of the Huron treachery, which apparently precipitated their flight, leads this writer to the opinion that the incident took place in the fall of 1670. If so, it is logical to argue that Marquette and his flock fled from Saint-Esprit the moment they could do so in the early spring of 1671. Since Marquette was not at the Sault on June 4, 1671, it may be reasonably presumed that he had already left there to escort the Indians to Mackinac Island. We know for certain that he was back at Sainte-Marie-du-Sault on July 2, and probably long enough before that date to have made a retreat of eight or ten days. This would mean that he had to be at the Sault at least by June 22. If he and the Huron refugees reached the Sault originally after June 4, there would hardly have been time for Marquette to go to Mackinac Island, settle the Indians, and return to the Sault by June 22. Also, the Indians would be anxious to move soon enough in the spring to allow them time to plant the corn so that they would have a crop in the fall. They would have been obliged to have finished the planting before late June, if they hoped to have a crop in the fall.

The canoe voyage back to Sainte-Marie-du-Sault in the spring of 1671 was not the pleasant, swift journey which Jacques Marquette had made the year before. This time the flotilla was unwieldy, hampered in movement by the presence of the women and children. Keeping the whole party reasonably joined together for mutual protection tried the patience of the older men. Equipment constantly got lost; some child was always falling out of a canoe; a pet dog couldn't be found when it was time to set out in the morning; one of the women always forgot a pot or a blanket. Day by day, however, the flotilla, like a giant inch worm, slowly drew closer to the Sault. Every evening the Blackrobe gathered the Indians for evening prayers and each day he tried to move up and down the line of canoes, settling disputes, encouraging the lazy, helping with the sick, and putting new heart into everyone. At long last the flotilla arrived at Sainte-Marie where it was expected, for news of its impending arrival had been sent on ahead by messenger. That evening great bonfires were lighted to warm the newcomers, and big black pots, filled with fish and coarse corn flour, bubbled over hot coals so that the weary travelers could eat their fill. In the morning Father Dablon, fresh from his winter on Mackinac Island, held council with the elders. The land chosen for them, he said, was very good. It was an island on which the oldest among them had once lived. They knew it as Michilimackinac. There they could plant their corn and watch it grow in peace. Great, fat fish splashed in the waters of the little coves around the island. Stands of birch with good bark for constructing houses and canoes, as well as fine willow trees furnishing struts for canoes and frames for cabins, were plentiful. Best of all, the island, as some knew, had a high, rocky ridge whereon they could build an almost impregnable fort for their protection in case of need. The few Indians now living there were friendly and quite willing to share their island home with the refugees. Father Marquette would go with them, and the Blackrobes, as well as all the French at Sault-Sainte-Marie, would help protect them. The Hurons, perhaps influenced by the oldest among them, agreed to go on the sixty miles southeast, fully determined to settle on Mackinac Island, which, surely the women hoped, would finally be a permanent home. Some of the older

Hurons grumbled, recalling that corn didn't prosper on that island, it never did and it never would. The Ottawa, however, formed other plans. Since reaching the Sault, perhaps, some of them had been talking to other Ottawa, recently come from Manitoulin Island. Ottawa from Chequamegon Bay fled there a whole year ago. After all, that island was the ancient home of the Ottawa. They would, therefore, go back to their original home and begin again with Father André. Once the decision was reached, there was no time to lose if cabins were to be erected and, especially, the corn planted in time for a harvest in the fall.

During his stay at Sainte-Marie-du-Sault, Jacques Marquette reported on his winter's activities to his superior. In the *Relation* of 1670-1671, Dablon recorded them thus: "And, as in transmigrations of this sort, people's minds are in no very settled condition, so Father Marquette, who had charge of that mission of Saint-Esprit, had more to suffer than to achieve for those people's conversion; for what with baptizing some children, comforting the sick, and continuing the instruction of those professing Christianity, he was unable to give much attention to converting others. He was obliged to leave that post with the rest, and to follow his flock, undergoing the same hardships and incurring the same dangers."[19]

Marquette must have brought up the previously proposed mission to the Illinois. Should he continue gathering information about the area, doing what he could to master the Illinois dialect? Or was the possibility of opening such a mission so remote that Marquette should forget about it? Quite the contrary! Dablon probably related to Marquette everything that he had learned from the Illinois. Piece by piece the route to the Illinois, and to the great river, was being unfolded. The journey to the river, it now seemed certain, could be made entirely by water. The great river actually did empty into a sea, though no one knew yet exactly which one. The Illinois seemed to be a friendly, docile folk, ripe for conversion. If they accepted the Faith, probably neighboring tribes would do likewise. Soon all the nations of the river's great valley would adore the true God. For the present, however, the missionaries

[19] *Relations*, LV, 171.

must patiently await the outcome of the threatened conflict between the Sioux and their eastern and southern neighbors. Marquette, Dablon quite possibly assured him, was the logical candidate for the Illinois mission when the time was ripe. For now, Marquette should settle the Huron at the new mission of Saint-Ignace. During the early summer the Sieur de Saint Lusson was coming to the Sault to claim the whole West for the crown and to inquire about its geography.[20] Dablon possibly hoped that the news of the great ceremony, to which all the tribes of the West were being invited, might, somehow, deter the Sioux and their enemies from an open conflict. But Marquette should not count on that; rather, let him go down to Mackinac Island and set to work. And, Father Dablon added somewhat enigmatically, he would see him there soon.

The Huron exiles accompanied by their missionary, Marquette, departed from Sainte-Marie-du-Sault for their new home on Mackinac Island probably in late April, 1671. Riding the swift current of the Saint Mary's River, they rapidly passed through Munuscong Lake and De Tour Passage into Lake Huron. Thence they slowly worked their way southwestward, hugging the shore for protection against rough waters until, at Morin Bay, they were opposite their destination. Then they dashed, as quickly as possible, across the five miles of open water separating Mackinac Island from the mainland. They found the mission Father Dablon had prepared for them on a stretch of quite level ground near the southern tip of the island. Behind the mission the land swooped abruptly upward to a high limestone outcropping from the top of which, on a clear day, one could see for miles out across Lake Huron. Father Dablon had chosen well, as the Huron elders agreed, after they had explored the island by land and water. Satisfied with the site, the women gathered willow branches and stripped bark from birch trees for the new cabins while the braves fished the waters off shore. When the cabins were completed, the fields were laid out and the precious seed corn planted. This year there would not be

[20] *Ibid.*, 105-15. Saint Lusson's primary concern was to investigate Allouez's report of copper mines in the area. Allouez's account of the mines may be read in *ibid.*, LI, 65.

a long summer hunt nor would the braves go to Montreal since there had been little time during the previous winter to lay in a store of peltries. Instead, the braves went off each day exploring the island and bringing back what small game they captured. Silver-haired old elders and ancient squaws, warming themselves in the sun, rambled on to the children, and anyone else who would listen, relating how when they were young the Hurons lived here, always fearful that the Iroquois would slaughter them. Now, with the Iroquois subdued by the French, a group of canoes spied out in the lake was not a cause for alarm. The occupants of the crafts were probably only Frenchmen bound for Sainte-Marie-du-Sault on some mysterious business of their own.

There was a great deal of going and coming past Mackinac Island during the early spring of 1671. When Jean Talon, New France's first and most able intendant, came back to Canada in August 1670, after an absence of two years, he carried instructions from the court to continue searching for iron, lead, copper, and tin mines, enjoining him to consider ". . . this work as most important for the prosperity of Canada."[21] On September 3, 1670, Talon appointed Simon François Daumont, Sieur de Saint-Lusson, leader of an expedition to the West with instructions to go as far westward as possible, looking for waterways leading to the ". . . Sea of the South which separates this continent from China; but only after he has given his first attention to the copper mine which is the main object of the expedition . . ."[22] To aid Saint-Lusson in the undertaking Talon procured the services of Nicolas Perrot, whom the western Indians greatly respected, to act as interpreter as well as to induce delegates from the tribes to meet with Saint-Lusson at Sault-Sainte-Marie in the early summer of 1671.[23] Concurrently, Louis Jolliet, a mature man of twenty-six, procuring a license to trade with the Ottawa, set out from Montreal in the summer of 1670 and, it appears, settled at Sault-Sainte-Marie where he carried

[21] *Rapport de l'archiviste de la Province de Québec pour 1930-31,* 112. This work is hereafter cited as RAPQ. The statement was included in the *Mémoire succinct* issued to Talon at Paris on May 18, 1669.

[22] *Ibid.,* 136. Talon's memoir to Colbert, November 10, 1670.

[23] Perrot, *Mémoire,* 126.

on trade with the Indians until the summer of 1671.[24] After wintering on the northern shore of Lake Huron opposite Manitoulin Island, Saint-Lusson and Perrot came to the Sault at the beginning of May, 1671. Perrot made a hurried visit to all of the nations whom he knew, inviting them to gather at Sainte Marie ". . . to hear the message from the king that Sieur Saint-Lusson was carrying to them and to all the tribes."[25]

On June 4, 1671, in the presence of representatives from some fourteen nations, four missionaries, Allouez, André, Dablon, and Druillettes, and fifteen or more Frenchmen, including Louis Jolliet, the impressive ceremony of taking possession of the West was solemnly enacted. Claude Allouez, the most fluent in the native tongues, delivered a long, flowery eulogy on Louis XIV, extolling the might of his arms and his paternal good will towards the Indians. Father Dablon blessed a great cross which was raised and, beside it, a tall, dressed cedar pole bearing the royal arms of France. Then the Sieur de Saint-Lusson appeared, dressed in the gorgeous uniform of a French military officer, his sword flashing at his side and a burnished helmet glittering on his head. Solemnly and sonorously he declared that, in the name of Louis XIV, he took possession of ". . . Sainte-Marie-du-Sault, Lake Huron, Lake Superior, Manitoulin Island, and all the rest of the country with its rivers, lakes, the rivers and lakes contiguous and adjacent, and their tributaries, as well those discovered as to be discovered, bounded on the one side by the northern and western seas and on the other by the South Sea, this land, in all its length and breadth. *Vive le Roi!*"[26] Afterwards a bountiful feast was served to all present and in the evening a fine bonfire was lighted, around which ". . . the *Te Deum* was sung to thank God on behalf of those poor people, that they were now subjects of so great and powerful a monarch."[27]

The Jesuits on the Ottawa mission did not retain their excellent superior, Dablon, for many days after the ceremony of June 4.

[24] Jean Delanglez, "Louis Jolliet: Early Years: 1645-1674," *Mid-America*, XVI (1945), 20.

[25] Perrot, *Mémoire*, 127.

[26] O'Callaghan, *Documents*, IX, 803-04.

[27] *Relations*, LV, 115.

Dablon had barely reached Sainte-Marie in 1669 when he received a letter from Father Le Mercier, directing him to return to Quebec in the late spring of 1671.[28] Le Mercier, who would be sixty-seven on October 4, 1671, was due to be relieved of the trying office he had held from 1653 to 1655 and again from August 6, 1665, until 1671. On August 26, 1670, he wrote to the Jesuit general, John Paul Oliva: "About ten months ago, I wrote to Father Claude Dablon, superior of the Algonquin mission among the Ottawa, to return next spring [1671], since he was needed here for many reasons . . . I do not know any [other] of our Fathers . . . who, in the present state of affairs, can conveniently be made superior . . . All the Jesuits rightly wish him for superior, because he lacks none of the qualities necessary to acquit himself perfectly of these functions . . ."[29] Within a few days after the ceremony of taking possession of the West, Dablon bade farewell to his Jesuit companions at Sainte-Marie-du-Sault and departed for Quebec, possibly in the company of Louis Jolliet who went down to Montreal that summer, evidently to cash in his peltries.[30] On their way back to the Saint Lawrence River valley, the two must have stopped at Mackinac Island to visit Father Marquette and see how things were going at the only mission which Dablon personally founded. The mission was going well, except that Marquette and the Indians were beginning to be worried about the corn, which, as Dablon could see, was not thriving at all. No one was hungry because the waters surrounding the island teemed with fish which were easily caught. But Indians could no more be content without corn than Frenchmen could without wine. Father Marquette had scouted the island testing the soil, only to discover that on the level stretches the ground was barely a thin cover for the solid rock under it. Probably it would be wiser to move the mission to the

[28] Jean Delanglez, "Claude Dablon, S.J. (1619-1697)," *Mid-America*, XV (1944), 99-100.

[29] *Ibid.*, 99. Dablon was installed as superior at Quebec on July 12, 1671.

[30] That Jolliet traveled with Dablon is pure conjecture. It is historically demonstrable, however, that Jolliet was in Montreal in the summer of 1671. See Delanglez, "Louis Jolliet: Early Years," 21.

mainland, if the corn didn't ear out come September.[31] Agreeing with Marquette's tentative plan, Dablon gave the young missionary permission to use his own judgment, assuring him that should a new superior be appointed for the Ottawa mission Dablon would inform him of the proposal. Perhaps revealing his own impending assignment, Father Dablon informed Marquette that it was time for him to pronounce his "last vows" as a Jesuit.[32] The young Blackrobe was, therefore, directed to go up to Sainte-Marie-du-Sault later in the summer to make his retreat. And at the completion of that spiritual exercise, he would pronounce his vows before Father Gabriel Druillettes, whom Dablon had, probably, delegated to receive them in the name of the general of the Jesuits.

With the Hurons settled at their new village and the corn planted, Father Jacques Marquette left them, perhaps about June 20, 1671, for a short stay at the Sault. During eight days there the young Blackrobe, withdrawing from all apostolic work, devoted himself to examining his own progress in virtue. On the feast of the Visitation of the Blessed Virgin Mary, July 2, Jacques Marquette knelt on the altar steps in the chapel at Sainte-Marie while old Father Gabriel Druillettes celebrated the Mass of the feast in

[31] The soil cover on Mackinac Island is so notoriously poor that the golf course owned by the Grand Hotel was made by bringing earth to the island from the mainland.

[32] The term "last vows" requires some explanation because it has a unique meaning which, in Marquette's day, applied only to the Society of Jesus, though presently it is applicable to other religious orders and congregations. Previous to the approval of the Jesuit constitutions, written by Saint Ignatius between 1539 and 1552, those who entered religious orders universally pronounced perpetual solemn vows at the completion of a year's testing of their vocations. These vows not only imposed obligations on the candidate but likewise gave rise to certain obligations to him on the part of the order he joined. Saint Ignatius introduced a new departure in that custom whereby candidates for his order spent two years of novitiate, or testing period, after which they pronounced simple vows, perpetually binding for the candidate, but only provisionally binding for the Society of Jesus. These vows came to be called "first vows." The Ignatian constitution provides that after a Jesuit finished his lengthy training he pronounced vows perpetually binding on him as well as on the Society of Jesus. These came to be called "last vows." In essence, the "last vows" differ little from the "first vows." See Martin P. Harney, *The Jesuits in History*, 100-12, for a satisfactory elaboration of this point.

the presence of a few Frenchmen. After consuming the Sacred Species himself, the celebrant, holding a host in his gnarled hands, faced his kneeling fellow Jesuit who solemnly pronounced the formula of his final vows:

> I, Jacques Marquette, promise Almighty God, in the presence of His Virgin Mother and the whole court of heaven, and you Reverend Father Gabriel Druilletes [*sic*] representing the General of the Society of Jesus and his successors, God's representative, perpetual poverty, chastity and obedience as well as unswerving dedication to the instruction of youth delineated in the Apostolic letters and in the constitutions of the Society. At Lake Superior of the Algonquins, in the town of Saint Mary's, the 2nd day of July, 1671. Jacques Marquette.[33]

If the ceremony had occurred in France there would have been a modest feast in the house in which he pronounced his vows. But at Sainte-Marie on the frontier, Brother Louis Boëme could do no more than provide a haunch of gamy venison, a little wine, and a salad from his precious kitchen garden. Perhaps the next day Father Marquette hurried back to his Hurons who must have felt bereft without him.

All through the summer and early fall the Indians anxiously inspected the growing corn day after day. For a time they hoped for a bountiful harvest, since the tender young stalks grew rapidly. But soon the Hurons noted that only a few plants showed the tell-tale bulging, presaging the budding ears of corn. By late August it was undeniably evident that the corn simply would not ear out. The doddering old squaws and the equally ancient braves shook their heads sadly over the stupidity of the younger generation. Hadn't they warned the elders that corn wouldn't grow on Mackinac Island! It never had and it never would! What was worse, there was no hope of the people lasting out the winter on the available game. There were a few deer on the island and perhaps a few more might wander over from the mainland when iron winter froze the straits, but a continued, dependable food supply from

[33] Garraghan, "Unpublished Marquettiana," 23, reproduces Marquette's handwritten formula of his vows. This document is preserved in ARSJ, Camp. *Vota ultima.* The translation of the Latin document given here is not that which Garraghan offers in his article.

game alone could not be relied upon. At last the elders, facing the desperate situation, came to their Blackrobe seeking advice. Would it not be better, there and then, to move to the mainland before it was too late to organize an effective fall hunt? The coming winter would be bad without corn, but it would be a desperate one unless the Indians could provide food by a successful hunt. Understanding full well the cogency of the leaders' argument, Father Marquette agreed; the Hurons must move to the mainland, and the sooner the better. Taking with him a few stalwart braves, Père Marquette scouted the mainland, perhaps from Groscap to Foley Creek. The most attractive location available was a deep, shallow bay, almost directly opposite Mackinac Island. There a wide, sandy beach led gradually to a broad meadow surrounded by a range of hills which provided shelter from the bitter, northwest winter winds. So it was decided, and perhaps in September 1671, Saint-Ignace was moved, bag and baggage, to its new site.[34]

Establishing the Hurons at another new village and buoying up their sagging spirits through their first winter away from Chequamegon Bay kept Marquette so occupied that he was unable to prepare a formal report of the mission of Saint-Ignace for inclusion in the *Relation* of 1671-1672. In that issue, Father Claude Dablon reviewed the history of the Huron migration and added:

> Father Jacques Marquette, who followed them from Point Saint-Esprit, continues in charge of them. As he has not furnished us any special account of the occurrences at that mission, all that can be said about it is that, this nation having been trained in Christianity years ago, before the Huron's destruction, those who have continued in the Faith now display great fervor. They fill the chapel daily, visit it often during the day, and sing God's praises there with a devotion that has commu-

[34] In his article, "Location of the Mission of Saint Ignace from 1670 to 1673," *Michigan History*, XLII (1958), 260-66, Raphael N. Hamilton expresses the opinion that Saint-Ignace was established on the mainland where St. Ignace, Michigan, stands today before Claude Dablon left Sainte-Marie-du-Sault for Quebec where he arrived at least by July 12, 1671. Hamilton's major argument is the fact that Dablon's map of the Ottawa country, which appeared in the *Relation* of 1670-1671, shows the mission as already existing there. This map may be consulted in *Relations*, LV, facing 94. The actual date on which the mission was established on the mainland cannot be determined from any extant documentary source.

nicated itself in no small measure to the French who have witnessed it. There the grown people have been baptized, and the old people set the children an example in their assiduous attendance at prayers. In a word, they observe all the exercises of piety that can be expected from a Christian body organized more than twenty years ago,—although it has been, most of that time, without church, without pastor, and without other teacher than the Holy Ghost.[35]

The *Relation* for the following year, 1672-1673, contains a lengthy report on the mission of Saint-Ignace submitted to Dablon by Marquette. Perhaps no other document from his hand reveals Marquette's character so effectively. After announcing that the 380 Hurons at Saint-Ignace enclosed their village, including the chapel, within a palisaded fort, perhaps in fear of a Sioux attack, Marquette registered a paternally charitable estimate of his people:

They have been more assiduous at prayer, have listened more willingly to the instructions that I gave them, and have acceded to my requests for preventing grave misconduct and their abominable customs. One must have patience with savage minds who have no other knowledge than of the devil, whose slaves they and all their forefathers have been; and they frequently relapse into those sins in which they have been reared. God alone can give firmness to their fickle minds, and place and maintain them in grace, and touch their hearts while we stammer into their ears.[36]

Continuing his report, Marquette recorded the arrival at Saint-Ignace of the Sinagaux Ottawa, with whom he worked so unsuccessfully at Chequamegon Bay three years previously. A sincerely humble man, the young Blackrobe announced that this Ottawa band, after spending a winter at the mission of Saint-François-Xavier under the direction of Father Louis André, now appeared ". . . to be very different from what they were when I saw them at the Point of Saint-Esprit. The zeal and patience of that Father have won over to the Faith hearts which seemed to us to be very adverse to it. They desire to be Christians, they bring their children to the chapel to be baptized, and they are assiduous in attending prayers."[37] Apparently, it did not once occur to Jacques Marquette

[35] *Ibid.*, LVI, 117-19.
[36] *Ibid.*, LVII, 249.
[37] *Ibid.*, 251.

to arrogate to himself any small credit for his own influence on the Sinagaux. In retrospect, however, it must have been in great measure due to Marquette's own sterling virtues that the stiff-necked Sinagaux were drawn to embrace Christianity so readily by Father Louis André.

One can sense with pleasure the consolation and satisfaction Marquette derived from the great majority of his Huron neophytes, when reading his account of their conduct while he was absent at Sainte-Marie, during the summer of 1672, while making his annual retreat. "Last summer," he related, "when I was obliged to go to Sainte-Marie-du-Sault with Reverend Father Alloués [*sic*], the Hurons came to the chapel during my absence, as assiduously as if I had been there, and the girls sang the hymns that they knew. They counted the days that passed after my departure, and continually asked when I was to return. I was absent only fourteen days; and, on my arrival, all proceeded to the chapel, to which many came expressly from their fields, although these were very far away."[38]

Much of Father Marquette's extensive report of the activities at Saint-Ignace has the flavor of the diary of a country pastor. After the harvest was gathered in the fall of 1672, Marquette was the guest of honor at the "feast of the squashes," clearly the equivalent of a modern Thanksgiving Day. Describing the event he wrote: "I cheerfully attended their feasts of the squashes, at which I instructed them and called upon them to thank God, who gave them food in abundance while other tribes, who had not yet embraced Christianity, had great difficulty in preserving themselves from hunger."[39] A highly respected savage, who gave a feast to which Marquette was invited, pleased the missionary by making to all the guests a public declaration of belief in Christianity. Thus the Huron host's announcement was recorded: "After calling each [of those present] by name, he told them that he wished to state his intention to them, so that all might know it—namely, that he was a Christian; that he denounced the god of dreams and all their

[38] *Ibid.*
[39] *Ibid.*

dances replete with lasciviousness; that the Blackgown was the master of [his] cabin; and that he would not abandon that resolution, whatever might happen."[40] Marquette added a homey little touch, saying: "As soon as anything has been said at a meeting, it is at once spread among all the cabins. This I soon recognized by the assiduity of some at prayer and through the malice of others, who endeavor to render our instructions useless."[41] If the noteworthy Huron's party was a stag affair, we may rightly judge that then, as now, men enjoyed gossip as much as women.

Speaking of women, it would be failing to complete Father Marquette's description of life at the mission of Saint-Ignace if the humorous little story regarding the distaff side of life there were not included. When the two hundred braves went off on the fall hunt in 1672, the women, it appears, felt that now was their chance to beard the Blackrobe. With a typically feminine oblique approach, the women asked their pastor what dances met with his approval. Weaving his way around the loaded question, the missionary recounted: "I replied in the first place that I would not permit those which God forbids, such as indecent ones; that as regards the others, I would decide about them when I had seen them."[42] Apparently those remaining in the village were immediately willing to demonstrate a whole repertory of dances, beginning with one called the bear dance which was requested by a sick woman who thought this would cure her. The whole thing turned into an embarrassing fiasco because the singers ". . . had great difficulty in carrying out the sick woman's design . . . for that dance was not in vogue among the Hurons."[43] Marquette had little difficulty persuading the Hurons to refrain from the bear dance with its pagan overtones, since the Indians didn't know it very well anyway, but he ". . . did not forbid others which are of no importance . . ." And possibly everybody was satisfied.

As to his apostolic labors during the season 1672-1673, Marquette could not report a great number of conversions since the

[40] *Ibid.,* 253.
[41] *Ibid.*
[42] *Ibid.,* 255.
[43] *Ibid.*

greater number of his charges were already Christians. Twenty-eight infants were baptized, but only two adults. The prudence he exercised in conferring baptism on an adult indicates that Marquette intended to have no part in creating a generation of rice Christians. Concerning the baptism of one of the adults, a woman, the missionary explained that she had come regularly for instructions for over a year. Whenever the persevering squaw asked for the grace of baptism, ". . . I always put her off until at last, when I saw that she was fully resolved to serve God, I baptized her on the day of the Annunciation. She does not fail to come, as a rule, three times a day to the chapel, where she remains longer than the others to finish her prayers."[44]

One last intimate glimpse of Jacques Marquette in his cherished role of pastor to the savages appears in a brief, but moving, passage in his account forwarded for inclusion in the *Relations* of 1672-1673:

> I did not fail during the autumn to go and visit them in their fields where I instructed them and made them pray to God, and told them what they had to do. I also made frequent and regular visits to them,—especially those who, owing to their advanced age, could not come to the chapel. . . .
>
> Since there was as yet no bell for the chapel, I went to notify them on the vigils of all the feasts. When time permitted, I delivered a short discourse to them, in which I always included what they were obliged to believe, and the principal things from which they should abstain.[45]

Marquette's account of his mission closed on a note of mixed regret and joy. "This . . . is all I can write to Your Reverence respecting this mission, where men's minds are more gentle, more tractable, and better disposed to receive instructions that are given them than in any other place. Meanwhile, I am preparing to leave it in the hands of another missionary, to go by Your Reverence's command and seek towards the South Sea new nations that are unknown to us, to teach them to know our great God, of whom hitherto they have been ignorant."[46] This time, please God, there would be no disappointment. Finally, after years of waiting, Jacques Marquette would realize his dream of going to the Illinois.

[44] *Ibid.*, 261. The feast of the Annunciation is celebrated on March 25.
[45] *Ibid.*, 259.
[46] *Ibid.*, 263.

JEAN TALON AND LOUIS JOLLIET

The mighty Mississippi River and the thousands of natives dwelling in its valley might not have been reached by Frenchmen for decades after Father Marquette first expressed his determination to go there if it had not been for the penetrating foresight of Jean Talon, first intendant of New France, and the calculated daring of Louis Jolliet, the official leader of the expedition which explored the Mississippi in 1673. Each of these extraordinary men deserve more than passing attention in any study of Jacques Marquette.

Jean Talon[1] was the scion of a family devoted to the law and noted for its staunch support of Gallicanism, a theory which, in

[1] Thomas Chapais, *Jean Talon, intendant de la Nouvelle-France (1665-1672)*, 5.

effect, made the king the practical head of the Catholic Church in France. Born at Châlons-sur-Marne in about 1625, Jean was educated at the Jesuit college of Louis-le-Grand at Paris, the most respected educational institution in France during that era.[2] While he was attending school there Jean could have become acquainted with the future first bishop of Quebec, François Laval who was a theological student during Talon's time at the school. Certainly young Jean came to know quite well several Jesuits whom he later met in New France. When he finished college Talon entered the administrative service of the government, through the good offices of his older brother, Philippe, who had influence with Cardinal Mazarin. By 1654 Jean had done so well that he was appointed military commissary to the army of the great Tourenne. A year later, when he was thirty, Talon became intendant of Hainault. This was a difficult post because this intendancy included much of Flanders, bordering the Low Countries, where trouble was always just under the surface. Talon administered that office with outstanding success until he was appointed intendant of New France on March 27, 1665.

What sort of person was the forty-year-old Talon when he reached Quebec on September 12, 1665? If one judged the man from his portrait, the conclusion would be far wide of the mark. The picture portrays an overbearing, foppish savant wearing a carefully curled, luxuriant wig, his head turned coyly to the viewer, his effeminate face characterized by dark, melting, almond-shaped eyes, a hair-line mustache and cupid-bow lips. A cloud of rich, crisp white lace swirls at his throat while a perfectly tailored, richly

[2] *Ibid.*, 15. Rochemonteix, *Jésuites*, III, 84-85, includes an interesting exchange of letters between the Jesuit general, John Paul Oliva, and Talon on the occasion of the latter's appointment as intendant. In his exaggeratedly florid Latin letter of January 19, 1666, Oliva expressed the gratitude of the Jesuit for Talon's appointment. Talon replied, on November 10, 1666, disclaiming any right to the high praise Oliva had heaped on him. Concerning his student days under the Jesuits at Louis-le-Grand, Talon told Oliva: "I am very grateful that I received my education from their [the Jesuits] obliging hands, having been a student in their schools. If I had preserved the fruits of their training I would have the honor of replying in Latin. Though I have become a bad student of a good master, it is my wish to serve well."

embroidered jacket covers his shoulder. Actually, Jean Talon was an exceptionally capable administrator with surprising ability to grasp the problems of the colony and offer practical solutions. In dealing with the clergy of New France his Gallican background caused him to be suspicious of them. He was, nonetheless, a morally good man, even a devout one. While at Quebec it was his custom to call frequently at the Hôtel-Dieu to visit the sick poor, striving to alleviate their distress, physical as well as financial.[3]

When Talon reached New France the colony had nearly expired. The royal government, introduced in 1663 when the country became a crown colony, had failed to function efficiently chiefly due to personality clashes between Governor de Mézy and Bishop Laval. The Iroquois had become so disdainful of the ability of the French to defend themselves that many colonists thought it to be only a matter of time before the Five Nations slaughtered all the French out of hand. During the nearly sixty years the French had been occupying the Saint Lawrence River valley, they had not even been able to produce enough food locally to avoid starvation. The colonists' only export was furs which were becoming a glut on the market. As intendant, in complete charge of the colony's internal affairs, it was Talon's responsibility somehow to stabilize the colony's economy, organize an effective civil government, strengthen internal defenses, and generally revitilize Canada. Talon accomplished most of these exceptionally well. He was the first royal appointee in New France to perceive the value of Canada's hinterland.

Jacques Marquette's zealous ambition to evangelize the Illinois was paralleled by Talon's eagerness to effect the exploration of the great river of the West and claim the area for France. During his first term as intendant (1665-1668), Talon was at Quebec hardly a full month before he called the attention of the king's minister, Jean-Baptiste Colbert, to the importance of the Canadian hinterland, writing: ". . . Canada is of a very vast extent; . . . I know not its limits on the north, they are so great a distance from us, and on the south there is nothing to prevent his Majesty's name and

[3] Pierre-Georges Roy, *La ville de Québec sous le régime français,* I, 346.

arms being carried as far as Florida, New Sweden, New Netherlands, and New England; and that through the first of these countries access is had even to Mexico."[4] Unaware of the importance of the intendant's observation, Colbert replied, curbing Talon's enthusiasm and directing him to confine French activities in Canada within an area that could be held securely rather than claiming a vast empire which France might some day be forced to relinquish ". . . with some loss of prestige to his Majesty."[5] Instead of feeling rebuffed Talon quite boldly suggested that Louis XIV could well profit by buying New Netherlands from the Dutch, thereby gaining complete control of access to the West as well as the generally ice-free port of New Amsterdam.[6] By the time Talon learned that his suggestion would not be acted upon, he had at hand a new, enticing reason for exploring the hinterland. When Father Claude Allouez came back from the Ottawa country in August 1667, he gave Talon some samples of copper ore he had found on the shores of Lake Superior.[7] When Talon informed the court of the valuable discovery, Colbert directed, as certainly the intendant expected: ". . . if it is reasonably certain that copper has been found in the lake of the Hurons [Lake Superior] and that it can be mined easily, this would be a thing worth following up . . ."[8] This encouragement to search for the copper mine could legitimately be stretched to justify having *voyageurs* explore the West as far as they could go. When Colbert's communication reached him, in the summer of

[4] RAPQ, 1930-31, 39. Talon to Colbert, October 14, 1665. Talon reached Quebec on September 12, 1665.

[5] *Ibid.*, 43. Colbert to Talon, April 5, 1666.

[6] *Ibid.*, 61. Talon to Colbert, November 13, 1666. In August 1664 Colonel Richard Nicoll, commanding four ships and a considerable body of troops from New England, captured the town of New Amsterdam. The following year, when the Dutch War broke out between England and the Dutch Republic, France supported the latter. Knowing this, Talon suggested that a treaty to end the war might well include a demand on the part of the Dutch for the return of their colony, with the secret understanding that France would buy it once it was back in Dutch hands. By the terms of the Treaty of Breda, which ended the war in 1667, England retained the former Dutch colony and renamed it New York.

[7] *Relations*, L, 265.

[8] RAPQ, 1930-31, 97. Colbert to Talon, February 20, 1668.

1668, the intendant appointed a Sieur Jolliet and Jean Péré, whom he subsidized with 400 and 1,000 livres respectively, to ". . . go and find out whether the copper mine . . . is rich and easy to exploit, and whether the ore can easily be brought here . . ."[9] Though Talon was recalled, at his own request, before the two explorers returned, at least the intendant had the satisfaction of making a start at opening New France's western stretches. Talon left for France shortly after November 5, 1668, to the nearly universal regret of the colonists who had no expectation that he would ever return.[10]

During Talon's absence a missionary expedition, proposing to penetrate the West, was initiated, with the permission of Bishop Laval and Governor Courcelle, by two Sulpicians, the abbé François Dollier de Casson and René François de Bréhant de Galinée. The governor induced them to join forces with Robert Cavelier, Sieur de La Salle who ". . . had long been premeditating [making a voyage] towards a great river, which . . . had its course towards the west, and at the end of which . . . the river falls into the sea."[11] Born at Rouen on November 21, 1643, La Salle entered the Jesuit novitiate at Paris on October 5, 1658. A little over eight years after he became a Jesuit, La Salle was released from his vows at his own request, and came to New France where, through the influence of his brother, Jean Cavelier, a Sulpician, he was granted a seigniory at the western end of the island of Montreal.[12] Leaving Montreal on July 9, 1669, La Salle and the two Sulpicians advanced to the western end of Lake Ontario. At that point La Salle and the fourteen men of his party separated from the Sulpicians on September 30, 1669. La Salle's activities for the following few years are difficult to follow with certainty. Perhaps he discovered the Ohio River after he left the Sulpicians and before the summer of 1670 when Nicolas Perrot encountered him on the Ottawa River.[13] If La Salle's

[9] Margry, I, 81. Patoulet, Talon's secretary, to Colbert, November 11, 1669.
[10] Chapais, *Jean Talon,* 302-03.
[11] Kellogg, *Early Narratives,* 168.
[12] Garraghan, "Newly Discovered Letters," 275-77.
[13] Perrot, *Mémoire,* 120.

travels were otherwise fruitless, perhaps they kept alive the importance of exploring the West during Talon's absence in France.

Fortunately for New France, Jean Talon did not lose interest in the colony when he arrived at the court of Louis XIV. Nor could he have reached there at a more propitious moment. The king, fresh from his first military victory, the successful conclusion of the War of Devolution (1666-1668), was in an expansive mood, favorably disposed to approve measures tending to strengthen and expand his colonial empire. With Colbert's support Talon procured generous grants of money for the colony, a promise of more troops, an increase in the number of immigrants, and, perhaps most importantly, abolition of the trade monopoly which the *Compagnie des Indes Occidentales* held regarding Canada. Having obtained these benefits, Talon was no doubt quite pleased to be reappointed on May 10, 1669, intendant of New France. Included in his instructions was a directive ordering Talon to continue searching for mines of various sorts, an effort he was to consider ". . . most important for the advancement of Canada . . ."[14] Adverse weather and shipwreck prevented Talon from reaching Quebec until August 18, 1670. But at last he had another opportunity to encourage the exploration of the West, this time with a sanction of sorts arising from his mandate to search for mines. And one mine, at least, was known to exist in the West.

Jean Talon was hardly comfortably settled in the intendant's palace at Quebec before he wrote to Louis XIV: "Since my arrival, I have sent resolute men to explore farther than has ever been done in Canada, some to the west and north-west, others to the south-west and south. They will all, on their return, write accounts of their expeditions and frame their reports according to the instructions I have given them. Everywhere they will take possession of the country, erect posts bearing the king's arms, and draw up memoranda of these proceedings to serve as title-deeds."[15] The first of these "resolute men," apparently, was Simon François

[14] RAPQ, 1930-31, 112. Louis XIV to Talon, May 18, 1669.

[15] Margry, I, 82. Talon to Louis XIV, October 10, 1670. Talon returned to Quebec on August 18, 1670.

Daumont, Sieur de Saint-Lusson, whose activity at Sainte-Marie-du-Sault in 1671 has already been described. Announcing the results of that expedition, Talon reported: "The place to which the said Sieur de Saint-Lusson has penetrated is supposed to be no more than three hundred leagues from the extremities of the countries bordering on the Vermilion or South Sea."[16] In the same communication the intendant informed the court that he had sent Paul Denys, Sieur de Saint-Simon, with the Jesuit, Father Charles Albanel, to Hudson Bay to claim the area for France as well as to determine ". . . whether there may be any means of wintering ships in that quarter, . . . that will possibly hereafter discover, by that channel, the communication between the two seas – the North and the South."[17] Leaving Quebec in August 1671, Saint-Simon and Albanel successfully completed their mission by August 1672.[18] By that date time was running out for Jean Talon. Besides his declining health, he and the governor, Courcelle, were on such bad terms that the only solution for the situation was the recall of both officials. Before leaving New France, however, Jean Talon was determined to plant the king's arms on the banks of the great river of the West. During the summer of 1672 the intendant commissioned Louis Jolliet to accomplish that feat.

Louis Jolliet was one of the newly emerging race of native-born Canadians, children of French immigrants. His father, Jean Jolliet was reputedly born at Sézanne, a French town located some fifty miles southeast of Reims. The place was noted for the quality furniture produced by its craftsmen. The existence of a Recollet convent at Sézanne may have had something to do with Jean's father, Nicolas, bringing his family to New France when Jean was a young boy.[19] The Recollets, it will be remembered, were the first missionaries at Quebec, coming at Champlain's invitation in 1615.

[16] RAPQ, 1930-31, 158. Talon to Louis XIV, November 2, 1671. In the same communication, Talon was careful to inform the king that Saint-Lusson's expedition cost the crown nothing since the furs given by the Indians as presents were sufficient to pay all expenses.

[17] *Ibid.*

[18] *Relations*, LVI, 149-217, Albanel's journal of that expedition.

[19] *Ibid.*, XXX, 304. Jean Jolliet's year of birth is said to have been 1574. If so, he was sixty-five when he married and seventy-seven when he died.

Various documents tell us that Jean Jolliet was a wheelwright in the employ of the Company of New France (the Hundred Associates). If so, Jean must have made wheels for handcarts; for previous to 1647 there was not a single horse in New France and that year one lone horse was sent over for the governor. Since the French word *charron* can also mean a ploughwright, perhaps Jean made more plows than wheels. Apparently, Jean Jolliet's usual place of residence was Beaupré where he owned 756 arpents (equivalently, acres) of land. On October 9, 1639, Jean married Marie d'Abancour, the daughter of Simone d'Orgeville and Adrien d'Abancour *dit* La Caille (the Quail) who owned land adjoining the Jolliet holdings. A year after the marriage, apparently when Marie's father died, the two properties were merged. Jean may not have been much of a farmer for thirty years later, when the land was sold, it was described as ". . . of little value because overgrown with wild rice and the buildings (two houses and a barn) were in ruins."[20] However, Jean seems to have done fairly well for when he lay dying in the Hôtel-Dieu on April 23, 1651, he willed sixty livres to the nuns, to show his appreciation for their care of him, and thirty-eight livres to the parish church, obviously to have Masses said for the repose of his soul.[21]

Marie d'Abancour Jolliet, a sturdy little frontier lady, presented her husband with four children: Adrien, probably born in 1640; Louis born in 1645; Marie, a couple of years younger than Louis; and Zacharie, born on December 23, 1650, four months before his father's death. Six months after Jean's sad demise, Marie Jolliet married Geoffroy Guillot *dit* La Valé who took his ready-made family to live on Ile d'Orleans where he had property.[22] By 1662 the Guillots were parents of a son, Jean, and two daughters, Louise and Elizabeth. Three years later on June 30, 1665, Geoffroy Guillot was drowned in the Saint Lawrence off the Ile d'Orleans in a kind of freakish accident. Early in the morning that day the people on the island spied the ships from France beating up the river to

[20] Amédée Gosselin, "Jean Jolliet et ses enfants," Royal Society of Canada *Proceedings and Transactions*, 3rd ser. XIV (1921), sec.1, 68.

[21] *Ibid.*, 65-66.

[22] *Ibid.*, 67.

Quebec. Impetuously, five men from the island jumped into a canoe intending to race up river and report the joyous event at Quebec. That was rather foolish since, unless the river was befogged, anyone in upper Quebec could have seen the ships very clearly. There was a strong wind on the river that day, so strong that the canoe was swamped and three of the men, including Guillot, were drowned.[23] Widowed a second time, Marie (Jolliet) Guillot married, on November 8, 1665, Martin Prevost of Beauport, a recent widower with a brood of six. His deceased wife was Marie-Olivier Manithabehich, an Algonquin who died on September 10, 1665.[24] Marie Jolliet Guillot Prevost lived to be quite an old lady, considering her times. Presuming that she was about twelve when she wed Jean Jolliet, the usual age when girls married in New France, she was about fifty-five at her death which is thought to have occurred in 1681. By then her son Louis Jolliet was a prominent man in Canada.

Louis Jolliet's childhood must have been the sort that small American boys once dreamed of having. He was born a few days before September 21, 1645, the day on which he was baptized at Quebec by Father Barthélemy Vimont. When he was five he was taken to Ile d'Orleans where, presumably, he lived until he was about nine or ten. Just a few months before the Jolliet children were brought to the home of their new stepfather, the Jesuits moved 600 Huron refugees from Quebec and settled them on the island.[25] As a boy Louis must have often visited the Indian village, especially since his family could fulfill their religious obligations at the chapel there. It may well have been during that period of his life that Louis acquired fluency in the native dialects, a facility he was said to have possessed as a grown man. At the age of about nine, Louis was sent off to attend the Jesuit *collège* at Quebec, as it is believed,

[23] *Ibid.*, 67-68.

[24] *Relations*, XI, 91; Roy, *La ville de Québec*, I, 365; RAPQ, 1936, 3. Prevost's marriage to his Algonquin spouse took place on November 3, 1644. Father Vimont was the officiating priest.

[25] *Relations*, XLI, 139-43, gives an excellent description of life at the Huron village.

did his older brother Adrien before him and Zacharie after him.[26] The curriculum at the college was a duplicate of that undergone by Jacques Marquette when he was a student at Reims.[27] Musically talented, Louis was fortunate to be at the college with Father Claude Dablon, himself a musician, who was there from 1658 until 1669.[28] Their mutual interest in music must have made these two fast friends. Dablon may well have buoyed up the boy's spirits during the trying days of the summer of 1658 when Adrien Jolliet was a prisoner in the hands of the Iroquois. Adrien and two other youths were captured at Three Rivers on June 13, 1658, at five in the morning. A little over three months later Adrien and one of his companions were returned, safe and sound.[29] The incident probably fired the imagination of the thirteen-year-old Louis who could boast to his school fellows that his brother not only stood up bravely to Iroquois threats of torture but that he was one of the few Frenchmen who could speak the Iroquois language. Three years later, in 1661, Adrien saw the Ottawa country with Father René Menard. That young Frenchman was with the missionary at Keweenaw Bay on Lake Superior on June 2, 1661.[30]

Perhaps Louis Jolliet's intellectual ability plus his musical talent linked together with close association with his Jesuit teachers ex-

[26] In his *Life of Jolliet*, 2, Delanglez suggests that Jolliet may have "worked his way through college" with his musical ability. Students at Jesuit colleges in those days were not charged any tuition, though they paid for room and board if they stayed at the college, as Jolliet probably did. If Jolliet received board and room in exchange for music, he did not play the organ in the college chapel. There was no organ in New France before 1663 when Bishop Laval brought one. See L. B. de La Tour, *Mémoires sur la vie de Mgr. de Laval, premier évêque de Québec*, 172. However, that Jolliet had some official position at the college seems certain from an entry in the house journal, *Relations*, XLIX, 157: ". . . on new-year's day . . . in the evening we invited the sieurs Morin and Jolliet, our musicians, to supper." The Morin mentioned was Germain Morin, the first Canadian to be ordained a priest. The date of the dinner was January 1, 1665.

[27] See Rochemonteix, *Jésuites*, I, 208-18.

[28] Dablon was on the Iroquois mission from 1655 to 1658. After that he was at the college continually until 1669, except for the summer of 1661 when he made a trip up the Saguenay with Father Druillettes.

[29] *Relations*, XLIV, 101, 109, relates the details of the capture and release.

[30] *Ibid.*, XLVI, 145.

ercised undue influence, inclining him to embrace an ecclesiastical career for which he may well not have been temperamentally suited. The warm relationship which sprang up between Louis and Bishop Laval, who reached Quebec in June 1659, may also have been an important factor. On August 10, 1662, when Louis was not quite seventeen, he received the tonsure and minor orders from Bishop Laval who was on the eve of leaving for France to confer with the crown.[31] On his return to Quebec in 1663, Laval established a seminary at Quebec which for a century after its founding was no more than a hostel for aspirants to the priesthood who attended classes at the Jesuit college. Jolliet, officially a cleric, was probably required to reside there. Perhaps his living expenses were met from funds furnished by the Jesuits, as was the case with Germain Morin, also a cleric.[32]

While Louis Jolliet was a seminarian we have one interesting glimpse of him participating in a scholastic function held in public. For generations in European schools the most hallowed academic exercise for displaying student ability was the disputation, a form of public debate which had a sacrosanct liturgy all its own. One of the more able students, known as a defendant for the occasion, formulated a series of philosophical or theological propositions, called theses, which he proposed to expound and defend against all comers. On the day of the disputation, the defendant explained his theses according to a rigid code of procedure. When the defendant finished his exposition, opponents challenged the conclusions, using an equally rigid formula. The defendant and opponent argued alternately, distinguishing and sub-distinguishing one another's declarations. Members of the audience were at liberty to participate in the discussion, provided they could speak fluent Latin and observed the rigid rules of argumentation. On July 2, 1666, the first such disputation was held in the Jesuit college at Quebec, in the presence, one may be sure, of the colony's distinguished citizens. The student participants were Louis Jolliet and Pierre Francheville. Jean Talon ". . . presented some very good arguments . . ." which

[31] Auguste Gosselin, *Vie de Mgr. de Laval, premier évêque de Québec,* II, 689.

[32] *Relations,* XLIX, 157.

the two students handled ". . . very well."[33] That intellectual séance was a landmark. Undoubtedly the *haut monde* at Quebec felt that New France was finally becoming a civilized, cultured center.

No documentary source has survived which throws any light on Louis Jolliet's decision, during the summer of 1667, to abandon the ecclesiastical career on which he had embarked five years before. Apparently both Bishop Laval and the Jesuits approved for both were helpful to him afterwards.[34] Instead of immediately finding employment Jolliet's first step after leaving the seminary was to make a trip to France, in the fall of 1667, using money which Bishop Laval lent him.[35] Why Jolliet went to France and what he did there is still a mystery. Ernest Gagnon, for long Jolliet's most respected biographer, surmised that the young man went to Paris to take a course in hydrography, a subject he later taught in the college at Quebec.[36] Louis certainly spent some time at Paris, since he paid 161 livres for board and lodging while living there, but he also lived at La Rochelle for an extended period. Though his sister Marie, who married François Fortin in 1660, was living permanently in France, at Dieppe, Louis doesn't seem to have visited her.[37] Nor did he make a pilgrimage to Sézanne, his father's native place, though one would have expected him to do so. It cannot be ascertained with certainty exactly when Jolliet returned to Quebec, but he was there on October 9, 1668. On that day he bought from Charles Aubert de la Chesnaye, again with money borrowed from the bishop, a dozen ells of cloth, a hat, two pair of shoes, as well as a large supply of trade goods, wampum, hatchets, small bells, coarse cloth, canvas, and forty pounds of tobacco.[38] Purchase of the large supply of trade

[33] *Ibid.*, L, 157. Pierre de Francheville, the eldest son of Martin Terrier de Repentigny, sieur de Francheville, was ordained in 1676. For a time he was Bishop Laval's secretary.

[34] Oddly enough, Louis Jolliet's oldest son, Louis, acted in the same manner. Born at Quebec on August 11, 1676, he entered the seminary on April 12, 1687, and left it on March 2, 1694. He became a sea captain. See Gosselin, "Jean Jolliet," 71.

[35] Delanglez, *Life of Jolliet*, 4.

[36] Ernest Gagnon, *Louis Jolliet*, 41.

[37] Gosselin, "Jean Jolliet," 77.

[38] Delanglez, *Life of Jolliet*, 6.

goods clearly indicated that Louis had decided to make his living as a fur trader, following in the footsteps of his brother Adrien.

Where Louis Jolliet was and what he did from November 9, 1668, to June 4, 1671, has never been satisfactorily documented. Since he and Adrien were at Cap-de-la-Madeleine on November 9, 1668, one presumes that Louis went there with his trade goods to begin his new career. But what did Louis do then? It may be recalled here that Talon, during the summer of 1668, paid a Jolliet 400 livres to search for the copper mine in the Ottawa country. This Jolliet actually went to the Ottawa country, but not necessarily in 1668. On April 13, 1669, Adrien gave his brother Louis power of attorney, a common practice in those days when men were departing on long, dangerous voyages from which they were not certain to return.[39] This legal action would indicate that Louis remained at Three Rivers or Cap-de-la-Madeleine at least until the spring of 1670 while Adrien went out in the summer of 1669 to search for the copper mine. Accepting this assumption, Adrien left Montreal a little before July 6, 1669, taking with him a supply of trade goods. On September 24, 1669, the Sulpicians, Dollier and Galinée with La Salle, met Adrien at the western end of Lake Ontario. Adrien announced that he had not found the mine but he had encountered trouble between the Iroquois and the Ottawa who had endangered the precarious peace by taking some Iroquois prisoners.[40] Father Allouez had persuaded the Ottawa to surrender the prisoners, some of whom he brought with him to Montreal.[41] Adrien Jolliet was returning to Montreal with one of the prisoners who showed the Frenchman the easier route to the Saint Lawrence by way of Lake Huron, the Detroit River, and Lake Erie. Adrien parted from the Sulpicians before October 1, 1669, and reached the colony, but not before November 11, on which date Patoulet, Talon's secretary, reported that nothing had been heard from either Péré or Jolliet. Early in 1670 Adrien and Louis Jolliet drew up a contract to engage in a trading expedition to the Ottawa country, but before their de-

[39] *Archives Judiciaires, Quebec,* Greffe Rageot, no. 339. This source is hereafter referred to as AJQ.

[40] Kellogg, *Early Narratives,* 192.

[41] *Relations,* LII, 197.

parture Adrien died, probably previous to March 22, 1670, when his wife, Jeanne Dodier, is called a widow in an official document signed that day at Cap-de-la-Madeleine.[42]

Louis Jolliet was undoubtedly saddened by the loss of his older brother, but Adrien's wife, who had two small children to support, needed whatever money the trading expedition, already organized, could earn. Hence, Louis and his partners set out in the summer of 1670 for Sault-Sainte-Marie where they set up a trading post. Perhaps they followed the easier, shorter route west, avoiding the difficult rapids in the Ottawa River, since their baggage contained such heavy, cumbersome objects as a forge.[43] Later that same year Saint-Lusson and his party, including Nicolas Perrot, left for the West seeking the elusive copper mine, but bad weather prevented them from reaching the Sault before May of 1671. In the summer of 1670 when Jolliet stepped ashore below the rapids of the Saint Mary's River, he was warmly greeted by his intimate friend of long standing, Father Claude Dablon, who had been superior of the western missions since the summer of 1669. Establishing headquarters close to the mission of Sainte-Marie-du-Sault, Jolliet set up his forge, arranged the trade goods, and was open for business. The trading partners probably fanned out visiting Indian villages, making friends, renewing old acquaintances, and trading their European products for furs, especially pelts the Indians had used as clothing. These furs, supple from body oil and pliant from constant use, commanded better prices than green pelts.[44]

The spring of 1671 brought an unusual amount of activity to Sainte-Marie-du-Sault. Ottawa refugees, fleeing the wrath of the Sioux, flocked in, keeping Jolliet busy supplying their needs in return for their furs. When Father Marquette arrived with his band of frightened Hurons, he and Dablon must have spent long hours with Louis Jolliet discussing the geography of the vast, unexplored areas to the west and south of the Sault. In May came Nicolas Perrot to prepare for the *prise de possession* to take place as soon

[42] Delanglez, *Life of Jolliet*, 12. As authority for this, Delanglez quotes *Archives Judiciaires, Trois Rivières*, Greffe Jean Cusson, March 22, 1670.

[43] Delanglez, "Louis Jolliet: Early Years," 27.

[44] Perrot, *Mémoire*, 128.

as he could summon representatives from all the tribes to the meeting at the Sault. Then Saint-Lusson and his campanions arrived for the splendid ceremony. When Saint-Lusson took possession of the West in the name of Louis XIV on June 4, 1671, six of the fourteen laymen listed as witnesses of the formal act of annexation were members of Louis Jolliet's trading partnership. These were: Jacques Maugras, Pierre Moreau *dit* La Taupine (the Mole), François de Chavigny, Jacques Largillier *dit* Le Castor (the Beaver), and Pierre Porteret. Maugras and Largillier were old trading partners of Adrien Jolliet with whom they had associated for the past five years.[45]

Before that assembly of hardy Frenchmen disbanded there was much discussion of the unexplored West and the great river supposed to be flowing there. Nicolas Perrot, and possibly others, of Saint-Lusson's company must have urged their leader to extend his voyage westward, but Saint-Lusson already had enough of that raw existence. He was commissioned to determine whether there was a copper mine in the West. Well, there was one, even a rich one, but who could transport heavy copper ore over those terrible portages back to Quebec? As to the supposed water route to the Sea of the South, it was at least 300 leagues away. Let somebody else find it. Saint-Lusson packed up the rich supply of peltry the Indians presented to him and unceremoniously departed for Montreal and Quebec. Jolliet, who also went down to cash in some of his peltries, was unwilling to dismiss exploration of the West so lightly.[46] There simply had to be some reality behind all the rumors of a great river. There even existed a few maps, crude and inaccurate to be sure, which showed that the great river was separated by only ". . . fifteen hundred leagues of navigation from Tartary, China and Japan . . ."[47] Whatever anyone else might decide, Louis Jolliet determined that he would have a go at finding the river and exploring its whole

[45] Margry, I, 99.

[46] Shortly before October 11, 1671, Adrien's widow married Antoine Baillargé. When he died on December 19, 1672, she married Mathurin Normandin *dit* Beausoleil. When Louis Jolliet came back to Montreal in 1674, after the voyage down the Mississippi, Normandin sued him because he had not brought back, in 1671, all the pelts collected. See Delanglez, *Life of Jolliet*, 16-17.

[47] RAPQ, 1930-31, 158. Talon to Louis XIV, November 2, 1671.

length. Father Dablon favored the project and was willing to appoint Father Marquette as Jolliet's companion, knowing full well for how many years Marquette had longed to establish a mission among the Illinois.

Sometime during the summer of 1672 Talon summoned Louis Jolliet to his palace at the head of the Côte de la Montagne. Resplendent in his great wig, a frothy, stiffly starched jabot at his throat, M. l'Intendant received the twenty-seven-year-old Louis Jolliet. Always the suave diplomat, Jean Talon expounded grandly on the glorious future of New France, the vast, wealthy empire it could be when its still unknown areas were explored. Who knew what such explorations would unfold? Perhaps the Sea of China really was at the end of the mysterious river of the West. For the glory of France and God any true Frenchman would exult at the opportunity to open the way to such an important route. Would the Sieur Jolliet wish the honor of exploring the length of that mighty river to its very mouth?[48] Though such a privilege was reward enough in itself, M. l'Intendant was prepared to grant Jolliet a trading license, allowing him to defray expenses. Surely Jolliet would find half the men at Quebec only too willing to go shares with Jolliet on such a venture. As M. Jolliet knew, a priest always accompanied such expeditions to care for the souls of the explorers as well as to contact the aborigines, laying the foundation for missions among them. Father Dablon, the intendant was certain, would be willing to assign a Jesuit missionary to accompany the expedition, if Jolliet chose to undertake it. So what was M. Jolliet's answer, queried M. l'Intendant? The young fur trader's reply, possibly enunciated a bit too hastily, was that he would happily accept the commission, which, he was certain, would be completed successfully to the great glory of France and God.

[48] Jolliet was probably commissioned by Talon previous to September 7 or 8, 1672, on one of which days Frontenac reached Quebec, the seventy-first day after he left La Rochelle on July 1 or 2. On November 2, 1672, Frontenac wrote Colbert: "He [Talon] also considered it expedient for the good of the service to send the Sieur Jolliet to discover the sea of the South by way of the country of the Mashoutins [Mascoutens] and the great river which they call Michissipi [Mississippi] which is thought to empty into the sea of California. He [Jolliet] is well suited for this sort of discovery . . ." *ibid.*, 1926-27, 18.

Trudging down the Côte de la Montagne on his way to the *basse ville,* Louis Jolliet mulled over the practicalities of fulfilling his commission. How much money would be required to launch the venture; whom should he invite to join the expedition; what supplies were needed; and what Jesuit missionary would Father Dablon appoint to accompany him? The *congé* or trading license granted by Talon permitted Jolliet to organize a trading partnership, but financing the operation was his own responsibility. Custom dictated that the holder of the *congé* furnish the canoes, victuals for all who went on the expedition, and all of the trade goods required for bartering with the Indians. At the completion of the enterprise profits were divided according to the agreement made before the partners set out. The holder of the *congé* usually received a full half of all profits, since he took the greatest financial risk. The other partners, together with the leader, each received an equal portion of the other half of the profits. The total cost of Jolliet's expedition was 3,000 livres.[49] Of that amount Louis Jolliet furnished a large portion. Two of his partners, François de Chavigny, who didn't go on the expedition, and Zacharie Jolliet, invested capital.[50] Two others, Louis-Théandre Chartier de Lotbinière and the "Demoiselle de la Tesserie," claimed, in 1674, that they had each invested 300 livres in the project.[51] Louis Jolliet probably thought he was saving money when he borrowed a canoe from his brother Adrien's widow. A good, stout Algonquin canoe could be purchased from the Indians who made them for ". . . nine or ten escus . . . ," but French owners of such crafts charged other Frenchmen as much as eighty livres for the same item.[52] Jolliet regretted that

[49] *Jugéménts et délibérations du conseil souverain de la Nouvelle-France,* I, 864.

[50] Chavigny could not have gone down the Mississippi with Jolliet since he was at Cataracoui (Kingston, Ontario) with Frontenac in July 1673 when Jolliet was far down the Mississippi. See O'Callaghan, *Documents,* IX, 113, Frontenac's journal of his voyage to Lake Ontario, July 1673.

[51] *Jugéménts et délibérations,* I, 864. On October 3, 1674, Chartier and the Demoiselle Tesserie, who was François Chavigny's mother, sued Jolliet claiming that each had invested 300 livres in the expedition, but had received no share in the profits. The court disallowed the claim.

[52] Kellogg, *Early Narratives,* 172.

economy, in 1674, when his sister-in-law sued him, demanding rent for her canoe.[53]

Besides the financing, Louis Jolliet recruited trading partners willing to undertake the hazardous journey. One of the seven members of the partnership, Jacques Largillier, was associated with Adrien Jolliet in 1666.[54] Two others, François Chavigny and Pierre Moreau, were partners of Louis Jolliet's trading venture of 1670-1671. Three partners, Morin, Plattier, and Tiberge, had not been associated with Jolliet before. The last partner, Zacharie Jolliet, deserves more than passing mention. By the time his stepfather, Geoffroy Guillot, was drowned in 1665, Zacharie, then a stripling of almost fifteen, had probably completed a few years of school with the Jesuits in their college at Quebec. When his mother married Martin Prevost in November 1665, and went to live with her new husband's brood of little half-breeds, Zacharie, along with his half-sister, Louise Guillot, was foisted off onto his sister Marie and her husband François Fortin.[55] That arrangement ended in 1666 or 1667 when the Fortins left Canada permanently to take up residence in France.[56] The question of what to do with Zacharie was solved by making him an apprentice of Noël Morin, a wheelwright who had bought Zacharie's father's tools for 45 livres back in 1652.[57] Whether the boy learned the trade, no one knows, but the apprenticeship was dissolved in 1668.[58] What Zacharie did after that until 1672 has not yet come to light. Whatever it was, in 1672, when Zacharie was almost twenty-one, he had enough money to invest some of it in Louis Jolliet's trading partnership.

When all the necessary arrangements were completed Louis Jolliet and his partners met at Jacques Cailhault de la Tesserie's

[53] Delanglez, "Louis Jolliet: Early Years," 26-27. In July 1674 Mathurin Normandin, the third husband of Adrien Jolliet's widow, Jeanne Dodier, sued Louis Jolliet, claiming, among other things, rent for a canoe loaned him in 1672. Delanglez presents this complete document.

[54] Gosselin, "Jean Jolliet," 74.

[55] *Ibid.*, 79.

[56] *Ibid.*, 68.

[57] *Ibid.*, 67.

[58] *Ibid.*, 79.

house where, in the presence of Gilles Rageot, a notary, they signed the following contract:

Before Gilles Rageot, notary, . . . were present the Sieur Louis Jolliet, François Chavigny, escuyer, Sieur de la Chevrotière, Zacharie Jolliet, Jean Plattier, Pierre Moreau, Jacques Largilier [*sic*], Jean Tiberge, all now in this town, who of their own free will have entered into partnership and society to make together the voyage to the Ottawa country [there to] trade with the Indians as profitably as possible and all binding themselves *en droit soy* [?]. [Since they] are leaving tomorrow for the said voyage, therefore the said Sieur Louis Jolliet promises and binds himself to furnish at his expense and cost all the merchandise, [all the] appropriate and suitable goods to carry on the said trade, and as much as they can take along with them; similarly [Louis Jolliet binds himself to furnish] suitable victuals to the said Sieurs Chavigny, Zacharie Jolliet, Plattier, Moreau, Largilier [*sic*] and Tiberge, . . . and when returning from the said voyage, all beaver, otter, marten and moose pelts acquired from the said trade, as well as any other pelts that may be had will be shared as follows: half of all the said pelts will be divided into seven shares, a share each, and the other half will be for the said Sieur Jolliet, because he is paying for the said merchandise, goods and victuals as well as for the canoes; [this half] is over and above his share [of one seventh of the one half] which he will have like the others, as said above. Also if it is necessary to make presents to the Indians during the voyage, and if some presents are received [in return], these will similarly be shared as said above, as well as [the money proceeding from the sale of] the canoes after their return, namely: half as for the said pelts, and the other half [to be divided] into seven shares . . . Done and drawn up in the said Quebec in the forenoon in the house of M[essi]r[é] Jacques de Cailhault, escuyer, Sieur de la Tesserie, royal counciller in the king's Sovereign Council in New France, the first day of October 1672, in the presence of Jean Mainguy and of Baptiste Morin, witnesses, who with the contractants and the notary have signed [this act], except the said Tiberge who, upon being formally asked as required by law, declared that he did not know how to write nor how to sign his name.

Jolliet-François Chavigny-Pierre Moreau-Plattier-Zacharie Jolliet-Morin-Jacques Largillier-J. Mainguy- Rageot.[59]

Though Jolliet planned to leave that day, the following day, October 2, 1672, he appeared before the notary, Rageot, and de-

[59] AJQ, Greffe Rageot no. 939. Jacques de Cailhault, Sieur de la Tesserie, was François Chavigny's stepfather.

clared that the share which Chavigny and his brother Zacharie were to have in the one-half of the trade profits would be proportionate to the investment each had made in the partnership and not merely a one-seventh share. The reason for this further official declaration, as Louis Jolliet explained, was that Zacharie and Chavigny had contributed money to the venture while the others were giving only their services.[60] Finished with that last-minute business, Jolliet and his partners set off for Sault-Sainte-Marie and eventual departure on the voyage of exploration. Buried under the packs of trade goods heaped in Louis Jolliet's canoe was his strongbox containing a letter, carefully wrapped in oilskin, addressed to Father Jacques Marquette from his superior, Claude Dablon.[61] This was the order so long awaited by Marquette; he was to go with the Sieur Louis Jolliet on his voyage of exploration.

[60] *Ibid.*, no. 943.

[61] Delanglez, *Life of Jolliet*, 107. Jolliet actually had such a box which he lost when his canoe overturned at Sault Saint Louis above Montreal in 1674. Marquette himself says he received orders directly from Dablon to accompany Jolliet. See *Relations*, LVII, 263.

". . . the grace . . . to visit
the nations who dwell
along the Mississippi . . ."
Relations LIX, 89.

NATIONS ALONG THE MISSISSIPPI

On the afternoon of December 8, 1672, the feast of the Immaculate Conception, an occasion deeply cherished by Jacques Marquette, Louis Jolliet swung his light canoe onto the sandy beach at the foot of a path leading to the rough bark chapel of the mission of Saint-Ignace. A good half-hour before, the little Huron children looking for all the world like round balls of fur, so completely were they swathed in their winter peltry, came running to tell the Blackrobe that a canoe with a Frenchman in it was rounding the point to the north, clearly bound for the mission. Père Marquette, welcoming his visitor, placed Jolliet's wet moccasins near the fire to dry, offered him food with a warm drink, and prepared to listen to the news. Had Jolliet come from Sainte-Marie-du-Sault and how were the Fathers there? All in good time, Jolliet replied. Yes, he had come from the Sault and everyone was well, even old Father Druillettes who was a little more stooped, perhaps, but still strong and active. Jolliet reached the Sault some three weeks previously and since then he had been occupied cleaning out his old trading post, storing merchandise, and assigning trading areas to his partners. Young Zacharie, his brother, was keeping store, learning the business. Since the Indians were still very friendly, business prospects were good. All of this was not the best news; the really important announcement was contained within the oilskin package which Jolliet slowly, dramatically unwrapped. First he read in solemn, sonorous tones M. l'Intendant's commission, appointing Louis Jolliet to lead an expedition southward to the great river of the West which Talon commanded Jolliet to locate and follow to its very mouth. Enthusiastically congratulating him, Father Marquette asked, a little fearfully, whether a missionary was to accompany the Sieur Jolliet and, if so, to which of the Jesuits had the blessed assignment been given? Smiling enigmatically, Jolliet handed the Jesuit a letter sealed with a great blob of wax. One glance was enough for Père Jacques; the letter was addressed to him in the familiar scrawl of his superior, Claude Dablon. Delighted as a small boy receiving a new red sled on a white Christmas, Marquette wrote as the first entry in his journal of the voyage down the Mississippi:

The feast of the Immaculate Conception of the Blessed Virgin—whom I have always invoked since I have been in this country of the Outaouacs, [*sic*] to obtain from God the grace of being able to visit the nations who dwell along the Missisipi [*sic*] River—was precisely the day on which Monsieur Jollyet [*sic*] arrived with orders from Monsieur the Count de Frontenac, our governor, and Monsieur Talon, our intendant, to accomplish this discovery with me. I was all the more delighted at this good news, since I saw that my plans were about to be accomplished; and since I found myself in the blessed necessity of exposing my life for the salvation of all these peoples, and especially of the Illinois, who had very urgently entreated me, when I was at the Point of Saint-Esprit, to carry the word of God to their country.[1]

[1] *Relations*, LIX, 89-91. The writer is well aware that the manner in which the account of the voyage down the Mississippi in 1673 is introduced here assumes that Father Jacques Marquette was the author of "*Récit des voyages*

When Marquette's first flush of great joy subsided the two Frenchmen, deep in the fastness, hundreds of miles from any source of supplies, began serious consideration of the physical requirements for their coming penetration of the unknown wilderness. Since all Indians offered presents to visitors and expected them in return, and there was no reason to believe that the custom was not universal, the stores in Jolliet's warehouse at the Sault would be drawn on to supply these. Food would not be a problem for the rivers and lakes were bound to be stocked with fish and on shore game would probably be found, and much of the sort perceived in the area of Lake Huron and Lake Superior. There were rumors that some sort of cattle were grazing in large herds in the country through which the river flowed, but just what this informa-

et des découvertes du Père Jacques Marquette . . ." Previous to 1928 no historian questioned the authorship, assuming that Marquette wrote the whole of the account. In 1928 Francis Borgia Steck, in his *The Jolliet-Marquette Expedition, 1673,* 261-301, held that Marquette was not the author. Jean Delanglez, in a series of articles in *Mid-America,* as well as in his *Life and Voyages of Louis Jolliet (1645-1700),* agrees with Steck that Marquette was not the author, but disagrees with the reasons Steck offers for his conclusions. This writer holds that Marquette was, in very truth, the author of the account. This matter will be discussed in depth in an appendix.

Steck made a signal point of Marquette's official, or unofficial, relationship to the expedition. Much of Steck's argument hinges upon Marquette's remark, ". . . to accomplish this discovery with me . . ." The phrase, ". . . *pour faire auvec moy cette decouuerte . . .,*" was taken by Steck to be an assertion by Marquette that he was at least a co-leader of the expedition. The French should be translated: ". . . to make this discovery and I accompanying him . . ." This is the practically identical phrase which Talon himself used in reporting that he had sent Saint-Simon to discover a land route to Hudson Bay in company with Father Charles Albanel. See RAPQ, 1930-31, 158.

As to how Marquette learned that he was to accompany Jolliet, there is no ironclad evidence. Delanglez in his *Life and Voyages of Louis Jolliet* makes a good case for Marquette receiving his orders as described here. There is, however, the possibility that Dablon sent orders with Father Pierre Bailloquet who came to the Ottawa mission sometime during the summer of 1673. If he came up with the Indians returning from trading, he would have left Montreal in late August or early September. If Dablon knew by that time that Jolliet was to make the expedition, Marquette was the logical missionary to send and he could have informed Marquette by a letter carried by Bailloquet. However, the fact is that documentation is lacking, or has not yet come to light, on this point. Certainly Marquette would not have gone without having been given permission by his own superior.

tion really meant remained to be seen. It would certainly be prudent to take along a supply of jerked meat and some Indian corn, just to be on the safe side.[2] Certain scientific instruments were essential if they expected to construct a map of the river which others could use after them. Compasses were common enough, so procuring a fairly accurate one would be no problem.[3] Without an astrolabe they could not locate themselves on the face of the earth; and with the astrolabe they needed a set of declination tables supplying celestial readings for the period of the year they planned to make the journey.[4] Above all, they must draw a tentative map showing ". . . the rivers which we were to navigate, the names of the peoples and of the places which we were to pass, the course of the great river, and the direction we were to follow when we reached it."[5] For the moment more proximate preparations were deferred until spring, except that Marquette began readying his neophytes for the transfer of Saint-Ignace into the hands of another missionary whom he hoped would arrive before his own

[2] *Relations*, LIX, 91.

[3] In his *Father Marquette*, Reuben Gold Thwaites included a picture of a seventeenth-century compass which was found in January 1902 by two hunters who discovered it on the site of an old Indian village on the southeast shore of Green Bay, just above Point Sable. See the photograph facing 158.

[4] An astrolabe, roughly speaking, is a simple form of a sextant. Since the position of the sun in the celestial sphere is considered to vary in the course of the year, knowledge of the distance of the sun from the celestial equator, that is, the projected circle in the sky directly above the earth's equator, is necessary in order to determine latitude on the earth from a sighting of the sun's position. Such information is derived from declination tables.

[5] It was common practice for those setting out on such expeditions to prepare tentative maps. See *Relations*, XLIV, 237; the journal of the *Badine*, Margry, IV, 178; the journal of the *Marin, ibid.*, IV, 269. A reasonably accurate map of the Mississippi could have been conjectured from Dablon's description of it in the *Relation* of 1670-1671. See *Relations*, LV, 207-09. In 1656 Nicolas Sanson d'Abbeville published a map of North America which, though inaccurate, would have furnished Jolliet and Marquette with a working tool. Sanson's map appeared in his *L'Amérique et plusieurs cartes et en divers traites de geographie et de l'histoire*. See a reproduction of this map in Kellogg's *The French Régime*, 92.

departure.[6] Spiritually, however, Marquette promptly petitioned celestial aid. "Above all," he wrote, "I placed our voyage under the protection of the Blessed Virgin Immaculate, promising her that, if she granted us the favor of discovering the great river, I would give it the name of the Conception, and that I would also make the first mission that I should establish among those new peoples bear the same name."[7] For the rest, Jacques Marquette must possess his soul in peace through the long, cold, bitter winter until spring.

Finally, winter relaxed its iron grip on the land. Mountainous masses of lake ice, driven into the bay by relentless winds off Lake Huron, gradually melted under warm breezes and bright sunshine. During the second week of May Louis Jolliet with his five pledged companions reached Saint-Ignace, come to pick up Père Jacques. These were sturdy, blocky men, thick in the shoulders, narrow-waisted, short of limb, tireless, enured to hardship and steady in the face of danger. Jacques Largillier, called the Beaver, was to be with Marquette almost constantly until the latter's death. Pierre Moreau, known as the Mole, later became involved in some of Frontenac's less savory enterprises.[8] Jean Tiberge was, perhaps, a simple, plodding man, unlettered, but probably devoted. Of Jean Plattier nothing is known, except his name, which is more than historians can record of the fifth man. His only claim to fame, poor fellow, is that in 1674, when Jolliet's canoe was swamped above Montreal, he was drowned.[9]

The last few days at Saint-Ignace were busy ones for the departing adventurers. Jolliet and Marquette squatted together for

[6] *Relations,* LVII, 263. Marquette already knew that if the expedition succeeded he would not return to Saint-Ignace, but would open a new mission among the Illinois.

[7] *Ibid.,* LIX, 93.

[8] W. J. Eccles, *Frontenac, the Courtier Governor,* 315.

[9] Neither Marquette nor Jolliet named the five men who accompanied them. Historians argue that Zacharie Jolliet was not one of the five because it is unlikely that Louis Jolliet would have failed to mention Zacharie if he had gone along. That Largillier was one of the five is known from a letter of Father Pierre Cholenec, dated October 10, 1675. (See Rochemonteix, *Jésuites,* III, 607.) Since Moreau, Plattier, and Tiberge were under contract to Louis Jolliet, it is quite reasonable to assume that they were members of the party.

long hours examining their tentative map, questioning Indians who claimed to know something about the far country, extracting the last scintilla of information from them. The others arranged the baggage into firm bundles of about a hundred pounds each, so shaped as to fit snugly into the canoes. One package contained presents for Indians to be met, who would expect such courtesy, as the French, in turn, would be offered presents. Powder and shot were packed in several bundles so that the chance loss of some would not leave the travelers unable to bag game or defend themselves if need be. Then there were reams of paper, needed for taking notes, squat bottles of ink, Father Marquette's sturdy, scarred box containing his chalice, vestments, a small missal, the all-important bottle of Mass wine, and a supply of hosts. Finally, after much packing and rearranging, all was ready. On Wednesday, May 17, 1673, Louis Jolliet, Father Jacques Marquette, and their five companions pushed off, bound for the unknown.

A tourist wishing to follow the first leg of the Jolliet-Marquette expedition could do so by car on Michigan's Highway 2 and, with the exception of about fifty miles, never be more than about a half-mile off the route. Leaving Saint-Ignace, the travelers rounded Groscap and followed the northern shore of Lake Michigan to Point Detour, averaging about thirty miles a day. Rather than risk the sixteen miles of open water at the mouth of Big Bay De Noc, they probably headed southward, island-hopping from Point Detour to Washington Island at the mouth of Green Bay. Coasting along the eastern shore of Green Bay to Eagle Harbor, they could easily cross westward to Strawberry Island, thence to Chambers Island, and reach the western shore of the great bay without facing more than seven miles of open water at any point.[10] About two weeks after leaving Saint-Ignace Marquette and his party reached the Menominee River where they stopped briefly to visit the *Folle Avione* or Menominee to whom Allouez and Dablon had preached in the summer of 1670.[11] On learning the objective of the journey

[10] Arthur C. Neville, "Some Historic Sites about Green Bay," *Proceedings* of the State Historical Society of Wisconsin for 1905, 151.

[11] *Relations*, L, 183.

the Menominee strove to dissuade the French, warning that the country to which they were bound was inhabited by people ". . . who never show mercy to strangers, but break their heads without any cause . . ."[12] Besides, the great river ". . . was full of horrible monsters, which devoured men and canoes together; that there was even a demon, who was heard from a great distance, who barred the way, and swallowed up all who ventured to approach him; . . ."[13] Thanking them for their advice, the missionary explained that he could not follow it ". . . because the salvation of souls was at stake, for which I would be delighted to give my life . . ."[14] Wherewith, the Frenchmen bade farewell to the Menominee who, doubtless, agreed among themselves that all Frenchmen were crazy and deserved the fate they were bound to meet.

Approaching the foot of Green Bay, Father Marquette looked forward with joyful anticipation to reaching the mission of Saint-François-Xavier where he expected to visit his fellow Jesuit missionaries Claude Allouez and Louis André. Reaching the end of the Bay, where great flocks of ducks scolded them for invading the stands of wild rice, the voyagers pushed up the lower Fox River to the first rapids near which the mission of Saint-François-Xavier stood, arriving on about May 27.[15] Father André was absent, evangelizing the Indians living near the mouth of the Oconto River on the western shore of Green Bay.[16] But Father Allouez was home to welcome the callers, having just returned from a visit to the Mascouten whose village was on the upper Fox River.[17] The sixty-year-old Allouez had important information for the explorers. Some

[12] *Ibid.*, LIX, 95.

[13] *Ibid.*, 97.

[14] *Ibid.*

[15] The distance by canoe from Saint-Ignace to the mission of Saint-François-Xavier is about 300 miles. That portion of the journey consumed about ten days. Hence, the travelers would have reached the mission at Green Bay on about May 27, since they left Saint-Ignace on May 17.

[16] *Ibid.*, 65.

[17] *Ibid.*, LVIII, 59-65. Allouez's account of his visit to the Mascouten from May 5 to 22, 1673. He left them to go to Green Bay, a distance of something under a hundred miles by water, all of it with the current. It is, however, not absolutely certain that Allouez met Marquette, since neither mentions meeting the other.

Illinois Indians, calling themselves the Kaskaskia, who had been frequenting the mission of Saint-François-Xavier for the past couple of years, informed Allouez that in their country there was a tributary of the Mississippi (the Illinois) which greatly shortened the distance between the mission and their homeland.[18] Of course Marquette and Jolliet would not want to follow that route on their outward voyage, since their objective was to explore as much of the great river as possible; but on their homeward journey the river mentioned by the Indians might offer a short cut as well as an opportunity for Father Marquette to contact the nation of the Kaskaskia. Grateful for this important addition to their geographical knowledge of the country to which they were bound, the travelers, after a brief rest at the mission, were on their way again.

The next thirty miles of their outward journey were the most difficult which the travelers would meet. The lower Fox River, from Lake Winnebago to its mouth at Green Bay, falls 169 feet, rushing over five dangerous rapids, Rapid des Père at De Père, Petit Kakalin at Little Rapids, La Croche at Kimberly, Grand Chute at Appleton, and Winnebago Rapids at Doty's Island where Lake Winnebago drains into the lower Fox. At each of these the canoes were, perforce, unloaded and dragged empty through the rapids. Then all of the baggage had to be carried laboriously around the portage and reloaded, repeating the tiresome process over and over. Emerging, at last, onto broad, shallow, odoriferous Lake Winnebago, the voyagers followed the western shore southward for twenty miles to the marshy entry of the upper Fox and continued up that pleasant stream forty-nine miles to the great village of the Mascouten,[19] ". . . the limit of the discoveries which the French have made, for they

[18] *Ibid.*, 265. See also Delanglez, *Life of Jolliet*, 125.

[19] *Relations*, LIX, 101. Claude Allouez, the first missionary to visit the Mascouten, reached their village on April 24, 1670. (See *ibid.*, LIV, 219.) Allouez spent eight days traveling to the village from the mouth of the lower Fox where it empties into Green Bay. Allouez spent the whole of April 24 traveling from the mouth of the upper Fox, where it empties into Lake Winnebago, to the Mascouten village. (See *ibid.*) That fall, on September 15, 1670, Dablon was at the Mascouten village with Allouez. (See *ibid.*, LV, 199.) The population of the village then numbered 3,000. Jones located the village as the present Berlin, Wisconsin. (See Jones, "The Site of the Mascoutin," 175-82.)

have not yet gone any farther." The travelers arrived there on Wednesday, June 7, twenty-two days and some four hundred miles southwest of Saint-Ignace.

Cooperation of the Indians at the Mascouten village was vital to Marquette and Jolliet for these natives knew the route to a river, thirty leagues from their village, which was believed to flow into the mighty river of the West.[20] As soon as the Frenchmen came into the village Jolliet assembled the elders, telling them that he and Father Marquette were ambassadors, the one from the governor of New France, the other from God, sent ". . . to discover new countries . . . to illuminate them with the light of the holy Gospel."[21] Offering a present, Jolliet asked for two guides to lead his party to the river which flowed into the Mississippi. "To this they very civilly consented; and they also spoke to us by means of a present, consisting of a mat to serve us as a bed during the whole of our voyage."[22] After three days of rest, surely a welcome respite, on Saturday, June 10, the explorers, accompanied by two Maumee guides, ". . . embarked . . . in the sight of a great crowd, who could not sufficiently express their astonishment at the sight of seven Frenchmen, alone and in two canoes, daring to undertake so extraordinary and so hazardous an expedition."[23] With the expert help of the Indian guides the party threaded its way for thirty leagues up the sluggish Fox River, through many swamps and numerous stagnant lakes. "For this reason," reported Marquette, "we greatly needed our two guides, who safely conducted us to a portage of 2,700 paces, and helped us to transport our canoes to enter that river; after which they returned home, leaving us alone in this unknown country, in the hands of providence."[24]

When the two helpful Maumee guides disappeared down the barely perceptible portage trail on their way back to the Mascouten village, the seven venturesome Frenchmen finally severed the last

[20] *Relations,* LIX, 105.

[21] *Ibid.*

[22] *Ibid.*

[23] *Ibid.*

[24] *Ibid.,* 105-07. Historians generally agree that the portage was made a little south of the present Portage, Wisconsin.

tenuous ties with lands and people in any manner familiar to them. The profound sense of utter separation from the world they knew and their complete dependence on heavenly aid during their excursion into the unknown shine forth clearly in Marquette's entry in his journal on that occasion.

> Thus we left the waters flowing to Quebec, 4 or 500 leagues from here, to float on those that would thenceforth take us through strange lands. Before embarking thereon, we began all together a new devotion to the Blessed Virgin Immaculate, which we practiced daily, addressing to her special prayers to place under her protection both our persons and the success of our voyage; and, after mutually encouraging one another, we entered our canoes.[25]

With very little effort of the imagination one can see those seven Frenchmen grouped hesitantly on the banks of the Wisconsin, looking a little fearfully down the stream. Where did this new river really go? Was there, by chance, anything to the Indian tales of monsters and giant whirlpools, dangers they could not hope to evade? Were they not being very foolhardy to go on? This was Ultima Thule, the end of the known world! Why go farther and for what purpose? One can almost hear Father Marquette encouraging his companions. Think of the glory their expected discovery would reflect on France and God! Think of the stories the Indians told of the vast, rich country ahead of them. But above all, think of the souls of the poor, benighted Illinois, and God knows how many other hitherto unknown nations, sitting in darkness and idolatry waiting so anxiously for the light of the Gospel to be brought to illuminate their stygian darkness. "Let us kneel together," he urged them, "in this vast wilderness and commend ourselves to the Mother of God. We will ask her today, and every day, to intercede with her Son to protect us and guide us safely through this perilous journey." Steadied by Father Marquette's confident trust in the protection of heaven, the six laymen knelt with the missionary, making their promise to the Mother of God. Rising, they boarded the canoes and pushed off into the unknown.

[25] *Ibid.*, 107.

Whatever trepidation and uneasiness the French explorers might have experienced was quickly eliminated by the very character of the boisterous, capricious Wisconsin River. For long stretches it rushes through weird rock formations, growling at its stony banks as if angered to be so rigidly contained. Again, it meanders across gently rolling prairies, whimsically changing its course for all the world like a small boy wandering down a country road, stopping here and there to splash through a puddle, dragging his feet as he dreams of high adventure. For a week Marquette and his companions paddled a hundred and eighteen miles down the Wisconsin in which shoals and low islands sometimes made their passage troublesome. But for the most part they glided by colorfully wooded hills and pleasant meadows where deer grazed in idyllic solitude. At last, forty leagues below their point of entry, on Saturday, June 17, 1673, ". . . at 42 and a half degrees of latitude, we safely entered the Mississippi . . . with a joy that I cannot express."[26] Though he does not tell us so, Father Jacques Marquette must have celebrated Mass the next day, a Sunday, with unwonted fervor in gratitude to God and the Virgin Immaculate for bringing him and his companions safely and successfully to the great river of the West which the French had desired to locate for so many years.

As the first Frenchmen to reach the Mississippi, it devolved upon the explorers to report in detail everything about the river, the country through which it flowed, the flora, the fauna, the nature of the soil, and the character of the aborigines dwelling there. Addressing himself at once to that responsibility, Marquette recorded that opposite the mouth of the Wisconsin River, across the breadth of the Mississippi, was a chain of high mountains, but on the river's left bank the land rolled away to the south as an open, pleasant prairie.[27] They measured the depth of the main channel of the Mississippi and found it to have a depth of ten fathoms.

[26] *Ibid.* The true latitude of the confluence of the Wisconsin and the Mississippi is forty-three degrees.

[27] The limestone cliffs on the right bank of the Mississippi at the mouth of the Wisconsin hardly deserve to be called mountains. They are about four hundred feet high.

Paddling with the slow, gentle current of the river, the voyagers observed deer and "cattle" on shore, flocks of ducks, and, later, turkey, but no people. The river was well stocked with sturgeon, whiskered catfish, and at least one tiger-fish which rammed Marquette's canoe so hard that he thought the fragile craft had been struck by a large tree.[28] The most impressive animals observed were the buffalo herds, one of which numbered four hundred by actual count. Marquette was the first European to give an eyewitness description of these great, lumbering beasts and the uses which the plains Indians made of the buffalo's hair, hide, skeleton, and flesh.[29] Nearly two centuries after Marquette saw buffalo herds, Indians were still hunting the animals in almost exactly the same manner as he described.

The continued absence of any sign of humans during the first hundred leagues of their journey down the river caused such concern that the travelers became very cautious. Each evening they went on shore, cooked a hasty meal over a very small fire, and spent the night in the two canoes which they anchored in the river some distance from shore. Throughout the night each member of the party stood sentry duty in turn ". . . for fear of surprise."[30] Eight days after leaving the mouth of the Wisconsin River, on Sunday, June 25, one of the Frenchmen noticed men's footprints on the right bank of the river, and a beaten path leading off into the prairie. Should they glide quietly on, hoping to escape detection, or should they risk contacting the natives who might well kill them out of hand? Missionary to the core, Marquette had joined the expedition, welcoming the ". . . blessed necessity of exposing my life for the salvation of all these peoples . . ."[31] Very well, here and now was the "blessed necessity" literally facing him; this was the time and the place to begin. Louis Jolliet was no less brave. If the valley of the mighty river was to be possessed effectively by the French, the first essential was opening contact with the Indians

[28] *Ibid.*, 109. Tiger-cat are now rarely caught in the Mississippi.

[29] *Ibid.*, 111-13. Dablon reported the existence of buffalo, but it is not certain that he actually saw one. See his description of them in *ibid.*, LV, 195-97.

[30] *Ibid.*, LIX, 113.

[31] *Ibid.*, 91.

dwelling there. And here was an opportunity to begin that contact. Besides, these Indians were bound to know something about the country and the people to the south of them. That fact alone was almost enough to induce Marquette and Jolliet to risk danger. "We, therefore," reported Father Marquette, "left our two canoes under the guard of our people, strictly charging them not to allow themselves to be surprised, after which Monsieur Jollyet [*sic*] and I undertook this investigation – a rather hazardous one for two men who exposed themselves alone to the mercy of a barbarous and unknown people."[32] Following the path for about two leagues, they discovered a village on the bank of a river and two more situated on a hill about half a league away. Without being detected, they came close enough to the first village to be able to hear the Indians talking. Commending themselves to God, they made their presence known by ". . . shouting with all our energy, and stopped, without advancing any farther."[33]

No more dramatic moment can be imagined than that facing Marquette and Jolliet as they stood awaiting the reaction of the Indians. Had the natives, who were Peoria, ever seen white men before? Would the aborigines mistake them for preternatural beings and grovel before them or would the Peoria promptly capture and torture them to death because some unknown, wandering *coureur-de-bois* had already enkindled fear and hatred of all white men? Hearing strange shouts, the Peoria poured out of their cabins to be greeted by the apparition of one tall man, bronzed and lithe, dressed in stained leather jerkin and breeches, and another, ramrod straight, thin and gaunt, seeming ten feet tall in his long black

[32] *Ibid.*, 115.

[33] *Ibid.* Locating the site of the Peoria village is difficult due to the proximity of the Iowa River to the Des Moines River. Just before meeting the Peoria, Marquette and his companions, according to their calculations, were at the ". . . parallel of 41 degrees, and as low as 40 degrees and some minutes, . . ." (*Ibid.*, 113.) All of the latitude calculations made are in error, but not consistently so. Hence, one could not simply raise Marquette's calculations one degree and thereby determine the location of the Peoria village. The preponderance of evidence seems to indicate that the village was four miles inland from the Mississippi on the Iowa River and near Oakville, Iowa. The true latitude of the mouth of the Iowa River is forty-one degrees and thirteen minutes. On Marquette's map it is slightly above forty degrees.

cassock. Both groups hesitated, eyeing one another, waiting. Finally the Indians took the initiative. Four dignified elders, detaching themselves from the multitude, gravely advanced towards the visitors, two of them bearing elaborately decorated calumets, which they ceremoniously raised to the sun, a universally accepted Indian symbol of friendship. Addressing them in the Illinois tongue, Marquette asked the Indians who they were. Replying that they were Illinois, the elders offered their visitors the calumet to smoke as a sign from the Frenchmen that they came in peace. Then the visitors were escorted to an ancient elder in the village who, though stark naked, greeted them with impressive solemnity, saying: "How beautiful is the sun, O Frenchman, when thou comest to visit us! All our village awaits thee and thou shalt enter all our cabins in peace."[34] After all of the elders of the village had smoked the calumet with the visitors, to do them honor, they were conducted in procession to meet the great captain of all the villages who had sent messengers to invite them to hold council with him.

Reaching the second village, the two Frenchmen were greeted by the great captain and two of his dignified elders, all equally naked. When all had smoked the calumet within the captain's cabin, a respectful silence fell on the gathering, awaiting the word the visitors brought. This was a thrilling moment for Jacques Marquette. At last, after years of waiting, he could begin to bring the word of God to the Illinois. And thus he addressed them:

> . . . I spoke to them by four presents that I gave them. By the first, I told them that we were journeying peacefully to visit the nations dwelling on the river as far as the sea. By the second, I announced to them that God, who had created them, had pity on them, inasmuch as, after they had so long been ignorant of him, he wished to make himself known to all the peoples; that I was sent by him for that purpose; and that it was for them to acknowledge and obey him. By the third, I said that the great captain of the French informed them that he it was who restored peace everywhere; and that he had subdued the Iroquois. Finally, by the fourth, we begged them to give us all the information that they had about the sea, and about the nations through whom we must pass to reach it.[35]

[34] *Ibid.*, 117.
[35] *Ibid.*, 119-21.

When the Blackrobe finished the great captain arose and, placing his hand on a young male slave, he replied:

> I thank thee, Black Gown, and thee O Frenchman . . . for having taken so much trouble to come and visit us. Never has the earth been so beautiful, or the sun so bright as today; never has our river been so calm or so clear of rocks, which your canoes have removed in passing; never has our tobacco tasted so good, or our corn appeared so fine, as we now see them. Here is my son whom I give thee to show thee my heart. I beg thee to have pity on me, and on all my nation. It is thou who knowest the great spirit who has made us all. It is thou who speakest to him and hearest his word. Beg him to give me life and health, and to come and dwell with us, in order to make us know him.[36]

Mindful of the sacrosanct custom of exchanging presents, the great captain offered Marquette four gifts in response to the presents tendered. The first was the slave boy; the second, ". . . an altogether mysterious calumet, upon which they place more value than upon a slave."[37] In presenting a third gift, the captain explained that it was tendered in the hope that the Frenchmen would not go farther ". . . on account of the great danger to which we exposed ourselves."[38] To that well-intentioned plea, Marquette replied that he did not fear death, but regarded no happiness greater than losing his life for the glory of him who made all. "This," the missionary noted, "is what these poor people cannot understand."[39] Nor were the Illinois alone in their misunderstanding for many do not understand it, even today.

At the conclusion of the council meeting the two Frenchmen were tendered a great feast at which the Indian master of ceremonies fed the honored guests as if they were children, spooning steaming sagamite and morsels of baked fish into their mouths. The guests were also offered portions of freshly killed dog, which they declined, and the fattest morsels of buffalo meat which the hosts obviously considered their most succulent delicacy. After the feast Marquette and Jolliet were given a tour of the village, fully three

[36] *Ibid.*, 121.
[37] *Ibid.*
[38] *Ibid.* Marquette mentions only three of the four gifts given him.
[39] *Ibid.*

hundred cabins, during which the people showered them with gifts, chiefly belts and bracelets woven from bear or buffalo hair, and dyed red, yellow, or gray. The following day the two visitors took their leave, escorted by nearly six hundred Indians who went to the river to see them off. Before bidding them farewell, Marquette solemnly promised that the following year he would come to live with them and instruct them.

Jacques Marquette was so delighted with the Peoria that he devoted a lengthy passage of his journal to eulogizing them. They were, he was convinced, gentle, docile, physically shapely, and very skillful. Their language was so closely related to Algonquin that the missionary readily understood them. Their country abounded in game and produced plentiful crops of corn, beans, melons, and squash. They dwelt in roomy, prefabricated cabins constructed of woven mats. As for clothing, the men wore nothing, but the women were modestly clothed. Though polygamy was universally practiced, women unfaithful to their husbands were punished by having their noses and ears cut off. For all their seeming gentility, these Indians were greatly feared by their neighbors to the south whom they frequently attacked to procure slaves. These poor victims were bartered for goods of European manufacture which the Peoria procured from nations north of them. The calumet was so honored among the Peoria that he who possessed one could travel safely even among nations at war. Solemn ritual dances and songs, centered around the calumet, were the core of the social and religious life of the Peoria.[40] Marquette carefully preserved the calumet he received from these Indians and found good use for it later in the journey.

Leaving the Peoria near the end of June, the seven French explorers followed the meandering course of the mighty Mississippi, knowing not what the next bend of the river might reveal. Day by day the sun sparkled on the water and the vast silence in the great valley of the river was broken only by the cry of birds or a *voyageur* chant sung softly by the paddling men. Frequently they could raise sail and run comfortably before a gentle breeze. Each warm June

[40] *Ibid.*, 131-37. See the music score for the calumet dance in *ibid.*, 311.

evening the small flotilla stopped on shore for the scant repast and the daily devotions in honor of the Virgin Immaculate. While Marquette and Jolliet worked on their notes in the fading light, their companions discussed endlessly the fertility of the land about them, imagining what bountiful harvests it would yield. They passed the mouth of the Illinois River, later so important to them, without Marquette's noting the fact. Yet, not twelve miles below that confluence they were astonished and not a little frightened by two grotesque monsters painted high on the face of a limestone cliff, so sheer as nearly to defy any human attempt to scale it let alone decorate an enormous area of it. Describing these creatures, Marquette wrote:

> They are as large as a calf; they have horns on their heads like those of deer, a horrible look, red eyes, a beard like a tiger's, a face somewhat like a man's, a body covered with scales, and so long a tail that it winds all around the body, passing above the head and going back between the legs, ending in a fish's tail. Green, red and black are the three colors composing the picture. Moreover, these 2 monsters are so well painted that we cannot believe that any savage is their author; for good painters in France would find it difficult to paint so well,– and, besides they are so high up on the rock that it is difficult to reach that place conveniently to paint them.[41]

Musing together over the meaning of the startling painting they had just seen, the Frenchmen were rudely awakened by the thunderous roar of what they thought to be a fearful rapid towards which the current of the Mississippi was pushing them at a frightening rate. Shortly they perceived that a giant of a river, flowing from the west, the Missouri, was roughly shouldering its way into the placid Mississippi, creating a great vortex at the confluence.[42] Once the threatening whirlpool was safely avoided, the questing instinct of the explorer immediately arose within the French voyagers. A river of such proportions obviously drained a vast area of land to the

[41] *Ibid.*, 139-41. The petroglyphs were on the face of a cliff near Alton, Illinois. For a discussion of these figures, which have long since disappeared, see Clara K. Bayliss, "The Significance of the Piasa," *Transactions* of the Illinois State Historical Society for 1908, 114-23.

[42] *Relations*, LIX, 139-41.

northwest. But from how far west did it come and how many aboriginal nations, previously undreamed of, dwelt on its banks? Could that river, which Marquette called the Pekitanoui, possibly be the route to the Vermilion Sea? The missionary promptly announced his intention of exploring the newly discovered stream, saying:

Judging from the direction of the course of the Mississippi, if it continues the same way, we think that it discharges into the Mexican gulf. It would be a great advantage to find the river leading to the southern sea towards California; and, as I have said, this is what I hope to do by means of the Pekitanoui, according to the reports made to me by the savages. From them I have learned that, by ascending this river for 5 or 6 days, one reaches a fine prairie 20 or 30 leagues long. This must be crossed in a northwesterly direction, and it terminates at another small river,– on which one may embark, for it is not very difficult to transport canoes through so fine a country as that prairie. This 2nd river flows towards the southwest for 10 or 15 leagues, after which it enters a lake, small and deep . . . which flows towards the west, where it falls into the sea. I have hardly any doubt that it is the Vermillion [*sic*] Sea and I do not despair of discovering it some day, if God grant me the grace and the health to do so, in order that I may preach the Gospel to all the peoples of this new world who have so long groveled in the darkness of infidelity.[43]

A little less than twenty leagues below the mouth of the Missouri Marquette and his companions encountered the great ox-bow bend of the Mississippi where it turns sharply and runs nearly due north for about ten miles and then, just as abruptly, reverses itself and flows southward, crowding the great volume of water into a narrow millrace. Indians believed that this area was the domain of a powerful, angry manitou who devoured travelers daring to invade his home.[44] The Illinois had good reason to fear that stretch of white water on their mighty river. Since their country afforded no birch bark for canoes, they constructed very cumbersome boats from a single log, producing a large unwieldly craft which very easily overturned in troubled waters. Just as the French voyagers emerged from the great ox-bow bend of the Mississippi, they came to the

[43] *Ibid.*
[44] *Ibid.*, 145.

mouth of the Ohio River.[45] Stopping long enough to calculate its latitude, Marquette placed the mouth of that river at thirty-six degrees north latitude, an error of a full degree. The true latitude of the mouth of the river is thirty-seven degrees. By then it was full summer, hot, muggy, enervating with mosquitoes at their maddening worst. Noticing how the natives fought the pests by inhabiting raised, shaded platforms with smudge fires under them, the French travelers tried to imitate the Indians by making tents of sailcloth over their canoes, hoping that breezes off the river would blow the mosquitoes away. Perhaps, also, the voyagers discovered that smoking the calumet discouraged their insect tormenters.

Drifting down the sluggish Mississippi, the attention of the Frenchmen was drawn to some Indians on shore who, armed with guns, seemed ready to attack them. Marquette displayed his calumet and addressed them in Huron while his companions prepared to defend themselves. When it became clear that the Indians were inviting them ashore, the French landed and were offered ". . . meat from wild cattle and bear's grease, with wild plums which were very good."[46] Jolliet and Marquette inquired from their hosts whence these Indians acquired the guns, cloth, knives, hoes, and glass beads they possessed. The Indians replied that they purchased these things from Europeans living towards the east who ". . . had rosaries and pictures; that they played upon instruments; that some of them looked like me [Marquette] and had been received . . . kindly [by them]."[47] As far as the missionary could determine,

[45] *Ibid.*, 143. Marquette called the Ohio River the Ouaboukigou. It was many years after Marquette's time before the French made a clear distinction between the Ohio and the Wabash. As everyone knows, the Wabash joins with the Ohio well over a hundred and fifty miles by water northeast of the confluence of the Ohio and the Mississippi.

[46] *Ibid.*, 145.

[47] *Ibid.*, 149. Who these Indians were has never been satisfactorily determined. Since Marquette addressed them in Huron, it is likely that something about them reminded him of the Hurons. These Indians may have belonged to the Chickasaw family. Their vague knowledge of Christianity would have been gained through at least indirect contact with Franciscan missionaries in the present Georgia. The labor of the Franciscans in Georgia is discussed by John Tate Lanning in his *The Spanish Missions of Georgia.* On his map Marquette called these Indians the Mons8pelea. Their village was located on or near the site of the present Memphis, Tennessee. See Jean Delanglez, "Marquette's Autograph Map of the Mississippi River," *Mid-America*, XVI (1945), 51.

however, the Indians had been given no religious instruction. When the Indians told their callers that the sea was only ten days away, the French believed that statement, chiefly because the whole character of the country had been gradually changing. Open prairies had given way to heavily wooded areas, cane brakes, and subtropical bird life. All of these signs indicated that the explorers were nearing their journey's end which arrived, sooner perhaps than they anticipated.

The voyagers set out from the small aboriginal band they had just met with light hearts. Ten days of paddling would see them at their goal. The weather was hot, but clear; the banks of the river were lined with great tall trees, cottonwoods, elm, and basswood. Behind the screening of trees they could hear wild cattle bellowing, a sure sign of prairie country which should mean fine farm land when France populated this new territory they were discovering. Small game, especially quail, fell under the gun of the hunter as, probably by accident, did a gorgeous little parakeet with a saucy red head, golden neck, and green body. But the pleasant pastoral scene changed abruptly as they neared, according to Marquette's reckoning, the thirty-third degree of latitude. There the travel-worn voyagers spied a village on the bank of the river and Indians, called the Michigamea, milling about in a hostile attitude. Braves in staunch wooden barks surrounded the Frenchmen's two canoes; warriors on land marched back and forth menacingly and a few hotheads leaped into the river, determined to swim out and overturn the canoes of the Frenchmen. "We had recourse," recorded Marquette, "to our Patroness and guide, the Blessed Virgin Immaculate; and we greatly needed her assistance . . ."[48] Marquette stood up in his canoe and ostentatiously displayed his calumet only to have a young brave throw a war club at the missionary, barely missing him. Just when Marquette fully expected to be pierced by a shower of arrows, the visitors drew close enough to shore for the elders to recognize the calumet. Two of these ancients approached and placed their weapons in the canoes of the French as a clear sign of peaceful intent. Then the

[48] *Relations*, LIX, 151.

French were invited to come ashore. Once landed, Marquette sought to communicate with these natives, employing in turn each of the six Indian languages he spoke, but in vain. At last one old man was brought forward who understood a little Illinois. Through that interpreter, the missionary made presents to the Indians and explained the purpose of the journey. Though they understood ". . . very well what we wished to say to them, . . ."[49] the Indians would tell their visitors only that they could learn what they desired to know at another large village called Arkamsea [*sic*] eight or ten leagues lower down. In spite of their uncommunicativeness on matters geographical, the Indians fed their visitors bountifully and invited them to stay the night, which they did, but with some anxiety. Father Marquette was particularly saddened at this meeting because, as he said: ". . . I know not whether they apprehended what I told them about God, and about matters pertaining to their salvation. This is a seed cast into the ground, which will bear fruit in its time."[50]

The following morning, accompanied by the old interpreter and a native canoe containing ten men, the French voyagers set out for the Arkansa village. Half a league above the village the small flotilla was met by two cumbersome log canoes, in one of which a welcoming dignitary stood erect, bearing a calumet and making signs of peaceful intent. Convoyed to shore, the French were conducted to the cabin of the chief warrior, a very clean scaffold carpeted with fine rush mats where the elders, the warriors, and the common people were assembled to welcome the visitors. Luckily, the French discovered a young lad among the people who spoke quite fluent Illinois. Through this youngster Marquette announced the purpose of their coming and spoke to the people ". . . about God and . . . instructed them."[51] The Indians revealed that, though

[49] *Ibid.*, 153.

[50] *Ibid.*

[51] *Ibid.*, 155. Historians, previous to 1945, generally agreed that Marquette and Jolliet went as far south as an Arkansas Indian village at the mouth of the Arkansas River. However, Jean Delanglez, in his "Marquette's Autograph Map," 42-43, makes a good case for Tongigua, an Arkansas village on the east bank of the Mississippi. Delanglez's conclusion, however valid, does not offer an apodictic answer because of the seventeenth-century French concept of

the sea was only ten days away, they had no contact with the people dwelling below them because these were their enemies, preventing them from trading with the Europeans. The hatchets, knives, and beads which the French saw among the Arkansa came partly from nations to the east and partly from a village of Illinois four days journey to the west. The Arkansa were generous with what they had, but their diet was limited to corn and melons. Though the country was overrun with wild cattle, the Arkansa did not hunt them for fear of their enemies. On the evening of their arrival the visitors were entertained by the chief who ". . . danced the calumet . . . as a token of our entire safety."[52] But just before the entertainment the Indians held a secret meeting ". . . in regard to the design entertained by some to break our heads and rob us; but the chief put a stop to all these plots."[53]

Having now come far enough south to be, at least figuratively, within sound of the sea, it behooved Father Marquette and Louis Jolliet to determine whether they should ". . . push on, or remain content with the discovery which we had made."[54] Having reached the latitude, according to their calculations, of thirty-three degrees and forty minutes, and being of the opinion that the Gulf of Mexico, into which the Mississippi surely flowed, was at thirty-one degrees and sixty minutes, only two or three days away, it would be imprudent to go on. If hostile savages killed them France would lose all the valuable knowledge of the Mississippi which they had gathered. If they fell into the hands of the Spaniards certainly Jolliet and the other five laymen would be thrown into prison, nobody knew for how long. Finally, they had already obtained all the pertinent information about the Mississippi and the country through which it flowed. The great river of the West did not flow into the Atlantic near Virginia or Florida, but into the Gulf of

where one located the mouth of the Arkansas. The French considered the mouth of the Arkansas to be the place where it is joined by the White River, a good ten miles from the Mississippi. We consider that the mouth of the Arkansas is below Big Island.

[52] *Relations*, LIX, 159.

[53] *Ibid.*

[54] *Ibid.*

Mexico. Jolliet had not been able to do any trading, it was true, but he could probably stay over at the Sault another season and recoup the financial losses this important exploratory journey had obliged him to incur. As for Father Marquette, his dream was realized; he had met the Illinois whom he had ambitioned converting for so long. As soon as the party reached the mission of Saint-François-Xavier, Marquette could complete his journal and then be off to work among the Illinois. Thus it was that Jacques Marquette wrote in his journal: "After a month's navigation, while descending the Missisipi [*sic*] from the 42nd to the 34th degree, and beyond, and after preaching the Gospel as well as I could to the nations that I met, we start on the 17th of July from the village of the Akensea [*sic*] to retrace our steps."[55] When they turned the prows of their canoes northward that Monday, July 17, 1673, the voyagers were nearly 1,700 miles from home.

On that bright, hot Monday in mid-July, Marquette and his friends could not help expressing their exuberent spirits at starting home, bearing important information, the solution of the mystery of the great river of the West. During the whole voyage down the river not a single one of the seven Frenchmen had suffered a serious accident and no Indian nation had been hostile. God was surely in his heaven and all was right with the world, thanks, indeed, to the intercession of the Immaculate Virgin whose protective mantle had sheltered them from all harm. With paddles flashing rythmically in the sun, the voyagers breasted the placid surface of the Mississippi while lustily singing hymns to the Mother of God. There was no need now for stealth and caution; they knew every bend of the river and had many friends among the peoples dwelling on it. And, as they advanced up the river against the current, they were confident of meeting more people whose friendship they would gain. Soon the travelers passed the village of the Michigamea

[55] *Ibid.*, 161. The exact latitude at which Marquette and Jolliet started for home will, perhaps, always remain conjectural. If Marquette's last observation was accurate, allowing him the very minimal error of six minutes, the party turned back at the place we call the mouth of the Arkansas River which is exactly at thirty-three degrees and forty-six minutes. Marquette calculated that he and his companions went as far south as latitude thirty-four degrees.

where the old man had acted as their interpreter. On Friday, August 4, 1673, the small flotilla of Frenchmen reached the Chickasaw village at which they had eaten such luscious plums. There Jacques Marquette made a latitudinal reckoning and wrote a letter which he asked the Indians to deliver to the Europeans to the east with whom they traded. He wrote:

> I salute in the Lord whoever receives this letter
> I, who am nothing, except by the virtue of obedience, seeking to lead anyone I could to Christ, our Saviour, happened, under divine direction, to meet Indians whom I believe are in contact with Europeans. Since they could not give me any information about this, I should like to learn who you are, where you live and who these Indians are. In the meantime know this about me. God called me to the Society of Jesus so that in this region of Canada I might spend my life working for the salvation of the Indians whom He redeemed with his Blood. I am certain that if the Immaculate Virgin Mother of God were present to me in this pitiable country, she would not wish me to render up my soul, which Christ saved with such bitter torment and she preserves, until I succeeded. Let us each pray that if we do not meet in this life we may do so in heaven.
> Done on the River of the Conception
> At the 35th latitude and
> Approximately the 275th longitude
> 4 August, 1673
>
> Your servant in Christ Jesus
> and the Immaculate Conception
> Jacques Marquette Societ. Jesu.[56]

Forging northward the French explorers toiled through the waters spilling out of the Ohio, fought their way through the roaring ox-bow bend of the Mississippi, and battled their way across the mouth of the angry Missouri. Again they examined the puzzling petroglyphs and passed on to the mouth of the Illinois River. There Father Marquette broke out his compass and astrolabe to make a careful latitudinal fix for if that river proved to be the short-cut which Father Allouez had learned about, it would be

[56] Clarence W. Alvord, "An Unrecognized Father Marquette Letter," *American Historical Review*, XXV (1920), 676. The translation given in the article, which also contains the Latin, is not used here. With chances many thousands to one that the Indians would actually pass the letter on, it came into the hands of William Byrd of Virginia.

very important to mark its exact position on the map so that others could find it. According to his calculations Marquette recorded that the mouth of the Illinois was at ". . . about the 38th degree."[57] Entering the Illinois, the voyagers were promptly taken by the country through which they passed with surprising ease. Unfurling their sails they traveled sixty-five leagues up the new stream in the greatest comfort. About two hundred miles up the river the French came upon a village of Illinois known as the Kaskaskia. The inhabitants of this little cluster of seventy-four cabins received the Frenchmen graciously, extracting a promise from Marquette that he would return to instruct them. And here the missionary fulfilled a promise he had made when he first heard that he was to accompany Jolliet. Marquette named the village, and the mission he expected to open there shortly, in honor of the Immaculate Conception just as he named the great river by that title on his map.[58] On leaving the Kaskaskia, the French were accompanied by the chief of the village and some of his young warriors who escorted their visitors to the Lake of the Illinois (Lake Michigan). Parting from their helpful Kaskaskia guides, Marquette and his companions went northward along Lake Michigan's beautiful western shore until they were opposite Sturgeon Bay. There they beached their two well-worn canoes and carried them, together with their now depleted baggage, about two miles over a faint portage trail to Sturgeon Bay. Possibly they spent the last night of their journey there, contentedly reminiscing about their many experiences, joshing one another regarding incidents which now seemed humorous in retrospect. The following morning the seven intrepid explorers set out for the mission of Saint-François-Xavier, a good day's paddle down Green Bay. Though we would wish Father Marquette had described his joyful homecoming, he merely remarked, quite prosaically: ". . . at the end of September, we reached the Bay des Puantz [*sic*] from which we had started at the beginning of June."[59]

[57] *Relations*, LIX, 161. True latitude of the mouth of the Illinois is thirty-eight degrees and fifty-five minutes.

[58] *Ibid.*, 165. The site of the village is disputed, but Utica, Illinois, would seem to be the most likely location.

[59] *Ibid.*, 161-63.

Jacques Marquette's final comment on the venturesome and eminently successful voyage of exploration merits inclusion:

> Had this voyage resulted in the salvation of even one soul, I would consider all my troubles well rewarded, and I have reason to presume that such is the case. For, when I was returning, we passed through the Illinois of the Peouarea [*sic*], and during three days I preached the faith in all their cabins; after which, while we were embarking, a dying child was brought to me at the water's edge and I baptized it shortly before it died, through an admirable act of providence for the salvation of that innocent soul.[60]

[60] *Ibid.*

THE MISSION OF THE IMMACULATE CONCEPTION AMONG THE ILLINOIS

No welcoming committee was waiting on the right bank of the lower Fox on that chilly evening in late September 1673, eager to welcome Father Jacques Marquette and his six travel-worn companions as they reached the mission of Saint-François-Xavier whence they had departed three months before. Negotiating the last troublesome rapid, the seven weary men paddled to shore, disembarking only a few steps from the mission building. Quite probably they found the place deserted and the ashes cold in the hearth. Autumn was, after all, the vital fall hunting season when most of the tribes took to the woods searching for deer and bear. Dressing out the carcasses, the Indians smoked the meat over slow fires or dried it in the sun, preserving it for the winter provender when corn ran low and fish were difficult to catch through the ice.

More than likely Father Louis André was sixty miles up the western shore of Green Bay following the Menominee.[1] For the same reason Father Claude Allouez may well have paddled away to spend the autumn and, indeed, the whole winter, with the Mascouten.[2] However disappointing the lack of a welcome may have been, with not even a single Frenchman available to listen to their thrilling saga, Marquette and Jolliet both had pressing occupations awaiting them. Louis Jolliet, already heavily in debt from expenses incurred for the exploratory voyage, had been prevented during the whole summer from trading with the Indians or even from watching over his business interests at Sault-Sainte-Marie. Since it was already too late in the season for Jolliet to take down to Montreal whatever peltry his brother Zacharie might have collected, there was nothing for it but to spend the coming year in the West. Perhaps the delay was providential since the Sieur Jolliet was in no position to settle with his creditors, though he expected to be able to do so by the fall of 1674, the end of the coming trading season.[3]

Father Jacques Marquette also had his work cut out for him. Even before he departed on the exploratory expedition the missionary knew that he would not return to Saint-Ignace, but, provided the journey was successful, would remain at Saint-François-Xavier until he could go off again, the following spring, to open a new mission among the Illinois.[4] While waiting for spring Marquette would care for the Indians in the neighborhood of Saint-François-Xavier and use his free time preparing his journal and map for forwarding to Father Dablon at Quebec. Louis Jolliet stayed with Father Marquette the few days requisite for the two explorers to compare notes, supplementing the information which each had gathered independently. But, at least by the middle of

[1] *Relations*, LVIII, 273-79.

[2] *Ibid.*, 267-69.

[3] Delanglez, *Life of Jolliet*, 130.

[4] *Relations*, LIX, 69. Dablon to Pinette, October 24, 1674: "Since his return, the Father has remained in the Ottawa country, that he may be fully prepared to establish missions among the Illinois, the nearest and the most docile of the tribes that he has discovered."

October, Louis Jolliet packed his notes into his strongbox and set off with his men for Sault-Sainte-Marie.[5] When Jacques Marquette bade farewell to his cherished friend, Louis Jolliet, on a raw October morning, neither was aware that they were never again to meet on earth. Of the other five men who made the journey down the Mississippi, Jacques Largillier would not only meet Father Marquette again, but that pious layman would sorrowfully place the body of his Jesuit friend in its lonely grave nineteen months hence.

Left alone at Saint-François-Xavier, Father Jacques Marquette was busy during much of each day ministering to the Indians residing near the mission or entertaining passing French traders and aboriginal visitors who stopped begging a handout. One of his major apostolic charges, it can be assumed, was a village of Potawatomie situated about twelve miles above the mouth of the lower Fox River, on the eastern shore of Green Bay, a short distance up the Red River.[6] Though sacerdotal duties filled most of his day, in the evenings Jacques Marquette, closing the door of his crude cabin, excluding Indians of all sizes and shapes, could spread his voluminous notes on a rude table and compile his journal, reporting the details of his history-making voyage. Sheet after sheet of his account, penned in his clear, regular hand, piled up as he recorded events in his unusually attractive style. Then he selected a large sheet of good rag paper, measuring 467 by 350 mm., on which he drew his map.[7] The projection employed was the simple, cylindric, equally spaced *plate-carrée* familiar to us today. On each side of the sheet, beginning at the top, he marked off degrees of north latitude from 30 to 48 degrees. On the top and bottom of the page he indicated longitudinal divisions, but did not assign degrees to them. Since a photographic reproduction of the original map is

[5] No documentary evidence has yet been discovered outlining Louis Jolliet's activities from the end of September 1673 until late June or early July 1674. Quite likely he went back to Sainte-Marie-du-Sault as quickly as possible after reaching Green Bay, since he had business interests there.

[6] The village was situated not far from Dykesville, Wisconsin.

[7] Marquette's original map is in the possession of the Collège Sainte-Marie, Montreal.

available in this volume, the reader may be spared a detailed verbal description of this first geographic delineation of the Mississippi River. It is, however, quite in order to include the remarks of a recognized expert concerning it. In his *Contribution of the Canadian Jesuits to the Geographical Knowledge of New France, 1632-1675*, Nellis M. Crouse avers that the map

> . . . represents, with the exception of Lake Superior, merely the route traversed by Marquette, even the eastern shore of Lake Michigan being traced by a dotted line, so careful was the author to show only those places with which he was personally acquainted. But this defect, if we can call it such, is compensated for by a style of execution that would do credit to a skilled designer. The Mississippi is shown only from its junction with the Wisconsin to the mouth of the Arkansas where the party turned back. Marquette has drawn those tributaries of the great river, as he described them in his journal, and he makes no attempt to trace them back to some imaginary sources or to decorate them with possible affluents. It is refreshing to turn to such a work executed with strict attention to detail, erected on a firm foundation of fact, and one in which the author attempts to impart his knowledge unadorned by any flights of fancy.[8]

As spring approached Père Jacques began preparations for what he surely considered the realization of his long-cherished dream of opening a mission among the Illinois. Soon Father Allouez came in from the Mascouten village with a glowing account of religious success not only with the Mascouten but with some of the Fox, the Maumee, and even a few Kaskaskia and Peoria.[9] Father André, returning from the Menominee River and the tribes dwelling along the Oconto River, was equally enthusiastic about the success of his apostolate.[10] To the surprise of his brethren Father Marquette seemed to have lost much of his wonted vigor. He was noticeably wan and drawn for one whose physical endurance was a byword among his fellow Jesuits. Father Allouez, himself a vigorous sixty-one, was no little concerned at discovering that Marquette was really ailing. By the end of May even Père Jacques was willing to

[8] Nellis M. Crouse, *Contributions of the Canadian Jesuits to the Geographical Knowledge of New France, 1632-1675*, 114.

[9] *Relations*, LVIII, 265-71.

[10] *Ibid.*, 273-81.

admit that he was not himself.[11] He was frequently afflicted with chills and fever; he took almost no nourishment, though a small sip of the precious supply of altar wine seemed to help a little.[12] When the young man grew worse rather than better, Father Allouez sent word to Father Nouvel, the superior, who resided at Sainte-Marie-du-Sault, that Father Marquette was in no condition to go off by himself, undertaking the arduous task of opening a new mission. The superior promptly replied, directing Father Marquette to defer his departure until he regained his usual, robust health.[13] Along with the order came the sad news of a disaster at Sainte-Marie which would eventually effect Jacques Marquette.

Since 1671 when bands of Ottawa fled from the Chequamegon Bay area to escape possible annihilation by the fierce, powerful Sioux, imprudent young Ottawa warriors, settled with their people around Sainte-Marie-du-Sault, continued playing with fire, raiding into the Sioux country where frequent skirmishes occurred. On one such occasion, eighty Sioux braves were taken by surprise and brought captive back to Sainte-Marie. To save their fellow tribesmen, the Sioux offered to conclude a peace which would embrace not only the Ottawa but the Cree as well. The Cree, no mean war-

[11] ARSJ, Gallia 110, II, f.195. Lettre circulaire du R. P. Jacques Marquette, October 13, 1675. Marquette's illness, in the early summer of 1675, began at the end of May and lasted until September.

[12] In an effort to discover the nature of Father Marquette's malady, this writer gathered every reference to his illness, either by himself or others, and submitted the material to Maximillian J. Fox, M.D., of Milwaukee, an internist of international repute. On April 22, 1967, Dr. Fox, after consultation with other respected physicians, reported: "The most plausible reasoning would be that his terminal disease was typhoid fever. His diet and the types of food ingested are consistent with this enteric 'bloody flux,' I am positive that he could not have had any other than a para-typhoid disease. If there were an opportunity to culture his bowel, we would find that he suffered from that tragic illness which maimed thousands of people living among Indians in the Great Lakes region . . . Previous to his 1673 experience, he apparently had satisfactorily prepared foods. He most likely contracted the disease during his voyage of 1673, from improperly prepared food furnished him by Indians. The 1674-75 trip to the Illinois Indian tribe again proposed either a repeat or a fresh infection of a para-typhoid typhoid syndrome. The entire picture is consistent with this gastro-intestinal disease and his demise, in complete control of his senses is quite consistent with the typhoid fever."

[13] *Relations,* LIX, 165.

riors themselves and sworn enemies of the Sioux, determined to frustrate the peace effort by slaughtering the ambassadors sent by the Sioux. When ten Sioux representatives reached Sainte-Marie in the spring of 1674, they were housed in the Jesuit residence under the protection of Father Gabriel Druillettes who profited by this opportunity to instruct them, hoping thereby to open the Sioux country to evangelization. At the peace parley held in the Jesuit residence, a Cree treacherously murdered one of the Sioux, and a bloody conflict followed, during which someone set fire to the building, burning it to the ground.[14] In that senseless conflagration a copy of Louis Jolliet's journal of his voyage down the Mississippi with Father Marquette went up in flames, leaving only the copy Jolliet carried with him when he went down to Quebec in the summer of 1674. That copy, too, found a watery grave before Jolliet reached Quebec. After the disaster headquarters of the Ottawa mission were moved to Saint-Ignace, though the mission of Sainte-Marie-du-Sault continued, but on a reduced scale. The Kiskakon and other Ottawa bands ". . . withdrew and left them [the Cree] exposed to the fury of the enemy."[15] The Kiskakon settled in a village of their own adjacent to the mission of Saint-Ignace and became the special charge of Father Henry Nouvel. It was the Kiskakon, converted for the most part by Father Marquette in 1671, who brought his remains back to Saint-Ignace from their original resting place.

The summer of 1674 was a very trying one for poor Jacques Marquette. After five long years of waiting, praying, and hoping for the privilege of evangelizing the Illinois, on the very threshold of realizing his dream his hitherto healthy, tireless body betrayed him. Instead of paddling joyfully off as soon as the ice was out of Green Bay, he lay at Saint-François-Xavier burning with fever and weak as an infant. His brethren anxiously nursed him, bleeding him and dosing him with vile-tasting herb tea while all through June, July, and half of August he languished, unable to take nourishment and plagued with an embarrassing diarrhea. But finally, in mid-

[14] *Ibid.*, LVIII, 255-63.
[15] *Ibid.*, LVII, 263.

August, he began to mend, though his recovery, it seemed to him, took an unconscionably long time. Through September he slowly regained his strength until at last he was back on his feet, chafing at the bit, anxious to be on his way. When it appeared that the young missionary was really recovered, a message was sent to Father Nouvel at Saint-Ignace, the new mission headquarters, reporting that Père Jacques, his old, vigorous self again, was well able to undertake the mission to the Illinois and might he please have permission to set out at once? "The Reverend Father Superior of the Ottawa missions permitted him to go, sending him for that purpose, eight days after the feast of Saint Michael, from Michilimackinac, where the superior usually resides, two of our domestics, *donnés,* attached to our mission, one of whom had made the [previous] voyage with him. They brought the permission to him at Green Bay where he was living and whence they set out at the beginning of November."[16]

Thus, at last, Jacques Marquette with his two assistants, Jacques Largillier and Pierre Porteret, pushed off into the lower Fox River on October 25, 1674, a Thursday, bound for the great village of the Illinois and the realization of the missionary's most cherished dream. There was barely enough room in the canoe for Marquette and his aides, so laden was the fragile little craft with everything requisite for establishing a new mission. Besides the essential equipment for a crude chapel, the canoe was crammed with presents for the

[16] Rochemonteix, *Jésuites,* III, 607. Cholenec to Fontenay, October 10, 1675. Pierre Cholenec was born at Saint Pol de Lêon in Brittany on July 29, 1640, and entered the Jesuit novitiate at Paris in 1658. He came to Canada in 1674 and died at Quebec in 1723. He could not have met Marquette in Canada. Jean de Fontenay, also a native of Saint Pol de Lêon, was born on February 17, 1643. He entered the Jesuit novitiate at Paris on October 11, 1658, and was, thus, a classmate of Cholenec's. If these two Jesuits were really friends of Father Marquette, as Cholenec says, each met him possibly once. When Marquette was on his way to sail for New France, he might have passed through Orleans where Fontenay was teaching. If Marquette stopped at La Flèche, he could have met Cholenec there for the latter was at that institution in 1666, studying philosophy. See ARSJ, France 23, 199. Fontenay volunteered for the foreign missions, but was not sent until 1687 when he went to China. He died at La Flèche on January 16, 1710. The feast of Saint Michael which Cholenec mentions, falls on October 6.

Indians, a roll of Chinese taffeta to be employed as a backdrop for a lovely picture of the Immaculate Conception, a supply of paper and ink, a scarred Mass-kit, a spare blanket or two, and ammunition needed for bagging game for the pot or, in direst need, warding off hostile Indians, none of whom they expected to encounter.

That Thursday, October 25, was a raw, blustery day with a strong wind blowing across Green Bay, creating a chop which made paddling the balky little canoe a tricky business. By noon when the travelers had advanced only about twelve miles, they were obliged to put in at the mouth of the Red River, on the eastern shore of Green Bay, where they were held landbound until the next morning.[17] At the mouth of the river the Frenchmen came upon a group of Potawatomie who were disputing among themselves regarding where they should spend the winter. The young braves, who had obtained a supply of trade goods at Montreal, were determined to take their wares to the Illinois where they would be paid good prices in pelts to say nothing of being able to trap beaver there themselves. The elders opposed the plan, fearing that, come spring, the young men would not dare come back home lest they be set upon by marauding Sioux. In that event the Potawatomie band would not only not profit economically, but they would also be deprived of the military help the young warriors afforded in case of an enemy attack.[18] Forced by the inclement weather to spend the night with the Potawatomie, Father Marquette did what he could to resolve their differences. The following morning, Friday, October 26, Marquette and his companions continued northward up the bay to Point Sable, stopping there to call briefly on the friends the missionary had made at the small Indian village located there for these Indians must have been frequent visitors at the mission of Saint-François-Xavier during the previous fall and winter. The missionary was somewhat surprised to find most of the people still in residence at the village. He would have expected the greater number to be gone off on their traditional fall hunting expedition. The Indians told him that only two cabins from

[17] *Relations*, LIX, 165. Marquette located this village on his own map.
[18] *Ibid.*

the village were spending the winter *"a la gasparde."*[19] Learning where Father Marquette was bound, the Indians told him that five canoes of Potawatomie and four of Illinois had just left the village on their way to the Illinois. If the Frenchmen wished to join that flotilla they could overtake it with ease. Since Indians could never be hurried, all the talking consumed so much of Friday that Marquette and his party were unable to set off until the next morning. Then a cold rain delayed him until noon when, finally, the wind died down and the sun came out. By evening, Friday, October 26, the French travelers reached the western end of Sturgeon Bay, catching up there with the Indian flotilla.[20]

Joining forces with the approximately fifty Potawatomie and Illinois afforded Father Marquette an excellent opportunity for instructing these traveling companions, but their presence also gave rise to the inevitable annoying delays attendant on voyaging with a group of aborigines. Greeting the members of the flotilla with the proper aboriginal courtesy and discussing plans with them wasted so much precious time that night fell before the whole group crossed the length of Sturgeon Bay to the land portage separating it from Lake Michigan. Starting early the following morning, Sunday, October 28, the whole group finally arrived at the portage. In the process, one canoeload of eager Indians raced ahead of the flotilla. When hunters wanted to shoot game in the woods, to avoid going hungry to bed, they feared to do so lest they endanger the lives of the impatient few who had gone on ahead of them. Pierre Porteret, hoping, undoubtedly, to avoid that danger, went off by himself, seeking something for the pot at a safe distance. For his pains, he got lost in the woods and thoroughly soaked in a thunderstorm which was followed by snow. After reporting that series of annoyances, Father Marquette added: "We began our portage and slept on the other shore where the stormy weather gave us much trouble."[21] As soon as the sun rose on Monday, October 29, the missionary and his companions, as well as the Indians,

[19] *Ibid.*
[20] *Ibid.*, 167.
[21] *Ibid.*

began the tiresome business of transporting baggage and canoes from Sturgeon Bay to Lake Michigan, a distance of ". . . nearly a league and . . . very difficult in many places."[22] That evening the Indians, perhaps sensing the annoyance of the French because the aborigines had not completed the portage in one day, came to Père Marquette and ". . . asked us not to leave them, as we may need them, and they know the lake better than we do."[23] The missionary assured the Indians that the French would not desert them, though certainly Marquette and Largillier knew the lake as well as they since both had traveled up Lake Michigan's western shore from the mouth of the Chicago River thirteen months before. After wasting two days waiting for the Indians to complete their portage, and being delayed for another half day by a strong wind, the party was ready to start traveling down the lake towards their objective.

As the first pale light of dawn brightened the sky on Wednesday, October 31, Father Marquette was up, urging everyone to be off. That late in the year when the days were so short, travelers could not afford to waste even a small part of the daylight hours. With ". . . tolerably fair weather . . ." the flotilla advanced perhaps twenty-five miles, stopping for the night ". . . at a small river."[24] The following morning, Thursday, November 1, the feast of All the Saints, after Father Marquette said Mass, the company advanced until nightfall when camp was made at ". . . a river,

[22] *Ibid.*

[23] *Ibid.*

[24] During the first day's journey on Lake Michigan, the flotilla would seem to have traveled as far south as the Kewaunee River which empties into Lake Michigan at Kewaunee, Wisconsin. The first river south of the Sturgeon Bay portage is the Ahnapee, which is about fifteen miles from the portage. Even in the only tolerably fair weather Marquette says they had that day, the flotilla would have traveled as far as possible. An average day's travel by canoe in fresh water was ten leagues or thirty miles. The distance from the Sturgeon Bay portage to the Kewaunee River would be about twenty-five miles. Chiefly due to the devotion of the late Henry J. Baumeister to Marquette, Kewaunee erected a monument to the missionary just a little north of the town. The tablet on the monument reads: "Father Marquette Served Holy Mass on This Spot, November 1, 1674." Kewaunee also has a small museum featuring Father Marquette.

whence one goes to the Poutewatamis [*sic*] by a good road."[25] That evening an Illinois named Chachagwessiou, a man ". . . greatly esteemed among his nation, partly because he engages in the fur trade, arrived . . . with a deer on his back, of which he gave us a share."[26] Friday, November 2, All Souls Day, dawned clear and crisp. After saying Mass the missionary and his party traveled all day. On the way two raccoons were killed for the pot, but when the carcasses were dressed out they were found to be ". . . almost nothing but fat."[27] When the fine weather continued on Saturday, November 3, Father Marquette went ashore on a wide beach of hard-packed fine sand to walk a while, stretching his legs. Coming to a river much too deep to wade, he summoned his companions to bring the canoe in to take him aboard. The two Frenchmen entered the river, picking up the missionary, but a strong wind prevented them from working their way out of the river back to Lake Michigan.[28] All of the Indian canoes continued on, except one which stood by to help. It was noon, Monday, November 5, before the French managed to exit from the river and continue on their way. More than likely Father Marquette and his companions did

[25] *Relations*, LIX, 165. The site at which the party camped for the night of November 1-2 was probably the mouth of Twin Rivers at Two Rivers, Wisconsin. Marquette says: ". . . we came for the night to a river, whence one goes to the Poutewatamis [*sic*] by a good road." He was speaking of the Potawatomie village on the eastern shore of Green Bay. The "good road" mentioned is not a land route, but one by water. One can paddle northward on the East Twin River to a short portage which brings one to the upper reaches of the Kewaunee. One can paddle up the Kewaunee to within a couple of miles of Dykesville, the approximate site of the Potawatomie village.

[26] *Ibid.* On November 2 the flotilla traveled all day in "very fine weather." Since voyagers could travel only from dawn to dusk, they would have voyaged, at that time of year, about ten hours. If they covered about thirty miles, they would have stopped at a location about even with Haven, Wisconsin.

[27] *Ibid.*

[28] *Ibid.*, 169. The description given by Father Marquette of the Lake Michigan shore on which he was walking would apply to almost any stretch of beach from Point Beach State Forest, four miles south of Two Creeks, Wisconsin, to Terry Andre State Park, a little less than fifteen miles below Sheboygan, Wisconsin. Given the point from which he seems to have started on the morning of Saturday, November 3, the river Marquette was unable to wade would be the Sheboygan at Sheboygan, Wisconsin.

not mind the delay since it allowed the priest to say Mass on Sunday and Monday without the presence of the Indians.

When he overtook the Indian flotilla Marquette found the Illinois engaged in a pagan ritual, honoring a wolf-skin. One of the Indians, named Nawaskingwe, was giving a feast for that purpose. "I seized the opportunity," recorded the missionary, "of instructing the Illinois on account of the feast . . ."[29] These Indians, after all, had little knowledge of the true God and not much more of Christianity. The score or so Illinois traveling with him were, to the missionary's mind, good, kindly people. Gathering them around him, he addressed them gently. It was useless and even foolish to honor the poor wolf's pelt since it could neither harm nor help them. The wolf's spirit was by no means some sort of divinity hovering over them. Only the true God of the Christians ought to be thus honored. And He was a loving God who cherished each one of them. Watching them, Marquette felt certain that, though still ignorant and uninstructed, these Illinois would become exemplary Christians and even apostles of their people. The Illinois, squatting around a dying fire, their serious faces turned toward the Blackrobe, listened with open hearts, wondering at this good man whose devotion to their welfare showed clearly for all to see and believe.

On Tuesday, November 6, the unwieldy flotilla ". . . performed a good day's journey."[30] However during the day when some of the Indians were ashore hunting, human footprints were observed. These might have been made by a roving band of Sioux warriors, the Indians conjectured. Since the Potawatomie and Illinois together were not numerous enough to stand off an enemy attack, it was more prudent to take cover in the woods for a while. It was noon on Friday, November 9, two and a half days later, before the Indians felt it safe to start southward again. During the afternoon the group advanced to a ". . . good camping ground." Where they

[29] *Ibid.* On Monday, November 5, Marquette and his men got out of the river at noon and journeyed until they came up with the Indian flotilla which had not stopped at the Sheboygan River. Since the Frenchmen could travel at most fifteen miles that day, they probably found the Indians at Bar Creek, near Cedar Grove, Wisconsin.

[30] *Ibid.* A "good day's journey," which was made that day, Tuesday, November 6, would put the party at Fox Point, Wisconsin, by nightfall.

were ". . . detained . . . for 5 days on account of the great agitation of the lake, although without any wind; and afterwards of the snow, which was melted on the following day by the sun and a breeze from the lake."[31] When the canoes were able to proceed, Thursday, November 15, the party advanced ". . . a sufficient distance . . ." to a camp ". . . at a favorable place, where we were detained 3 days."[32] At that point, the missionary had been traveling for twenty-one days and had covered perhaps 170 miles, averaging hardly more than eight miles per day.

The remaining fourteen days of travel were increasingly difficult. Setting off again on Tuesday, November 20, the buffetted voyagers after a cold, raw day of paddling ". . . slept near the bluffs . . ." where they were ". . . very poorly sheltered."[33] For the next two and a half days the thoroughly chilled travelers were unable to advance because of a strong wind which made it unsafe to risk going ahead. While thus delayed Pierre Porteret scouted the country and discovered that they were ". . . 20 leagues from the portage," or about sixty miles above the mouth of the Chicago River.[34] Embarking again at noon on Friday, November 23, the party had difficulty reaching a small river where it was again necessary to take shelter on land for three days.[35] The wretchedness of their situation may be gathered from Marquette's remark: "Then the cold began, and more than a foot of snow covered the ground;

[31] *Ibid.* The first "good camping-ground" below Fox Point would be the mouth of the Milwaukee River at Milwaukee, Wisconsin, about eighteen miles south of Fox Point. The party could have easily covered that distance from dawn to "about 2 o'clock," when they landed.

[32] *Ibid.* On Thursday, November 15, the party voyaged "a sufficient distance." The French *assez de chemin,* in its context, really means they traveled as far as they could in the bitter weather. They probably camped at the mouth of Oak Creek, somewhat less than fifteen miles south of the mouth of the Milwaukee River.

[33] *Ibid.*

[34] *Ibid.* Porteret's observation that the party was "20 leagues from the portage," that is, the Chicago portage, locates them at about Racine, Wisconsin, which is sixty-six miles, or a little over twenty leagues, north of the Chicago portage.

[35] *Ibid.*, 171. Since the party traveled only a part of the afternoon of Friday, November 23, and then put in at a river, they probably stopped at the mouth of Pike Creek at Kenosha, Wisconsin.

it has remained ever since."[36] Though the voyagers certainly suffered intensely from the bitter cold, everyone, except the missionary, ate well for Porteret bagged a deer, three ducks, and three turkeys ". . . which were very good."[37] Perhaps his companions managed to make a little broth for the priest whose insidious enemy, the old affliction again began to plague him. On Friday, November 23, he recorded in his journal: "Here I had an attack of diarrhea."[38] Jacques Marquette would never again be well.

Starting again on Tuesday, November 27, the travelers covered only three leagues, nine miles, before strong winds and unbearable cold drove them off the water. Trying again on Saturday, December 1, the three Frenchmen embarked ahead of the Indians ". . . so that I might celebrate holy Mass."[39] On that day and the next very little distance was covered, if any. On December 3, after traveling only a few miles, the flotilla encountered such masses of floating ice that they dared not continue lest their paper-thin canoes be ripped to pieces. To avoid that threatening disaster they were ". . . compelled to make for a point, so that we could land . . ."[40] The following day, Tuesday, December 4, aided by a favorable wind, the exhausted voyagers reached the mouth of the Chicago River, finding it ". . . frozen to the depth of a foot; there was more snow there than elsewhere . . ."[41] Utterly spent from the exertions of their incredibly difficult journey, the Frenchmen hastily threw together a rude shelter and settled down for eight days to regain

[36] *Ibid.*

[37] *Ibid.*

[38] *Ibid.*

[39] *Ibid.* On Tuesday, November 27, they covered only three leagues or nine miles. This distance would put them at Winthrop Harbor, Illinois.

[40] *Ibid.* The most likely point of land would be at Waukegan, Illinois, where there is a point of land behind which is a sheltered harbor. As everyone familiar with Lake Michigan knows, lake ice drifts back and forth all winter, driven by the wind. In this occasion the wind was driving the lake ice toward the Illinois shore.

[41] *Ibid.*, 173. The distance from the harbor at Waukegan to the mouth of the Chicago River is very close to thirty miles.

their strength.[42] The two laymen surely did what they could for the ailing missionary, but their efforts were fruitless. Undoubtedly, Father Marquette hoped that on the feast of the Immaculate Conception, December 8, his "Virgin Immaculate," whom he loved so tenderly, would cure him. But of that day he wistfully recorded: "We were unable to celebrate holy Mass on the day of the Conception, owing to the bad weather and cold."[43]

Since it was all too obvious that Father Marquette, even after a week's rest, was entirely too unwell to attempt continuing on another twenty leagues to their destination, the Illinois village, the Frenchmen decided to move two leagues up the Chicago River, the site of the portage between that stream and the Des Plaines River, where they spent the winter. Recording their decision on December 14, Marquette wrote: "Having encamped near the portage, 2 leagues up the river, we resolved to winter there, as it is impossible to go further, since we are too much hindered and my ailment did not permit me to give myself much fatigue."[44] The physical sufferings endured by the heroic missionary during that horrible winter nearly beggar description. To the bone-chilling cold was added wretched shelter from the wind and driving snow as well as Marquette's recurring fever and, a crowning, embarrassing indignity, "After the fourteenth of December my disease turned into a bloody flux."[45] In the midst of that almost nightmarish, frigid purgatory, the devout

[42] *Ibid.* The spot where Marquette spent eight days at the mouth of the Chicago River is at the intersection of Chicago's Wacker Drive and Michigan Avenue. His presence there is commemorated by a bas-relief on one of the pylons of the Michigan Avenue bridge. The artist who did the work was J. E. Fraser who apparently knew little about Marquette since he portrays the Jesuit in a Franciscan habit.

[43] *Ibid.*

[44] *Ibid.* Marquette's winter camp was situated a few steps away from where Chicago's Damen Avenue crosses the Sanitary and Ship Canal. A bronze relief commemorating the event is to be seen attached to the Damen Avenue bridge. The relief is the work of E. P. Seidel who worked from a sketch submitted by Thomas A. O'Shaughnessy. It is worth noting that Damen Avenue honors a well-known nineteenth-century Jesuit, Father Arnold Damen, S.J. The most scholarly investigation of the location of the Chicago portage was done by Robert Knight and Lucius H. Zeuch in their *The Location of the Chicago Portage Route of the Seventeenth Century.* See their map following 128.

[45] *Relations,* LIX, 175.

missionary made his annual eight-day retreat, an obligation his illness during the previous summer had prevented him from fulfilling. His two companions later reported to Father Pierre Cholenec that Father Marquette made his retreat ". . . with particular fervor and great spiritual consolation. The remainder of the time, he spent writing an account of his voyages. [Except for that] he was entirely consumed with spiritual matters, avoiding commerce with anything earthly in that wretched place, except for his two companions, whose confessions he heard and gave them Communion, exhorting them as earnestly as his strength permitted."[46]

Father Cholenec's description of Marquette's occupations during the winter is quite inaccurate. Far from leading a wholly ascetical, eremitical life, Marquette received a surprising number of visitors. The Illinois contingent of the flotilla remained with the Frenchmen until December 15 when they went on ". . . to join their people and give them the goods that they had brought, in order to obtain their robes."[47] Chachagwessiou, leader of the Illinois band, who was ". . . esteemed among his nation, partly because he engages in the fur trade . . .," had already come to understand the effect the law of supply and demand could have on prices. Noting that fact, Marquette remarked that the shrewd Illinois leader and his followers ". . . act like the traders, and give hardly any more than do the French."[48] Perhaps the missionary perceived Chachagwessiou's business acumen when the Indian dickered with him, or the two French laymen, trading ". . . 3 fine robes of ox-skins for a cubit of tobacco; . . ."[49] That aboriginal business man knew quite well that he would profit handsomely selling the French tobacco to the Indians. Father Marquette was probably quite well aware of this for he remarked: "I do not think that I have ever seen any savages more eager for French tobacco than they [the Illinois]. They came and threw beaver-skins at our feet, to get some pieces of it; . . ."[50]

[46] Rochemonteix, *Jésuites*, III, 607.
[47] *Relations*, LIX, 175.
[48] *Ibid.*
[49] *Ibid.*
[50] *Ibid.*

Two weeks after the departure of the Illinois band with their shrewd leader, Jacques Largillier visited a group of Illinois wintering six leagues away, and learned that Pierre Moreau, the Mole, who had accompanied Father Marquette on his voyage down the Mississippi, was trading in the area with his partner who is known only as "the surgeon." Appraised of the missionary's illness, the surgeon walked eighteen leagues, over fifty miles, bringing the patient ". . . some blueberries and corn."[51] After staying a few days, to offer the sick priest what medical aid he could as well as to receive spiritual ministration, he departed with Largillier who returned, on January 24, ". . . with a sack of corn and other delicacies which the French had given him for me. He also brought the tongues and flesh of two cattle, which a savage and he killed near here."[52] These visitors spread the news of Father Marquette's presence at the portage among the Indians and soon the missionary was waited upon by a delegation of Illinois who were spokesmen for the elders of the great village to which Marquette was enroute. These dignified ambassadors presented the Blackrobe with ". . . 2 sacks of corn, some dried meat, pumpkins, and 12 beaver-skins: 1st, to make me a mat; 2nd, to ask me for powder; 3rd, that we might not be hungry; 4th, to obtain a few goods."[53] The ailing priest replied that having come to instruct them in the ways of God, he would give them no powder, since he sought to obtain peace. Explaining that he was not a merchant, he promised to encourage French traders to come to them. Then, presenting them with a hatchet, two knives, three clasp-knives, ten brasses of glass beads and two double mirrors, he promised to visit their village, ". . . for a few days only, if my illness continued. They told me to take courage, and to remain and die in their country; and that they had been informed that I would remain there for a long time."[54]

At the beginning of February 1675, Jacques Marquette's health began to improve somewhat. "Since we addressed ourselves to the Blessed Virgin Immaculate," he recorded on February 9, "and

[51] *Ibid.*
[52] *Ibid.*, 177.
[53] *Ibid.*
[54] *Ibid.*, 179.

commenced a novena with a Mass, at which Pierre and Jacques, who do everything they can to relieve me, received Communion, to ask God to restore my health, my bloody flux has left me, and all that remains is a weakness of the stomach. I am beginning to feel much better and to regain my strength."[55] Perhaps the missionary's improved health was in some measure due to a lessening of the iron cold of winter. That such might have been the case seems indicated by the fact that Indians in the area, who were therefore, weather wise, were beginning to abandon their winter quarters. A group of them, who had camped for a month near the Frenchmen, took ". . . the road to the Potawatomies . . ." on their way to Green Bay to trade.[56] Some Illinois bands were already camped on the shore of Lake Michigan, waiting for navigation to open. To one of these groups Marquette entrusted a letter ". . . for our Fathers at Saint-François."[57] In it he reported to his superior, Father Nouvel: "The Blessed Virgin Immaculate has obtained for me the favor of reaching this place in good health, and with the resolve to correspond to the intentions which God has respecting me, since he has assigned me to the voyage towards the south. I have no other thought than that of doing what God wills. I dread nothing – neither the Nadoissis, nor the reception awaiting me among the nations, dismay me. One of two things will happen: either God will punish me for my crimes and cowardice, or else he will give me a share in his Cross, which I have not yet carried since my arrival in this country. But this Cross has been, perhaps, obtained for me by the Blessed Virgin Immaculate, or it may be death itself, that I may cease to offend God. It is that for which I try to hold myself in readiness, surrendering myself altogether into his hands. I entreat Your Reverence not to forget me and to obtain for me of God that I may not remain ungrateful for the favors which he heaps upon me."[58]

At long last on the feast of the Annunciation, March 25, 1675, vice-like winter loosed its grip on the land and the world began to

[55] *Ibid.*
[56] *Ibid.*
[57] *Ibid.*
[58] *Ibid.*, 209-11.

thaw. Three days later ice floes choked the river, causing a flood from which the three Frenchmen were obliged to flee in haste.[59] When the water subsided and the missionary was about to depart for the Illinois village, he recorded his own reaction to the hardships endured during the winter: "The Blessed Virgin Immaculate has taken such good care of us during our wintering that we have not lacked provisions, and have still remaining a large sack of corn, with some meat and fat. We also lived very pleasantly for my illness did not prevent me from saying holy Mass every day. We were unable to keep Lent, except on Fridays and Saturdays."[60] After Mass on Saturday, March 30, 1675, Father Marquette and his two aides set out for the Illinois village twenty leagues to the southwest. Enroute, the missionary made one last entry in his journal, predicting: "If the French procure robes in this country, they do not disrobe the savages, so great are the hardships that must be endured to obtain them."[61] Marquette was a far better missionary than prophet. Within a little more than a decade his prediction was proven to have been completely wrong.

When Father Marquette first saw the Illinois-Des Plaines river system, sailing up it in 1673, he wrote enthusiastically: "We have seen nothing like this river that we enter, as regards its fertility of soil, its prairies and woods; its cattle, elk, deer, wildcats, bustards, swans, ducks, parroquets and even beaver. There are many small lakes and rivers [flowing into it]. That on which we sail is wide, deep and still for 65 leagues."[62] Descending to the great village of the Illinois, Marquette and his men paddled down the slow, meandering Des Plaines River which ambles through quite level, uninteresting prairie land until it joins with the Kankakee, a few miles northeast of Morris, Illinois, where the Illinois truly begins. Within less than ten miles of its source, the Illinois begins falling, a foot per mile, through a picturesque gorge it has gouged out of a limestone outcropping. Then it widens out, creating a lovely valley averaging a mile and a half wide. Gliding effortlessly down the Illinois, Pierre

[59] *Ibid.*, 181.
[60] *Ibid.*
[61] *Ibid.*, 183.
[62] *Ibid.*, 161.

Porteret, who was seeing that river for the first time, must have been struck by its resemblance to the upper reaches of the Rhone or even some stretches of the Moselle. Some day, Pierre could conjecture, this powerful stream, too, would have its barge traffic when the French had populated its valley. During the eleven days the three Frenchmen spent descending to the village of the Illinois, Father Marquette felt well enough to enjoy the voyage, pointing out to Jacques places where amusing little incidents happened and showing Pierre where the party had stopped for the night on their way up the river in 1673.

Reaching his destination on April 10, 1675, the Wednesday of Holy Week, the missionary was received ". . . as an angel from heaven."[63] When he stopped at the village in 1673 Marquette reported that it contained seventy-four cabins.[64] Since then the population increased until it was now composed of ". . . 5 or 600 fires . . .," the inhabitants numbering ". . . more than 1,500 men without counting the women and children who are always numerous . . ."[65] After formally greeting the multitude Father Marquette summoned the chiefs and elders of each clan within the village and gave each group religious instructions individually so that ". . . he might sow in their minds the first seeds of the Gospel . . ."[66] Then, following a practice employed by all Jesuit missionaries evangelizing an aboriginal village, he began systematically visiting each of the cabins. But such multitudes followed him, attempting to crowd into every cabin, that he abandoned the approach as simply impractical. The truth was, the Indians had no intention of allowing this long awaited visitor out of their sight; wherever the Blackrobe went hordes of aborigines followed, anxious to witness his every act. Discovering a stretch of level prairie close to the village, the missionary selected that site for a gathering of all of the people so that he might address them. When the chiefs and the elders were appraised of Father Marquette's plan, they had the area adorned

[63] *Ibid.*, 189. The village was located on the Illinois River, a few miles from Utica, Illinois, probably within the confines of Starved Rock State Park.

[64] *Ibid.*, 161.

[65] *Ibid.*, 189.

[66] *Ibid.*

". . . after the fashion of the country, covering it with mats and bear-skins."[67] On Holy Thursday morning the final, dramatic preparations were added to the open-air church when Largillier and Porteret, setting poles in the ground, broke out the roll of rich Chinese taffeta which had been brought for just this purpose. Draping the dazzling cloth over a line strung between the poles, they mounted the picture of the Immaculate Conception against that striking background. Before it were then assembled ". . . 500 chiefs and elders, seated in a circle around the Father, and . . . all the young men who remained standing."[68] In serried ranks behind the menfolk were the women surrounded by their children. When the whole village was thus gathered together, a great hush fell on the people, waiting eagerly to hear the word of the Blackrobe.

After nine years living in daily contact with the Indians, Jacques Marquette was a past master at the art of aboriginal oratory, choosing just the right physical "present" to convey precisely the abstract idea he wished to implant in the minds of that primitive assembly. Drawing on the extensive theatrical training he received during his student days at Reims, the tall, ascetical Jesuit staged his religious drama in the wilds of France's colonial empire with a skill which the French dramatist Molière, Marquette's contemporary, might well have envied.[69] "The Father addressed the whole body of the people, and conveyed to them 10 messages, by means of ten presents which he gave them. He explained to them the principal mysteries of our religion and the purpose that had brought him to their country. Above all, he preached to them Jesus Christ, on the very eve (of that great day) on which He died upon the Cross for them as well as for all mankind . . ."[70] At the completion of his colorful discourse, Father Marquette celebrated the Mass of Holy Thursday, the liturgy so movingly commemorating the institution of the sacrament of Holy Eucharist. The Illinois, of course, were

[67] *Ibid.*

[68] *Ibid.*

[69] Molière (Jean-Baptiste Poquelin) was an alumnus of the Paris Jesuit college of Louis-le-Grand. His most controverted play was *Le Tartuffe.*

[70] *Relations*, LIX, 189.

incapable of grasping the solemn significance of the action they witnessed, but they certainly must have understood that the Black-robe, so devoutly attentive in all his solemn actions, was offering a sacrifice of propitiation, in their behalf, to his Manitou, the God of the Christians about whom the missionary had just spoken to them so long and so earnestly.

Through Good Friday and Holy Saturday, April 12 and 13, Marquette continued to evangelize the Illinois, probably realizing full well that his days of mortal life were drawing to a close.[71] But come what may, he had voyaged many miles over a hundred leagues, enduring wracking illness and terrible cold, to realize his long-cherished desire of ". . . . founding a mission [among the Illinois] to the glory of God and for the salvation of those poor Indians . . . under the glorious Virgin Mary . . ."[72] And this he would do at whatever cost to himself. When Easter Sunday, April 14, dawned the enfeebled missionary celebrated the glorious Easter liturgy in the presence of the whole population as well as his companions and ". . . two other Frenchmen who were in the area . . .," all four of whom received Holy Communion during the Mass.[73] "That was the last Mass he offered to God during his life and certainly the most pleasing to the Divine Majesty and most consoling to himself. During the Mass his companions were deeply impressed by his great spiritual fervor which they could not help but notice."[74]

For the remainder of Easter Sunday, while Pierre Porteret and Jacques Largillier assembled the baggage and packed it away in their battered canoe, Father Marquette attended a last council meeting of the Illinois chiefs. "He informed them that he was obliged to return to Michilimackinac where the Father Superior had scheduled a meeting of all the missionaries of that area. They begged him to return as quickly as possible and he promised to do so or at least to send another in his stead. The latter he added, realizing his condition, knowing that his strength was ebbing away,

[71] *Ibid.*, 187.

[72] Rochemonteix, *Jésuites*, III, 608.

[73] *Ibid.* The two other Frenchmen must have been Pierre Moreau and the surgeon.

[74] *Ibid.*

little by little, even as they spoke."[75] At the conclusion of the council Jacques Marquette, accompanied by the whole population, slowly made his way to the bank of the river where his companions awaited him. The Indians sought to shower him with gifts, stripping themselves of their poor best, hoping thus to demonstrate their gratitude and their sincere desire for his prompt return. But the missionary, determined to impress the Illinois ". . . with one idea, the integrity of those who have no other interest than their salvation, coming to preach to them no matter what the labor or danger, . . ." gently declined all of their proffered gifts. "But these good savages, intent on showing him how grateful they were, could not do enough for him while he was with them. They competed over his light baggage and, when he went up the river, escorted him for thirty leagues. Then they returned his baggage at the portage which they accomplished for him. Then they took leave of the Father, filled with affection for him as well as enthusiasm for the Gospel and a burning desire for him to return soon."[76]

[75] *Ibid.*
[76] *Ibid.*

". . . dying, as he always hoped,
in a wretched hut
in the midst of the wilderness . . ."

DEATH IN THE WILDERNESS

During the eleven or twelve days spent paddling up the Illinois River to the Chicago portage, Jacques Largillier and Pierre Porteret became more and more concerned about the distressing state of Father Marquette's health. Each morning at dawn they watched him board the canoe, impelled only by the force of sheer will-power. Throughout each day the Blackrobe sat erect and alert lest he appear unable or unwilling to converse with the canoe loads of Indians constantly surrounding his own battered craft. Every hour of every day, however, the missionary, to the discerning eyes of his assistants, was visibly fading away. At night, when the gabble and bustle of Indian camp life died down, the two French laymen consulted anxiously together, trying to devise some means of hastening the long voyage back to Saint-Ignace. Their one desire was to get Père Jacques home so that he might at least die among his Jesuit brethren, surrounded by what small comforts they could provide. Much more importantly, they yearned to reach their destination in time to procure for their saintly charge all the consolations of the Church for those departing this life. It just wasn't right that this holy priest should expire without receiving the last sacraments, surrounded by his brethern who could recite for him the prayers for the dying. It was highly improper, almost sacrilegious, to contemplate burying Father Marquette's poor, wasted body in unhallowed ground on some lonely hillside, with only two unlettered laymen mourning him. If the missionary was just another Frenchman, well, you did what you could in that wild land. You helped the dying man to make an act of contrition and, when he died you buried the body and said some prayers over the grave. Then you did your best to erase all traces of the tomb lest some wild animal or a wandering band of pagan Indians disturbed the poor soul's eternal rest. But that was no way to bury a priest who ought to have all the rites of the Church, a requiem Mass, a sad solemn procession to a proper graveyard with the church bell tolling mournfully. Discussing their problem, night after night, the two worried men determined that, once freed of their aboriginal escort, they would paddle like fiends, hoping to reach Saint-Ignace before Father Marquette expired. It was probably Largillier, who urged that they return by way of the eastern shore of Lake Michigan, a route hitherto unexplored by any Frenchman. His purpose in choosing that direction was reasonably sound. Since Father Marquette must be brought to Saint-Ignace to attend a meeting of all the Jesuit missionaries assigned to the Ottawa mission, following Lake Michigan's eastern shore ought to make the voyage much shorter. Jacques already knew, from having traversed it with Father Marquette in 1673, that at its northern end Lake Michigan was a good hundred and fifty miles wide. The lake simply had to be narrower than that at the southern extremity, a fact which would surely shorten the journey. Choosing an unknown route was risky, of course, but if following it cut days off the travel time they just might make Saint-Ignace before their ailing charge died.

Perhaps on April 25, 1675, the three Frenchmen and their honor guard of Illinois reached the Chicago portage. There the Indians engaged in almost endless bickering over which of them should have the honor of carrying the scant baggage over the short portage to the Chicago River.[1] And when the portage was finally accomplished each dignified chief must deliver one final, sonorous address. And, sick as he was, Father Marquette was obliged out of courtesy to reply, rolling out picturesque phrases, thanking the Illinois for their hospitality and congratulating them on accepting, so sincerely, the message he brought them. Again and again he assured his hearers that if he were able, he would return soon to dwell with them. If he, himself, could not come back, he solemnly promised that another Blackrobe would soon arrive to stay with them.[2] At long last Jacques Marquette could board the canoe and he and his companions pushed off, bound for Lake Michigan and home.

The moment Father Marquette was sure he had passed out of sight of the Illinois, he was ". . . no longer a man of this world, but a citizen of heaven, one about to receive an award at his return from an embassy on which he had served his master brilliantly."[3] At the end of their brief six-mile voyage to the mouth of the Chicago River, Porteret and Largillier discovered, to their distress, that Father Marquette was so weak that ". . . he was unable to assist or even move himself, and had to be handled and carried about like a child."[4] How humiliating to the once strong, vigorous Marquette, now burning with fever and plagued with a painful, demeaning bloody flux, to be unable to tend his needs or even turn himself to a more restful position! How much more bearable it would have been to suffer the unbelievably cruel martyrdom meted out to Jean de Brébeuf who at least faced his diabolical tormentors standing valiantly on his own two feet! But God did not ask Jacques Marquette to shed his blood at the hands of a hate-crazed mob of Indians, skilled at inflicting exquisite torture. He was called to

[1] *Relations*, LIX, 191.
[2] *Ibid.*
[3] Rochemonteix, *Jésuites*, III, 609.
[4] *Relations*, LIX, 193.

endure humiliating helplessness. For nine years known as the great, towering, untiring giant, now, just a few weeks short of his thirty-eighth birthday, he was physically degraded to the helplessness of an infant. But, "All of this he bore with joy and resignation, consoling and encouraging his companions to bear all for Jesus Christ . . ."[5]

At dawn the morning after their arrival at Lake Michigan, Jacques and Pierre, gulping down a hasty breakfast, prepared to shove off as early as possible, determined to cover as many miles as they could between first light and darkness. Quite likely they tempted their ailing charge with a little warm *sagamité,* encouraging him to try to swallow even a spoonful, just to keep up his strength. He tried, only to please them, but it was no use. His tortured digestive system rejected even the bland, warm mush. Then, carrying him to the canoe and settling him as comfortably as possible, the two devoted followers leaped aboard and bent their backs to the paddles. Though Saint-Ignace, according to their calculations, was over a hundred leagues away, they resolved to eat up the miles, covering the distance in record time.[6] They swept down Lake Michigan, passing the barren sand dunes, scarcely noticing the scenery. In a day or so the two straining paddlers were encouraged to notice the morning sun full in their faces, proving to them that they were moving eastward across the southern extremity of the lake. Slowly the scenery on shore changed from bleak, wind-sculptured sand dunes to rich wooded meadows. Each day one of the two laymen took to the shore, snaring game for their supper. At night, at lonely camp fires, they tried to concoct a broth, feeding their patient a few spoons full of the none too palatable results of their cooking. Then they chafed Father Marquette's wasted limbs, bathed his face and cleansed his feverish body as best they could. While ministering to him each evening they exchanged glances with one another, knowing, without communicating, that they were running a losing race. They would never reach Saint-Ignace on time; Jacques Marquette would die on their hands. Expending themselves to the ut-

[5] Rochemonteix, *Jésuites*, III, 610.

[6] *Relations*, LIX, 191. By land, Chicago is over 400 miles from Saint-Ignace.

most each day, Pierre and Jacques inched around the great circle of Lake Michigan's lower shore until the morning sun was to their right. They passed the mouths of several attractive streams, the Saint Joseph, the Black, and the Kalamazoo, with barely a glance at them. Every day one or other of the paddlers climbed the highest elevation they spotted, intently examining the country to the north, hoping against hope that they might find themselves closer to Saint-Ignace than they knew in their hearts they were. But all they could discern was vast stretches of attractively wooded, level country with rolling hills off to their right.

Though Pierre and Jacques would not let themselves admit it, Jacques Marquette well knew that for him the journey would end, not at Saint-Ignace, the mission he had begun, but in heaven. As the small party moved over the water in the soft air of late spring, the wasted, uncomplaining missionary ". . . began to make more special preparations for death."[7] Unaware of doing so, he frequently prayed aloud, ". . . conversing sometimes with our Lord, sometimes with His holy Mother, or with his guardian angel or with all paradise. He was often heard to repeat . . .'I believe that my Redeemer lives,' or 'Mary, Mother of God, remember me'."[8] Though he was surely sick unto death, "He recited his breviary every day; and, although he was so low that his sight and strength were greatly enfeebled, he continued to do so to the last day of his life, despite the remonstrances of his companions,"[9] who sought to persuade him that his desperate physical condition excused him from any such obligation. Every day he had one of his companions read a passage or two from a pious book he had brought along with him. During the last few days of his life, the dying Jesuit requested his friends to read him some reflexions on death which he had composed himself and always carried with him.[10] Then, indeed, he ". . . began to hope that God would soon grant him the favor he besought so often . . .

[7] *Ibid.*, 193.
[8] *Ibid.*
[9] *Ibid.*
[10] *Ibid.*

to let him die while making a missionary journey, deprived of all human comfort."[11]

The evening before his death, which was a Friday [May 17, 1675], he told them, very joyously, that it would take place on the morrow. He conversed with them during the whole day as to what they would have to do regarding his burial; about the manner in which they should inter him; of the place that should be chosen for his grave; how his feet, his hands and his face should be arranged; and that they should erect a cross over his grave. He even went so far as to counsel them, three hours before he expired, that as soon as he was dead they should take the little hand-bell from his Mass-kit and ring it while he was being buried. He spoke of all these things with such great tranquility and peace of mind that one might have supposed he was concerned with the death and burial of another person rather than his own.

He conversed with them thus as they made their way along the lake until, perceiving a river on whose shore stood an eminence which he deemed well suited as the place of his interment, he told them that that was the place of his last repose. They wanted, however, to proceed farther, as the weather was favorable, and the day was not far advanced, but God raised a contrary wind, which compelled them to return, and enter the river which the Father had pointed out. They accordingly brought him to the land, lighted a little fire for him, and prepared for him a wretched bark shelter. They laid him down therein, in the least uncomfortable manner that they could; but they were so overcome with sorrow that, as they since said, they hardly knew what they were doing.

The Father being thus stretched out on the ground in much the same way as St. Francis Xavier, as he had always so passionately desired, and finding himself alone in the midst of these forests, for his companions were occupied with the disembarkation, he had leisure to repeat all the acts which he had repeated during these last days.

His cherished companions, having afterwards rejoined him, all disconsolate, he comforted them, and inspired them with confidence that God would take care of them after his death, in these new and unknown countries. He gave them some final instructions, thanking them for all the charity they exercised in his behalf during the whole journey and asking pardon for the trouble he had given them. He charged them to ask pardon for him, also, of all our Fathers and Brothers who lived in the Ottawa country. Then he undertook to prepare them for the sacrament of penance, which he administered to them for the last time. He gave them also a paper on which he had written all his faults since his own last confession, that they might place it in the hands of the Father Superior, so that

[11] Rochemonteix, *Jésuites,* III, 611.

the latter might be urged to pray fervently to God for him. Finally, he promised not to forget them in paradise. And, as he was very considerate, knowing that they were much fatigued from the hardships of the preceding days, he bade them go and take a little repose. He assured them that his hour was not yet so very near, and that he would awaken them when the time should come, as, in fact, two or three hours afterward he did summon them, when he was about to enter his agony.

They drew near him and he embraced them once again, while they burst into tears at his feet. Then he asked them for holy water and his reliquary; and having himself removed his crucifix, which he always carried suspended around his neck, he placed it in the hands of one of his companions, begging him to hold it before his eyes. Then, feeling that he had but a short time to live, he made a last effort . . .[12]

Fixing his eyes on the crucifix, he declared in clear, calm tones that he died a Christian, a son of the Holy Roman Catholic Church . . .,[13] and gave thanks to the divine majesty for the great favor accorded him of dying in the Society of Jesus, of dying in it as a missionary of Jesus Christ, and, above all, of dying, as he had always prayed, in a wretched cabin in the midst of the forests and bereft of all human succor.

After that he was silent, communing within himself with God. Nevertheless, from time to time he let escape these words: "My soul is sustained by His word"; or these: "Mother of God, remember me," which were the last words he uttered before entering his agony, which was, however, very mild and peaceful.

He charged his companions to remind him, when they saw he was about to expire, to repeat frequently the names of Jesus and Mary, if he could not do so himself. They did as they were bidden; and when they believed him to be near his end, one of them called aloud, "Jesus, Mary!" The dying man repeated the words distinctly, several times; and, as if at these sacred names, something appeared to him, suddenly he raised his eyes above his crucifix, holding them riveted on that apparition, which he appeared to regard with pleasure.[14] So, with a countenance beaming and aglow, he peacefully rendered his blessed soul to his creator on Saturday, May 18, between eleven and midnight.[15]

He lacked fourteen days of being thirty-eight years old.

Our two men, shedding copious tears over the body, having satisfied their devotion and sorrow, . . . buried it in the place and manner di-

[12] *Relations*, LIX, 193-99.
[13] Rochemonteix, *Jésuites*, III, 602.
[14] *Relations*, LIX, 199.
[15] Rochemonteix, *Jésuites*, III, 612.

rected.[16] . . . they carried him devoutly to his grave, ringing the little bell as he had bidden them . . .[17] At the feet they planted a great cross to mark the place for the future. The next day, Sunday, they set out on their journey with what sentiments you may surmise, sad and regretful at having lost the source of their consolation. One of the two was so heart-sick all night that in the morning he was severely ill . . . Obliged to go on, he had recourse, with consummate faith, to the dead missionary, whom he felt sure was in heaven. Saying nothing to his companion, who was readying the canoe to depart, he knelt at the foot of the body and prayed earnestly, at the same time swallowing a pinch of earth from the grave. He was cured at once. The man himself told me this in confidence. Then the two men went their way, filled with trust, inspired by their good Father.[18]

On that sad Sunday morning, May 19, 1675, Jacques and Pierre knelt together at the grave of their dear departed friend, neither wishing to be the first to leave. But life must go on; the bereft must somehow find the courage to take up the burden of living without the beloved departed. Sadly, regretfully, Marquette's two devoted companions slowly descended the high, sandy hill where their cherished Father lay at rest and, embarking in their canoe, started for Saint-Ignace, nearly seventy leagues to the north. In no hurry now, each paddled quietly, buried in his own grief. Had they done everything possible to save the life of that valiant missionary whose death was such a serious blow to the Ottawa mission? Which of the Jesuits left behind possessed Father Marquette's extraordinary gift for the native languages? Who could carry on the evangelization of the Illinois begun so propitiously by Père Jacques? And what would Father Nouvel say to them? He had selected them especially to assist and protect Father Marquette. Now they must report that the very apple of his eye was buried on a wind-swept hill, far from home. Occupied with these disheartening thoughts the two Frenchmen, the first to see the whole of Lake Michigan's eastern shore, had no eyes for the passing scenery which was at its fresh, attractive best during the late spring and early summer. The delta of the Manistee River,

[16] *Ibid.* Marquette was buried on a hillside adjacent to and near the mouth of the Père Marquette River at Ludington, Michigan.

[17] *Relations,* LIX, 199.

[18] Rochemonteix, *Jésuites,* III, 612.

enticing Grand Traverse Bay, lovely Beaver Island, off to their left, none held any interest for them. Rounding Waugoshance Point, they soon realized that the millrace of the Straits of Mackinac were not far away. Saint-Ignace would soon be reached.

Jacques Largillier and Pierre Porteret carried their travel-worn canoe ashore at Moran Bay near the mission of Saint-Ignace on or about June 1, 1675. Disconsolately they announced the distressing news of the death of Father Jacques Marquette to the Jesuits at the mission. After hearing them out Father Nouvel consoled the dejected travelers, assuring them that they most certainly had been loyal, devoted assistants to whom no blame could possibly be attached.[19] They must always remember that Father Marquette died as he wished, on an apostolic mission, at a lonely spot, in imitation of Saint Francis Xavier, whom he strove to emulate. Surely the lately departed missionary would be a staunch advocate for the Ottawa missions before the throne of God where he could accomplish much more for them all than even his boundless zeal had effected while he was among them. They must not brood over his loss, unjustly indulging in self-recrimination. Let them continue serving the mission zealously, helping the missionaries to bring all of the Indians to the feet of Christ our Lord. To help distract them from their sorrow, Father Nouvel sent them down to Quebec for the supplies needed for the coming winter. On their way down, as well as returning, Jacques and Pierre stopped at the sedentary Indian colony of Saint-François-Xavier at La Prairie-de-la-Madeleine, near Sault-Saint-Louis, opposite Montreal where Father Pierre Cholenec was stationed. It was he who after questioning Father Marquette's companions closely wrote his lengthy letter to Father Jean de Fontenay, a Jesuit at Nantes, from which we learn the minute details of Jacques Marquette's last days. Though history loses track of Pierre Porteret, Jacques Largillier, who was three years older than Father Marquette, became a Jesuit Brother in 1690. Undoubtedly to his great delight, Frère Jacques was assigned to the mission of the Immaculate Conception among the Illinois. There he lived out his days, dying at the age of eighty on Novem-

[19] No historical evidence places Nouvel at Saint-Ignace at that moment.

ber 4, 1714.[20] Jacques Largillier lived to see Father Marquette's dream of converting the Illinois come true.

Jacques Marquette's pledge to the Illinois, to return soon himself or to send another Blackrobe to instruct them, was promptly fulfilled. In his report to the provincial of the Province of France, Father Claude Dablon announced in 1677: "A successor to the late Father Marquette was needed who should be no less zealous than he. To fill his place, Father Claude Allouez was chosen, who had labored, the leader in all our missions to the Ottawas, with untiring courage. He was engaged, at the time, in that of Saint-François-Xavier in the Bay des Puants, and was soon ready to set out."[21] The aging, yet sturdy, Allouez left Green Bay towards the end of October, 1676 ". . . in a canoe with two men, to attempt to go to winter with the Illinois."[22] Before advancing very far an early winter obliged Allouez to ". . . go into camp and wait until the ice was strong enough to bear us."[23] In February 1677, when thick ice bridged the rivers and lakes, Allouez again began his voyage, employing ". . . a very unusual mode of navigation, for, instead of putting the canoe into the water, we placed it upon the ice over which the wind, which was in our favor, and a sail made it go as on water. When the wind failed us, in place of paddles we used ropes to draw it along, as horses draw carriages."[24] Reaching Lake Michigan, by way of the Sturgeon Bay portage, on the eve of the feast of Saint Joseph, March 18, 1677, Allouez named that great body of water Lake Saint Joseph, a name which he alone applied to it.[25] Arriving at the great village of the Illinois on April 27, he ". . . entered, at once, the cabin in which Father Marquette had lodged; and the old men being assembled there with the entire population, I made known the reason for which I had come to them, namely, to preach to them the true God, living and immortal, and His only Son, Jesus Christ. They listened very attentively to

[20] *Relations,* LXXI, 149.

[21] *Ibid.,* LX, 149.

[22] *Ibid.,* 151. Perhaps the two men were Largillier and Porteret.

[23] *Ibid.*

[24] *Ibid.*

[25] *Ibid.,* 153.

my whole discourse and thanked me for the trouble that I was taking for their salvation."[26] The visit was a brief one, made primarily ". . . to acquire the information necessary for the establishment of a complete mission."[27] Allouez returned to the Illinois in 1678 and remained with them for two years.[28] Between 1680 and 1688 the Illinois were evangelized only sporadically until the arrival among them of Father Jacques Gravier in 1688. From that date until 1763 the mission of the Immaculate Conception, founded by Jacques Marquette, was maintained under Jesuit auspices, through several migrations from its original location near Utica, Illinois to the mouth of the Kaskaskia.[29]

How correctly Jacques Marquette estimated the adaptability of the Illinois to the ways of civilization and the sincerity of their expressed desire to embrace Christianity may be gathered from a description of the mission of the Immaculate Conception written only thirty-seven years after Father Marquette founded it:

> To return to our Illinois: they are very different from these savages, and from what they themselves were formerly. Christianity, as I have already said, has softened their fierce habits, and they are now distinguished for certain gentle and polite manners that have led the Frenchmen to take their daughters in marriage. Moreover we find in them docility and ardor in the practice of Christian virtues . . . They often approach the sacraments and the custom among them is to confess and communicate every fortnight . . . we have, not infrequently, the satisfaction of seeing them die in great peace and in a lively hope of being very soon united to God in Heaven.[30]

If that report be held suspect because it emanated from the pen of Father Gabriel Marest, a Jesuit missionary working among the Illinois, we add the testimony of André Pénicault, soldier, adventurer, and sometime ship's carpenter, who reported what he

[26] *Ibid.*, 159.

[27] *Ibid.*, 163.

[28] *Ibid.*, 167.

[29] Clarence W. Alvord, *The Illinois Country, 1673-1818*, 132. In 1692 the mission was moved to the vicinity of Peoria, Illinois. In 1700 it was moved to a site near Kaskaskia, Illinois.

[30] *Relations*, LXVI, 241.

saw at the mission of the Immaculate Conception when he visited it in 1711:

> The Kaskaskia Illinois are hard-working and skilled in tilling the fields. They plow them with a plow, which has not yet been done elsewhere in the lower Mississippi. They acquired a knowledge of the plow from the Reverend Jesuit Fathers . . .
>
> The region in which they are presently settled is one of the finest . . . and one of the best for fertility of the soil. Wheat grows there as fine as any in France, and all kinds of vegetables, roots and grasses. Also, they have many varieties of fruit, of an excellent taste . . . On these prairies . . . they have a great deal of livestock, such as bullocks, cows etc. Also there are many fowls of every kind at their settlement . . . Near their village they have three mills to grind their grain . . . The Illinois are quite fond of good eating and very often feast one another . . . The majority of the Illinois are Catholic Christians. In their village they have a rather large church in which there is a baptismal font. The church is quite clean on the inside . . . They attend high Mass and vespers regularly.[31]

For two years after interment in a lonely grave two hundred and fifty miles south of Saint-Ignace, only the stark wooden cross planted beside it stood vigil over the mortal remains of Jacques Marquette. And there his bones might have remained were it not for the Kiskakon Christians whom Marquette had converted at Saint-Esprit over five years before his death. Most of these Indians had migrated in 1671 to a site within a league of the mission of Sainte-Marie-du-Sault.[32] There, under the tutelage of Father Gabriel Druillettes, the Kiskakon became exemplary Christians with whom "Prayer . . . gained more favor than ever."[33] After the unfortunate destruction of Sainte-Marie in 1674, the Kiskakon Christians migrated to Saint-Ignace, establishing their own village near the mission and coming under the special care of Father Henry Nouvel.[34] Regarding the religious fervor of these Christians, Father Nouvel enthusiastically reported to Father Claude Dablon in 1678: "Their village . . . is near our chapel of Saint-Ignace at Michilimackinac.

[31] André Pénicault, *Fleur de Lys and Calumet*, 137-39.
[32] *Relations*, LVII, 223.
[33] *Ibid.*
[34] *Ibid.*, LIX, 217.

Their chiefs and most notable elders perform their spiritual duties well, as do also the majority of the women and children . . . I am occupied from morning till night in cultivating this church . . ."[35] The Kiskakon, who certainly knew of Father Marquette's death and the general area in which he was buried, laid claim to what we call the lower peninsula of Michigan as their winter hunting ground. In the spring of 1677, when they were in the vicinity of the grave of their well-loved Father, ". . . God . . . put it into their hearts to remove his bones and bring them to our church at the mission of St. Ignace at Missilimakinac [*sic*], where those savages made their abode."[36]

They repaired, then, to the spot, and resolved among themselves to act in regard to the Father as they are wont to do towards those for whom they profess great respect. Accordingly, they opened the grave, and uncovered the body; and, although the flesh and internal organs were all dried up, they found it entire, so that not even the skin was in any way injured. This did not prevent them from proceeding to dissect it, as is their custom. They cleansed the bones and exposed them to the sun to dry; then, carefully laying them in a box of birch-bark, they set out to bring them to our mission of St. Ignace.

There were nearly 30 canoes which formed, in excellent order, that funeral procession. There were also a goodly number of Iroquois, who united with our Algonquin savages to lend more honor to the ceremonial. When they drew near our house, Father Nouvel, who is its superior, with Father Piercon [*sic*], went out to meet them, accompanied by the Frenchmen and savages who were there; and having halted the procession, he put the usual questions to them, to make sure that it was really the Father's body which they were bringing. Before conveying it to land, they intoned the *De profundis* in the presence of the 30 canoes, which were still on the water, and of the people who were on the shore. After that, the body was carried to the church, care being taken to observe all that the ritual appoints in such ceremonies. It remained exposed under the pall, all that day, which was Whitsun-Monday, the 8th of June; and on the morrow, after having rendered it all the funeral rites, it was lowered into a small vault in the middle of the church, where it rests as the guardian angel of our Ottawa missions. The savages often come to pray at his tomb. Not to mention more than this instance, a young girl, aged 19 or 20 years, whom the late Father had instructed, and who had been

[35] *Ibid.*, 69.
[36] *Ibid.*, 203.

baptized in the past year, fell sick, and applied to Father Nouvel to be bled and to take certain remedies. The Father prescribed to her, as sole medicine, to come for 3 days and say a *Pater* and three *Aves* at the tomb of Father Marquette. She did so, and before the 3rd day was cured, without bleeding or any other remedy.[37]

There is no more fitting manner to close the study of the life of Jacques Marquette than to quote, in part, the eulogy written of him by Claude Dablon:

Father Jacques Marquette of the Province of Champagne, died at the age of 38 years, of which 21 were passed in the Society [of Jesus] namely, 12 in France and 9 in Canada. He was sent to the missions of the upper Algonquins . . . and labored therein with the zeal that might be expected from a man who had proposed to himself St. Francis Xavier as the model of his life and death. He resembled that great saint, not only in the variety of barbarian languages which he mastered, but also by the range of his zeal, which made him carry the Faith to the ends of this new world, and nearly 800 leagues from here into the forests, where the name of Jesus Christ had never been proclaimed . . .

We might say much of the rare virtues of this noble missionary: of his zeal, which prompted him to carry the Faith so far, and proclaim the Gospel to so many people who were unknown to us; of his gentleness, which rendered him beloved by all, and made him all things to all men, a Frenchman with the French, a Huron with the Hurons, an Algonquin with the Algonquins; of the childlike candor with which he disclosed his heart; of his angelic chastity; and of his uninterrupted union with God.

But that which apparently predominated was a devotion, altogether rare and singular, to the Blessed Virgin, and particularly toward the mystery of her Immaculate Conception. It was a pleasure to hear him speak or preach on that subject. All his conversations and letters contained something about the Blessed Virgin Immaculate—for such he always called Her.

So tender a devotion toward the Mother of God merited some singular grace; and she accorded him the favor that he always requested—to die on a Saturday. His companions never doubted that she appeared to him at the hour of his death, when, after pronouncing the names of Jesus and Mary, he suddenly raised his eyes above his crucifix, holding them fixed on an object which he regarded with extreme pleasure, and a joy that showed itself upon his features; and they had, at that time, the impression that he had rendered up his soul into the hands of his good Mother.[38]

[37] *Ibid.*, 205.
[38] *Ibid.*, 305-09.

Appendix one

JACQUES MARQUETTE, PRIEST

The title of this appendix is borrowed from an article by Raphael N. Hamilton, S.J., archivist of Marquette University, which appeared in the March 1949 issue of *Revue de l'Université Laval* in response to a previous study in the same publication by Father Joseph C. Short, entitled "Jacques Marquette, S.J., Catechist."[1] In his article Father Short, then pastor of Saint Patrick's Church, New London, Wisconsin, declared that Marquette had never been ordained and, consequently, the whole journal of his second voyage to the Illinois, 1674-1675, was a "charming bit of fiction" foisted on an unsuspecting world by Claude Dablon, Marquette's superior. Short had al-

[1] Joseph C. Short, "Jacques Marquette, S. J., Catechist," *Revue de l'Université Laval*, III (1948-1949), 436-43.

ready proposed the central argument of his article in a review of Father Jean Delanglez's *Life and Voyages of Louis Jolliet* which appeared in the December 1948 issue of the *Wisconsin Magazine of History.*[2] In that review, commenting on Delanglez's statement that Marquette was not at Sault-Sainte-Marie when Saint-Lusson took possession of the West in the name of Louis XIV, on June 4, 1671, Short declared that, though Marquette was present, he did ". . . not sign the *procès-verbal* because, unlike the four Jesuit Fathers who did, he was not an ordained priest."[3] Neither of Short's extraordinary assertions was left long unanswered. In the June 1949 issue of the *Wisconsin Magazine of History,* Hamilton refuted the statements contained in the review of Delanglez's book, indicating why Short was in error. He was joined in the lists by Father Paul Desjardins, S.J., archivist of the Collège Sainte-Marie, Montreal, whose response, "Jacques Marquette était-il prêtre?" was published in the March 1949 issue of *Revue de l'Université Laval.*[4] The scholar most competent to refute Short's assertions, Jean Delanglez, S.J., died suddenly on May 9, 1949, without formulating a reply to Short. Jerome V. Jacobsen, S.J., editor of *Mid-America,* the publication in which much of Delanglez's valuable research appeared, published a reply to Short, "Attempted Mayhem on Père Marquette."[5] In a subsequent issue of *Mid-America,* Jacobsen published a "followup" article entitled "Documents: Marquette's Ordination."[6]

With the publication of Jacobsen's last article, which included a reproduction of a document proving the fact of Marquette's ordination, the controversy might well have been laid to rest had it not been for a chapter in a series of essays relating to the Jolliet-Marquette expedition, privately published in mimeograph form, in

[2] Joseph C. Short, Review, *Wisconsin Magazine of History,* XXXII (1948-1949), 227-29.

[3] *Ibid.,* 228.

[4] Paul Desjardins, "Jacques Marquette était-il prêtre?" *Revue de l'Université Laval,* III (1948-1949), 346-49.

[5] Jerome V. Jacobsen, "Attempted Mayhem on Père Marquette," *Mid-America,* XX (1949), 109-15.

[6] Jerome V. Jacobsen, "Documents: Marquette's Ordination," *Mid-America,* XXXII (1950), 46-54.

1953, by Francis Borgia Steck, O.F.M.[7] Chapter VI of that opus casts doubts on the factual objectivity of Marquette's priesthood. By way of reply, Father Ernest J. Burrus, S.J., of the Jesuit Historical Institute at Rome, published an admirable, scholarly study of the question, "Father Jacques Marquette, S.J.: His Priesthood in the Light of the Jesuit Roman Archives."[8] That excellent presentation ought to have been the last word on the subject; but Father Steck saw fit to re-open the question, at least obliquely, in his *Marquette Legends* which appeared in 1959.[9] Since then, off and on, this question is re-opened in many unusual places. It seems apropos, therefore, in a new biography of Father Marquette, to review the arguments proposed pro and con as well as to present, again, the evidence demonstrating that Jacques Marquette was, unquestionably, a validly ordained priest and clearly functioned as such. This effort will, undoubtedly, not prove to be the final, apodictic answer to the absurd allegation that Marquette was not a priest. Flamboyant errors of this nature die hard simply because it is more interesting to gossip than it is to face the prosaic truth. A similar situation exists regarding John Paul Jones. People would sooner believe he replied to the British demand for surrender: "I have not yet begun to fight," rather than to accept the unprintable remark he actually uttered on that dramatic occasion.

To approach discussing the controversy in an orderly manner, it seems proper first to consider Father Short's article in *Revue de l'Université Laval* which originated the discussion. Short characterized Marquette as ". . . crabby, melancholic . . ." and thoroughly disgruntled, in 1665, at having been ordered ". . . instead of going on to dogmatic theology, . . . to repeat his philosophy . . ."[10] These conclusions were drawn both from a misunderstanding of the technical terminology employed in the triennial catalogues of the Society of Jesus and from a lack of knowledge of the normal course of studies pursued by young Jesuits destined for the priest-

[7] Francis Borgia Steck, *Essays Relating to the Jolliet-Marquette Expedition, 1673.*

[8] Burrus, "Marquette, Priesthood," 257-71.

[9] Steck, *Marquette Legends.*

[10] Short, "Marquette, Catechist," 437.

hood. Because he had some familiarity with Latin, Short should not have attempted to interpret the Latin terms used in technical reports any more than he would be competent to define terms proper to topology because he once studied algebra. Marquette was not sent, in 1665, to "repeat philosophy" but to complete his three-year study of the subject and to submit to an hour's oral examination on the whole field of philosophy. Interpreting Marquette's letter of March 19, 1665 to the Jesuit general, Short found in it a declaration that Marquette no longer wished to be a priest, based on the future missionary's statement that he believed himself unsuited for speculative subjects. This is a gratuitous assumption arising from ignorance of procedures within the Society of Jesus. The true meaning of the statement was that, in order to go on the missions sooner, Marquette was ready to forego the opportunity to be professed of four solemn vows, one essential requirement for which is the completion of four years of speculative theology with distinction.

Deferring for the moment Father Short's conclusions regarding Marquette's not having any formal theological training, we call attention to that author's errors pertaining to Father Marquette's family. Short, quite injudiciously, accepted Arthur J. O'Dea's historically inaccurate statement that Nicolas Marquette, the missionary's father, ". . . had espoused the cause of Henry of Navarre with so much ardor that he was banished from Laon only to return honored and with added wealth and powers when Henry became king."[11] If Short had checked the date of Nicolas Marquette's birth, he would have known that O'Dea's statement was absurd. Nicolas Marquette was born on September 15, 1597, six years after Henry of Navarre conquered Laon in 1591. The Marquette who espoused the cause of Henry of Navarre was neither Nicolas, Father Marquette's father, nor Michel, his grandfather, but another Nicolas Marquette, a distant cousin.[12] A similar error, made by Short regarding the Marquette family, was to characterize Father Jacques Mar-

[11] Arthur J. O'Dea, "The Observance of the Marquette Tercentenary," *Mid-America*, XX (1938), 17.

[12] Public Archives of Canada, Collection Ste. Marie, Montreal, M.G. 17, 6, 3.

quette as a ". . . rich man's baby boy . . ."[13] Nicolas Marquette may have been financially well off, but Jacques was not the "baby boy" of the family. This error arose from assuming that Hamy's genealogical chart of the Marquette family listed the children of Nicolas Marquette and Rose de la Salle according to the chronological order of their births.[14] The composition of the chart was dictated not by exact familial relationships within a family but by considerations of space. Two of Father Marquette's brothers, Louis and Jean-Bertrand, appear to be the eldest children of Nicolas Marquette only because each had progeny. Placing these two first allowed more convenient space on the chart to list their descendants. We might add that Hamy's genealogical chart of the Marquette family is almost wholly untrustworthy.

In his review of Delanglez's *Life and Voyages of Louis Jolliet,* Short declared that Marquette was ". . . ineligible for the priesthood because of his lack of theological training in France."[15] Since it is indisputably true that Father Marquette had no formal theological training, Short could have argued that in the face of the strictures of the Council of Trent regarding adequate training for aspirants to the priesthood, what bishop would be so brash as to ordain a man who had no formal training at all? Though Short did not employ this argument, except obliquely, the question deserves an answer. The Council of Trent, in its twenty-third session, July 15 to November 11, 1563, encouraged bishops to establish seminaries and outlined a program of theological studies lasting about four years, but no sanctions were attached to these decrees.[16] Previous to the Council of Trent, Paul III in his *Licet debitum* issued October 18, 1549, granted major Jesuit superiors the right to present candidates for ordination to any bishop and whenever superiors considered subjects properly prepared for holy orders. This privilege was renewed by Gregory XIII, in his *Pium et utile* of September 22, 1582, almost twenty years after the close of the

[13] Short, "Marquette, Catechist," 440.

[14] Hamy, *Au Mississippi*, 36-37.

[15] Short, *Wisconsin Magazine*, 228.

[16] Henry J. Schroeder, *Canons of the Council of Trent: Original Text with English Translation*, 446-50.

Council of Trent.[17] Jesuit provincials frequently exercised the privilege and not always in favor of subjects who volunteered for the missions. One of Marquette's fellow novices, Jean Bordois, was ordained in the spring of 1667 without any theological training, though he was never sent to a foreign mission.[18] The frequency with which the privilege was invoked in favor of just one missionary area, Paraguay, may be discovered in "Jésuites, Wallons, Flammands, Français, missionnaires au Paraguay," an article by Pierre Delattre and his brother Edmond which was published in the *Archivum Historicum Societatis Jesu.*[19]

In his review of Father Delanglez's book, Father Short further argues that Marquette was obviously not a priest since he ". . . took his final vows as a spiritual coajutor and formed lay-brother . . ." which automatically excluded him from the priesthood. To that display of ignorance concerning the organization of the Society of Jesus, the benign Father Paul Desjardins replied with restrained asperity: "For anyone who knows the slightest thing about the Society of Jesus – and it was easy for the author [Short] to inform himself on this point, if his association with the Jesuits at Innsbruck had not already made him aware of it – that the title spiritual coajutor is an infallible indication of the sacerdotal character of the Jesuits to whom the title pertains."[20] While the observation is certainly true, the information might never have come to Father Short's attention during his years of theological study under the Jesuits at Innsbruck. A very brief explanation of the so-called (and incorrectly so) grades within the Society of Jesus will be helpful to the uninitiated reader. Before Saint Ignatius founded the Society, all members of every religious order, lay-brothers and priests alike, e.g. Franciscans, Dominicans, Benedictines, etc., pronounced solemn, perpetual vows of poverty, chastity, and obedience at the completion of a year of novitiate training. Saint Ignatius originally

[17] *Institutum Societatis Jesu,* I, 16, 85, 86.

[18] Carrez, *Catologi,* VI, 83, 100.

[19] *Archivum Historicum Societatis Jesu,* XVI (1947), 98-176.

[20] Desjardins, "Marquette, prêtre?" 346. Father Short did his theological studies at the famous Canisianum conducted by the Jesuits at Innsbruck in Austria. He was ordained there on July 27, 1913. He died on June 30, 1951.

intended his order to be composed only of priests, all of whom would take solemn vows. However, when he and his early companions found that ". . . because of the fewness of their numbers much sacred ministry had to be neglected, in the spirit of the apostles choosing deacons, they set forth to Paul III their need for helpers (coajutors) . . . ,"[21] laymen to help in temporal tasks and priests to assist in the spiritual work. On January 5, 1546, Paul III, by his decree *Exponi nobis,* granted the petition. When he wrote his constitutions, Saint Ignatius ordered that the spiritual coajutors, whose very reason for existing required that they be priests, should take simple, not solemn, final vows. Ignatius himself composed the formula for the vows Jesuits of whatever "grade" pronounce. The formula for each "grade" immediately identifies the fact that he who pronounced it was or was not a priest. On July 2, 1671, Jacques Marquette pronounced the final vows of a spiritual coajutor at Sault-Sainte-Marie before Father Gabriel Druillettes, who was delegated to receive them in the name of the general of the Jesuits. The formula of Marquette's vows, written in his own hand, is extant. From it any Jesuit would immediately know that Jacques Marquette had unquestionably received holy orders. In his "Some Hitherto Unpublished Marquettiana," Gilbert J. Garraghan included a reproduction of the holograph copy of Marquette's vows which, therefore, may be examined by anyone.[22] The formula of the vows pronounced by all Jesuit priests contains the clause, ". . . et secundum eam [obedientiam], peculiarem circa puerorum eurditionem . . .," a clause which must be omitted from the formula of vows pronounced by lay-brothers, or temporal coajutors. The reason for the omission of the clause in the vow formula of temporal coajutors is that they do not normally devote themselves to the education of youth, as do Jesuits priests who, by the clause in the formula of their vows, bind themselves to that work, if superiors direct them to undertake it. There is, of course, no such grade in the Society of Jesus as "spiritual coajutor and formed lay-brother" which Short asserted to be the status of Jacques Marquette.

[21] Burrus, "Marquette, Priesthood," 265.
[22] Garraghan, "Unpublished Marquettiana," 23.

All of the foregoing is, quite evidently, a merely negative approach which leaves the positive problem unanswered. If Jacques Marquette received holy orders, where was he ordained, when, and by whom? If he was ordained an official, authentic record of the fact should be found in the archives of the Jesuit Province of Champagne as well as in the general archives of the Society of Jesus at Rome. Also there should be some incontestable evidence of his ordination in the diocesan archives of the diocese in which he was raised to the priesthood. Since Pont-à-Mousson, where Marquette was residing when he was said to have been ordained, was then within the diocese of Toul, one of the notorious Trois-Evêches, the archives of that diocese could be expected to contain an official record of Marquette's ordination. However, the now suppressed diocese of Toul had a stormy history. From 927 to 1552 the bishops of Toul held the title of count and exercised civil sovereignty within the diocese. In 1552 Henry II of France seized the Trois-Evêches, Metz, Toul, and Verdun, making them territorial possessions of France. During the French Revolution ecclesiastical records everywhere in France suffered vandalistic destruction at the hands of unruly mobs. When Napoleon I made his Concordat with Pius VII, in 1801, Toul, along with many other ancient dioceses in France, was suppressed. Nancy became the episcopal see of the area which included the governmental departments of Meurthe, Meuse, and Vosges. The archives of the diocese of Nancy-Toul, as it is now called, contain no documents dated earlier than the first decade of the nineteenth century, a good century-and-a-half after the date of Marquette's ordination. A similar disappointment should be expected regarding the records of the French Jesuit Province of Champagne. When the property of the Society of Jesus was confiscated by the French crown between 1763 and 1773, government agents, who assumed jurisdiction over the property, usually destroyed all documents pertaining to spiritual affairs as simply useless.[23] One would surmise that the archives of the Province of Champagne, which were housed in the Jesuit college at Nancy where the provincial normally resided, would have met the

[23] Jacobsen, "Documents," 48-49.

sad fate of all such valuable documents. Providentially, however, the public library at Nancy has a collection of Jesuitica pertaining to the old Province of Champagne, including a holograph codex of the *Annals of Ordinations* of Jesuits raised to holy orders between 1655 and 1667.[24] In this document Jacques Marquette is listed as having been ordained at Toul, forty miles from Pont-à-Mousson, on March 7, 1666. Though in Marquette's case, the document does not indicate the name of the officiating bishop, he was, most probably, André du Saussay who held the see of Toul from 1649 to 1675. This bishop, who was a prolific author, was one of the co-consecrators of François de Laval, first bishop of Quebec, when he was consecrated by the papal nuncio to France, Piccolomini, at Saint-Germain-des-Prés on December 8, 1656.[25]

Documentary evidence, corroborating the *Annals of Ordinations* at Nancy, is found in abundance in the archives of the Society of Jesus at Rome. Provincials of every province of the order made two kinds of reports to the Jesuit general who always resided at Rome. These were: letters and catalogs. The latter were submitted in two forms. The first was, and still is, an annual listing of every member of a given province indicating the full name of each Jesuit pertaining to the province; his ecclesiastical status, e.g. a priest, a lay-brother, or one studying for the priesthood, the current address of each person, and in what work he was then engaged. The second form of catalog, called a *catologus triennialis*, because submitted, ideally, every third year, was a far more complete report consisting of several divisions, one of which named all those ordained to the priesthood since the last such report. In the triennial report submitted by the provincial of the Province of Champagne in 1669, among those ordained since the last such report is listed Jacques Marquette, ordained at Toul on March 7,

[24] Archives de la bibliothèque publique de Nancy, Manuscrit 560 (138). J. Favier, in his *Manuscrits de la bibliothèque de Nancy*, also notes the existence of this manuscript.

[25] Bishop du Saussay was the son of very poor parents. He risked royal displeasure by acting as a coconsecrator for Bishop Laval. The crown wished Laval appointed as dependent on the archbishop of Rouen. But Rome chose to give Laval independent status.

1666.[26] The following year, in 1667, the annual catalog of the Province of Champagne reports Marquette as a priest who has been transferred to the Province of France and as then in New France. The five subsequent annual catalogs of the Province of Champagne, 1668, 1669, 1671-1672, 1672-1673, and 1673-1674, all list Marquette as a priest "applied" to the Province of France.[27] Concurrently, the annual catalogs of the Province of France, from 1667 to 1674, list Marquette as a priest engaged in missionary work among the Indians in New France.[28] The triennial catalogs submitted by the Province of France, in 1669 and 1672, also indicate that Marquette was a priest. One last piece of documentary evidence reposing in the Jesuit archives at Rome may be noted. At regular intervals each Jesuit province forwarded to Rome a list of all who had died since the last report of this nature. The obituary notice forwarded by the Province of Champagne for the period 1675 to 1678 is entitled: "A summary of the lives of those Jesuits of the Province of Champagne who have died . . . first: Father Jacques Marquette . . . a formed spiritual coajutor . . ."[29]

The evidence presented above should demonstrate, unquestionably, that Jacques Marquette was ordained a priest on the feast of Saint Thomas Aquinas, March 7, 1666, in the cathedral at Toul by, in all likelihood, the illustrious Lord André du Saussay, bishop of Toul. One could overwhelm the reader by listing from the *Jesuit Relations* the many instances on which Marquette functioned as a priest, administering the sacraments, celebrating Mass and such like functions which the Catholic Church empowers only validly ordained priests to perform. Of these many examples the reader is asked to bear with the investigation of only one, the authenticity of which was questioned by Francis Borgia Steck in his *Marquette Legends,* that of completing the ceremonies of baptism in favor of an Indian infant performed by Father Marquette at Boucherville on May 20, 1668. Steck branded the document reporting the ceremony as a forgery, declaring: "To all appearances, the so-called

[26] Jacobsen, "Documents," 51.
[27] Burrus, "Marquette, Priesthood," 259.
[28] *Ibid.,* 260.
[29] *Ibid.,* 264.

Marquette baptismal entry was inscribed on the title page of the Boucherville parish registry by the same person (and in the same handwriting) who wrote the Journal of the Second Voyage, with a view to bolster the alleged Marquette authorship of the Journal of the Second Voyage."[30] The entry to which Steck refers is three-and-a-half lines of writing found at the top of the title page of the registry of baptisms and marriages for the parish of Boucherville. The village, located some fifteen miles below Montreal on the right bank of the Saint Lawrence River, was founded by Pierre Boucher in 1667. Boucherville had no pastor until 1669 when the abbé Hughes Pommier, a diocesan priest, was appointed. On the first page of the still-extant registry we find inscribed in French: "This book of records contains the baptisms, marriages and burials performed in the parish of Boucherville." Above the title is written, again in French: "I, Jacques Marquette of the Society of Jesus, have conferred the ceremonies on Marie, daughter of Victor Kiouentaoue and Antoinette de Miskouminich, at the age of two months and baptized privately at Sorel by Monsieur Morel, a priest, the godfather being Ignace Boucher and the godmother Marie Boucher. May 20, 1668." Though he never personally examined the document, Steck holds it to be a forgery for many reasons. The placing of the entry above the title of the registry indicates to him that it was made long years after the registry was begun. The position of the entry probably proves, if anything, that Pierre Boucher, knowing the need for such a registry furnished one. The book could not have been properly called a parish registry in 1668 since Boucherville as yet had neither pastor nor parish. Steck also doubts that there ever was such an Indian child who was baptized by the abbé Morel, pastor of Holy Family Church on the Ile d'Orleans, a good 165 miles down the Saint Lawrence from Boucherville. Why would the parents take such a small child so far from home? And what was the abbé Thomas Morel doing at Sorel, a village at the mouth of the Richelieu River, 125 miles above Quebec? Father Steck failed to keep in mind the frequency with which Indians moved about as he also forgot that after the arrival of Bishop Laval

[30] Steck, *Marquette Legends*, 205.

care of the spiritual life of French villages came into the hands of the diocesan clergy who were thereby obliged to travel up and down the Saint Lawrence a great deal caring for their flocks. Steck also argues that if the entry were authentic Marquette would not have called the godmother Marie Boucher but Madam Gauthier since the Jesuit ought to have known that Pierre Boucher's daughter Marie married René Gauthier, Seigneur de Varennes, at Three Rivers on September 26, 1667. On the contrary, Marquette would call her exactly what appears in the registry, as Steck could discover if he read any of the innumerable documents of various characters pertaining to New France in the *Reports of the Archivist of the Province of Quebec.* Invariably, married women are referred to by their maiden names. Accepting the word of Father Joseph C. Short, who examined the document, Steck asserted that the freshness of the ink used in the Marquette entry demonstrates that it was made many, many years after the date noted in the document, i.e. 1668. This writer not only examined the entry personally and at length, in the summer of 1966, but had it photographed to its exact size as well as enlarged to the approximate dimensions of the reproduction of Marquette's last vows as they appear in *Mid-America,* XVIII (1935), 23. The photography was done by Armour Landry, an internationally respected freelance photographer. One can safely say that the ink in the Marquette entry is certainly darker than that of the other writing on the page. It cannot be said to be "fresher" than the rest of the script on the page. What can be said is that the ink used by Father Marquette was of a better quality than that used by others whose writing appears on the same page.

If one wished to "plant" a forged document, imitating the handwriting of the journal of Marquette's second voyage, it would have been necessary for the forger to be aware of several other unquestionably authentic samples of Marquette's handwriting, most of which did not come to light until after 1935. Such foresight could only be attributed to someone with preternatural powers. Speaking finally, then, on the question of the priesthood of Father Marquette, the evidence that he was validly ordained on March 7, 1666, is so conclusive that no honest scholar would presume to deny it. We may close this discussion by relating an amusing incident pertaining to the subject. Father F. Paul Prucha, S.J., of the history faculty of Marquette University met, not long ago, Father Athanasius Steck, O.F.M., brother of Father Francis Borgia. As was practically inevitable, the question of whether Marquette was a priest arose for discussion. Father Athanasius insisted that Marquette could not possibly have been a priest because he was a "spiritual coajutor and formed lay-brother." Father Prucha replied that he, himself, who had not as yet taken his final Jesuit vows, was certainly a priest and might possibly be directed to pronounce the vows of a spiritual coajutor. The living, breathing argument before him did not convince Father Athanasius Steck that Jacques Marquette was in very truth a priest.

Appendix two

JACQUES MARQUETTE, AUTHOR OF THE JOURNAL OF THE EXPEDITION OF 1673

Previous to 1927 historians universally agreed that the *Récit des voyages et des découvertes du Père Jacques Marquette,* which chronicled the Jolliet-Marquette expedition of 1673, was Jacques Marquette's personal journal of that historic voyage.[1] In 1927, however, Father Francis Borgia Steck, O.F.M., published his *Jolliet-Marquette Expedition, 1673* in which he declared: "In its present

[1] The *Récit,* as is later explained in detail, was included in Dablon's report to his provincial on the state of the missions for the period 1677-1678. This document contained the following divisions: (1) Dablon's report on all the missions of New France; (2) the *Récit;* (3) Marquette's journal of his visit to the Illinois, 1674-1675; (4) Allouez's report of his trip to the Illinois in 1676. In the Thwaites edition of the *Relations* these divisions do not appear as a unit. No. 1 is found in *Relations,* LXI, 19-87; No. 2, *Relations,* LIX, 87-164; No. 3, *Relations,* LIX, 165-211; No. 4, *Relations,* LX, 149-67.

form the narrative of the 1673 expedition is the work of the Jesuit superior, Claude Dablon; furthermore, it is in the main Jolliet's journal, which Marquette transmitted to Quebec and which Dablon eventually recast and, in 1678, sent to Paris."[2] When Father Jean Delanglez's lengthy study of the *Récit* appeared in *Mid-America* nineteen years later, many were surprised to find the author saying: "As we shall see, Father Steck's conclusion is certain, but the hypothesis, for which he claims great probability, is most improbable."[3] This writer maintains that the hypothesis proposed by each of the writers noted above is equally improbable. Further, this biographer holds that Jacques Marquette was, in very fact, the author of the *Récit*. To support that position it is requisite to describe, in some detail, the document being dealt with here, as well as to review and appraise the hypothesis which each author proposed and to assess the validity of each.

At the outset it is to be noted that there is no holograph copy of a journal of the voyage of 1673 which came from the hand of either Marquette or Jolliet, though all historians, except Steck, agree that such a document from the hand of each did exist.[4] It is certain that Louis Jolliet composed a journal because both Father Claude Dablon and Governor Frontenac reported its existence, as well as of at least one copy of it, though both the original and the one known copy were lost to posterity probably before August 1, 1674.[5] It is equally certain that Marquette wrote an account of the expedition for in the journal of his second voyage, 1674-1675, he reported that he had complied with Dablon's request to furnish a copy of his journal of the expedition of 1673.[6] Also, a copy of that journal by Marquette was used by Father Jacques Gravier who, in the fall of 1700, journeyed down the Mississippi from Chicago to the Gulf of Mexico. In his account of that voyage, Gravier made

[2] Steck, *Expedition*, 306.

[3] Jean Delanglez, "The *Récit des voyages et des découvertes du père Jacques Marquette*," *Mid-America*, XVII (1946), 173.

[4] Steck, *Expedition*, 306-07.

[5] *Relations*, LVIII, 93. On November 11, 1674, Frontenac reported to Colbert that Jolliet had left a copy of his journal ". . . at Sault-Sainte-Marie with the Fathers . . ." See Margry, I, 258.

[6] *Relations*, LIX, 165.

several references to Marquette's journal. For example, an Arkansas chief, when asked by Gravier if he had ever before seen a Frenchman dressed as the missionary was, replied that many years before one had visited his people who ". . . had danced to him the captain's calumet . . ."[7] Gravier commented: ". . . I have found in the Father's journal that they had indeed danced the calumet to him."[8]

Had it not been for the existence of the Chinese Rites controversy, coupled with Louis XIV's conflict with the Holy See over the matter of the *regale* just when the Mississippi River was explored, there never would have been a problem regarding Marquette's journal of the expedition of 1673.[9] Since the last *Relation* to be published was that of 1672-1673, which appeared before Marquette made a report of the expedition, any document regarding the voyage of 1673, whether from the pen of Marquette, Dablon, or any other Jesuit in New France, was a private communication to superiors in Europe and not intended for public consumption.[10] The first Jesuit source of information regarding the Jolliet-Marquette expedition is found in a letter, dated August 1, 1674, which Father Claude Dablon wrote to his provincial in France, Father Jean Pinette.[11] The information contained in the letter, as the writer informs us, was obtained from Louis Jolliet, who reached Quebec shortly before the date of Dablon's letter. Before relating what the expedition had accomplished, Dablon informed the provincial: "We cannot this year give all the information that might be expected regarding so important a discovery, since Sieur Jolliet, who was bringing us the account of it, with a very exact chart of these new countries, lost what he had in a shipwreck . . . However, while waiting the arrival of the account, of which Father Marquette pos-

[7] See *ibid.*, LXV, 121. Anastase Douay, a Recollet, also had a copy. See Steck, *Expedition*, 264.

[8] See *Relations*, LIX, 159, for the original account of the incident.

[9] For an explanation of the effect of these two problems on the publication of the *Relations*, see Joseph P. Donnelly, *Thwaites Jesuit Relations, Errata and Addenda*, 35-37.

[10] Léon Pouliot, *Etude sur les Relations des Jésuites de la Nouvelle-France (1632-1672)*, 9.

[11] Dablon to Pinette, August 1, 1674. The letter may be consulted in *Relations*, LVIII, 93-109.

sesses a copy, here is what we have been able to put together."[12] Dablon's letter constituted the introduction to his report on the state of the missions in New France for the period 1672-1673 and was not intended for publication.[13] Dablon's next report was called "*The Present Condition of the Missions of the Fathers of the Society of Jesus in New France, during the Year 1675*,[14] a part of which was Dablon's lengthy account of Father Marquette's effort to establish the mission among the Illinois and his death.[15] There is no further reference to Marquette in subsequent reports of the superior of the Jesuit missions in New France until his so-called *Relation* of 1677-1678. That document contained the *Récit des voyages et des découvertes du P. Jacques Marquette*.[16]

While there is no existing autograph copy of Dablon's *Relation* of 1677-1678, there exists one complete manuscript copy of it and five fragmentary copies, one of which was corrected by Dablon. Four of the fragmentary copies are in the archives of the Jesuit Province of France at Chantilly and one is in the archives of the Collège Sainte-Marie, Montreal. The only complete copy of the document is at Chantilly where it is identified as Fonds Brotier 159,

[12] *Ibid.*, 93. The translation given here is this author's, not that found in *Relations*, LVIII.

[13] Jean Delanglez, "The 1674 Account of the Discovery of the Mississippi," *Mid-America*, XV (1944), 302. Dablon composed a *Relation* for 1672-1673, but apparently did not send it once he learned, quite probably with the arrival of the fleet in the spring of 1673, that the *Relations* would no longer be published. There is a copy of Dablon's *Relation* of 1672-1673 in the archives of Collège Sainte-Marie, but no copy is found in ARSJ, Rome or at Chantilly. In 1674 Dablon revised his *Relation* of 1672-1673 and prefaced the revision with his letter of August 1, 1674. In the article noted above, Delanglez explains why Thwaites, lacking the information given above, did such an unsatisfactory job of editing the *Relation* of 1672-1673 in *Relations*, LVII, 36-305—LVIII, 20-89, separating Dablon's letter of August 1, 1674, from its proper position as the introduction of the *Relation* of 1672-1673.

[14] Thwaites put the *Relation* of 1675 in *Relations*, LIX, 216-91—LX, 26-65.

[15] Thwaites printed Dablon's account of Marquette's last apostolic effort, his death, and the translation of his bones to Saint Ignace in *Relations*, LIX, 185-211.

[16] Dablon's complete *Relation* of 1677-1678 was not published in the Thwaites' edition of the *Relations* as a unit. To assemble it, the student would be required to read it from the following volumes in the order set down: *Relations*, LIX, 216-91; LX, 25-65; LIX, 87-211; LX, 149-67.

Canada 5.[17] The manuscript consists of sixty-eight pages, numbered 1 to 67 on the recto of each page. The first twenty-four pages give a resume of the state of all the Jesuit missions in New France. Pages twenty-three and twenty-four are blank. Then follows the *Récit,* pages twenty-five to fifty-two. This portion has come to be known as Marquette 5. Pages fifty-two to sixty-one of the Chantilly manuscript contain a copy of Marquette's journal of his voyage to the Illinois, 1674-1675. The remaining pages of the manuscript contain a copy of Claude Allouez's account of his visit to the Illinois in 1676. In 1681 a Paris publisher, Melchisedech Thévenot, brought out a summarized version of the *Récit* as part of a volume called *Recueil de voyages de M. Thévenot.*[18] In his *Discovery and Exploration of the Mississippi Valley,* published in 1853, John Gilmary Shea included the *Récit* for which he used the manuscript in the archives of Collège Sainte-Marie.[19] Fortuné De Montézon republished the *Récit* in 1861 and Father Alfred Hamy did likewise in his *Au Mississippi* which appeared in 1903.[20] With the above information before us, we may review and assess the hypotheses proposed by Steck and Delanglez.

A discussion of Father Steck's theory, concerning the authorship of the account of the expedition of 1673, should be prefaced with Steck's own statement of his hypothesis as well as his estimate of its validity. Steck summarized his position thus: "That Marquette could not have written the narrative of the 1673 expedition as it exists today has been demonstrated. At the same time, however,

[17] See the schema composed by Delanglez showing what portions of the whole each of the five fragments include, Delanglez, *Récit*, 179.

[18] From which manuscript Thévenot made his summary is not known.

[19] John Gilmary Shea, *Discovery and Exploration of the Mississippi Valley*, 231 ff. The manuscript in the archives of Collège Sainte-Marie has a total of seventy-eight pages. Pages one to thirty-seven contain the *Récit*, except pages four and five which are missing and have been replaced by copying, in modern script and ink, the proper portion from Thévenot's published edition. Pages thirty-seven to fifty-one contain Dablon's account of Marquette's last voyage. Pages sixty-one and sixty-two are blank. Pages sixty-three to sixty-eight contain Marquette's journal of his last expedition.

[20] Fortuné M. de Montézon, editor, *Mission du Canada: Relations inédites de la Nouvelle-France (1672-1679) pour faire suite aux anciennes relations (1615-1672)*, 241-89. Hamy, *Au Mississippi*, 224-55.

the conclusion that it is a compilation by Dablon with Jolliet's journal as a basis remains a theory."[21] Given the status of research in this field previous to Steck's work, plus the comparative difficulty of access to several key documents, Father Steck did not deserve the highly critical reviews his study received. In fairness to Steck, it is to be remembered that there were difficulties regarding the authorship of the *Récit*, some of which had then not been completely solved.

Father Steck's hypothesis was based on his interpretation of two letters of Claude Dablon, a reference to a journal in Marquette's chronicle of his voyage of 1674-1675, Jolliet's letter of October 10, 1674, to Bishop Laval, plus Steck's interpretation of Dablon's motivation for composing the *Récit* and casting it in a style which inevitably led readers to presume that Marquette and not Dablon was the author. In the first of Dablon's letters to Pinette, he was reporting information procured from Louis Jolliet who probably reached Quebec only a few days before August 1, 1674. Explaining that because of Jolliet's accident the news contained in the missive was not very precise, Dablon informed Pinette that he would forward more exact information when he received ". . . an account of which Father Marquette possesses a copy . . ."[22] Steck assumed that the account was a copy of Jolliet's journal which he supposedly left with Marquette at Green Bay.[23] That conclusion was hardly justified in the face of Frontenac's report to Colbert on November 14, 1674, of which Steck was well aware. Frontenac announced that Jolliet had left a copy of his journal with the Jesuits at Sault-Sainte-Marie where it was destroyed in the fire which consumed the mission in the spring of 1674.[24] Steck circumvented Frontenac's clear statement by declaring that the governor ". . . misunderstood Jolliet when the latter told him in a general way of his having left copies of the lost papers with the

[21] Steck, *Expedition*, 310.

[22] The student should consult Delanglez's edition of the letter in "The 1674 Account of the Discovery of the Mississippi," 317-24.

[23] Steck, *Expedition*, 291.

[24] RAPQ, 1926-27, Frontenac to Colbert, November 14, 1674. See also Margry, I, Frontenac to Colbert, November 11, 1674.

Jesuits."[25] Steck conjectured that without inquiring, ". . . Frontenac very naturally presumed that . . ."[26] Jolliet's journal had been left at Sault-Sainte-Marie because that mission was the general headquarters of the Jesuits in the Ottawa country. If Jolliet actually had left a copy of his journal with Marquette at Green Bay, Frontenac would have told Colbert so if only because the journal was the official record of the expedition, a document of immense value, the basis of France's claim to the area explored. Frontenac would hardly have failed to inquire diligently as to exactly where a copy was to be procured nor would he have failed to inform Colbert when the copy would be forwarded to France.

Regarding Dablon's second letter to his provincial, that of October 24, 1674, Steck stresses the fact that, though Dablon refers to Marquette's voyage of 1673, ". . . he says nothing whatever about a narrative that the missionary had written of the enterprise . . ."[27] The absence of such a reference hardly proves that Marquette had no journal, either of his own or a copy of one written by Jolliet. Since Dablon had already told the provincial, in a letter written three months before, that Marquette possessed a journal, there was little reason for repeating that information in a subsequent communication. Significantly, in this same letter of October 24, 1674, Dablon reviewed the hazardous voyage Father Charles Albanel had made to Hudson Bay, 1671-1672, without mentioning that Albanel wrote a journal of that voyage. Dablon had included Albanel's journal in the *Relation* of 1671-1672.[28]

Steck contends that Marquette did not write a journal of the expedition of 1673 but compiled only a few scattered notes which, at Dablon's request, he forwarded to Quebec.[29] This opinion required Steck to offer some explanation of Marquette's unequivocal statement found at the opening of his account of his journey to the Illinois in 1674-1675: "After complying with Your Reverence's re-

[25] Steck, *Expedition*, 291-92.

[26] *Ibid.*

[27] Dablon's letter of October 24, 1674, may be consulted in *Relations*, LIX, 64-84.

[28] See *ibid.*, LVI, 148-217, for Albanel's journal.

[29] Steck, *Expedition*, 306.

quest for copies of my journal concerning the missisipi [*sic*] River, I departed . . . on the 25th of October, 1674, about noon."[30] Though it would seem abundantly clear that Marquette wrote a journal of the expedition of 1673, Father Steck declared: "He had no journal, illness having all year prevented him from composing one."[31] Illness was not the cause of Marquette's not composing a journal since he wasn't sick all year, but only from the end of May to late September.[32] If the journal to which Marquette referred was not his own, but Jolliet's, Marquette could not have honestly called it "my journal" for that statement would be an untruth.

The letter which Jolliet wrote to Bishop Laval on October 10, 1674 supports the existence of a journal composed by Jolliet, but does not, of itself, prove that the *Récit* is substantially Jolliet's journal, as Steck contends. The pertinent portion of Jolliet's missive to Laval reads: "On returning, being about to disembark at Montreal, my canoe upset and I lost two men and my strong box wherein were all the papers and my journal with some rarities of those distant countries."[33] Perhaps Father Steck considered Jolliet's letter to Laval so vastly important because he accepted Henry Harrisse's assertion that the copy of the *Récit* in the archives of the seminary of Saint-Sulpice at Paris, to which a copy of Jolliet's letter is attached, ". . . is all in the hand of Jolliet . . ."[34] However, none of the manuscript is in Jolliet's hand.[35] Hence, it does not follow, from the argument of silence, as Steck contended, that the document in Marquette's possession at Green Bay was Jolliet's journal. Steck reasoned that when, supposedly, Jolliet made a copy of the *Récit* for Bishop Laval he would have corrected any errors, including the remark that Marquette had a copy of the Jolliet journal at Green Bay, if the journal had actually been left at Sault-Sainte-Marie. The whole of this supposition, therefore, rests on an unsound premise.

[30] *Relations*, LIX, 165.

[31] Steck, *Expedition*, 306-07.

[32] *Relations*, LIX, 165.

[33] Steck, *Expedition*, 290.

[34] Henri Harrisse, *Notes pour servir à l'histoire . . . de la Nouvelle-France*, 323.

[35] Delanglez, "The 1674 Account of the Discovery of the Mississippi," 309.

Supposing that Father Dablon, with malice aforethought, deliberately purloined Jolliet's journal and so edited it that it would appear to be the work of Marquette, what would his motive have been? Steck suggested that Dablon feared that LaSalle would bring Recollets into the Mississippi Valley, excluding the Jesuits from a field of evangelization which bade fair to be the most successful ever opened in New France. Thus wrote Father Steck:

> Accordingly, to establish a priority of claim to this new field of missionary endeavor, the Jesuit Superior drew up a narrative in the name of the missionary who with Jolliet had explored the great river in 1673. To the use of his own journal as a basis Jolliet consented, when Dablon proposed the matter to him, especially since hopes were held out to him of acquiring territorial claims in the fertile Illinois country and of settling there with twenty other Frenchmen. He did not reckon with the possibility that Dablon would compose the narrative in a way that would represent Marquette as the author and that the original copies together with Marquette's notes would be destroyed.[36]

It is to be hoped that Father Steck did not advert to the moral implications of his hypothesis. If Dablon really followed that course of action, he was guilty of lying to his superior who could not possibly have guessed that the *Récit* was not the work of Marquette. Dablon risked being unmasked by Jolliet if or when the latter came upon a copy of the *Récit.* Though Steck offered no answer to the morality of Dablon's supposed deception, he did propose a solution for the problem of Jolliet resenting the *Récit.* Steck surmised: "Due respect for the memory of Marquette, however, the news of whose death must have touched him deeply, sealed the lips of the explorer. After all, his future prosperity did not depend on his having written the narrative of the expedition which he had undertaken in 1673."[37] On the contrary Jolliet's future prosperity might well have been greatly advanced if he could have claimed the *Récit* as his own when he asked the crown for a grant of land in the Mississippi Valley. In summary, then, Steck's hypothesis that the *Récit* is not Marquette's own account of the expedition of 1673 but Jolliet's journal edited by Father Claude Dablon is simply untenable.

[36] Steck, *Expedition,* 307.
[37] *Ibid.*

During the past three decades no historian interested in the history of New France did more to advance knowledge of that area of history than Father Jean Delanglez, S.J. One should not lightly take issue with Delanglez's opinion that the *Récit* is not Marquette's journal of the voyage down the Mississippi but entirely the work of Claude Dablon. In his long, scholarly article on the authorship of the *Récit,* Delanglez first discusses each of the existing copies of the document. Then Delanglez announces, without any evidence offered for the conclusion: "Since there is no doubt that Dablon wrote the *Relation* of 1677-1678, of which the *Récit* is an integral part . . ., our main problem is to ascertain what material he had at hand for composing the *Récit* of 1678."[38] It is unquestionably true that Dablon was the author of the *Relation* of 1677-1678, but he was not the author of the *Récit* any more than he was the author of Allouez's account of his visit to the Illinois in 1676. Demonstrating conclusively that Marquette composed his own account of the expedition of 1673, Delanglez maintains that Dablon never received a copy of Marquette's journal.[39] After waiting in vain until 1678, Dablon, says Delanglez, ". . . had given up hope of ever receiving this important document, and wrote the *Récit* on the basis of what he had."[40] What Dablon "had," from which to compose the *Récit* was in Delanglez's opinion: 1) Dablon's own letter of August 1, 1674; 2) a copy of Jolliet's map drawn from memory; 3) further conferences with Jolliet, held between 1674 and 1678; 4) talks with Jacques Largillier who was at Quebec in 1675 and again in 1676; 5) Marquette's map as well as his journal of the voyage of 1674-1675; 6) a set of the Jesuit *Relations,* at least those published from 1655 to 1672.[41] Undoubtedly Dablon had all of these documents and people available, but if he had a copy of Marquette's map, or even the original, why did he not also have the missionary's journal which Delanglez insists Marquette wrote. If the map reached Dablon, why not also the journal? One would be rather inclined to believe that the map would not have been separated from the journal.

[38] Delanglez, "*Récit,*" 183.
[39] *Ibid.*, 190.
[40] *Ibid.*
[41] *Ibid.*, 183-84.

Delanglez's explanation of why Father Dablon did not receive Marquette's journal is neither satisfactory nor clear. Delanglez reasons that Dablon learned from Jolliet, in late July 1674, that Marquette had a copy of Jolliet's journal. The superior then sent a letter to Marquette requesting that the journal be forwarded. That suppositious missive, Delanglez thinks, reached Saint-Ignace probably during the latter part of September 1674, whence it was forwarded to Green Bay by Jacques Largillier and Pierre Porteret who also brought with them, according to Delanglez, permission from the local superior, Father Henri Nouvel, for Marquette to undertake the journey to the Illinois.[42] At that point in his article, Delanglez switches the context of his argument, changing from Dablon's asking for Jolliet's journal to a discussion of Marquette's own journal of the expedition of 1673. Instead of saying, as one would expect from what went before, that Marquette complied with Dablon's request for a copy of Jolliet's journal, Delanglez says that between the time Marquette received Dablon's request at Green Bay and his departure for the Illinois, the missionary had ample time to ". . . defer to the wishes of Your Reverence for copies of my journal concerning the missisipi [*sic*] River . . ."[43] Thenceforth, Delanglez apparently completely forgot about copies of Jolliet's journal, reminding the reader that Marquette did not have a copy of that document, but only his own journal which he transcribed for Dablon. If Dablon really did ask for a copy of Jolliet's journal, Marquette would hardly have ignored his superior's request. He would have explained that he had no copy of Jolliet's work, but was sending a copy of the journal he wrote himself. However, Marquette unquestionably replied that he was sending a copy of his own journal and made no reference to any work of Jolliet's. Therefore, it is at least reasonable to argue that Dablon knew as early as August 1, 1674, that Marquette had a journal and requested a copy of it.

The most unfortunate portion of Delanglez's discussion of the *Récit* is his attempt to explain why Dablon, if he be the author of

[42] *Ibid.*, 188-90.
[43] *Ibid.*, 190.

the document, cast it in a style which inevitably led the reader to presume it was Marquette's own work. Even the merest tyro reading the *Récit* would immediately assume that Father Marquette was the author. Delanglez offers the most unsatisfactory of explanations in defense of Dablon's employing such a deception. After quoting a lengthy paragraph from Langlois and Seignobos in defense of such a device, Delanglez remarks that Dablon, in good conscience, considered it proper to compose a whole journal of a very important expedition and pass the result off as the work of Marquette.[44] Dismissing the question of Dablon's honesty, Delanglez avers: "Once this is understood [i.e. that Dablon employed the literary device of using the first person, though composing the journal himself] the question of the authorship of the *Récit* no longer involves . . . the honesty of Père Dablon."[45] Not only is that conclusion unjustified, it should discredit, entirely, everything Dablon wrote or edited, including his own journal of his voyage up the Saguenay, 1660-1661 and all of the *Relations* from 1671 to 1680.

With a kind of myopic intensity, Delanglez appears to have misinterpreted the one key document in which, it would seem, Dablon quite clearly indicates that the *Récit* was Marquette's own personal journal of the expedition of 1673. On October 25, 1678, Dablon wrote to Father Claude Boucher, French assistant to the Jesuit general at Rome: "I gathered together all the writings of the late Father Marquette pertaining to his discoveries. I put these in order together with all the rarities and curiosities of the voyage and the establishment of the mission of the Illinois. I sent this little work to Father Ragueneau who will see that you get it."[46] Delanglez arbitrarily declared that by "this little work" Dablon meant only the *Récit* which was but one section of the whole sixty-seven page manuscript of the *Relation* of 1677-1678. On the contrary, if words mean anything, Dablon told Boucher that he included all the writings of Father Marquette on his voyages, one of which was his journal of the trip down the Mississippi in 1673.

[44] Charles V. Langlois and Charles Seignobos, *Introduction aux études historiques*, 258.

[45] Delanglez, *"Récit,"* 219-20.

[46] ARSJ, Gallia 110, I, f.62v. Dablon to Claude Boucher, October 25, 1678.

If Dablon wished Boucher to understand anything else he would have been obliged to be very explicit, which he was not.

The major portion of Delanglez's study of the *Récit* is taken up with a textual analysis, showing that much of what is contained in the *Récit* may be found in material previously published by Dablon. From this erudite exposition, Delanglez concluded that Dablon inserted into the *Récit* large sections of his own writings. There are, certainly, striking similarities between passages written by Dablon before 1673 and sections of the *Récit,* but why must this prove that Dablon authored the *Récit*? Why was it impossible for Marquette to have paraphrased Dablon's writings? Were there no copies of the *Relations* anywhere but Quebec? The *Relations* were as much a newsletter to Marquette at Saint-Ignace as they were to Jesuits in France. By 1674 Marquette had been away from Quebec for six years. He and the rest of the Jesuits on the Ottawa mission were more out of touch with the rest of the missions of New France than the Jesuit provincial at Paris. To say that Dablon's admittedly distinctive style can be discerned in passages of the *Récit* proves no more than that Marquette quite likely had available copies of the *Relations* in which Dablon described his own journey to Green Bay and the Mascouten village in the autumn of 1670.[47] Why could not Marquette, who did not have a facile pen, have paraphrased what Dablon wrote in 1670? In summary, this portion of Delanglez's article is simply not convincing. Neither is his whole hypothesis.

Having attempted to review the literature regarding Father Marquette, after studying the available documents, this biographer firmly believes that there is no mystery about the *Récit.* This is Marquette's own account of the expedition of 1673. There is no valid reason to suppose that it is not. To come to any other conclusion maligns Dablon, casts doubt on the integrity of the *Relations,* and reflects on the honesty of Jacques Marquette. There is one simple, obvious answer to the question of the authorship of the *Récit.* This is the journal of the expedition of 1673 which Jacques Marquette wrote during the long winter evenings at Green Bay, 1673-1674.

[47] *Relations,* LV, 183-219.

Appendix three

A LETTER OF FATHER PIERRE CHOLENEC TO FATHER JEAN DE FONTENAY

A Letter of Father Pierre Cholenec, Missionary in Canada, to Father de Fontenay, at Nantes, from the residence of Saint Francis Xavier, October 10, 1675

Though I have a thousand reasons to be grateful to you and much to tell you, I defer all of that to a later time so anxious am I to give you the most joyful news you could receive from me. Courage, my dear colleague, rejoice, we have a new apostle, a new Saint Francis Xavier in paradise, assuredly praying for us in a very special manner. He is your dear friend, Father Marquette, who, departing this life, has gone to join the angels. You may wonder why I urge you to rejoice at the loss of such a dear friend. I do so, my dear Father, because his death was so saintly and precious in the sight of God. Indeed, that grand man, that zealous missionary died the death of an apostle, another Saint Francis Xavier, expiring in a rude cabin, beside the water, abandoned by all, as he always prayed that he would.

You know about the important voyage he made last year to the great river, flowing from [the Lake of the] Illinois, descending, they say, to within thirty leagues of [the Gulf of] Mexico. He met the Illinois living on a very beautiful river which flows out of the lake bearing their name and courses southward. He believed that those Indians were so gentle, so moral, so disposed to receive the Gospel and so anxious to have one of our Fathers with them that he promised them he would return himself, after reporting the results of his voyage to the superior, or he would procure another for them. Though most of the time, after returning, he was very unwell, because of a bloody flux brought on by his exhausting labors, he recovered somewhat. The Reverend Father Superior of the Ottawa mission permitted him to go, sending him for that purpose, eight days after the feast of Saint Michael, two of our domestics, *donnés* of our mission, one of whom had made the [previous] voyage with him, bringing the order to him at Green Bay, where he was, and whence he set out with them at the beginning of November. Entering that bay at its southern end, after a brief journey, reaching the Lake of the Illinois, he traveled southward, paralleling the shore corresponding to Green Bay. He voyaged many days on that lake, always southward, finally reaching the entrance to a river bearing the same name, that is to say Illinois. There he was obliged to winter because of the snow. You can imagine the courage of that great man undertaking a journey of two hundred leagues in the face of death, still recovering from a severe illness which was bound to recur. Even though he was so weak that he doubted that he was strong enough to undertake the journey, still for a long time he had been asking God to let him die while making a missionary journey, deprived of all human comfort. He generously undertook that painful voyage, thinking only of his dear mission to the Illinois where he hoped, not without some presentiment, to lay down his life in that glorious enterprise, as indeed he did.

While dwelling in a cabin on the banks of that river, his malady, which had improved somewhat eight days before [the feast of] Saint Francis Xavier, grew increasingly worse after the eve [of the feast of the Immaculate] Conception. Then he understood clearly that God was granting him the favor he had so many times besought from Him. He even told his companions very plainly that he would certainly die of that malady, and during that voyage. In spite of his great physical indisposition, in order to prepare his soul to die well, he began that cruel winter by [making] the Exercises of Saint Ignatius which he performed with great devotion and much celestial consolation. The remainder of the time he spent writing an account of his voyages. [Except for that], he was entirely taken up with spiritual concerns, eschewing commerce with anything earthly in that wretched place, save for his two companions whose confessions he heard and to whom he gave Communion, exhorting them as earnestly as his strength permitted. I saw these same two domestics, *donnés,* here when they were going down to Quebec from the Ottawa [country] as well as when they came back. I had them tell me themselves, at their leisure, every detail regarding the man and his death, certain that I could do nothing which would be more gratifying to you.

I leave it to you to conjecture the suffering the Father endured, passing the winter at that place, but with such heroic courage, joy, and peace of soul, that the two men could not help admiring him. Breaking camp on March 19, [1675,] after ten days on the road, sixty leagues to the south they found the great village of the Illinois where the Father was received as an angel from Heaven. He summoned a great council at which he offered presents according to the custom of the Indians. Because it was a large village of five or six hundred fires and everyone wanted to see and hear him, he held the meeting in an open field. There the grand, brave apostle, after planting a row of poles in the ground, to which he attached the beautiful lengths of taffeta he had brought along, displayed a lovely picture of the glorious Virgin Mary, holding her Son in her arms. It was there that he announced to the great assembly the purpose of his voyage, proclaiming and preaching to them Christ crucified. [This he did] on the very eve of the day on which He died for them on the Cross. Then he said holy Mass. Three days later, which was Easter Sunday (he arrived there on the previous Wednesday), everything was arranged in the same manner as on Thursday. He celebrated the same mysteries for the second time, saying Mass in the presence of all the people, giving Communion to his companions and to two Frenchmen who were in the area. By these two [holy] Sacrifices, which had never before been offered to God [in that area] he took possession of the country in the name of Jesus Christ to the glory of God and for the salvation of those poor Indians. The mission, which he wished placed under the protection of the glorious Virgin Mary, dedicating it to Her Immaculate Conception towards whom he had an inexpressible affection and devotion, so great that everything was measured by the honor and cult of that Queen of Heaven and earth. That was the last Mass he offered to God during his life and certainly [it must have been] the most pleasing to the Divine Majesty and most useful to himself. His companions were profoundly impressed with his deep spiritual fervor during the Mass, a fervor they could not help but notice. After spending the morning in such a gloriously holy manner, to the great astonishment and admiration of the Indians, who were impressed by the novelty and grandeur of these [sacred] mysteries, in the afternoon he attended their council for the last time. He informed them that he was obliged to return promptly to Michilimackinac where the Father Superior had convened a meeting of all the missionaries of the area. They begged him to return as quickly as possible and he promised to do so or, at least, to send another [missionary] in his stead. This latter he added, aware of his condition, knowing that his strength was ebbing away, little by little, even as he spoke to them. After that he became completely the apostle, refusing all of the gifts they pressed on him. They were so docile, so well disposed, so inclined to accept the Gospel that he wished to leave them with one impression, the integrity of those who have no other interest than their salvation, coming to preach to them no matter what the labor or the danger. But these good savages, determined somehow to show him how grateful they were, could not do enough for him. Since he declined to accept anything they offered him, they competed with one another for [the honor of carrying] his light baggage. They followed him up the river for thirty leagues. Returning his baggage on the far side of a portage he was obliged to make, which they made for him, they bade farewell to the Father, filled with affection for him, enthusiastic about the Gospel and burning with a desire for his prompt return to their village. But God disposed otherwise. After bidding the Indians farewell with as much ceremony as possible, Father Marquette was no longer a man of this world, but a citizen of Heaven, one about to receive a reward at his return from an embassy on which he had served his master brilliantly. He was well aware of this himself for when he reached the Lake of the Illinois and started along the southern shore, returning by a route not previously followed, his strength waned so alarmingly that his companions lost all hope of his reaching their destination. Then he began to hope that God would soon grant the favor he had besought so often. This was what consoled him during an illness which brought him so low that he could no longer move but had to be handled and carried like a child. All of this he bore with joy and resignation, consoling and encouraging his companions to bear all for Jesus Christ Who would not abandon them after his death. Finally, when his demise was approaching, going ashore in the evening, on a Friday, he told them that he believed he would die on the morrow. He exhorted them to have courage and resign themselves to the will of God. This gave him great happiness, but caused profound sorrow to his two companions. The following day, continuing their journey, all the while he spoke of his death, the place for his burial, the manner of burying him and how to mark his grave, speaking of all this with such sweetness and tranquility of spirit that one would have thought he was talking about the death and burial of another rather than of his own. Having always hoped to be buried at some notable site on that lake, when they encountered a suitable place, at about 3 in the afternoon, he asked them to go no farther, saying that it was time to go ashore at a river so that he might have a little time to prepare for his last hour which was approaching. So they obliged him. They hurriedly threw up a rude bark shelter, making him as comfortable as they could, though, as they told me, they were so overcome with sadness at the death of their Father, who loved them dearly, that they scarcely knew what they were doing. Stretched on a couch of sorts, the first thing he did was console his companions, exhorting them to have confidence in God, who would not abandon them in that solitude, adding a few precepts and some instructions. Then he gave them a little time to prepare for the sacrament of penance which he wished to administer to them. In the meantime, he recited his breviary, which he did daily to the last day of his life, though he was not obliged to this, considering his weakness.

Finishing his own devotions, he satisfied the piety of his loving companions, hearing their confessions. He thanked them for their continued kindness to him throughout the voyage and asked their pardon for all the trouble he gave them, promising not to forget them in heaven. Then he embraced them for the last time, causing the two poor men to fall at his feet dissolved in tears. He took the crucifix, which he always wore suspended around his neck, and asked one of the two men to hold it so that he could see it, as well as not to forget, when he was about to expire, to repeat frequently the names of Jesus and Mary, if he didn't do so himself. Then, when he felt his last hour approaching, gathering his feeble strength, he made a profession of faith, in a strong voice, his hands joined and his eyes resting lovingly on the crucifix. He added all the other prayers proper to such an occasion and finished, thanking the Blessed Trinity for the incomparable grace of dying a Jesuit, a missionary of Jesus Christ and, above all, dying, as he always hoped, in a wretched hut in the midst of the wilderness, and, at the end, bereft of all human succor, except his two companions, who could do nothing for him in his extremity, except pray. After that he remained silent, communing within himself with God, except for a word uttered now and then, revealing the admirable sentiments of his heart. Finally, a little later, he began his agony, which was very mild and peaceful. At that, one of his men obeyed his order to repeat the names of Jesus and Mary in a loud voice. The dying man repeated them distinctly several times. While he was pronouncing those two adorable names, something appeared to him a little above the crucifix, which, until then, had held his attention. So, with a countenance beaming and all aglow, he peacefully rendered his blessed soul to his Creator on Saturday, May eighteenth, between eleven and midnight.

Such, my dear Father, was the death of your good friend, the Reverend Father Marquette, in the flower of his manhood. He was consummated in Christ.

Our two men, shedding copious tears over the body, having satisfied their devotion and sorrow, which was profound, buried it at the place and in the manner directed. At the feet they planted a great cross to mark the spot for the future. The next day, Sunday, they set out on their journey with what sentiments you can guess, sad and regretful at having lost the source of their consolation. One of the two was so heartsick all night that in the morning he was severely ill at his stomach. Obliged to go on, he had recourse, with consummate faith, to the dead missionary, whom he felt sure was in heaven. Saying nothing to his companion, who was readying the canoe to depart, he knelt at the foot of the body and prayed earnestly, at the same time swallowing a pinch of earth from the grave. He was cured at once. The man himself told me this in confidence. Then the two went on their way, filled with confidence, inspired by their good Father.

With all respect and affection for Your Reverence,
Your very humble and obedient servant in our Lord,
Pierre Cholenec of the Society of Jesus.[1]

[1] Archives of the Province of France of the Society of Jesus, Séminaire Missionnaire, "Les Fontaines," Chantilly (Oise), France, Fonds Brotier 166 (Canada 12), 4.

Appendix four

THE MARQUETTE DEATH SITE

Since 1684 there has been intermittent discussion regarding the exact place where Father Jacques Marquette breathed his last and was originally buried. In 1683 René-Robert Cavelier de La Salle, who had an intimate knowledge of the geography of both shores of Lake Michigan from his own travels as well as those of his loyal lieutenant, Henri de Tonty, petitioned authority from the crown to set up, on the Gulf of Mexico, a trading colony which would exploit the economic possibilities of the Mississippi Valley. Entwined in La Salle's grandiose project was the ambition of one of his friends at court, the abbé Claude Bernou, who dreamed of establishing a new episcopal see for the colony with himself as the obvious candidate for the position of bishop. The vast extent of La Salle's proposal was dramatically illustrated by an excellent map, prepared and published in 1684 by Jean-Baptiste Franquelin, currently France's most competent cartographer, who probably gleaned most of his detailed information about the Lake Michigan area from La Salle and Tonty.[1] At the very time La Salle was at court seeking permission to establish his new colony, Bishop Laval was also there arranging his own resignation in favor of Jean-Baptiste de la Croix de Chevrière de Saint-Vallier, who was appointed to the see of Quebec in 1685. When the newly nominated bishop learned of the abbé Bernou's ecclesiastical designs on the lower Mississippi Valley, he promptly protested, declaring in a *mémoire* to the crown that any proposal to establish a new ecclesiastical jurisdiction within the territory owned by France on the mainland of North America was an invasion of the rights of the bishop of Quebec whose authority was coextensive with France's possessions there. Saint-Vallier adduced as proof of his position the fact that, among other things, not only had Father Marquette and Louis Jolliet explored the Mississippi, but the missionary had died at a ". . . mission located near the middle of the lake of the Illinois, as can be seen, in the original, in Paris, of the map outlined and entitled in the hand of Sr. Joliet [*sic*]."[2] Since Jolliet did not make a map showing any noteworthy geographical features of the eastern shore of Lake Michigan, quite possibly Saint-Vallier was referring to Franquelin's map. On it, south of a great inlet resembling Grand Traverse Bay, there are two small, unnamed rivers below which are the Rivière Aramone, the Rivière du P. Marquette and then six more rivers, the last of which is the Rivière des Miamis, now called the St. Joseph.[3] Saint-Vallier was probably unaware that Marquette had not established a mission on the river bearing his name, but since that missionary was a vicar-general of the bishop of Quebec, Saint-

[1] Franquelin's map was called *Carte de la Louisiane, ou des voyages du Sr de La Salle et des pays qu'il à découverts depuis la Nouvelle-France jusqu'au Golfe Mexique, les années 1679, 80, 81 et 82*. A reproduction of the map may be examined in *Relations*, LXIII, frontispiece.

[2] Raphael N. Hamilton, "The Marquette Death Site: the Case for Ludington," *Michigan History*, XLIX (1965), 242. The *mémoire* itself is found in the Bibliothèque Nationale, Paris, Clarambault, 1016: 629.

[3] The Rivière Aramone received its name from an inexpensive French table wine called Aramon.

Vallier could correctly argue that his see did extend to the mouth of the Mississippi because an ecclesiastic holding spiritual faculties from the bishop of Quebec had exercised his priestly ministry in the area.

Locating the mouth of Franquelin's Rivière du P. Marquette by latitude and longitude is not readily done from the map itself since its author did not include a mileage scale on it. But Minet, an engineer who accompanied La Salle on his disastrous voyage of 1684, made a sketch of Franquelin's map on which the engineer included a gauge for measuring distances.[4] From Minet's sketch one can determine that the Rivière du P. Marquette was sixty leagues, as the crow flies, from Michilimackinac and about the same distance from the mouth of the Rivière des Miamis. The river bearing Marquette's name empties into a broad, shallow bay formed by a cape at the north, closely resembling the present Big Sable Point, and at the south by one quite similar to Little Sable Point. Since Saint-Vallier declared that Marquette's "mission" was near the middle of the lake of the Illinois, the mouth of Franquelin's Rivière du P. Marquette would coincide with the place where Marquette breathed his last.

In 1688 Franquelin produced a second map of French North America, known as the *Carte de l'Amérique Septentrionale.*[5] On it the Rivière Marquette is forty leagues from Michilimackinac. Thirty years later, in 1718, Guillaume Delisle, a famous French cartographer, published his *Carte de la Louisiane et du cours du Mississippi.*[6] On this map, though the eastern shore of Lake Michigan is abbreviated to ninety leagues, the Rivière du P. Marquette is again placed at a bit more than forty leagues south of the Straits of Mackinac.

The first European known to have visited the site of Father Marquette's demise was Father Pierre François Xavier de Char-

[4] See Sara J. Tucker's *Indian Villages of the Illinois Country,* plate 7 for a reproduction of Minet's sketch.

[5] There is a copy of Franquelin's map of 1688 in the William L. Clements Library, University of Michigan, Ann Arbor.

[6] A reproduction of Delisle's map may be examined in Louis C. Karpinski's *Bibliography of Printed Maps of Michigan, 1804-1880,* plate xi.

levoix, a Jesuit of no mean historical attainments. A native of Picardy, Charlevoix was born in 1682 and entered the Jesuit novitiate at Paris on September 15, 1698. Seven years later, in 1705, he was sent to Quebec for the usual period of teaching done by young Jesuit aspirants to the priesthood previous to their theological studies. Jacques Marquette, at that time in his grave only twenty-seven years, would still be fresh in the memories of the older Jesuits in New France. This would be especially true of Father Antoine Silvy, who lived with Marquette at Green Bay, and Pierre Cholenec, whose letter of October 10, 1675, gave us the details of the great missionary's last days. Both Silvy and Cholenec were still living when Charlevoix was at Quebec.[7] Returning to Paris in 1709, Charlevoix, after completing theology and being ordained, taught at Louis-le-Grand. At the conclusion of the War of the Spanish Succession (1701-1714), when the Treaty of Utrecht granted England the territory of Acadia (Nova Scotia), according to the ancient boundaries of that area, Charlevoix was commissioned, in 1719, to draw up for the French crown an historical report proving what the ancient boundaries of Acadia had been since France first claimed the area. Charlevoix's document may have been very scholarly, but it didn't help his country much because France lost Acadia to the English and with it undisputed control of the mouth of the Saint Lawrence River.[8]

Fearing that the English might blockade the mouth of the Saint Lawrence, depriving France of access to Quebec, the colonial office at Paris determined to discover, if possible, a western entry to her colony by way of the Pacific Ocean and a rumored inland waterway

[7] Silvy lived with Charlevoix in the college at Quebec. See *Relations*, LIX, 307.

[8] No full-length biography of Charlevoix has ever been done. The biographical details given here are taken from the preface to the reprint edition of Charlevoix's *History and General Description of New France* issued by Loyola University Press in 1962. Charlevoix's first major historical work was his *Histoire de l'etablissement, des progrès et de la décadence du Christianisme dans l'empire du Japon*, published in 1715. His other major publications were: *La vie de la Mère de l'Incarnation*, 1725; *Histoire de l'Isle Espagnol ou Saint-Domingue*, 1730-1731; *Histoire et déscription générale de la Nouvelle-France, avec le journal historique d'un voyage fait par ordre du roi dans l'Amérique Septentrionale*, 1744; and *Histoire du Paraguay*, 1756.

leading thence to Quebec. When the cost of a properly equipped expedition for that venture proved prohibitive, as well as diplomatically imprudent, it was decided to send Father Charlevoix to Canada, ostensibly to investigate the condition of the Jesuit missions there, but actually to search for a trans-Canada water route to the Pacific. On hearing of Charlevoix's commission, the Duchess de Lediguière, a generous benefactor of the Jesuits, asked him to keep her informed of the adventures he might encounter on the expedition. Charlevoix complied with the lady's request by writing a series of letters. Reaching Canada during the autumn of 1720, the visitor was unable to embark on his expedition until the spring of 1721. During his enforced delay, Charlevoix interviewed experienced *voyageurs* and old missionaries, seeking information which might lead to the discovery of a water route to the Pacific. Setting out by boat in the spring of 1721, the Jesuit reached Michilimackinac and started down the east coast of Lake Michigan on July 29, 1721. On August 3 he entered ". . . the river of Father Marquette . . . ," visiting the site where the missionary was first buried, ". . . to see if what they told me about it was true." Charlevoix's description of the site was the first reasonably accurate one from which later historians could hope to identify the place. But exactly what site fits Charlevoix's description?

Because of its importance to the question under discussion, it seems useful to include Charlevoix's own account of his visit to the site of Marquette's death:

> The third [day of August, 1721], I entered the river of Father Marquette to see if what they told me was true. This is, at first, only a brook, but fifteen paces higher up, one enters a lake which is nearly two leagues in circumference. To allow it [the river] to discharge into Lake Michigan, one would say that they sliced with a pickax a large hummock which one leaves to the left on entering. And on the right the shore is quite low for about the length of a good musket shot. Then, all at once, it [the land] rises quite high. They described it accurately to me and concerning it [the site] here is the constant tradition of all our *voyageurs* and what our old missionaries told me.
>
> Father Joseph [*sic*] Marquette, a native of Laon in Picardy, where his family still holds a position of distinction, was one of the most illustrious missionaries of New France. He traveled over almost all of the area

and made many discoveries, of which the last was that of the Mississippi, which he entered with the Sieur Joliet [*sic*] in 1673. Two years after that discovery, of which he published the Relation, as he was coming from Chicago, which is at the bottom of Lake Michigan, to Michilimackinac, he entered on the eighteenth of May 1675, into the river of which I am speaking, whose mouth was then at the extremity of the low land, which, as I said, one leaves on the right on entering. There he prepared his altar and said Mass. Then he retired a little way to make his thanksgiving and asked the two men who paddled his canoe to leave him alone for half an hour. When the time was up, they went to look for him and were very surprised to find him dead. They remember, however, that on entering the river he had let slip a remark that he would end his journey there. Since it was too far to bring the body from there to Michilimackinac, they buried it very close to the bank of the river which, since that time, has moved, little by little, as out of respect, towards the headland, whose foot it now washes and where it has made a new channel. The following year, one of the two men, who had buried the servant of God, returned to the place where they interred him and, raising what remained, brought it to Michilimackinac. I was unable to learn, or I have forgotten, what that river was previously called, but today the Indians never call it anything but the River of the Blackrobe. The French have given it the name of Père Marquette and never fail to invoke his name when they find themselves in some danger on Lake Michigan. Many have assured me that they believe that they escaped very grave danger through his intercession.[9]

Charlevoix's published letters to the Duchess de Lediguière contained a map drawn, in 1744, by Jacques-Nicolas Bellin, Ingenieur de la Marine.[10] Bellin included a scale of miles on his map from which we learn that a French "common league" equals approximately 2.76 miles. Employing Bellin's scale, the Rivière du Père Marquette is a bit over forty common leagues from the mission of Saint-Ignace which was, in Charlevoix's day, located at the top of Michigan's lower peninsula. During the four decades following the publication of Bellin's map, a charting of the eastern shore of Lake Michigan appeared in several other geographical efforts. John Mitchell's *Map of British and French Dominions in North*

[9] Pierre François Xavier de Charlevoix, *Histoire et déscription générale de la Nouvelle-France*, VI, 19-21. The English translation is the work of the author of this biography.

[10] Charlevoix, *Nouvelle-France*, V, xvii.

America, 1755 includes a "Margurite R." which, according to the author's scale of miles, is ninety-one miles from the northernmost tip of the lower peninsula of Michigan.[11] John Fitch's *Map of the North West Parts of the United States of America, 1785* shows a "Pt. Marque R." at a distance of 150 miles from "Michilimackinac Ft. & Str."[12] None of these geographers had, however, actually visited the Rivière du Père Marquette. But such a pilgrimage was soon to be made.

Very early in the nineteenth century, Gurdon S. Hubbard, an American, was shown the original site of Marquette's grave. Hubbard, a New Englander by birth, came to the Lake Michigan area as a young boy. Apprenticed at sixteen to the American Fur Company, he spent a decade traveling the shores of Lake Michigan as a fur trader. In 1818, when Hubbard happened to be at the mouth of a stream on Lake Michigan's eastern shore, his companions, announcing that this was the river of Père Marquette, led him to the remains of a red cedar cross, which, Hubbard was told, marked the place where Marquette had originally been buried. The young American was informed that the place, then still a wilderness, was sacred to ". . . *voyageurs* who, in passing, paid reverence to it by kneeling and making the sign of the cross."[13] Hubbard and his companions restored the cross which, he tells us, was ". . . about where the town of Ludington now stands."[14] The first priest to visit the site of Marquette's demise in the nineteenth century was Father Gabriel Richard, a Sulpician *emigré* who reached the United States in 1792 and became pastor of the parish of Saint Anne at Detroit, an ecclesiastical jurisdiction including the whole of the present states of Michigan and Wisconsin. In 1819 while evangelizing settlements along the eastern shore of Lake Michigan, he was shown a site which, he was told, was the original grave of Father Marquette. In 1821, writing to the abbé Candide-Michel Le Saulnier, a mis-

[11] Charles O. Paulin, *Atlas of the Historical Geography of the United States*, plate 89.

[12] See P. Lee Philips, *The Rare Map of the Northwest, 1785, by John Fitch.*

[13] Gurdon S. Hubbard, *The Autobiography of Gurdon Saltenstall Hubbard, Pa-Pa-Ma-Ta-Be, the Swift Walker*, 31-32.

[14] *Ibid.*

sionary stationed near Montreal, Richard reported that the place shown him was forty-five leagues south of Arbe Croche (the present Spring Harbor, Michigan), at the entrance of a river named Père Marquet [*sic*].[15] Richard located the site as roughly 135 miles south of about the top of Michigan's lower peninsula. Significantly, he was guided to the place by Frederic Countryman and Charles Rousseau, two of the 600 Canadian *voyageurs* engaged in the fur trade with headquarters at Michilimackinac.

Richard's apostolic burdens were lightened, a year before his death in 1832, by the arrival of Father Frederick Baraga, who eminently deserved his title of Apostle of the Chippewa. Between 1831 and 1835 Baraga evangelized both Indians and whites along the eastern shore of Lake Michigan from Arbe Croche to Grand River, the present Grand Rapids, Michigan. During those years Father Baraga covered the territory extensively on foot and by water. From his own personal observation, he drew a map of the country which was published as an insert in the *Berichte der Leopoldinen-Stiftung im Kaiserthume Oesterreich,* appearing in 1834.[16] On Baraga's *Karte* the rivers shown below Grand Traverse Bay are, from north to south, the Carp, the Platte, the Betsie, the Manistee, the Sand, and the "Pater Marquette Fl." which latter is exactly in the middle of the coast of the eastern shore of Lake Michigan.

After the middle of the nineteenth century several historians, amateur as well as professional, published articles or works dealing with Marquette. In the biographical sketch of Marquette which Shea included in his *Discovery and Exploration of the Mississippi Valley,* that author located the site of Marquette's original grave at Ludington.[17] Three years after the publication of Shea's work, John Law, a legalist, wrote an article, "Jesuit Missionaries in the Northwest," in which he asserted that Father Marquette was first buried beside the ". . . third river south of Bay du Traverse, known on

[15] *Annales de la Propagation de la Foi,* III, 338.
[16] Hamilton, "Ludington," 246.
[17] Shea, *Discovery and Exploration of the Mississippi Valley,* lxxii.

modern maps as Rivière au Betsie."[18] Since Law later admitted that he had not been carefully accurate in using sources, not much importance attaches to his conclusion.[19] After Law, Francis Parkman, in his *La Salle and the Discovery of the Great West,* an interestingly written if not too accurate account of the subject, did not assign a name to the stream beside which Marquette was buried, but declared that the river was not the present Père Marquette.[20] Since Parkman did not visit the area, his testimony on this point is no more valuable than his famous diatribe of the Jesuits which he included in his *Jesuits in North America.*[21] Between 1883 and 1912 a series of articles or books dealing with local areas along the eastern shore of Lake Michigan appeared. In at least four of them the site of Marquette's original grave was assigned to locations other than Ludington.[22] Each of these authors may be praised for his good will, but hardly dignified with the respect due to the professional historian.

Parenthetically, we might call attention to a letter to the editor of *Woodstock Letters,* dated October 2, 1877, very shortly after Father Marquette's tomb at Saint-Ignace had been discovered:

> Now that the late discovery of Father Marquette's remains renewed the loving interest which we all feel in whatever relates to that noble son of our least Society, the following few items will, I trust, be acceptable to your readers, as they concern the present condition of the locality, where the great missionary died, and where his mortal remains first found a temporary resting place. I have gathered these items from one of our Fathers, who lately gave a mission on that venerated spot. The place was known for many years as Père Marquette, Michigan. This town contained, among other settlers, some hundreds of Catholics of various nationalities; but it had no regular attendance from any priest. Gradually the torch of faith had grown so dim that most of the Catholics had lost sight of its guidance, and many attended protestant church. For all these the Cath-

[18] John Law, "Jesuit Missionaries in the Northwest," Wisconsin *Historical Collections,* III (1857), 105.

[19] Hamilton, "Ludington," 230.

[20] Francis Parkman, *La Salle and the Discovery of the Great West,* 81-82.

[21] Francis Parkman, *The Jesuits in North America in the Seventeenth Century,* 8-13.

[22] See Catherine L. Stebbins, "The Marquette Death Site," *Michigan History,* XLVIII (1964), 347.

olic name of Père Marquette had lost its charm, and they readily parted with it in exchange for that of Ludington, the name of a wealthy man in the neighborhood, who promised them $500 as his part of the bargain.[23]

The writer related that when a pastor was appointed to Ludington he invited three latter-day missionaries of the Society of Jesus to help him revivify the faith among the people of Ludington. Three Jesuits spent a week with the pastor, Father C. L. Ceuninck, preaching alternately in English, German, and French, with highly consoling results. A full five hundred of the townspeople were restored to the religion of their ancestors. Before departing Ludington the three Jesuits visited the site traditionally pointed out as the first grave of Jacques Marquette. Describing that pilgrimage the writer remarked:

It was with deep emotions of gratitude, hope and love that the three missionaries knelt on the venerated spot where the body of Father Marquette had been first buried; and as they rose from their knees, they felt confident that from the height of heaven the blessed soul of their illustrious predecessor would guard and foster the precious seed which they had so hopefully dropped in that hallowed ground.[24]

Of itself, of course, the incident proves only that a tradition of long standing at Ludington held that there was the place Father Marquette had first been interred.

It was not until 1926 that the problem of the exact site of Father Marquette's original grave was investigated by a competent scholar. That year, Father Patrick Lomasney, chairman of the department of History at Marquette University, conducted a quite thorough examination of the various locations claiming to be the place where Marquette was first buried.[25] Father Lomasney's most valuable contribution towards solving the problem of the precise location of Marquette's original grave site was the information he acquired from Mrs. Dorleska Hull, a very alert old lady of eighty-five, who

[23] *Woodstock Letters*, VI (1877), 171-72. The author of the letter was probably Father John I. Coghlan, S.J., one of the Jesuits participating in the work. The letter is signed simply C.

[24] *Ibid.*

[25] Patrick J. Lomasney, "Marquette's Burial Site Located," *Illinois Catholic Historical Review*, IX (1927), 147-55, 348-62.

had resided for seventy-five years on the heights overlooking Ludington. Mrs. Hull reported that at the age of nine she had seen a cross marking the site which her mother told her stood over the original grave of Father Marquette.[26] Though no cross stood at the site in 1926, a Ludington resident, Bert Smith, showed Father Lomasney where it had been. In 1938 a large wooden cross was erected on the top of a noteworthy rise near the shore of Lake Michigan south of Ludington. Eighteen years later, in 1956, a quite attractive monument, surmounted by a stainless steel cross, was erected on the summit of the hummock, marking, at least to the satisfaction of the citizens of Ludington and many historians, the approximate site of Marquette's original grave.

Since that date occasional articles appeared questioning the accuracy of the Ludington site or defending it. Of these, the work of two historians deserves brief attention. In 1960 Catherine L. Stebbins published an interesting little pamphlet, *Here I Shall Finish My Voyage,* and four years later, in 1964, a rather scholarly article, "The Marquette Death Site,"[27] both defending the mouth of the Betsie River as the place of Marquette's original interment. To both of these, Raphael N. Hamilton replied with his "The Marquette Death Site: the Case for Ludington." The two periodical articles merit commendation for their restrained approach as well as the scholarship evidenced by their authors. Miss Stebbins seeks, by analyzing Charlevoix's narrative of his visit to the site, to locate precisely where that Jesuit was on August 3, 1721. However, at a crucial point in Charlevoix's account, August 2, one cannot determine how far he traveled, if he did so at all. Further, using the scale on Bellin's map, which was compiled for Charlevoix's work, the voyaging Jesuit was already at about the Betsie River by the night of August 1. Even supposing that Charlevoix did no traveling on August 2, he did so on August 3, and before reaching the site he examined. That fact alone casts doubts on Miss Stebbins' conclusions. She buttresses her position with an admirably erudite analysis of the precise meaning of certain French phrases used by

[26] A typed copy of the interview is in the archives of Marquette University.
[27] Stebbins, *Michigan History*, XLIX, 333-68.

Charlevoix and lays great stress on the Jesuit's statement that the distance between the hill, beside which Marquette was buried, and the next rise of ground beyond it could not be great because Charlevoix reported it to be the length of a musket shot. That distance, according to Miss Stebbins, could not have been much more than perhaps eighty feet. From that fact she argues that the Ludington site would not match Charlevoix's description, but the mouth of the Betsie River would. Considering the inefficiency of muskets in Charlevoix's day, the length of a good musket shot could be any distance from twenty feet to the greatest possible trajectory of the most excellently constructed eighteenth-century musket.

In this polite controversy Father Hamilton may be said to have the high ground. It can be, and we fondly hope has been, demonstrated that from very shortly after Marquette's demise there has existed a tradition, continually strengthened by competent research, that the site of Marquette's demise and burial was very near the Père Marquette River. Father Hamilton shows that the Betsie River site simply will not meet the geographical information which tradition and ancient maps give us. As for Charlevoix's description of the site, that evidence, as presented by Hamilton, is nearly as inconclusive as it is for the reader who studies Miss Stebbins' handling of it. Hamilton's argument from semantics is equally as learned as that of his gentle opponent's, but, to this writer's mind, equally inconclusive. In his article Father Hamilton, like Homer, also nods. His asserting that Dablon's imprecise description of the site of Marquette's burial was due to haste is quite incorrect. Dablon's report is, nearly word for word, taken from Cholenec's letter. To leave the impression, as Hamilton does, that Dablon ordered Largillier and Porteret to hasten back, disinter the body of Marquette, and bring it to Saint-Ignace has no documentary basis.[28] If one re-

[28] Between 1611 and 1800, 158 Jesuits died in New France. Eighty-two were buried at Quebec, seven were drowned, and three died at sea. Only six were buried at Montreal. The others were buried where they died, at such distant places as Tadoussac, Lake Saint John, Chicago, Hudson Bay, Fort Niagara, the Lake of the Woods, and the like. Jacques Marquette was the only Jesuit buried at Saint-Ignace mission in the upper peninsula of the state of Michigan. Two other Jesuits died and were buried at Sault-Sainte-Marie. See *Relations*, LXXI, 137-81.

views the history of the Jesuits in New France, he finds that, except for the martyrs of Huronia, and a handful of others, Jesuits were buried where they died. However important Jacques Marquette has since become, when he died he was just another of an heroic band. His mortal remains would probably have been left undisturbed had not the Kiskakon disinterred them out of respect for the man and because it was their tribal custom to collect the bones of the dead for burial in a common grave.

From this writer's own efforts concerning the location of Father Marquette's original grave, it is concluded that, until much more cogent evidence is available to the contrary, one has no choice but to hold that Jacques Marquette died and was originally buried only a few paces down the slope from his monument which looks out over Lake Michigan at Ludington. An examination of the sites claiming the honor of the missionary's original grave, done on foot, by car, from the air in a small plane, and by water seems to this biographer to demonstrate that no other location on Lake Michigan's eastern shore will satisfy. Documentary evidence, meagre as it is, favors Ludington. Local, long-standing tradition for the Ludington site is too precise to be ignored. Thus, at least for the present, one must accept the fact that Jacques Marquette died and was originally buried at the base of a quite large hummock just south of Ludington, near the shore of Lake Michigan.

Appendix five

THE DISCOVERY OF FATHER MARQUETTE'S GRAVE AT SAINT IGNACE, MICHIGAN

The Kiskakon, once the object of Jacques Marquette's zeal at the mission of Saint-Esprit, had, since 1671, migrated eastward until, by 1676, they were settled at the mission of Saint-Ignace.[1] In 1677 their pastor, Father Henri Nouvel wrote of them: "Their village . . . is near our chapel of Saint-Ignace at Michilimackinac. The chiefs and most notable elders of the Kiskakon are Christians, and perform their duties well, as do also the majority of the women and children. It may be said that Christianity is held in esteem among them and their ancient superstitions are despised. I am occupied from morning to night in cultivating this church, and I have only time to perform my spiritual exercises, especially in

[1] *Relations*, LX, 213.

winter."[2] Probably because the Kiskakon were latecomers to the Michilimackinac area, they were unable to acquire any more convenient hunting ground than one on the mainland south of the Straits of Mackinac. They must have learned of the death of Father Marquette very soon after the news reached Saint-Ignace just as they also were informed of the approximate location of his grave. During the winter of 1676 and the spring of 1677, the Kiskakon roamed their hunting ground until, on their way back to Saint-Ignace, ". . . they were greatly pleased to pass near the grave of their good father whom they tenderly loved; and God also put it into their hearts to remove his bones and bring them to our church at the mission of St. Ignace at Missilimackinac [*sic*], where those savages made their abode."[3] On opening Marquette's grave, the Indians found his body completely intact.[4] As was their custom, however, the Kiskakon, excising the skeleton, dried the bones and placed them in a small birch-bark casket, lovingly fashioned to receive them. Then, with solemn dignity befitting the circumstances, the Kiskakon brought their precious burden back to Saint-Ignace for burial. At Saint-Ignace, the superior, Henri Nouvel, and Father Philippe Pierson, pastor of the Huron colony at the mission, afforded Marquette's remains all the religious ceremonies proper to the occasion, including a day, Pentecost Monday, June 8, 1677, of lying in state in the mission chapel. The following morning, ". . . after having rendered to it [the small casket] all the funeral rites, it was lowered into a small vault in the middle of the church where it rests as the guardian angel of our Ottawa missions."[5]

[2] *Ibid.*, LXI, 69.

[3] *Ibid.*, LIX, 203.

[4] The incorrupt state of Marquette's body was probably due to the fact that it had been buried in a shallow grave and in sandy ground. The heat of the sun on the sand would dehydrate the body, causing it, in effect, to be mummified.

[5] *Relations*, LIX, 205. It has been flippantly suggested by an unthinking writer that the Jesuits were very credulous to believe that the Kiskakon really brought back the bones of Marquette. Perhaps, he conjectured, the Indians simply collected an assortment of animal bones. Father Nouvel was not so gullible as not to have made certain that the small casket actually contained the bones of Father Marquette. Nouvel, himself, answered the supposed doubt: "When they drew near our house, Father Nouvel, who was its superior, with

Between 1677 and 1690 Saint-Ignace expanded, not only as a successful mission center but as an economic emporium for the valuable fur trade which funneled through it from the West and the Illinois Country. In 1690, when the threat of a new Iroquois uprising endangered the post, Governor Frontenac sent Louis de la Porte, Sieur de Louvigny, with 150 Canadian troops, to build a fort, known as Fort Buade, for the protection of the settlement at Saint-Ignace as well as to maintain control of the Straits of Mackinac. Though the missionaries promptly found that the soldiers exercised a deleterious influence on their aboriginal neophytes, matters did not get utterly out of hand until 1694 when Antoine de la Mothe Cadillac was appointed commandant. In 1696, by a series of clever moves, Cadillac succeeded in transferring the center of trade from Saint-Ignace to Fort Pontchartrain on the Detroit River. When Cadillac succeeded in attracting to his new fort most of the Indians frequenting the mission at Saint-Ignace, that ecclesiastical establishment ceased to serve any useful purpose. Facing the reality of the situation, the two Jesuits stationed at Saint-Ignace, Etienne de Carheil and Gabriel Marest, set fire to the mission buildings, to save them from desecration, and returned to Quebec, probably in 1705.[6] If they had brought with them the small bark casket containing the bones of Jacques Marquette, that noteworthy fact would certainly have been remembered by Father Charlevoix, who was then a young cleric teaching in the Jesuit college at Quebec. Almost certainly, Charlevoix would have recalled such a striking incident and referred to it in his letter describing his visit to the site of Marquette's original grave. Charlevoix says nothing about the two returning Jesuits having brought with them Marquette's bones nor

Father Piercon [*sic*], went out to meet them, accompanied by the Frenchmen and savages who were there; and having halted the procession, he put the usual questions to them, to make sure that it was really the Father's body which they were bringing." (*Ibid.*, 205.) Future generations would learn that Dablon's French phrase, *au milieu de l'eglise*, could not have meant that Marquette's bones were buried in the geographic middle of the church, a small structure measuring 36 by 40 feet, but rather "within the church" as opposed to outside in a cemetery.

[6] Rochemonteix, *Jésuites*, III, 527. The exact date of the abandonment of Saint-Ignace is not known.

does any other document even hint that Marquette's relics were removed from the tomb when Saint-Ignace was burned and abandoned. In 1713, eight years after fire consumed Saint-Ignace, the French, realizing the strategic import of the Straits of Mackinac, sent Constant Le Marchand de Lignery, with a small force of soldiers and laborers, to construct a new fort there. This bastion was erected on the southern shore of the Straits, just south of the great new bridge which spans that picturesque expanse of water.[7] Thenceforward the old Saint-Ignace slumbered while its site slowly became a wilderness which blanketed every vestage of its former greatness. But French *voyageurs* and the Indians kept alive the fact of its existence and the knowledge that a great, holy man's remains rested there. But knowledge of the exact location of the mission church slowly faded from memory.

Happily, several seventeenth and eighteenth-century publications pointed out the location of the mission of Saint-Ignace. Dablon's map, included in the *Relations* of 1671, placed the mission on the mainland, to the west of Mackinac Island.[8] The same location was assigned the mission on Marquette's own map. Father Louis Hennepin's *Description de la Louisiane,* published in 1688, reported that he said Mass on August 28, 1678, in the mission chapel at Saint-Ignace. According to him, the mission was on the mainland, opposite Mackinac Island.[9] Chrestien Le Clercq's *Gaspesie,* published in 1691, contains a map showing the mission of Saint-Ignace on a point of land north of the Straits of Mackinac.[10] In his *Nouvel découverte,* Hennepin described Saint-Ignace mission thus: "There are Indian villages in these two places. Those who are established at the point of land of Missilimackinac [*sic*] are Hurons, and the others, who are five or six arpents beyond, are named Outtaouatz [*sic*]."[11] The Baron Lahontan, who equalled

[7] Walter Havighurst, *Three Flags at the Straits,* 48-49.

[8] *Relations,* LV, facing 94.

[9] Louis Hennepin, *Déscription de la Louisiane,* 59.

[10] John Gilmary Shea, "Romance and Reality of the Death of Father James Marquette and the Recent Discovery of His Remains," *Catholic World,* XXVI (1877), 274.

[11] Louis Hennepin, *Nouvelle découverte d'un grand pays situé dans l'Amérique le Nouveau-Mexique et la mer glaciale,* 134.

Baron Munchausen's ability to embroider the truth, included in his *Nouveaux Voyages* a map of the area around Mackinac. This map, almost certainly not Lahontan's own work, shows the mission of Saint-Ignace in detail, including the Jesuit residence, the chapel, and the villages of the French, Huron, and Ottawa as well as the cultivated fields surrounding the mission.[12] Unquestionably, this complex was located at Moran Bay.

Just two centuries after Jacques Marquette's relics were buried at Saint-Ignace, the long-forgotten place of repose was discovered. By 1823 the site of the mission had come into the hands of François La Pointe, who received his patent to it on his sworn statement to the government of the United States that he had occupied that land since before 1812.[13] The land was eventually bought by the Dousmans, a famous and wealthy fur trading family. They sold it to David Murray, an Irish immigrant from the county Mayo, who came to America in 1848 and settled in the Mackinac area.[14] In 1877, when David allowed his married son, Patrick, to use the land, the latter employed Peter D. Grondin, a half-breed, to clear the site of trees and underbrush in preparation for cultivating it.[15] On May 4, 1877, when Grondin found the remains of a limestone foundation, he called David Murray's attention to the discovery. Murray promptly informed the local pastor, Father Edward Jacker, that the foundation might be the site of the long-lost Jesuit mission of Saint-Ignace where, perhaps, even yet Father Marquette's relics reposed. Fortunately, Father Jacker took an immediate interest in the discovery.

Since Father Jacker was, in a true sense, a singular benefactor of Father Jacques Marquette, as well as a noted missionary in his own right, a brief word about him is in order. Edward Jacker, born at Wurtemberg in 1829, studied theology at the University of

[12] For a readily available reproduction of the map included in Lahontin's book, see George S. May, editor, "The Discovery of Father Marquette's Grave at Saint Ignace in 1877, as Related by Father Edward Jacker," *Michigan History*, XLII (1958), 277.

[13] Emerson K. Smith, *Before the Bridge*, 57.

[14] *Ibid.*

[15] *Ibid.*, 28, has a picture of Grondin.

Tubingen, but left before receiving holy orders. In 1854, Jacker came to the United States, planning to enter the Benedictine novitiate founded in 1846 by Father Boniface Wimmer, O.S.B. While at the novitiate, Jacker learned of the sad religious plight of the American Indian and determined to devote his life to them. Wherefore, he volunteered his services to Bishop Frederick Baraga who had been consecrated for the see of Sault-Sainte-Marie in 1853. Ordained on August 5, 1855, Jacker was assigned to work among the Chippewa, with headquarters at L'Anse, Michigan. After six years of that apostolic work Jacker was summoned to Marquette, Michigan as Bishop Baraga's vicar, an office Jacker exercised under Baraga until 1868 and under Bishop Mrak, Baraga's successor, until 1873. That year Father Jacker was appointed to care for Mackinac Island and the neighboring mainland. Having a bent for local history, Father Jacker was quite well prepared to understand the importance of the discovery made by Grondin.[16]

A carefully controlled examination of the site of the ancient mission of Saint-Ignace was not instituted until September 3, 1877, chiefly because David Murray ". . . had conscientious scruples in regards to having the presumable grave of a holy man disturbed . . ."[17] The pious Irishman adamantly refused to allow the site to be investigated unless ". . . the chief pastor of the diocese, upon his arrival here, should wish to have a search made . . ."[18] While awaiting a visit from Bishop Mrak, Father Jacker studied the *Relations* and other sources, gleaning as much detailed information as possible about the old mission. Throughout the summer, press releases, especially in the Michigan newspapers, played up the importance of the discovery, stressing the possibility that the plot of ground contained the bones of Father Jacques Marquette. As a result the little town of Saint-Ignace became a minor Mecca for tourists, many of whom, spade in hand, hoped to find a monetary treasure. Despite David Murray's efforts, some sporadic, perhaps even damaging, excavation went on before more competent hands took over.

[16] For biographical data concerning Father Edward Jacker, see Chrysostom Verwyst, *Life and Labors of the Rt. Rev. Frederick Baraga.*

[17] May, "Discovery of Marquette's Grave," 276.

[18] Shea, "Romance," 276.

Finally, on Monday, September 3, 1877, Bishop Ignatius Mrak ". . . dug out the first spadeful of ground . . ."[19] in the presence of some 200 people, ". . . many of them, though nearly white, being lineal descendants of the very Ottawas among whom Father Marquette labored at La Pointe du St. Esprit, and who witnessed his interment in this place two hundred years ago."[20]

The problem of where to begin the evacuation was solved by taking literally Father Dablon's statement that Marquette's bones were buried in the middle of the church. That phrase was strengthened by the physical fact that there actually was ". . . some apparent depression near the center of the ancient building . . ."[21] Evacuation of that site quickly disclosed that the subsoil, to the depth of three feet, had never been disturbed. The next likely location was ". . . a cellar-like hollow to the left . . ."[22] towards the back wall of the structure, where the altar certainly must have been. A trench, two or three feet deep, was dug from the depression first evacuated to the depression on the left. Father Jacker thus described what followed:

> Close to the ancient cellar-like evacuation a decayed piece of post, planted deeply in the ground, came to light. The bottom of that hollow itself furnished just the things that you would expect to meet within the cellar of a building destroyed by fire, such as powdered charcoal mixed with the subsoil, spikes, nails, an iron hinge (perhaps of a trap-door), pieces of timber, apparently of hewed planks and joists, partly burned and very much decayed. Nothing, however, was found that would indicate the former existence of a tomb, vaulted or otherwise. Our hopes began to sink (the good bishop had already stolen away), when, at the foot of the western slope of the ancient evacuation, fragments of mortar bearing the impress of wood and partly blackened, and a small piece of birch-bark, came to light. This was followed by numerous other, similar or larger, fragments of the latter substance, most of them more or less scorched or crisped by the heat, not by the immediate action of the fire; a few only were just blackened, and on one side superficially burned. A case or box of birch-bark (*une quaisse d'escorce de bouleau*), according

[19] *Ibid.*
[20] *Ibid.*, 278.
[21] *Ibid.*, 276.
[22] *Ibid.*

to the *Relation,* once enclosed the remains of the great missionary. No wonder our hopes revived at the sight of that material. Next appeared a small leaf of white paper, which, being quite moist, almost dissolved in my hands. We continued the search, more with our hands than with the spade. The sand in which those objects were embedded was considerably blackened, more so, in fact, than what should be expected, unless some digging was done here *after the fire,* and the hollow thus produced filled up with the blackened ground from above. Here and there we found small particles, generally globular, of a moist friable substance, resembling pure lime or plaster-of-paris. None of the details of our search being unimportant, I should remark that the first pieces of birch-bark were met with at a depth of about three and a half feet from the present surface, and nearly on a level, I should judge, with the floor of the ancient evacuation. For about a foot deeper down more of it was found, the pieces being scattered at different heights over an area of about two feet square or more. Finally a larger and well-preserved piece appeared, which once evidently formed part of the bottom of an Indian mawhawk (*wig-wass-makak, birch-bark box*), and rested on clean white gravel and sand. Some of our people, who are experts in this matter, declared that the bark was of unusual thickness, and that the box, or at least parts of it, had been double, such as the Indians sometimes, for the sake of greater durability, use for interments. A further examination disclosed the fact that it had been placed on three or four wooden sills, decayed parts of which were extracted. All around the space once occupied by the box the ground seemed to be little disturbed, and the bottom piece lay considerably deeper than the other objects (nails, fragments of timber, a piece of glass jar or large bottle, a chisel, screws, etc.) discovered on what I conceived to have been the ancient bottom of the cellar. From these two circumstances it seemed evident that the birch-bark box had not (as would have been the case with an ordinary vessel containing corn, sugar, or the like) been placed on the floor, but sunk into the ground, and perhaps covered with a layer of mortar, many blackened fragments of which were turned out all around the space once occupied by it. But it was equally evident that this humble tomb, for such we took it to have been, had been disturbed, and the box broken into and parts of it torn out, after the material had been made brittle by the action of the fire. This would explain the absence of its former contents, which, what else could we think? were nothing less than Father Marquette's bones. We, indeed, found between the pieces of bark two small fragments, one black and hard, the other white and brittle, but of such form that none of us could determine whether they were from the human frame.[23]

[23] *Ibid.,* 276-77.

Father Jacker's discovery evinced great disappointment because the evacuation had revealed so little, but some satisfaction since there was solid reason to hold that, besides finding what certainly must have been the small vault mentioned in the *Relations,* some of the contents of the tomb must have been part of the birch-bark casket and the few fragments of bone discovered were at least possibly from a part of the dead missionary's skeleton. While Jacker was absent from the site on September 4, assisting Bishop Mrak administer confirmation at Mackinac Island and at the parish church on the mainland at Saint-Ignace, the open pit was quite probably invaded by the curious who may have made other discoveries about which nothing was ever learned. On September 5, a young man named Joseph Marly brought Father Jacker a handkerchief containing ". . . over thirty small pieces of bone from different parts of the human frame . . .,"[24] all taken from the floor of the small vault. Other bone fragments were subsequently found before the evacuation was finally closed. On Tuesday, September 11, Father Jacker submitted the bone fragments to an examination by a Doctor Pommier, ". . . a good French surgeon . . .,"[25] who, ". . . declared the fragments of bone to be undoubtedly human and bearing the marks of fire . . ."[26]

At the time it was made public, a whole litany of questions arose regarding the authenticity of Father Jacker's discovery. Were Jacques Marquette's bones actually in the tomb awaiting discovery, or had they been previously removed? If Jacker actually discovered Marquette's tomb, why was it placed in such a seemingly peculiar location? Since the Jesuits who burned the building must have known that Marquette's bones were buried within it, why would they not have removed them, especially since they did not expect to return to Saint-Ignace? Supposing that the departing Jesuits deliberately left Marquette's relics, who violated the tomb, when and why? Could it not be maintained that the evacuation was handled so unscientifically that little can be relied upon concerning

[24] May, "Discovery of Marquette's Grave," 281.
[25] Shea, "Romance and Reality," 281.
[26] *Ibid.*

the results? In some degree, Father Jacker was unwittingly responsible for a certain amount of the adverse criticism launched against him. Though he wrote several accounts of the discovery, three of them quite lengthy, Jacker, probably through lack of time, did not publish a definitive article in which each minute detail of the whole episode was included and placed in its proper perspective. Criticizing a very active pastor for failing to have written a highly scholarly account of the discovery smacks of the pedantic. Those who blame Jacker for failing to employ the meticulous techniques of trained archaeologists conveniently ignore the existing circumstances in 1877. Neither Father Jacker nor David Murray commanded the resources requisite to isolate the site from the public nor were there available federal or foundation funds with which to employ skilled archaeologists, even supposing that these were available.

When Father Jacker discovered Marquette's tomb and found it apparently violated, an explanation, of some merit, was offered him on the spot by an Indian present who suggested that it would be surprising if, after the abandonment of the mission by the Jesuits, a pagan Indian did not open the grave and carry off some of its contents ". . . to use the great Blackgown's bones for superstitious purposes . . ."[27] Why the departing Jesuits did not take along with them the small box containing Father Marquette's relics was not Jacker's problem. No positive documentation proves that the relics were removed while reasonably sound negative arguments indicate the contrary. The position of the tomb within the confines of the church at Saint-Ignace also gave rise to some adverse criticism. Father Jacker believed that the spot chosen for the small vault was ". . . nearest to the altar or at least the statue of the Blessed Virgin, the most appropriate spot for the interment of the champion of Mary Immaculate."[28] Such might well have been Father Nouvel's reason for selecting it, but he might, equally as well, have felt that on a raw frontier the bodies of missionaries would be best protected against vandalism if they were buried within the church. In that case, he would probably have buried

[27] *Ibid.*, 277.
[28] *Ibid.*, 279.

the first of the dead near the altar on the left as one faces the front of the church, planning to bury the next to die beside the first and so on in turn. Such a plan would be sensible since Saint-Ignace, already headquarters for the Ottawa missions, bade fair to become a permanent center. No one knew, of course, that Jacques Marquette would be the only missionary to be buried there. Still less did anyone realize that Saint-Ignace itself would again be a wilderness within three decades of the day Jacques Marquette's small casket was laid in its miniature tomb.

The evidence supporting the claim that Father Edward Jacker discovered Jacques Marquette's tomb is unimpeachable. That the fragments of human bone found in the tomb were segments from the skeleton of Marquette is satisfactory, at least in the case of those pieces which show the effects of intense heat. This writer contends that Father Edward Jacker discovered Father Jacques Marquette's last resting place, and in it some portions, however minute, of Jacques Marquette's bones.

The final disposition of the relics discovered by Father Jacker should be recorded. In 1882, through the efforts of the Marquette Monument Association, founded at Mackinac Island in 1878, a modest monument was erected over the site of the small vault discovered five years previously. Some of the bone fragments were placed under that monument.[29] The rest were retained by Father Jacker who, in 1882, presented them to Marquette University. The collection consists of nineteen fragments, the longest measuring an inch and a quarter. The entire group of fragments together weighs less than an ounce.

[29] May, "Discovery of Marquette's Grave," 286.

Appendix six

GENEALOGY

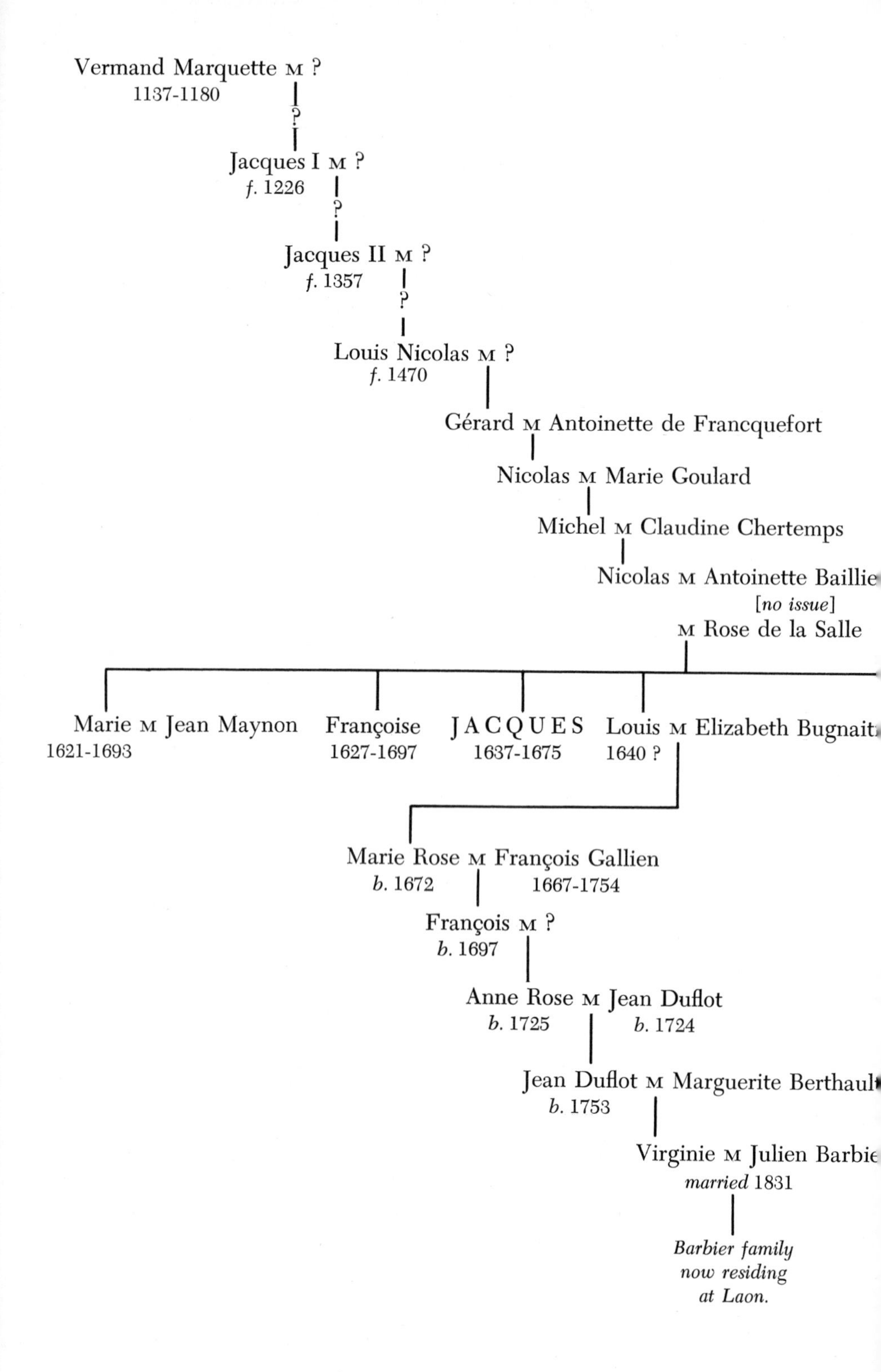

Vermand Marquette M ?
1137-1180
?
Jacques I M ?
f. 1226
?
Jacques II M ?
f. 1357
?
Louis Nicolas M ?
f. 1470
Gérard M Antoinette de Francquefort
Nicolas M Marie Goulard
Michel M Claudine Chertemps
Nicolas M Antoinette Baillie
[no issue]
M Rose de la Salle
Marie M Jean Maynon
1621-1693
Françoise
1627-1697
JACQUES
1637-1675
Louis M Elizabeth Bugnait
1640 ?
Marie Rose M François Gallien
b. 1672
1667-1754
François M ?
b. 1697
Anne Rose M Jean Duflot
b. 1725
b. 1724
Jean Duflot M Marguerite Berthaul
b. 1753
Virginie M Julien Barbie
married 1831
Barbier family
now residing
at Laon.

THE MARQUETTES OF LAON

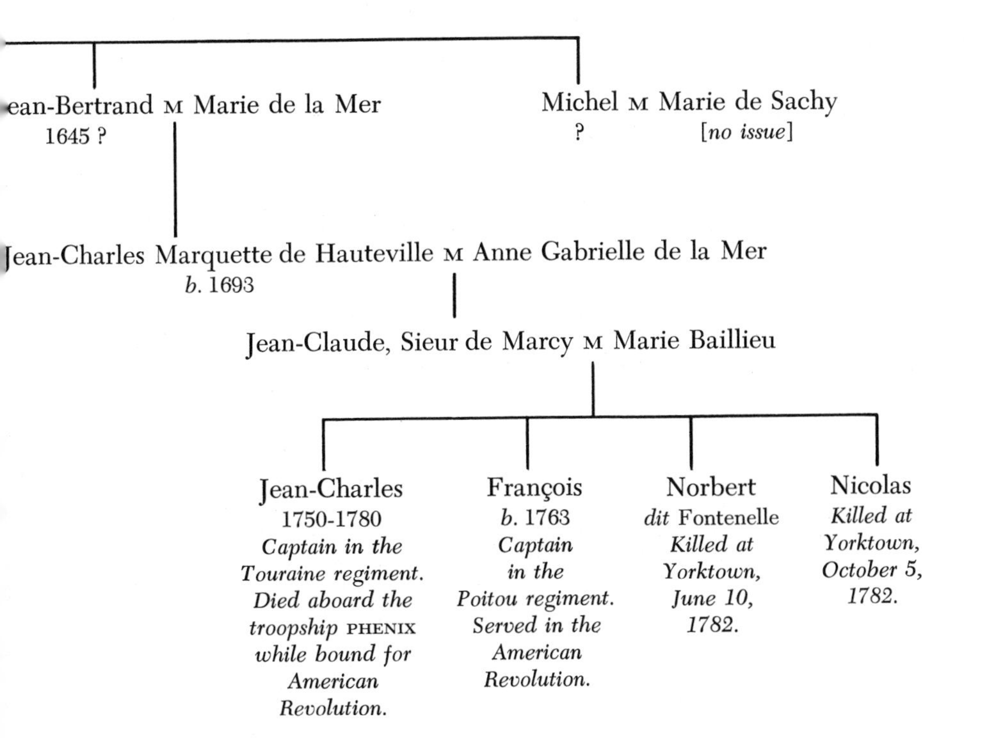

GENEALOGY OF FATHER JACQUES MARQUETTE

Vermand Marquette—1137-1180. Hamy, *Au Mississippi*, 31.

Jacques Marquette—flourished 1226, steward of Ferdinand of Portugal whose twelve years of prison in the Louvre Marquette shared. On Ferdinand's release in 1226, Jacques settled at Laon.

Jacques II—flourished 1357. He was sheriff of Laon when commissioned to deliver Laon's contribution to ransom France's king. For this service Jacques was personally ennobled and given permission to use the arms of the city of Laon as his family crest.

Louis Nicolas Marquette—flourished about 1470. He was the father of six sons, of whom the third, Gérard, was Father Marquette's direct ancestor.

Gérard Marquette—Tax collector of the *"election"* of Laon. He married Antoinette de Francquefort. Their third son, Nicolas, was Father Marquette's great-grandfather.

Nicolas Marquette—resided at Cressy-sur-Serre. He married Marie Goulard. Their second child, Michel, was Father Marquette's grandfather.

Michel Marquette, Vicomte de Beaurieux, treasurer and keeper of the seal, of the *"Baillage de Vermandois."* His first wife was Claudine Chertemps, his second Elizabeth Sureau. Claudine's second child was Nicolas, the father of Father Marquette.

Nicolas Marquette, Seigneur de la Tombelle, *"conseiller en l'election de Laon,"* was born at Saint-Remi Place on September 19, 1597. His first wife was Antoinette Baillieu, who had no children. His second wife was Rose de la Salle, daughter of Eustache de la Salle of Reims. Of this union there were six children, two girls and four boys:

Marie, born in 1621, who married Jean Maynon. Marie died in 1693.

Françoise (1627-1697) who founded the Soeurs Marquette at Laon in 1685.

Jacques (1637-1675) discoverer of the Mississippi River.

Louis, *dit* Le Catalan, born about 1640. He married Elizabeth Bugnaitre. Of the union there were three children:

Nicolas Hyacinthe, born at Saint-Remi-Porte on May 22, 1669. He married Barbe de la Mer on July 28, 1693. There was no male child of the union.

Marie Rose, born at Saint-Remi-Porte on June 14, 1672. On May 16, 1692, she married François Gallien. Her son François (born at Saint-Remi Place on March 2, 1697) was the ancestor of the Barbier family now residing in Laon.

Marie Françoise, born at Saint-Remi-Porte on March 25, 1674. She was married on July 29, 1696, to Dreincourt Cyr.

Jean-Bertrand, presumed to have been born in about 1645. He married Marie de la Mer. Their son, Jean-Charles Marquette, Seigneur d'Hauteville, *conseiller au presidial*, was born in 1693. His daughter, Marie-Rose died in 1792. Jean-Charles married Anne Gabrielle de la Mer. Their son was Jean-Claude Marquette, Sieur de Marcy (March 7, 1718-March 31, 1792). He was an infantry captain, Chevalier of the royal military order of St. Louis and mayor of Laon. He married Marie Charlotte Baillieu. Four of their sons fought in the American Revolution. These were:

Jean-Charles Marquette *dit* Du Buquois, an infantry captain in the Touraine regiment. He was born at Laon in 1750 and married Françoise Brance on March 8, 1773. He died in 1780 aboard the *Phenix* when the ship stopped at Santo Domingo on its way to America with troops to aid our cause.

François Guillaume Marquette, born at Laon in 1763, was an officer in the Poitou regiment which also campaigned in America during our revolution.

Norbert *dit* Fontenelle was killed at Yorktown on June 10, 1782.

Nicolas who was killed in the American Revolution on October 5, 1782.

SOURCES

Hamy, Alfred. *Au Mississippi*, 36-37.
Public Archives of Canada, Collection Ste. Marie, Montreal, M.G. 17, 6, 3.
Archives, Collège Sainte-Marie, Montreal, Collection Rochemonteix:
a) Tableau Marquette College
b) Tableau Brifoleaux-Rochemonteix
c) Tableau Lefebvre
d) Tableau "Napoléon," ou Janséniste
Woodstock Letters XXVIII (1898), 204-05.
Mérou. *Combattants français de la guerre Amérique*, 320, 325, 327.

DOCUMENTS

Father Marquette made this map at the mission of Saint François Xavier, near the present Green Bay, Wisconsin, after he returned there from his journey of 1673. The map is now in the archives of Collège Sainte Marie, Montreal.

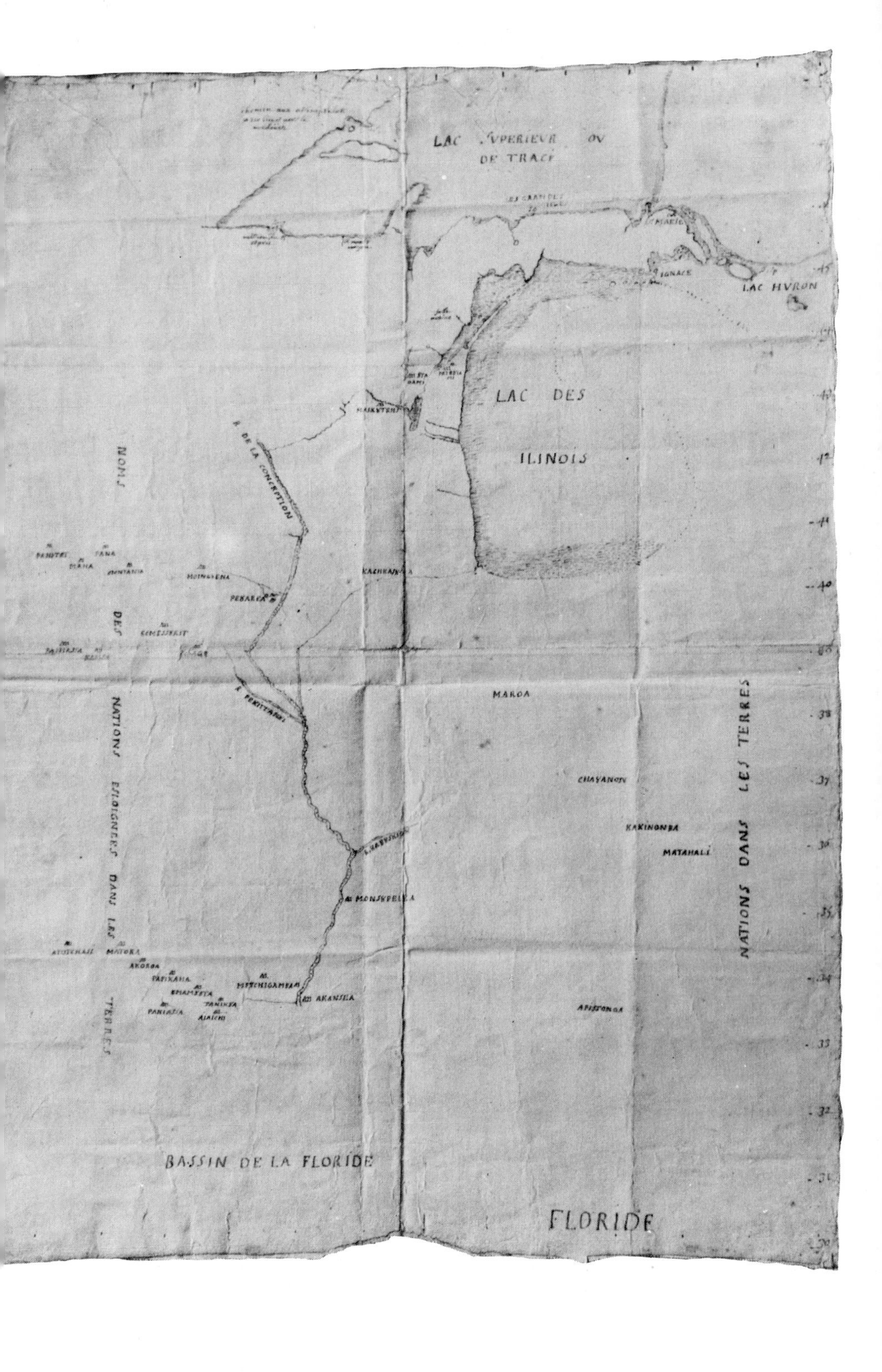

LAC SVPERIEVR OV DE TRACY
LAC HVRON
LAC DES ILINOIS
R. DE LA CONCEPTION
NOMS DES NATIONS ESLOIGNEES DANS LES TERRES
MAROA
CHAYANON
KAKINONBA
MATAHALI
APISTONGA
NATIONS DANS LES TERRES
BASSIN DE LA FLORIDE
FLORIDE

The first page of the baptismal register of the parish at Boucherville, Canada. The three and one-half lines at the top of the photograph are in Father Marquette's handwriting. See page 112 where the text of the document is given. The baptismal record is preserved in the archives of the parish of the Most Holy Family, Boucherville.

Jacque marquette de la compagnie de Iesus ay donne les ceremonies a
rie fille de Victor Kiȣentaȣe et Antoinette de michiȣminich, agee de 2 mois et
doyé a lauvel par monsieur morel prestre le parrain Ignace Boucher et la marraine
ie Boucher le 20 May 1668

Ce Livre des Registres, contient
Les Baptesmes, Les Mariages,
& Les Enterrements qui ont esté faits
dans La paroisse de Boucherville.

Depuis La page 1. Jusqu'au nombre de 90, sont
contenus Les baptesmes : Depuis La page 91 Jusques
au nombre 140, sont contenus Les Mariages,
& depuis La page 140 Jusques a la fin, sont contenus
les enterrements.

Le 1er Avril 1693 B. Pierre Sicle ba dos
Le 5 Avril B. Janne Cle
Le 6 Avril M. Adr. Lam. & Deny. ver
Le 9 Avril M. Bert. ui. et Rei. Robin
Le 9 Avr. B. Mar. Fran. Benoist

1669
1696

N.B. 1o Les mariages du 21 octobre 1670 au 28 avril
1681 soit de la page (feuillet) 44 ro au feuillet 48 ro.
2o Deux mariages du 14 oct 1681, ~~et du~~
sont inscrits au feuillet 14e ro.
P.Th. ptre vic.

Ego Jacobus Marquette promitto omnipotenti Deo coram eius Virgine Matre, et tota cœlesti curia, et tibi Reverendo Patri Gabrieli Druillettes vice Præpositi Generalis Societatis Jesu, et Successorum eius locum Dei tenenti perpetuam paupertatem, castitatem et obedientiam; et secundum eam peculiarem curam circa puerorum eruditionem, juxta modum in literis Apostolicis et constitutionibus dictæ Societatis expressum, ad lacum Superiorem Algonquinorum in oppido Sanctæ Mariæ Die 2a mensis Julii, anno 1671.

Jacobus Marquette.

Gal. 28-f.

A photo-reproduction of the holograph of Father Marquette's final Jesuit vows pronounced at Sault Sainte Marie on July 2, 1671. For a translation of the Latin formula, see page 178.

This document was the official report to the Jesuit General recording the fact of Marquette's ordination. The first reproduction shows page one of the document in which the ordination record is found in the archives of the Society of Jesus at Rome. The second reproduction lists those Jesuits ordained since the last such report. The second name listed as those recently ordained to the priesthood is Father Jacques Marquette, ordained at Toul on March 7, 1666.

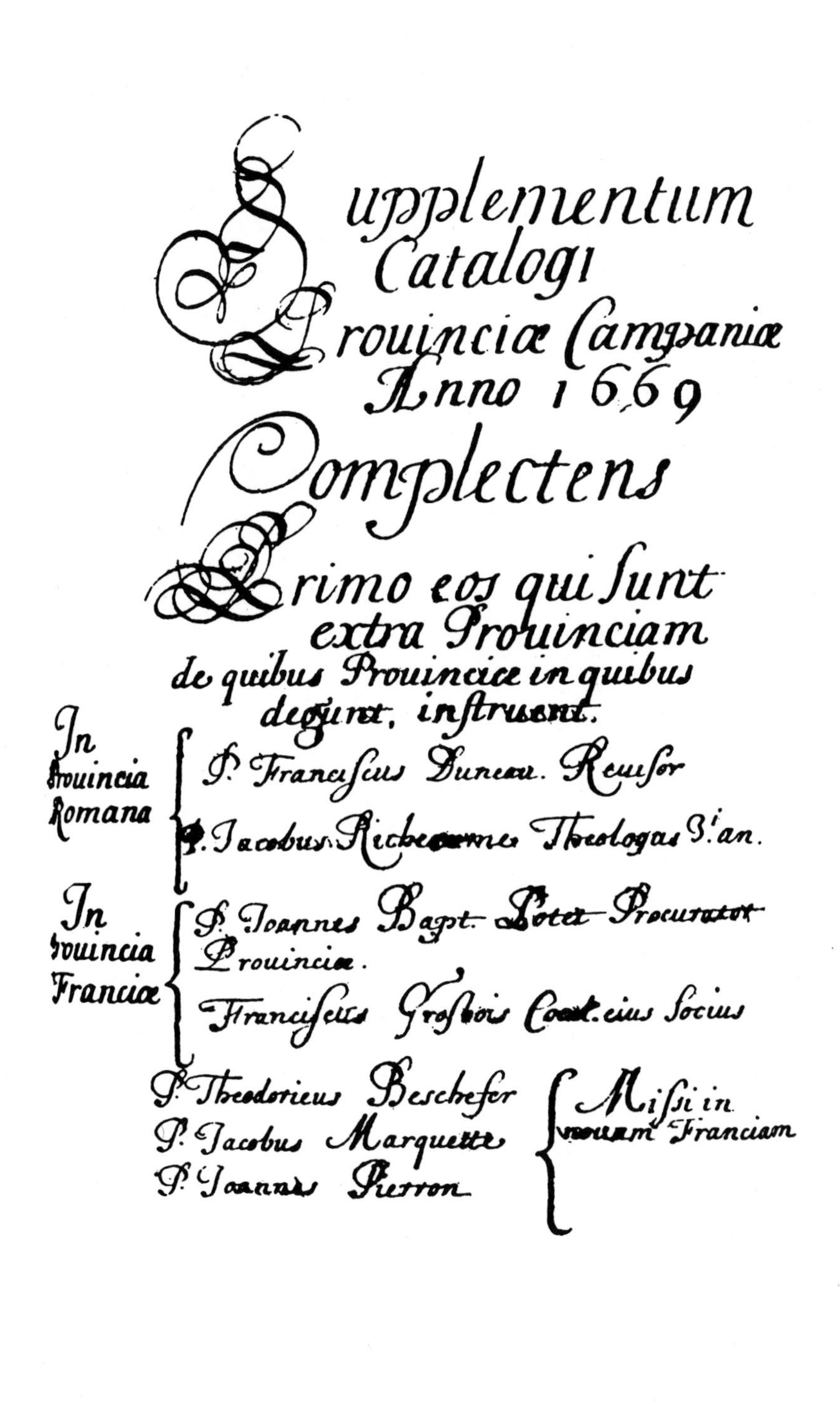

Supplementum
Catalogi
Prouinciæ Campaniæ
Anno 1669
Complectens
Primo eos qui sunt
extra Prouinciam
de quibus Prouinciæ in quibus
degunt, instruent.

In Prouincia Romana
- P. Franciscus Duneau. Reuisor
- P. Jacobus Richeomme Theologus 3.ⁱ an.

In Prouincia Franciæ
- P. Joannes Bapt. Potet Procurator Prouinciæ.
- Franciscus Grosbois Coad. eius socius

- P. Theodoricus Beschefer
- P. Jacobus Marquette
- P. Joannes Pierron

Missi in nouam Franciam

Sexto Sacerdotes initiatos

1666	P. Nicolaus Bardin. Tulli 24. Jan.	
	P. Jacobus Marquette Tulli 7. Mar.	
1666	P. Joannes Hardy	Tulli 21 Sept
	P. Remigius Poton	
	P. Nicolaus Domballe	
	P. Godefridus Thiery	
	P. Nicolaus Audry	
1667	P. Nicasius Rolland Tulli, 13. Martij	
	P. Renat.ˢ le Seur	Remis, 28.° Augusti.
	P. Claudius Nicolas	
	P. Claudius Faultrier	
	P. Petrus Josephus Aimé, Tulli. 9 Jan.	
	P. Nicolaus Coquot	Tulli. 18 Oct.
	P. Carol. Ant. Badoux	
	P. Franc Vignolles Bruntruti 25 Sept.	
	P. Desiderius de Chabut	
1668	P. Alexander Le Blanc	Tulli 9. Apr.
	P. Jacobus David	
	P. Joannes Robin. Tulli. 14 Octobr.	
	P. Joannes Bordois. Tulli. 30 Dec.	
	P. Nicolaus Jacquemin	Remis, 30.° Decbris.
	P. Edmundus Courcier	
1669	P. Theodoricus Thuret, Vitriacj, 6.° aprilis.	

BIBLIOGRAPHY

MANUSCRIPT SOURCES

Canada

Archives, Archdiocese of Quebec
    Registre de l'évêché de Québec, A, 166-167.
Collège Sainte-Marie, Montreal
    Collection Rochemonteix
        a) Tableau Marquette College
        b) Tableau Brifoleaux-Rochemonteix
        c) Tableau Lefebvre
        d) Tableau "Napoléon," ou Jansêniste.
Public Archives of Canada, Ottawa
    Collection Sainte-Marie, Montreal
        M.G. 17, 6, 3.

France

Chantilly, Archives of the Jesuit Province of France
  Fonds Brotier 158 (Canada 4)
  Fonds Brotier 159 (Canada 5)
  Fonds Brotier 166 (Canada 12)
Nancy, Archives de la bibliothèque publique
  Manuscrit 560, 138.
Paris, Archives de la Service Hydrographique
  5: 16.
Paris, Archives, Seminary of Saint-Sulpice
  Récit des voyages du P. Marquette
Paris, Bibliothèque Nationale
  Clarambault 1016: 48v.
  Moreau 842: 31-32v, 37.
  Mss.fr.n,a,7491:351-355.

Italy

Rome, General Archives of the Society of Jesus
  Camp. 8 (12),f.257, 428v, 441.
  Camp. 11, f.44-47, 82, 87, 123v, 132v, 148v, 180, 208, 239
  Camp. 12, 87
  Camp. 19, f.88,98, 123v, 148v, 175, 183v.
  Camp. Vota ultima
  Camp. Necrologia, f.40.
  Gallia 14, f.24-25.
  Gallia 28, f.42-42v.
  Gallia 110.I,f.40-41,44-47,48-49v,62v.
  Gallia 110.II,f.195-196v.
  France 14, f.172, 219r, 224, 285, 292v, 293v, 674.
  France 23, f.218-219, 232, 245, 261, 302v, 320, 336-340v.

PRINTED PRIMARY SOURCES

Annales de l'Association de la Propagation de la Foi. 82 vols. Lyons, 1822-1910.

Blair, Emma H., editor. *The Indian Tribes of the Upper Mississippi Valley and the Region of the Great Lakes.* 2 vols. Cleveland: Burrows, 1911-1912.

Brébeuf, Jean de. *The Travels and Sufferings of Father Jean de Brébeuf among the Hurons of Canada as Described by Himself,* edited and translated by Theodore Besterman. London: Golden Cockerel, 1938.

Carrez, Louis, editor. *Catologi sociorum et officiorum provinciae Companiae Societatis Jesu ab anno 1616 ad annum 1773.* 10 vols. Châlons-sur-Marne: Thouille and O'Toole, 1897-1914.

Charlevoix, Pierre François Xavier de. *Histoire et déscription générale de la Nouvelle-France, avec le journal historique d'un voyage fait par ordre du roi dans l'Amérique Septentrionale.* 6 vols. Paris: Nyon, 1744.

——— *The History and General Description of New France,* translated and edited by John Gilmary Shea. 6 vols. New York: John Gilmary Shea, 1870.

Chaumonot, Pierre Joseph Marie. *Un missionnaire des Hurons: autobiographie du père Chaumonet de la compagnie de Jésus,* edited by Felix Martin. Paris: Oudin, 1885.

Dablon, Claude. "Notes spirituelles du P. Claude Allouez," *Lettres du Bas-Canada,* VII (1953), 200-07.

Dollier de Casson, François. *The History of Montreal, 1640-1672, from the French of Dollier de Casson,* translated and edited with a life of the author by Ralph Flenley. Toronto: Dent, 1928.

Gavet, Gaston, editor. *Diarium universitatis mussipotaniae, 1572-1764.* Nancy: Berger-Levrault, 1911.

Hennepin, Louis. *Déscription de la Louisiane, nouvellement découverte au sud-ouest de la Nouvelle-France.* Paris: Huré, 1683.

——— *Nouvelle découverte d'un grand pays situé dans l'Amérique le Nouveau-Mexique et la mer glaciale.* Utrecht: Broedelet, 1697.

Incarnation, Marie (Guyard) de. *Lettres de la révérende mère Marie de l'Incarnation,* edited by F. Richaudeau. 2 vols. Tournai: Casterman, 1876.

Inventaire des registres de l'état civil conserves aux archives judiciaires de Québec. Beauceville: Eclaireur, 1921.

Jones, Arthur E. *Rare and Unpublished Documents Relating to Catholic Canadian History.* 2 vols. Montreal: Collège Sainte-Marie, 1893.

Jouvency, Joseph. *De la manière d'apprendre et d'enseigner,* edited by H. Ferté. Paris: Hachette, 1892.

Jugéménts et délibérations du conseil souverain de la Nouvelle-France. 6 vols. Quebec: Provincial Government, 1885-1891.

Kellogg, Louise Phelps, editor. *Early Narratives of the Northwest, 1634-1699.* New York: Scribner's, 1917.

Lahontan, Louis Armand de Lom d'Arce, baron de. *New Voyages to North America,* edited by Reuben Gold Thwaites. 2 vols. Chicago: McClurg, 1905.

Le Clercq, Chrestien. *Nouvelle relation de la Gaspesie, qui contient les moeurs & la religion des sauvages Gaspeiens Porte-Croix, adora-*

teurs du soleil & autres peuples de l'Amérique Septentrionale, dite le Canada. Paris: Auroy, 1691.

Lescarbot, Marc. *The History of New France*, translated and edited by W. L. Grant. 3 vols. Toronto: Champlain Society, 1907-1914.

Margry, Pierre, editor. *Découvertes et établissements des Français dans l'ouest et dans le sud de l'Amérique Septentrionale (1614-1674): mémoires et documents originaux.* 6 vols. Paris: Maisonneuve, 1876-1886.

Masson, Louis F. *Les bourgeois de la compagnie du Nord-Ouest; récits de voyages, lettres et rapports inédites relatifs au Nord-Ouest Canadien.* 2 vols. Quebec: Côté, 1889.

Migne, Jacques P., editor. *Patrologiae cursus completus, series Latina.* 221 vols. Paris, 1844-1864.

Montézon, Fortuné M. de, editor. *Mission du Canada: Relations inédites de la Nouvelle-France (1672-1679) pour faire suite aux anciennes relations (1615-1672).* 2 vols. Paris: Duniol, 1861.

Montini, Martino. *De bello tartarico historia; in qua pacto Tartari hac nostra aetate Sinicum imperium inuaserunt, ac fere totum occuparunt narratur, eorumque mores breviter describantur.* Rome: Lazeri, 1654.

——— *Novus atlas Sinensis.* 17 maps. Amsterdam: Blau, 1655.

O'Callaghan, Edmund B., editor. *Documents Relative to the Colonial History of the State of New York.* 15 vols. Albany: Weed, Parson, 1856-1887.

Pénicault, André. *Fleur de Lys and Calumet, Being the Pénicault Narrative of French Adventure in Louisiana*, translated and edited by R. G. McWilliams. Baton Rouge: Louisiana State University Press, 1953.

Perrot, Nicolas. *Mémoire sur les moeurs, coustumes et religion des sauvages de l'Amérique Septentrionale.* Leipzig, 1864.

Rapport de l'archiviste de la Province de Québec, 1926-27, 1930-31.

Rhodes, Alexandre de. *Voyages et missions du P. Alexandre de Rhodes de la compagnie de Jésus en la Chine et autres royaumes de l'orient.* Paris: Lanier, 1854.

Saint Ignace, Françoise (Juchereau) de. *Histoire de l'Hôtel-Dieu de Québec.* Montauban: Legier, 1751.

Sanson d'Abbeville, Nicolas. *L'Amérique et plusieurs cartes et en divers traites de geographie et de l'histoire.* Paris: The author, 1657.

Shea, John Gilmary. *Discovery and Exploration of the Mississippi Valley: with the Original Narratives of Marquette, Allouez, Mémbre, Hennepin, and Anastase Douay.* New York: Redfield, 1853.

Têtu, H., and C. O. Gagnon, editors. *Mandements, lettres pastorales et circulaires des évêques de Québec.* 6 vols. Quebec: The editors, 1887-1890.

Thévenot, Melchisedech. *Recueil de voyages*. Paris: Michallet, 1681.

Thwaites, Reuben Gold, editor. *The Jesuit Relations and Allied Documents: Travels and Explorations of the Jesuit Missionaries in New France, 1610-1791*. 73 vols. Cleveland: Burrows, 1896-1901.

Vernon, François. *Manuale sodalitatis Beatae Mariae Virginis, ac juventutis universae selectae gymnasiorum Societatis Jesu, miraculis dictae sodalitatis illustrum*. La Flèche: Rezè, 1610.

SECONDARY SOURCES

Adams, George B. *The History of England from the Norman Conquest to the Death of John (1066-1216)*. London: Longmans, 1905.

Alvord, Clarence W. *The Illinois Country, 1673-1818*. Springfield: Illinois Centennial Commission, 1920.

Arregui, Antonius. *Annotationes ad epitomen instituti Societatis Jesu*. Rome: Oeconomum generalem, 1934.

Ashley, Maurice. *Louis XIV and the Greatness of France*. London: English Universities, 1946.

Bald, F. Clever. *Michigan in Four Centuries*. New York: Harper, 1954.

Beers, Henry P. *The French in North America: a Bibliographical Guide to French Archives, Reproductions and Research Missions*. Baton Rouge: Louisiana State University Press, 1957.

Belting, Natalia M. *Kaskaskia under the French Regime*. Urbana: University of Illinois Press, 1948.

Brodrick, James. *Robert Bellarmine, Saint and Scholar*. Westminster, Maryland: Newman, 1961.

——— *Saint Francis Xavier (1506-1552)*. New York: Wicklow, 1952.

——— *Saint Ignatius Loyola*. New York: Farrar, 1955.

Brucker, Joseph. *Jacques Marquette et la découverte de la vallée du Mississippi*. Lyons: Pitrat, 1880.

Calvet, Jean. *Saint Vincent de Paul*, translated by L. C. Sheppard. New York: McKay, 1951.

Caruso, John A. *The Mississippi Valley Frontier*. Indianapolis: Bobbs-Merrill, 1966.

Casgrain, Henri R. *Histoire de l'Hôtel-Dieu de Québec*. Quebec: Brousseau, 1878.

Casper, Henry J. *History of the Catholic Church in Nebraska:* I, *The Church on the Northern Plains, 1838-1874*. Milwaukee: Bruce, 1960.

Chapais, Thomas. *The Great Intendant: a Chronicle of Jean Talon in Canada, 1665-1672*. Toronto: Glasgow, Brook, 1914.

——— *Jean Talon, intendant de la Nouvelle-France (1665-1672)*. Quebec: Demers, 1904.

Chaulanges, M. and S. *Histoire, 1610 à 1789.* Paris: Delagrave, 1961.
Costain, Thomas B. *The White and the Gold: the French Regime in Canada.* Garden City: Doubleday, 1954.
Crouse, Nellis M. *Contributions of the Canadian Jesuits to the Geographical Knowledge of New France, 1632-1675.* Ithaca: Cornell University Press, 1924.
Delanglez, Jean. *Life and Voyages of Louis Jolliet (1645-1700).* Chicago: Institute of Jesuit History, 1948.
Delattre, Pierre, editor. *Les établissements des Jésuites en France depuis quatre siècles.* 5 vols. Enghien: Institut superieur de theologie, 1955.
Devisme, Jacques F. L. *Histoire de la ville de Laon.* 2 vols. Laon: Courtois, 1822.
Disturnell, J., compiler. *The Island of Mackinac: Giving a Description of All the Objects of Interest and Places of Resort in the Straits of Mackinac and Its Vicinity.* Philadelphia, 1875.
Donnelly, Joseph P. *Thwaites Jesuit Relations, Errata and Addenda.* Chicago: Loyola University Press, 1967.
Driver, Harold E. *Indians of North America.* Chicago: University of Chicago Press, 1961.
Eccles, William J. *Canada under Louis XIV, 1663-1701.* Toronto: McClelland and Stewart, 1964.
——— *Frontenac, the Courtier Governor.* Toronto: McClelland and Stewart, 1959.
Faillon, Etienne Michel. *Histoire de la colonie française en Canada.* 3 vols. Villemarie, 1865.
Farrell, Allen P. *The Jesuit Code of Liberal Education: Development and Scope of the Ratio studiorum.* Milwaukee: Bruce, 1938.
Faucher de Saint-Maurice, Narcisse H. E. *Relation de se qui s'est passé lors des foulles faites par ordre du gouvernement dans une partie des fondations du collège des Jésuites de Québec, précédée de certaines observations.* Quebec: Darveau, 1879.
Ferland, Jean Baptiste Antoine. *Cours d'histoire du Canada.* 2 vols. Quebec: Côté, 1861-1865.
Fitzpatrick, Edward A. *La Salle, Patron of All Teachers.* Milwaukee: Bruce, 1951.
Fuller, George N., editor. *Historic Michigan.* 3 vols. Dayton, no date.
Funck-Brentano, Frantz. *The National History of France: the Middle Ages,* translated by Elizabeth O'Neill. London: Heineman, 1922.
Gagnon, Ernest. *Louis Jolliet, découvereur du Mississippi et du pays des Illinois, premier seigneur de l'Ile d'Anticosti.* Montreal: Beauchemin, 1946.
Ganss, George E. *Saint Ignatius' Idea of a Jesuit University.* Milwaukee: Marquette University Press, 1954.

Garraghan, Gilbert J. *The Catholic Church in Chicago, 1673-1871.* Chicago: Loyola University Press, 1921.

——— *Chapters in Frontier History.* Milwaukee: Bruce, 1934.

——— *Marquette: Ardent Missionary, Daring Explorer.* New York: America Press, 1937.

Gauthier, François. *Notice historique sur le collège de Langres.* Langres: Huiffier, 1856.

Gosselin, Auguste. *Mgr. Saint-Vallier et son temps.* Evreux: Eure, 1898.

——— *Vie de Mgr. de Laval, premier évêque de Québec et apôtre du Canada, 1622-1708.* 2 vols. Quebec: Demers, 1890.

Guibert, Joseph de. *The Jesuits: Their Spiritual Doctrine and Practice,* translated by W. J. Young and edited by G. E. Ganss. Chicago: Loyola University Press, 1964.

Hamy, Alfred. *Au Mississippi: la première exploration (1673).* Paris: Champion, 1903.

Harney, Martin P. *Good Father in Brittany: the Life of Blessed Julien Maunoir.* Boston: St. Paul Editions, 1963.

——— *The Jesuits in History: the Society of Jesus through Four Centuries.* New York: America Press, 1941.

Harrisse, Henri. *Notes pour servir à l'histoire, à la bibliographie, et à la cartographie de la Nouvelle-France et des pays adjacents, 1545-1700.* Paris: Tross, 1872.

Havighurst, Walter. *Three Flags at the Straits.* Englewood Cliffs: Prentice-Hall, 1966.

Hay, Malcolm. *Failure in the Far East: Why and How the Breach Between the Western World and China First Began.* Philadelphia: Dufour, 1957.

Hedges, Samuel. *Father Marquette, Jesuit Missionary and Explorer, the Discoverer of the Mississippi, His Place of Burial at St. Ignace, Michigan.* New York: Christian Press, 1903.

Hock, Conrad. *The Four Temperaments.* Milwaukee: Bruce, 1934.

Houyous, Joseph. *Routes canadiennes, '49.* Trois-Rivières: Bien Public, 1950.

Hubbard, Gurdon S. *The Autobiography of Gurdon Saltenstall Hubbard, Pa-Pa-Ma-Ta-Be, the Swift Walker.* Chicago: Lakeside Press, 1911.

Hurlbut, Henry H. *Father Marquette at Mackinac and Chicago: a Paper Read before the Chicago Historical Society, October 15, 1878.* Chicago: McClurg, 1878.

Hyde, George E. *Indians of the Woodlands from Prehistoric Times to 1725.* Norman: University of Oklahoma Press, 1962.

Illinois, a Descriptive and Historical Guide. Chicago: McClurg, 1946.

Institutum Societatis Jesu. 3 vols. Florence: SS. Conception, 1892-1893.

Jenness, Diamond. *The Indians of Canada.* Ottawa: National Museum of Canada, 1958.

Karpinski, Louis C. *Bibliography of Printed Maps of Michigan, 1804-1880.* Lansing: Michigan Historical Commission, 1931.

Kellogg, Louise P. *The French Régime in Wisconsin and the Northwest.* Madison: State Historical Society of Wisconsin, 1925.

Knight, Robert, and Lucius H. Zeuch. *The Location of the Chicago Portage Route of the Seventeenth Century.* Chicago: Chicago Historical Society, 1928.

Lalande, Louis. *Une vielle seigneurie Boucherville.* Montreal: Entandard, 1890.

La Monte, John L. *The World of the Middle Ages.* New York: Appleton-Century-Crofts, 1949.

Lanctôt, Gustave. *The History of Canada.* 3 vols. Cambridge: Harvard University Press, 1963-1966.

Langlois, Charles V., and Charles Seignobos. *Introduction aux études historiques.* Paris: Hachette, 1898.

Lanning, John Tate. *The Spanish Missions of Georgia.* Chapel Hill: North Carolina University Press, 1935.

La Roncière, Charles G. *Au fil du Mississippi avec le père Marquette.* Paris: Bloud et Gay, 1935.

Larousse du XXe siècle. 6 vols. Paris: Larousse, 1931.

La Tour, Louis B. de. *Mémoires sur la vie de Mgr. de Laval, premier évêque de Québec.* Cologne, 1761.

Lavater, Johann Kasper. *Aphorisms on Man.* Newburyport: Osborne, 1793.

Leach, Morgan L. *History of the Grand Traverse Region.* 1883.

Le Jeune, Louis, editor. *Dictionnaire général de biographie, histoire, littérature, agriculture, commerce, industrie du Canada.* 2 vols. Ottawa: Ottawa University Press, 1931.

Lough, John. *An Introduction to Seventeenth Century France.* London: Longmans 1954.

Luchaire, Achille. *Social France in the Time of Philip Augustus,* translated by E. B. Krehbiel. New York: Unger, 1957.

MacLennan, Hugh. *Seven Rivers of Canada.* Toronto: McMillan, 1961.

Mahoney, Mother Denis, O.S.U. *Marie of the Incarnation, Mystic and Missionary.* Garden City: Doubleday, 1964.

Marquis, Thomas G. *The Jesuit Missions, a Chronicle of the Cross in the Wilderness.* Toronto: Glasgow, Brooks, 1916.

Martin, Eugene. *L'Universite de Pont-à-Mousson (1572-1768) avec plan et vue d'ensemble.* Nancy: Berger-Levrault, 1891.

Mast, Doloreta. *Always the Priest; the Life of Gabriel Richard, S.S.* Baltimore: Helicon, 1965.

Melleville, Maximilien. *Histoire de la ville de Laon et ses institutiones civiles, judiciares, foedales.* 2 vols. Paris: Dumoulin, 1848.

Mérou, H., et al. editors. *Combattants français de la guerre Amérique, 1778-1783.* Washington: Imprimerie nationale, 1905.

Meschler, Moritz. *Die gesellschaft Jesu, ihre statzugen und ihre erfolge.* 2 vols. 1914.

Morin, Soeur Marie. *Annales de l'Hôtel-Dieu de Montreal.* Montreal: Imprimerie des editeurs, 1921.

Nute, Grace Lee. *Caesars of the Wilderness.* New York: Appleton-Century, 1943.

——— *The Voyageur.* St. Paul: Minnesota Historical Society, 1955.

The Oxford Companion to the Theatre, edited by Phyllis Hartnoll. London: Oxford University Press, 1957.

Paris, L. *Le thêatre au collège des Bons-Enfants et chez les pères Jésuites à Reims.* Paris, 1883.

Parkman, Francis. *The Jesuits in North America in the Seventeenth Century.* Boston: Little, Brown, 1860.

——— *La Salle and the Discovery of the Great West.* Boston: Little, Brown, 1904.

——— *The Old Régime in Canada.* Boston: Little, Brown, 1901.

Paulin, Charles O. *Atlas of the Historical Geography of the United States.* Washington: Carnegie, 1932.

Pfister, Christian. *Histoire de Nancy.* 3 vols. Paris: Berger-Levrault, 1902-1909.

Philips, P. Lee. *The Rare Map of the Northwest, 1785, by John Fitch.* Washington: Lowdermilk, 1916.

Pirenne, Henri. *Les villes et les institutions urbaines.* 2 vols. Paris: Alcan, 1939.

Plattner, Felix A. *Jesuits Go East.* Westminster, Maryland: Newman, 1952.

Pouliot, Adrien. *Aux origines de notre devotion à l'Imaculée-Conception.* Quebec: Société Historique de Quebec, 1956.

Pouliot, Léon. *Etude sur les Relations des Jésuites de la Nouvelle-France (1632-1672).* Montreal: Messager, 1940.

Quaife, Milo M. *Chicago and the Old Northwest.* Chicago: University of Chicago Press, 1913.

——— *Lake Michigan.* Indianapolis: Bobbs-Merrill, 1944.

Quimby, George I. *Indian Culture and European Trade Goods.* Madison: University of Wisconsin Press, 1966.

——— *Indian Life in the Upper Great Lakes, 11,000 B.C. to A.D. 1800.* Chicago: University of Chicago Press, 1960.

Repplier, Agnes. *Père Marquette: Priest, Pioneer and Adventurer.* New York: Doubleday, 1929.

Rezek, Antoine. *History of the Diocese of Sault Sainte Marie and Marquette.* 2 vols. Houghton, Michigan: The author, 1907.

Rochemonteix, Camille de. *Les Jésuites et la Nouvelle-France au XVIIe siècle.* 3 vols. Paris: Letouzy et Ané, 1895-1896.

——— *Un collège des Jésuites aux XVIIe et XVIIIe siècles: le collège Henri IV de La Flèche.* 4 vols. Paris, 1899.

Roy, Pierre-Georges. *La ville de Québec sous le régime français.* 2 vols. Quebec: Paradis, 1930.

Roy, Regis, and Gérard Malchelosse. *Le régiment de Carignan, son organization et son expedition au Canada, 1665-1668.* Montreal, 1925.

Sarazin, Charles. *Les Jésuites à Reims, 1606-1764.* Reims, 1923.

Schmitt, Louis. *Synopsis historiae Societatis Jesu.* Ratisbon: Pustet, 1914.

Schoolcraft, Henry R. *Narrative Journal of Travels from Detroit Northwest through the Great Chain of American Lakes to the Source of the Mississippi River in the Year 1820.* Albany: Hosford, 1821.

——— *Personal Memoirs of a Residence of Thirty Years with the Indian Tribes on the American Frontiers.* Philadelphia: Lippincott, 1851.

Schroeder, Henry J. *Canons of the Council of Trent: Original Text with English Translation.* St. Louis: Herder, 1950.

Scott, H. A. *Une paroisse historique de la Nouvelle-France, Notre-Dame-de Sainte-Foy.* Quebec: Laflamme, 1902.

Shea, John Gilmary. *The Catholic Church in Colonial Days.* New York: The author, 1886.

Smith, Emerson K. *Before the Bridge: a History and Directory of St. Ignace and Nearby Localities.* St. Ignace, Michigan: Kiwanis Club, 1957.

Societatis Jesu constitutiones et epitome instituti. Rome: Curia praepositi generalis, 1949.

Sommervogel, Carlos. *Bibliothèque de la compagnie de Jésus.* 12 vols. Paris: Province de Belgique, 1890-1898.

Stebbins, Catherine L. *Here I Shall Finish My Voyage!* Omena, Michigan: Solle's Press, 1960.

Steck, Francis Borgia. *Essays Relating to the Jolliet-Marquette Expedition, 1673.* 2 vols. Quincy, Illinois: The author, 1953.

——— *The Jolliet-Marquette Expedition, 1673.* Quincy, Illinois: Franciscan Fathers, 1928.

——— *Marquette Legends.* New York: Pageant Press, 1960.

Strickland, W. P. *Old Mackinaw: or the Fortress of the Lakes and Its Surroundings.* Philadelphia: Challen, 1860.

Sullivan, John J., editor. *The Autobiography of the Venerable Marie of the Incarnation, O.S.U., Mystic and Missionary.* Chicago: Loyola University Press, 1964.

Tanquerey, Adolphe. *The Spiritual Life: a Treatise on Ascetical and Mystical Theology,* translated by Herman Brandris. Tournai: Desclée, 1930.

Tessier, Albert. *Les Trois-Rivières: quatre siècle d'histoire, 1535-1935.* Trois-Rivières: Nouvelliste, 1934.

Thibout, Marc. *Eglises gothiques en France.* Paris: Amery, 1959.

Thiery, A. D. *Histoire de la ville de Toul et de ses évêques.* 2 vols. Paris: Rotet, 1841.

Thwaites, Reuben Gold. *Father Marquette.* New York: Appleton, 1902.

——— *How George Rogers Clark Won the Northwest and Other Essays in Western History.* Chicago: McClurg, 1903.

Tilley, Arthur, editor. *Medieval France: a Companion to French Studies.* Cambridge: Cambridge University Press, 1922.

Tucker, Sara Jones, compiler. *Indian Villages of the Illinois Country.* 2 vols. Springfield, Illinois, 1942.

Les Ursulines de Québec depuis leur établissement jusqu'à nos jours. 4 vols. Quebec: Darveau, 1863-1866.

Verwyst, Chrysostom. *Life and Labors of the Rt. Rev. Frederick Baraga, First Bishop of Marquette, Michigan.* New York: Benziger, 1900.

——— *The Missionary Labors of Fathers Marquette, Ménard, and Allouez in the Lake Superior Region.* Milwaukee: Hoffman, 1886.

Villaret, Emile. *Les congrégations mariales.* I: *Des origines à la suppression de la compagnie de Jesus (1540-1773).* Paris: Beauchesne, 1947.

Warren, William W. *History of the Ojibway Nation.* Minneapolis: Ross and Haines, 1957.

Waugh, Evelyn. *Edmund Campion.* Boston: Little, Brown, 1946.

Westercamp, Charles. *Le Laonnois pittoresque.* Laon: Editions des Tablettes de l'Aisne, 1930.

Wild, J. C. *The Valley of the Mississippi Illustrated in a Series of Views,* edited by Lewis Foulk Thomas, painted by J. C. Wild. St. Louis: The artist, 1841.

Wissler, Clark. *Indians of the United States: Four Centuries of Their History and Culture.* Garden City: Doubleday, 1940.

Wood, Edwin O. *Historic Mackinac.* 2 vols. New York: Macmillan, 1918.

PERIODICAL LITERATURE

Alvord, Clarence W. "An Unrecognized Father Marquette Letter," *American Historical Review,* XXV (1920), 676-80.

Arth, Sister Mary Columbière. "Marquette Memorials," *Mid-America,* II (1931), 291-303.

Barbin, René. "Le voyageur du Christ (Gabriel Druillettes, 1610-1681)," *Lettres du Bas-Canada,* VI (1952), 41-51, 81-97.

Bayliss, Clara K. "The Significance of the Piasa," Illinois State Historical Society *Transactions,* 1908, 114-23.

Brown, Charles E. "Indian Trade Implements and Ornaments," *Wisconsin Archaeologist,* XVII (1918), 61-97.

Burmeister, Charles. "Short History of Benzie County," Michigan *Historical Collections,* XVIII (1892), 502-06.

Burrus, Ernest J. "Father Jacques Marquette, S.J.: His Priesthood in the Light of the Jesuit Roman Archives," *Catholic Historical Review,* XLI (1955), 257-71.

Bussières, Marc-André. "Monseigneur de Laval et les Jésuites," *Lettres du Bas-Canada,* VI (1952), 151-66.

Campeau, Lucien. "Marquette Legends," *Revue d'Histoire de l'Amérique Française,* XIV (1960-1961), 282-86.

——— "Voyageurs et martyrs," *Lettres du Bas-Canada,* II (1948), 3-23.

Champris, H. G. de. "Le R. P. Marquette," *Canada Français,* XII (1925), 773-77.

Corrigan, Raymond. "Missions of New France: a Study in Motivation," *Mid-America,* VII (1936), 234-46.

Côté, Jean. "L'Institution des donnés," *Revue d'Histoire de l'Amérique Française,* XV (1961), 344-78.

Couture, Théotime. "Manitouline (1600-1800). Ses premiers habitants. Ses premiers missionaires," *Lettres du Bas-Canada,* III (1949), 175-85.

Delanglez, Jean. "The Cartography of the Mississippi," *Mid-America,* XXX (1948), 257-84; XXXI (1949), 29-52.

——— "Claude Dablon, S.J. (1619-1697)," *Mid-America,* XXVI (1944), 91-110.

——— "The Discovery of the Mississippi—Primary Sources," *Mid-America,* XVI (1945), 219-31.

——— "The Discovery of the Mississippi—Secondary Sources," *Mid-America,* XVII (1946), 3-29.

——— "The Jolliet Lost Map of the Mississippi," *Mid-America,* XVII (1946), 67-144.

——— "Louis Jolliet: Early Years: 1645-1674," *Mid-America,* XXVII (1945), 3-29.

——— "Louis Jolliet: The Middle Years: 1674-1686," *Mid-America*, XVI (1945), 67-96.

——— "Marquette's Autograph Map of the Mississippi River," *Mid-America*, XVI (1945), 30-53.

——— "The *Récit des voyages et des découvertes du père Jacques Marquette*," *Mid-America*, XVII (1946), 173-94, 211-58.

——— "Le révérend père Jacques Marquette, S.J., etait-il prêtre?" *Revue d'Histoire de l'Amérique Française*, II (1949), 581-82; III (1949), 73-74.

——— "The 1674 Account of the Discovery of the Mississippi," *Mid-America*, XV (1944), 301-24.

Delattre, Pierre and Edmond. "Jésuites, Wallons, Flammands, Français missionaires au Paraguay, 1608-1767," *Archivum Historicum Societatis Jesu*, XVI (1947), 98-176.

Desjardins, Paul. "Le donné Jean Guérin," *Lettres du Bas-Canada*, X (1956), 80-99.

——— "Jacques Marquette, était-il prêtre?" *Revue de l'Université Laval*, III (1948-1949), 346-49.

Dionne, René. "Les Jésuites dans la première lettre de Frontenac à Colbert (2 novembre, 1672)," *Lettres du Bas-Canada*, XIV (1960), 201-20.

Douville, Raymond. "Jacques Largillier *dit* 'le castor,' coureur des bois et 'frère donne,'" *Cahiers des Dix*, XXIX (1964), 47-69.

Dubroux, C. "Le collège des Jésuites de Charleville," *Revue Historique Ardennaise*, 1901 (May-June), 137-208.

Duffield, George. "On the Recent Discovery of the Long Lost Grave of Père Marquette," Michigan *Historical Collections*, II (1877-1878), 134-45.

Faye, Stanley. "Jolliet Goes West," Illinois State Historical Society *Journal*, XXVII (1934), 5-30.

Garraghan, Gilbert J. "Catholic Beginnings in Chicago," *Mid-America*, V (1933), 33-44.

——— "The Death of Father Marquette," *Mid-America*, XI (1940), 223-25.

——— "The Jolliet-Marquette Expedition of 1673," *Thought*, IV (1929), 32-71.

——— "Marquette's Titles to Fame," *Mid-America*, XX (1938), 30-36.

——— "Some Hitherto Unpublished Marquettiana," *Mid-America*, XVIII (1935), 15-26.

——— "Some Newly Discovered Marquette and La Salle Letters," *Archivum Historicum Societatis Jesu*, IV (1935), 268-90.

"A Genealogy of Father Marquette," *Woodstock Letters*, XXVIII (1899), 204-05.

Girardin, J. A. "The Life and Times of Gabriel Richard," Michigan *Historical Collections*, I (1877), 481-95.

Godbout, Archange. "Louis Jolliet et son dernier historien," *Culture*, XIV (1953), 223-46.

Gosselin, Amédée. "Jean Jolliet et ses enfants," Royal Society of Canada *Proceedings and Transactions*, 3rd ser. XIV (1921), sec. 1, 65-81.

Grady, Richard F. "Cenodoxus redivivus," *Woodstock Letters*, LXIX (1940), 133-39.

Greenman, Emerson F. "An Early Historic Cemetery at St. Ignace," *Michigan Archaeologist*, IV (1958), 28-35.

——— "Wintering in the Lower Peninsula, 1675-1676," *Michigan Archaeologist*, III (1957), 63-65.

Hamilton, Raphael N., S.J. "Father Jacques Marquette, S.J., Priest," *Revue de l'Université Laval*, III (1949), 640-42.

——— "Location of the Mission of Saint Ignace from 1670 to 1673," *Michigan History*, XLII (1958), 260-66.

——— "The Marquette Death Site: the Case for Ludington," *Michigan History*, XLIX (1965), 228-48.

——— "To the Editor of the *Wisconsin Magazine of History*," *Wisconsin Magazine of History*, XXXII (1949), 472-73.

Harris, Robert M. "Missionary Catechetics in New France," *Woodstock Letters*, LXXXVIII (1959), 37-56.

Healy, George R. "The French Jesuits and the Idea of the Noble Savage," *William and Mary Quarterly*, XV (1958), 147-67.

Hickerson, Harold. "The Southwestern Chippewa, an Ethnohistorical Study," American Anthropological Association *Memoir*, 92, LXIV (1926), 1-110.

Hoffman, Walter J. "The Midewiwin or Grand Medicine Society of the Ojibwa," Bureau of American Ethnology *Annual Report*, 1885-1886, 143-300.

Jacker, Edward. "Catholic Indians in Michigan and Wisconsin," *American Catholic Quarterly Review*, I (1876), 404-35.

——— "Father Henry Nouvel, S.J., the Pioneer Missionary of Lower Michigan," *United States Catholic Historical Magazine*, I (1887), 258-80.

——— "Father Marquette. Discovery of His Remains," *Woodstock Letters*, VI (1877), 159-72.

Jacobsen, Jerome V. "Attempted Mayhem on Père Marquette," *Mid-America*, XX (1949), 109-15.

——— "Documents: Marquette's Ordination," *Mid-America*, XXXII (1950), 46-54.

"Jacques Marquette et l'inauguration de son monument à Laon, le 13 juin, 1937," *Société académique de Laon,* 1937.

Jenks, Albert E. "The Wild Rice Gatherers of the Upper Lakes," Bureau of American Ethnology *Annual Report,* 1897-1898, 1019-1137.

Jenks, William L. "History and Meaning of the County Names of Michigan," Michigan *Historical Collections,* XXXVIII (1912), 439-77.

Jones, Arthur E. "The Site of the Mascoutin," State Historical Society of Wisconsin *Proceedings,* 1906, 175-82.

Kellogg, Louise P. "Marquette's Authentic Map Possibly Identified," State Historical Society of Wisconsin *Proceedings,* 1906, 183-93.

Knight, Robert, and Lucius H. Zeuch. "The Birthplace of Father Marquette," *Mid-America,* XIV (1932), 263-65.

Kohne, Christopher J. "James Marquette, the Soldier of the Cross," *Illinois Catholic Historical Review,* VI (1923-1924), 89-95.

Lamalle, Edmond. "Les catalogues des provinces et des domiciles de la Compagnie de Jésus," *Archivum Historicum Societatis Jesu,* XIII, 77-101.

Lambert, E. "La cathédrale de Laon," *Gazette des beau-artes,* I (1926), 361-84.

——— "L'Eglise de Templiers à Laon," *Revue Archéologique,* XXIV (1926), 224-33.

Law, John. "Jesuit Missionaries in the Northwest," Wisconsin *Historical Collections,* III (1857), 89-111.

Lecompte, Edouard. "Les Jésuites du Canada au XIXe siècle," *Lettres du Bas-Canada,* IV (1950), 73-94.

Lomasney, Patrick J. "Marquette's Burial Site Located," *Illinois Catholic Historical Review,* IX (1927), 147-55, 348-62.

Macdougall, Angus. "La réception de M. le Vicomte d'Argenson," *Lettres du Bas-Canada,* IV (1950), 95-104.

Maggiolo, L. "Le théâtre classique en Lorraine, répetroire chronologique et bibliographique," *Mémoires de l'Académie de Stanislas,* LV (1887), 265-302.

Marsden, Gerald K. "Father Marquette and the A. P. A.: an Incident in American Nativism," *Catholic Historical Review,* XLVI (1960), 1-21.

May, George S., editor. "The Discovery of Father Marquette's Grave at Saint Ignace in 1877, as Related by Father Edward Jacker," *Michigan History,* XLII (1958), 267-87.

Middaugh, Ruth B. "Father Marquette," *Illinois Catholic Historical Review,* VI (1923-1924), 22-27.

Neville, Arthur C. "Some Historic Sites about Green Bay," Wisconsin Historical Society *Proceedings,* 1905, 143-56.

O'Dea, Arthur J. "The Observance of the Marquette Tercentenary," *Mid-America,* XX (1938), 15-29.

Pouliot, Adrien. "Le congrégation huronne de 1653," *Lettres du Bas-Canada,* VII (1953), 159-70.

——— "Monseigneur de Laval et les Jésuites," *Lettres du Bas-Canada,* XIII (1959), 205-10.

——— "La plus vieille maison du Canada," *Lettres du Bas-Canada,* IV (1950), 25-39.

——— "Troisième centenaire de la congrégation des hommes de Quebec," *Lettres du Bas-Canada,* XI (1957), 28-36.

Pouliot, Adrien, and T. Edmond Giroux. "Ou est né Louis Jolliet?" *Bulletin des Recherches Historiques,* LI (1945), 334-46.

Pouliot, Léon. "Nombre et qualité des baptisés dans les *Relations des Jesuites,*" *Science Ecclesiastique,* X (1958), 473-95.

——— "La part du P. Claude Allouez dans les 'Sentiments' qui lui sont attribues," *Revue d'Histoire de l'Amérique Française,* XV (1961), 379-95.

——— "Le Père Paul Ragueneau (1608-1680)," *Lettres du Bas-Canada,* XVII (1963), 143-54.

Roquebrune, Robert La Roque de. "Uniforms et drapeau des régiments au Canada sous Louis XIV et Louis XV," *Revue de l'Université de Ottawa,* XX (1950), 327-42.

Roustang, François, editor. *An Autobiography of Martyrdom,* translated by Sister M. Renelle. St. Louis: Herder, 1964.

Roy, Pierre-Georges. "Jean Péré et Pierre Moreau *dit* La Taupine," *Bulletin des Recherches Historiques,* X (1905), 213-21.

Schmirler, A. A. A. "Wisconsin's Lost Missionary: the Mystery of Father René Ménard," *Wisconsin Magazine of History,* XLV (1962-1963), 99-114.

Shea, John Gilmary. "Romance and Reality of the Death of Father James Marquette and the Recent Discovery of His Remains," *Catholic World,* XXVI (1877), 267-81.

Short, Joseph C. "Jacques Marquette, S.J., Catechist," *Revue de l'Université Laval,* III (1948-1949), 436-43.

——— "To the Editor of the *Wisconsin Magazine of History,*" *Wisconsin Magazine of History,* XXXII (1948-1949), 227-29.

Spalding, Henry S. "The Grave and Relics of Father Marquette," *Messenger of the Sacred Heart,* February 1901.

——— "The History of the Marquette Statue Presented to Statuary Hall in the Capital by the State of Wisconsin," *Historical Records and Studies,* III (1904), 409-18.

——— "The Life of James Marquette," *Illinois Catholic Historical Review,* IX (1927), 3-17, 109-33, 223-64.

——— "Who Discovered the Mississippi," *Illinois Catholic Historical Review*, VI (1923-1924), 40-49.

"A Statue of Father Marquette in the Capital at Washington," *Woodstock Letters*, XVI (1887), 175-80.

Stebbins, Catherine L. "The Marquette Death Site," *Michigan History*, XLVIII (1964), 333-68.

Steck, Francis Borgia. "The Discovery of the Mississippi River," *Illinois Catholic Historical Review*, VI (1923), 50-65.

——— "Father Garraghan and the 'Jolliet-Marquette Expedition of 1673,'" *Fortnightly Review*, XXXVI (1929), 265-68, 301-05; XXXVII (1930), 5-8.

——— "Father Marquette's Place in American History," *The Americas*, V (1949), 411-38.

——— "The Real Author of the *Récit*," *The Americas*, IV (1948), 475-500.

——— "What Became of Jolliet's Journal?" *The Americas*, V (1948), 172-99.

Talbot, Francis X. "Le congrégation huronne de 1653," *Lettres du Bas-Canada*, VII (1953), 159-70.

Thompson, Joseph J. "Marquette and Jolliet," *Illinois Catholic Historical Review*, VI (1923-1924), 3-4.

Verwyst, Chrysostom. "The Chippewas, Their History, Religious Ideas, Missionaries and Needs," *Salesianum*, VI (1910), 19-24.

Walker, C. I. "Father Marquette and the Early Jesuits of Michigan," Michigan *Historical Collections*, VIII (1885), 368-92.

Warren, William W. "History of the Ojibways, Based Upon Tradition and Oral Statements," Minnesota Historical Society *Collections*, V (1885), 21-395.

Weld, L. G. "Jolliet and Marquette in Iowa," *Iowa Journal of History and Politics*, I (1903), 3-16.

Wittry, Warren L. "The Bell Site Wn 9: an Early Historic Fox Village," *Wisconsin Archaeologist*, XLIV (1963), 1-58.

Wolff, R. L. "Baldwin of Flanders and Hinaut, First Latin Emperor of Constantinople," *Speculum*, XXVII (1952), 281-322.

Woodstock Letters, VI (1877), 171-72.

——— XXVIII (1898), 204-05.

INDEX

About this book

Jacques Marquette, S.J., 1637-1675 was designed by William Nicoll of Edit, Inc. It was set in the composing room of Loyola University Press and Avenue Typographers. The text is 10/13 Caledonia; the reduced matter, 8/10 and 9/11. The display type is 12 Caledonia.

It was printed by Photopress, Inc., on Warren's 60-pound English Finish paper and bound by The Engdahl Company in Bancroft Arrestox #44000.

Imprimi potest Joseph D. Sheehan, S.J., Provincial of the Wisconsin Province, August 19, 1967. *Nihil obstat* John B. Amberg, S.J., *censor deputatus*, July 25, 1968. *Imprimatur* Right Reverend Monsignor Francis W. Byrne, Vicar General, Archdiocese of Chicago, August 2, 1968. The *nihil obstat* and *imprimatur* are official declarations that a book or pamphlet is free of doctrinal or moral error. No implication is contained therein that those who have granted the *nihil obstat* and *imprimatur* agree with the contents, opinions, or statements expressed.